Questions & Answers

Criminal Law

Questions & Answers Series

Series Editors: Rosalind Malcolm and Margaret Wilkie

The ideal revision aid to keep you afloat through your exams

Q&A Company Law
Stephen Judge

Q&A Criminal Law
Mike Molan

Q&A Employment Law
Richard Benny, Michael Jefferson, and Malcolm Sargeant

Q&A Equity and Trusts
Margaret Wilkie, Rosalind Malcolm, and Peter Luxton

Q&A EU Law
Nigel Foster

Q&A Evidence
Maureen Spencer and John Spencer

Q&A Family Law
Penny Booth with Chris Barton and Mary Hibbs

Q&A Human Rights and Civil Liberties
Steve Foster

Q&A International Law
Susan Breau

Q&A Land Law
Margaret Wilkie, Peter Luxton, and Rosalind Malcolm

Q&A Law of Contract
Adrian Chandler with Ian Brown

Q&A Law of Torts
David Oughton, Barbara Harvey, and John Marston

Q&A Public Law
Richard Clements and Philip Jones

- advice on exam technique

- summary of each topic

- bullet-pointed answer plans

- model answers

- diagrams and flowcharts

- further reading

Questions & Answers

Criminal Law

SEVENTH EDITION

Mike Molan

Professor of Legal Education and Executive Dean,
Faculty of Arts and Human Sciences,
London South Bank University

2010 and 2011

OXFORD

UNIVERSITY PRESS

Great Clarendon Street, Oxford ox2 6DP

Oxford University Press is a department of the University of Oxford.
It furthers the University's objective of excellence in research, scholarship,
and education by publishing worldwide in

Oxford New York

Auckland Cape Town Dar es Salaam Hong Kong Karachi
Kuala Lumpur Madrid Melbourne Mexico City Nairobi
New Delhi Shanghai Taipei Toronto

With offices in

Argentina Austria Brazil Chile Czech Republic France Greece
Guatemala Hungary Italy Japan Poland Portugal Singapore
South Korea Switzerland Thailand Turkey Ukraine Vietnam

Oxford is a registered trade mark of Oxford University Press
in the UK and in certain other countries

Published in the United States
by Oxford University Press Inc., New York

First published 1999
This edition 2010

British Library Cataloguing in Publication Data

Data available

Library of Congress Cataloging in Publication Data

Data available

Typeset by MPS Limited, A Macmillan Company
Printed in Great Britain
on acid-free paper by
Ashford Colour Press Ltd, Gosport, Hampshire

ISBN 978–0–19–957912–9

1 3 5 7 9 10 8 6 4 2

Contents

The Q&A series

Key features

The Q&A series provides full coverage of key subjects in a clear and logical way.

This book contains the following features:

- Questions
- Commentary
- Bullet point answer plans
- Suggested answers
- Further reading
- Flowcharts

 online resource centre
www.oxfordtextbooks.co.uk/orc/qanda/

Every book in the Q&A series is accompanied by an Online Resource Centre, hosted at the URL above, which is open-access and free to use.

The online resources for this title include revision and exam advice, a subject-specific glossary, and links to websites useful for the study of criminal law.

Preface

This seventh edition of the Q & A in Criminal Law reflects a number of key developments in criminal law that have occurred in the two years since the previous edition was published. Unusually, most of this has been the result of statutory changes. Some of these, such as the Manslaughter and Corporate Homicide Act 2007, are very welcome changes to the law, providing clarity where there was some confusion, and establishing a new framework for liability. Other changes are more changes of style rather than substance. Hence s 76 of the Criminal Justice and Immigration Act 2008 does not replace the common law and statutory forms of self-defence but seeks to 'clarify' certain aspects of these defences—in truth it is hard to see what changes if any have been achieved by this measure. Part 2 of the Serious Crime Act 2007, which is now in force, abolishes the common law form of incitement, replacing it with an offence of encouraging the commission of crime. This is not problematic in itself, but the wording of the statutory offences is incredibly complex, and further difficulty is caused by the fact that these statutory offences also introduce liability for assisting the commission of offences. This statutory form of secondary liability does not replace the common law principles on accessorial liability but sits alongside it, leaving prosecutors with an enviable array of possible charges, but leaving tutors and exam candidates with quite a headache as regards the offences that should be considered—not least within the constraints of the traditional time-limited examination answer.

Notwithstanding the substantial revisions to many chapters required to reflect recent changes in the law, the principal aim of the book remains unchanged. It is designed to help students who have a good basic knowledge of the criminal law to maximize their potential by adopting appropriate styles and structures for their answers.

There is, of course, no such thing as a model answer. What this text provides is examples of suggested solutions. So often good candidates fare badly simply because they have not mastered the techniques of adopting a logical structure and providing a concise analysis of the legal issues arising. The preponderance of problem-style questions is not accidental. Experience has shown that students tend to find identifying a clear and concise style of answering these questions quite a challenge—hence more examples of solutions to these types of question are provided.

Whilst the answers in the text are meant to provide the reader with a framework that can be used to tackle criminal law assessments, it must be borne in mind that any answer submitted for assessment on a criminal law course must be the student's own work. In short, emulate the style, but make the content your own!

In preparing this latest edition I would like to acknowledge the contribution made by students I have taught over the years to my understanding of their difficulties in dealing with criminal law assessments, and the comments of colleagues on drafts of the questions used.

Thanks also to colleagues at Oxford University Press for the very professional way in which they have dealt with the business of text production and publication, and my thanks to Alison, Grace, Joy, Miles, and Parker the mad lurcher for their forbearance whilst I was busy with the revisions to this work.

Mike Molan
London South Bank University
August 2009

Table of Cases

Table of Statutes

Introduction: exam technique

Many students mistakenly believe that techniques required to succeed in examinations are totally distinct from what they have learnt throughout the year-long course. This is not the case; although certain techniques may need to be modified for exam purposes, a student will be well served by applying the skills and disciplines that have been acquired during the course of study leading to an examination.

It is therefore very important to acquire good habits as early in your course as possible. When a problem or essay question is set for discussion in lectures or seminars, you should treat it as a possible exam question, but with the luxury that you are not under the pressure of the examination room. You will therefore have much longer to prepare, research, and consider your answer; but when this has been done, you will obtain the maximum future benefit if you tackle it in the same way as an examination question. In this way you will acquire good habits, which may need only minor modification in the examination.

The plan

Stage 1 is to plan your answer. For problem questions, identify the issues raised and make a list of all the offences you must consider, noting the *actus reus* and *mens rea* of each offence. Then briefly note the defences that may be available, and add the case names that you may be using as authority or discussing in detail. Then re-read the question and check your list to ensure that you have not missed anything. You are now in a position to put your list into logical order—in other words an organized plan—in which you can identify those issues which need to be discussed in detail and those which can be referred to briefly; which cases should be used to illustrate your points and which ones you will briefly quote as authority for a principle.

Lastly, still at the planning stage, you should consider your conclusion. More is said regarding the conclusion later, but the advantage of considering a conclusion at this stage is that it helps to crystallize your thoughts and identify any errors in your plan; and, possibly more importantly, it does give you confidence when you start to write your answer, because you know what conclusion you are working towards.

Answer the problem

Give more space to the more important points. If the problem raises various possibilities, start with the most serious or the most obvious.

It generally makes sense to deal with the *actus reus* of an offence before dealing with the *mens rea*. When these issues have been dealt with consider any defences.

Is there doubt about liability? If so, may a lesser offence be proved? Here again, deal with the key elements of liability for these offences.

The most important point is that you answer the question set, not the question you wish had been set! Apply the law to the facts given. Take the facts as stated in the problem as conclusive—you must examine the facts as proved. Sometimes the facts are deliberately vague or ambiguous, e.g., what exactly was D's state of mind when he killed V? If this is the case, you may have to discuss murder and manslaughter, or even advise that the death does not give rise to criminal liability. Do not be afraid in some circumstances to fail to reach a rock solid conclusion. It may be perfectly acceptable— indeed highly appropriate—to say, for instance: 'If…then he may be liable for murder, if…then he may be liable for manslaughter'. Identifying unclear areas is a skill in itself, where either the facts or the law itself are unclear. What you are effectively required to do in many problem questions is argue in the alternative. For example, if the harm done to the victim amounts to a wound, then the answer is…

On the other hand, if the harm is held not to amount to a wound the alternative lesser offences may be…

You may have a problem that involves the potential liability of several parties. If this is the case, there is no need, for instance, to reiterate the ingredients of, say, murder. There may, however, be differences which must be noted, e.g., one party being under ten, or one being an accomplice rather than a principal offender. Although it often helps to discuss the parties in order of their appearance in the problem, where you have a problem question involving significant issues of accessorial liability it is sensible to deal with the liability of the principal offender before looking at the liability of accomplices.

Your statements of law should be backed up by reference to authorities, statute, or case law. You may also refer to relevant articles and textbook theories, and draw an analogy or use hypothetical examples.

The question may say 'discuss'. This will require discussion of all the possibilities raised by the facts, all offences, all parties, and any possible defences. Alternatively, you may be asked to 'advise A' or 'discuss the criminal liability of D'. Your answer clearly will have to be tailored to suit. Often the rubric will provide gateways—e.g., it will ask you to advise on the liability of A for theft and the liability of B for criminal damage. It is never wise to ignore these pointers and provide advice on other offences. Irrelevant material, however well researched or presented, will gain no marks but will waste time and space.

Be prepared to see both sides of the question. For instance, give proper weight to defences that may be applicable. There is no need to discuss potential defences not raised by the facts, e.g., if the problem says 'A kills Y' you need not go into the question of whether perhaps A was nine years old. If you were required to discuss infancy, the problem should involve facts to lead you to do so. The permutations otherwise would be endless! Do not forget to deal with the burden of proof, where appropriate, for example in relation to diminished responsibility.

Where the question raises issues of fact that could be resolved either way be careful to avoid taking on the role of a jury member, as opposed to legal adviser. Your task is to advise on the possible offences, defences and any issues of fact that might have a bearing on the application of relevant legal definitions. For example, in dealing with theft it may well be unclear as to whether or not the defendant is dishonest. You will advise as to the direction to the jury on dishonesty, but you may not be able to indicate how the jury will deal with that direction. In such cases be prepared to say that the outcome depends on the view the jury takes of the facts in the light of the appropriate direction on the law as given by the trial judge.

Some identifiable pitfalls

A cardinal fault is irrelevance. Even if a question seems squarely on a certain area of law, it should not be a case of 'writing all you know' on such a topic. Instead, your answer should demonstrate your ability to recognize what is at issue and apply legal principles to it, backed up by authorities. Your ability in selecting the relevant areas for in-depth treatment will also be assessed; a problem question may contain minor points as well as central issues. Be selective in the way you answer, giving priority to the main points, dealing briefly with the rest.

Mistakes identified as common include illogical order, inadequate introduction and conclusion, repetition, poor or inappropriate use of authority, and a conclusion that does not follow from the evidence. Not only do such mistakes cost you marks, they give the marker a negative view of the rest of your answer or entire paper. So the favourable impression you may have created earlier quickly disappears. It is therefore essential to eliminate sloppy, fundamental errors. Most markers accept that in the heat of the examination certain errors will be made, but they heavily penalize errors that reveal a lack of technique or lawyerly skill.

Examination technique

Two central pieces of advice are these:

(a) Answer the required number of questions.

(b) Keep to time.

If you answer, for instance, three questions instead of the four required, you are immediately giving yourself an absolutely total potential maximum of 75% rather than 100%. If one takes 50% as an average secure pass, your 'score' (assuming such standard of answer to three questions) would be 50% of 75, i.e., 37 or 38, a *fail*. It cannot be stressed too strongly: it is vital that you attempt the required number of questions. Be careful to read through the 'rubric', the instructions on the examination paper. You may be asked to answer so many questions from part A, part B and so on. One or more questions may be compulsory. Some questions may have particular instructions built into them. Accurate interpretation of such instructions is *very important*. You should be given an indication by the relevant lecturer of what will be required, but do ask in advance if you are not sure. You ought to know when you are revising what exactly it is that you are revising for. If certain aids are allowed in the examination, you should know this—and be familiar enough with the aids to use them.

It is most important that you make the maximum use of time. The duration of the examination will vary according to the amount of material to be covered. For year-long criminal law courses exams will normally be of three hours' duration, with additional reading time. On semesterized modular courses examinations may be only 90 minutes plus reading time. Either way, it is rarely the case that a student will run out of time during a criminal law exam. The usual problem for a weak student is that he or she has completed the answers, and there is still some 30 minutes left. Obviously in some cases this is because the student does not possess enough knowledge, but in the vast majority of cases, the problem is that the student has panicked and rushed into the answer without preparing a plan. At the start of an exam, there is a feeling that, as there is so much to do, the answers must be started immediately. This temptation must be resisted, for it is at the start of your exam that you are freshest and best able to plan your answers, and the order in which you tackle them. You do not want to be panicking with 45 minutes to go, and it is therefore worthwhile considering leaving one of your stronger answers to the end, to enable you confidently to cover material you are sure of, rather than dealing with troublesome topics with a tired mind.

In an ideal situation, your four and five answers will all be strong, but unfortunately experience shows that on even the best of scripts, there is often one relatively weak answer. It is well worth using some calm time at the beginning of the examination to look through the *whole* paper. Read slowly through the questions, deciding which you will choose (or be forced) to answer. To do this at the outset saves a lot of potential 'dithering' time during the course of the examination. You may find as you initially go through the paper that certain issues or cases leap out at you as you read. It is worth making a marginal note of such matters as you go through, because it may be that you may not be able to bring them to mind later on.

Having stressed the importance of *timing,* the need to *read the questions carefully* must also be highlighted. You will be asked questions which are often quite specific in their terms. It is unlikely that you will be asked to write 'all you know about conspiracy, strict liability etc'. Much more likely would be a question investigating a certain aspect of the topic in question. It is here that you have to be very precise and concentrated in your reading of the question so that you answer the question that has been set.

If you have worked out the time allocation for each individual question, you can proceed to your first answer. It is strongly recommended that you stick strictly to your time plan, leaving one question and passing on to another when the allotted time is up. You can always return to add the finishing touches. Just leave a gap, start a new page and *press on*. Remember, when you are working out the amount of time you will allow for each question, you have to take into account thinking time, calming time and note-making time.

It is suggested that the making of an answer plan is essential. This should help to get your thoughts in order and promote the feeling of your being in control. Your answer structure will be greatly assisted by the formulation of a plan in advance. The best approach is to prepare plans for all answers before actually writing the first answer. This requires discipline and nerve, but arguably you are doing your most important thinking while your mind is at its freshest.

You will know your own strengths and weaknesses. You should, for instance, know if you are better at answering problems/writing essays; theory/practice; history/ modern angle; broad/detailed questions. You have to choose as far as you can in line with your knowledge of your own abilities generally, and the selection you see before you. (Of course, on the day you may see a wonderful essay question on a topic you have fully revised and decide to answer that instead of the problem you would normally go for.)

Some things should be watched out for, guarded against. Be careful to *answer* the *question*. This may sound trite, but it cannot be emphasized enough. If the question has several parts, make sure you answer *every part*. If there is a quotation to be discussed in an essay question, you have to really pick the quote to pieces so that you discuss every facet of it. Obviously, the angle you take will depend on the wording of the question— does it say 'Evaluate', or 'Contrast' or 'Critically analyse', for instance? Beware latching on to one key word in the question and writing all you can drag up about the subject.

This is a really crucial point. All you write has to be *relevant* in order to gain you marks. Irrelevancies lose you precious time and will gain no marks. You have to aim for balance in your answer, too. Devote most time to the central issues in a problem, for instance, making brief reference only to subsidiary points.

Problem questions

If you have a long problem question involving, say, several parties to a crime and several substantive offences, and you are told at the beginning of the question that 'A and B agree to…', then you would not be expected to enter into a lengthy discourse about conspiracy law. The question here calls for the briefest of references to that possible offence. It would be different if the question appeared to hinge largely on the issue of conspiracy. As a general rule it is best to deal with completed substantive offences first. You can then return to inchoate offences towards the end of your answer on the basis that, if the completed offences cannot be made out, there may be residual liability for inchoate offences.

If a problem gives you no indication of the possible relevance of a particular defence then you would not be expected to deal with that issue, otherwise the permutations would be endless. If the problem mentions, for instance, a serious injury to a person but there is no mention of death, there is no need to develop an argument about what the situation would be if the victim died.

What this really means is that you have to interpret what it is the examiner is trying to test. What is the question essentially about? Within that question, you then have to decide what emphasis you think should be accorded to various aspects of the question.

It is very important to include in your answer clear definitions where appropriate. For instance, if you are going to discuss insanity, make sure that you state what amounts to insanity; if you are discussing provocation, say what it is. Clear definitions set the tone of your answer and put the marker in an optimistic frame of mind. The same is true of a good, clear opening paragraph—it bodes well and is worth aiming for.

It is also very important to display your understanding clearly concerning the burden of proof, particularly in relation to defences. Be careful that you do not suggest that there is a burden of proof on the defence when there is not. As you revise, you should be very alert to this point.

While on the question of displaying your knowledge, if you have read a relevant article or have been swayed by a particular writer's approach, make sure that you state this. In the case of essay questions, show the marker that you have read widely. Capitalize on your research. Get the credit.

In answering a problem question, don't feel that you have to come to a rock solid conclusion. Very often it will be impossible to do so. It is perfectly acceptable to say, for example, 'If D is found to have intended grievous bodily harm then....' and so on. As long as you indicate what the issues are, what the relevant principles of liability are, that is sufficient. There is no need to predict the decision of the jury/magistrates, although you do have to indicate, where appropriate, how the jury should be directed, for instance.

Your conclusion may differ from that of another student, and may differ from that of the marker. This does not matter. So long as you can illustrate why you reach your conclusion by reference to authorities, analogy, and argument, that is fine. It is quite likely that you cannot, on the facts presented, reach a definite conclusion. It may depend, for instance, on whether the jury believed that A had the necessary intention to kill or cause grievous bodily harm. If they did, the verdict could be guilty of murder unless the jury considered that A had used reasonable force in self-defence, in which case he would be acquitted of all charges. In situations like this, it would be wrong to conclude that A was definitely guilty or not guilty. What you must do is cover the alternatives—this demonstrates your understanding of the position. In certain questions there may be many alternative outcomes. Remember that the marks allocated for the conclusion are not simply given for arriving at the same result as the examiner (e.g., A guilty of murder) but for analysis and awareness.

Essay questions

In answering essay questions it is necessary to include the traditional introduction, followed by discussion, followed by conclusion. Neither the introduction nor the conclusion need be lengthy. The advantage of the essay question is that you can play to your strengths—so long as what you write is relevant. Beware writing all you know on a topic; it is essential to be discriminating, to tailor your answer to the way the question is worded. Simply ask yourself: 'Am I answering the question set?'

Candidates sometimes tend to forget authorities when answering essay-style questions, particularly under examination conditions. You still need reference to case law, statutory definitions and general principles in an essay answer. The onus is more on you, since in a problem the facts will (or should) suggest which authorities you are being asked to discuss.

If the essay question revolves around a particular case, clearly you will need to concentrate on that decision—but the odds are that you will still need plenty of reference to other case law and statutory provisions, to place the case in its historical perspective, or to highlight the way in which the central decision will or may affect existing law.

The major task in essay writing, given that you know the subject matter, is to structure the material. You have to determine for yourself the scope and shape of your answer. It is easy to tell when marking essay answers whether the candidate has followed a plan—it really shows.

A good answer to an essay question, therefore, will go beyond simply describing or giving an account of those issues to which the question relates. A good answer will have a point to make—a view to express. It will present a polemic of some sort. It will seek to persuade the reader, by means of reasoned and supported argument, to agree with a particular view on the subject.

Conclusion

In an exam your goal must be to obtain the highest mark possible, given your knowledge and ability. Student A may have the same attributes as student B, but student A may obtain 10–20 more marks in the exam because of good exam technique. It is therefore essential that you incorporate into your answer the style and techniques covered in this chapter. So remember to:

- read the instructions thoroughly;
- answer the correct number of questions;
- prepare your answer plan;
- answer the question set;
- deal with one issue fully before going on to the next;
- write a logical conclusion which does not conflict with the rest of your answer;
- read through your answers at the end of the exam.

2

The elements of a crime: actus reus and mens rea

Introduction

The traditional starting point for the study of criminal law is the constituents of a criminal offence: *actus reus* (often referred to as the prohibited conduct, but more accurately described as the external elements of the offence) and *mens rea* (often referred to as the mental element, but more accurately described as the fault element). Commentators and students alike want to find consistency and certainty in the application and development of the criminal law, and most criminal law textbooks dealing with the elements of crimes try to state principles that the student should see consistently applied in later chapters covering specific offences. The main problem is that the offences have developed in a piecemeal fashion, exhibiting no underlying rationale or common approach. Thus in examining *actus reus,* the student might be covering an offence defined in modern terms, e.g., by the Criminal Damage Act 1971, or in obscure outdated language, e.g., in the Offences Against the Person Act 1861 or—the definition of *actus reus* may arise from the common law, perhaps amended or augmented by statute, e.g., murder.

Similarly, when we examine our approach to *mens rea,* we can see little common ground. If the offence requires the prosecution to prove intention, this must generally be left to the jury without detailed guidance from the trial judge (*R v Moloney* [1985] 1 All ER 1025); but if recklessness is the issue, a direction spelling out to the jury what they must find may be required. Prior to the decision of the House of Lords in *R v G* [2003] 4 All ER 765, a case involving criminal damage would have involved a court in trying to assess whether the defendant was reckless according to the definition laid down in *Metropolitan Police Commissioner v Caldwell* [1981] 1 All ER 961. But now, following the abandonment of '*Caldwell* recklessness', the issue has been simplified so that a court now has to concentrate on whether or not the defendant was aware of the risk in question and if so, whether or not, in the circumstances known to the defendant, it was unreasonable for him to take the risk.

If dishonesty is the *mens rea* (see Theft Acts 1968–1996) the jury must consider two specific questions (would ordinary people consider D dishonest?; if so, did D realize that they would?); but these are questions of fact for them to resolve (*R v Ghosh* [1982] 2 All ER 689). In other words, there are three different approaches in establishing the *mens rea* for different offences. A search for consistency is therefore a futile exercise!

Students should therefore be aware that studying the chapters on *actus reus* and *mens rea* can produce a distorted impression of the criminal law. One is dealing with concepts in isolation and could form the impression that these general principles are consistently applied.

One particular criticism is that the criminal law is not consistent in applying objective or subjective tests for liability. Objective tests consider what the reasonable person would have foreseen. Subjective tests judge the defendant on the facts as he honestly believed them to be. There appears to be an absence of any underlying rationale and the offences develop independently of each other. One can understand why Sir Henry Brooke (former head of the Law Commission) and many others wish for codification of some, if not all, of the criminal law (see [1995] Crim LR 911—'The Law Commission and Criminal Law Reform').

Even established concepts that have been applied by the courts for many years, may suddenly come under attack and be interpreted differently by the judiciary. Thus the House of Lords in *Attorney-General's Reference (No. 3 of 1994)* [1997] 3 All ER 936, reversed the Court of Appeal decision ([1996] 2 WLR 412), holding that the doctrine of transferred malice could not apply to convict an accused of murder when he deliberately injured a pregnant woman in circumstances where the baby was born alive but subsequently died. Lord Mustill criticized the doctrine as having no sound intellectual basis and involving a fiction, although the *Criminal Law Review* disagrees with his view ([1997] Crim LR 830).

In this chapter questions have been chosen to cover all major aspects of this area. There are some problem questions, but candidates should expect the essay questions in an exam to be selected from these topics. Essays are therefore included on the important aspects of *mens rea*: intention and recklessness.

Question 1

The practice of leaving the issue of intention to the jury without any judicial guidance as to its meaning is unworkable and likely to produce inconsistent decisions.

Discuss this statement with reference to decided cases.

Commentary

There have been so many important decisions on this important aspect of criminal law, that it is always likely to be the subject of an examination question.

Because the facts of *R v Moloney* **[1985] 1 All ER 1025** are so well known, there is a temptation simply to regurgitate them with the House of Lords' decisions. This must be resisted as there are many ingredients in the answer, which requires careful planning and organization.

In summary, this is a question where it is quite easy to obtain a pass mark but difficult to obtain a high grade.

 Answer plan

- *Mens rea*
- Intention—definition
- *Moloney* [1985]—'the golden rule'
- *Woollin* [1998]—direction on intention
- Law Commission No. 218

Suggested answer

Except with strict (or absolute) liability offences, in order for an accused to be found guilty of a criminal offence, the prosecution must prove that the accused committed the *actus reus* of the offence with the appropriate *mens rea*. *Mens rea* generally signifies blameworthiness, although in *R v Kingston* [1994] 3 All ER 353, the House of Lords confirmed that the accused was guilty of an offence requiring the prosecution to prove intention, although he was morally blameless. *Mens rea* is the mental element, which varies from one offence to another; but generally, for the more serious offences, it comprises intention or recklessness, with intention being reserved for the most serious crimes.

One would therefore think that, being of such fundamental importance, intention would be specifically defined and rigidly applied, but this is not the case. There have always been difficulties with the concept of intention within the criminal law. What is it? How should it be defined? How do the prosecution prove it? How does the trial judge direct the jury? These issues have been the subject of much judicial and academic debate in recent years.

Although the word 'intention' implies purpose or even desire, there have been many diverse definitions by the judiciary, and commentators have also identified different types of intention. First, direct intent, where it was the accused's purpose or motive to bring about a result. Thus in *R v Steane* [1947] 1 All ER 813, the accused, who assisted the enemy during the war, had his conviction quashed as the court decided that he did not intend to assist the enemy; he intended to protect his family, who would have been harmed had he not cooperated. Secondly, oblique intent, where the accused does not necessarily desire the result but foresees it as highly probable. Thus in *Hyam v DPP* [1974] 2 All ER 41, the House of Lords upheld a conviction for murder where the accused had set fire to the victim's house even though the accused's purpose had been only to frighten the victim. Because there was evidence that the accused foresaw that death or grievous bodily harm was highly probable the House of Lords felt justified in concluding that her state of mind could be regarded as a form of intent (on this matter the law is now as set out in *R v Woollin* [1998] 4 All ER 103—see below). Thirdly, ulterior intent, where it must be shown that in intentionally doing one act the accused has a related purpose. Thus to be guilty of burglary under s. 9(1)(a) of the Theft Act 1968, it is necessary for the prosecution to prove that the accused, when deliberately entering a building as a trespasser, did so with a specific related purpose in mind, e.g., to steal or commit criminal damage. It would not be sufficient if the accused intentionally broke into the house with the sole purpose of sheltering from the weather. The terms specific and basic intent, are also used in respect of the defence of intoxication to distinguish between those offences where intoxication is permitted as a defence and those where it is not (see further *DPP v Majewski* [1976] 2 All ER 142).

Although there is an overlap between intention on the one hand and motive and foresight on the other, and these latter concepts assist the jury in their deliberations on intention, it is clear that the concepts are not synonymous. Motive is the reason why a person acts, while intention is his or her mental awareness at the time of the act. Foresight can be evidence of intention, but it is not conclusive proof of it. Section 8 of the Criminal Justice Act 1967 states that a court shall not be bound in law to infer that the accused intended or foresaw a result of his actions by reason only of its being a natural and probable consequence of those actions, but 'shall decide whether he did intend or foresee that result by reference to all the evidence, drawing such inferences from the evidence as appear proper in the circumstances'.

The issue of intention was debated by the House of Lords in *R v Moloney* [1985] 1 All ER 1025 and *R v Hancock and Shankland* [1986] 1 All ER 641. In the former case, Moloney shot his stepfather from point blank range and was convicted of murder after the trial judge (following *Archbold Criminal Pleading Evidence and Practice*, 40th edn, para. 17–13, p. 995) directed the jury that:

In law a man intends the consequence of his voluntary act:

(a) when he desires it to happen, whether or not he foresees that it probably will happen, or

(b) when he foresees that it will probably happen, whether he desires it or not.

The House of Lords quashed the conviction on the basis that this was a misdirection, Lord Bridge stating that:

the golden rule should be that, when directing a jury on the mental element necessary in a crime of specific intent (i.e., intention), the judge should avoid any elaboration or paraphrase of what is meant by intent, and leave it to the jury's good sense to decide whether the accused acted with the necessary intent, unless the judge is convinced that, on the facts and having regard to the way the case has been presented to the jury in evidence and argument, some further explanation or elaboration is strictly necessary to avoid misunderstanding.

Although the decision may be criticized on the ground that their Lordships missed a golden opportunity to define intention, it is in keeping with the modern trend of leaving more and more issues to the jury, especially the meaning of words in common use. For example, *Brutus v Cozens* [1972] 2 All ER 1297 (insulting); *R v Feely* [1973] 1 All ER 341 (dishonestly).

This decision was followed by the House of Lords' ruling in *R v Hancock and Shankland*, where Lord Scarman also made the point that if intention required a detailed direction it was best to leave this to the discretion of the trial judge who would have had the benefit of hearing all the witnesses and gauging the ability of the jury. He added that the trial judge could not do as Lord Bridge suggested and simply direct the jury to consider two questions: first, was death or really serious injury in a murder case a natural consequence of the defendant's voluntary act?; secondly, did the defendant foresee that consequence as being a natural consequence of his act?— further instructing them that if they answer 'Yes' to both questions it is a proper inference for them to draw that the accused intended that consequence. Lord Scarman stated that the trial judge must refer to the concept of probability—the more probable the consequence, the more likely the accused foresaw it and intended it.

Despite clear House of Lords' *dicta* to the contrary, the Court of Appeal in *R v Nedrick* [1986] 3 All ER 1 did lay down some guidelines to the effect that the jury should not infer intention unless they considered that the accused foresaw the consequence as a virtual certainty. However, this decision has attracted criticism, and the Court of Appeal in *R v Walker and Hayles* [1989] 90 Cr App R 226 stated 'we are not persuaded that it is only when death is a virtual certainty that the jury can infer intention to kill'.

Nevertheless, the status of *Nedrick* was confirmed by the House of Lords' discussion in *R v Woollin* [1998] 4 All ER 103. The House, stating that where the simple direction was not enough, the jury should be further directed that they were not entitled to find the necessary intention unless they felt sure that death or serious bodily harm was a virtually certain result of D's action (barring some unforeseen intervention) and, that D had appreciated that fact.

This decision also illustrates one of the difficulties of the present approach, i.e., when is the issue of intention so complicated as to warrant a detailed direction? In *R v Walker and Hayles*, the Court of Appeal decided that 'the mere fact that a jury calls for a further direction on intention does not of itself make it a rare and exceptional case requiring a foresight direction'. On the other hand, in *R v Hancock and Shankland*, the House of Lords confirmed that the trial judge was right to give a detailed direction, even though the content of the direction was wrong.

A further problem is that different juries may have different ideas as to what constitutes intention, some insisting on purpose being necessary, while others are prepared to accept that only foresight of a probable consequence is required. There is clearly the risk of inconsistent decisions and it is therefore not surprising that the Law Commission (Nos 122 and 218) have recommended that the following standard definition of intention be adopted:

a person acts intentionally with respect to a result when

(i) it is his purpose to cause it; or

(ii) although it is not his purpose to cause that result, he knows that it would occur in the ordinary course of events if he were to succeed in his purpose of causing some other result.

Question 2

'*Mens rea* is, by definition, the defendant's state of mind.'

Discuss the accuracy of this statement using case law to support your argument.

Commentary

This question requires examination of some of the assumptions made about *mens rea* and the current trends in judicial thinking. Candidates would be expected to consider the main forms of *mens rea* and the extent to which courts are required to take an objective or subjective view of fault. Although '*Caldwell* recklessness' has now been effectively consigned to legal history (for the time being at least) a good answer will need to show an awareness of that decision and its impact on the *mens rea* debate. Consideration also needs to be given to the issue of mistake and its relationship with *mens rea*. Finally, the answer should encompass some consideration of negligence as a form of *mens rea* and the extent to which its use accords with notions of subjective fault.

Answer plan

- The nature of *mens rea*
- Intention—*R v Woollin*— House of Lords' decision
- The recklessness debate *R v G* [2003]—abandoning *Caldwell*
- The treatment of mistake and its effect on *mens rea*—*DPP v Morgan* [1976]
- Killing by gross negligence—whether objective or subjective

Suggested answer

Although *mens rea* translates literally as 'guilty mind', relying on this as the meaning given to that term in modern criminal law is likely to lead to error. This is because a defendant may be found to have *mens rea* even though he himself has not acted with the intention of committing an offence, or even with the awareness that this might be the result. The better approach is to regard *mens rea* as denoting the fault element that the prosecution has to prove. In the majority of cases this will involve proof of some positive state of mind on the part of the accused, but in other cases it may be enough to show that the accused failed to advert to something that would have been obvious to the reasonable person.

The two most important fault elements used in modern criminal law are intention and recklessness. It can now be said that, as far as these two forms of *mens rea* are concerned, liability cannot be established without evidence as to what the defendant foresaw when he committed the acts causing the prohibited results. Exactly what it is that the defendant has to have foreseen, and how much foresight he must be shown to have had, are questions that go to the core of the debate relating to where the dividing line between different types of subjective *mens rea* should be drawn.

The modern definition of intention can be derived from a number of House of Lords' decisions, notably *R v Moloney* [1985] 1 All ER 1025 and *R v Woollin* [1998] 4 All ER 103. A defendant cannot be guilty of murder unless he is proved to have acted with intent to kill or do grievous bodily harm. Where a direction on intent is deemed necessary, a jury should be instructed that they should consider the extent to which the defendant foresaw death or grievous bodily harm resulting from his actions. Only where there is evidence that he foresaw either consequence as virtually certain would it be safe for a jury to conclude that a defendant therefore intended either of those consequences. The key here is foresight. Section 8 of the Criminal Justice Act 1967 makes clear that foresight is a subjective concept—i.e., it is based on what the defendant actually foresaw—not on what he ought to have foreseen, or indeed what the reasonable person would have foreseen had he been in the defendant's shoes. Taken together, the definition of foresight in the 1967 Act, and the House of Lords' ruling in *Woollin* ensure that where intention is the required *mens rea,* there can be no doubt that it will be based on the defendant's state of mind—i.e., a subjective approach will be adopted.

The rationale for this is fairly obvious—it is hard to describe a defendant as having intended a consequence if there is no evidence of it having occurred to him. Even where there is such evidence, if the possibility of the consequence occurring has only fleetingly crossed his mind it would still be absurd to say he intended it. The law, therefore, requires a very high degree of foresight before a defendant's state of mind is labelled as having been intentional.

Recklessness, by contrast, implies risk taking, as opposed to the defendant foreseeing a consequence as a certainty. Here there has been great controversy over the past few decades as to the right approach to the determination of fault. The traditional approach to recklessness as a form of *mens rea* very much reflected the view that *mens rea* had to be based on the defendant's state of mind. In *R v Cunningham* [1957] 2 All ER 412, the Court of Appeal held that a defendant was reckless only if he took an unjustifiable risk and was at least aware of the risk materializing. The key point about this approach to recklessness was that there would be no liability if the risk never occurred to the defendant.

However, there was a radical departure from this approach as a result of the House of Lords' decision in *Metropolitan Police Commissioner v Caldwell* [1981] 1 All ER 961. The accused had a grudge against the owner of an old people's home, and while drunk he set fire to it. He was convicted under s. 1(1) of the Criminal Damage Act 1971 of recklessly damaging another's property, and of the more serious offence under s. 1(2) of the Act, destroying or damaging any property being reckless as to whether the life of another would be thereby endangered.

The House of Lords, by a majority, held that in relation to criminal damage, a person was reckless if:

(a) he did an act which in fact creates an obvious risk that property would be destroyed or damaged; and

(b) when he did the act he either did not give any thought to the possibility of there being any such risk, or had recognized that there was some risk involved and had nevertheless gone on to do it.

Lord Diplock clearly wanted to introduce liability for failing to think in the guise of this reformulation of recklessness, but this raised a number of issues.

First, what of the defendant who did not think of the risk because it would not have occurred to him even if he had stopped to think? In *Elliot v C (A Minor)* [1983] 2 All ER 1005, a 14-year-old schoolgirl of low intelligence, who was tired and hungry, spilt some inflammable spirit and then dropped a lighted match on the wooden floor of a garden shed. She was charged under s. 1(1) of the 1971 Act. It was argued that she did not foresee the risk of fire, nor would she had she addressed her mind to the possible consequences of her action. Although Goff LJ stated that a test for recklessness which allowed the court to take into account the individual characteristics of the accused had much merit, he felt bound by the doctrine of precedent to follow *Caldwell*, and therefore the magistrates should have convicted the accused as the correct test was 'whether this is an obvious risk to a reasonable man'.

Secondly, there was the argument that '*Caldwell* recklessness' was not acceptable as a form of *mens rea* because it was not based on the defendant's state of mind. In *R v Reid* [1992] 3 All ER 673, Lord Keith observed by way of response that: 'Absence of something from a person's state of mind is as much part of his state of mind as is its presence. Inadvertence to risk is no less a subjective state of mind than is disregard of a recognised risk.' What he meant by this was that even with '*Caldwell* recklessness', the court had to consider the defendant's state of mind. But, it is submitted, this is a piece of judicial sophistry, as all that was required was for the court to examine the defendant's state of mind and, on finding 'no thought', conclude that he had been reckless provided the risk would have been obvious to the reasonable prudent bystander.

Whilst many might have applauded Lord Diplock's efforts to penalize thoughtlessness in terms of a social policy initiative, the real question was whether he was right to pursue this via a radical judicial reinterpretation of the term 'recklessness'. It is significant that Parliament intervened shortly after *Caldwell* to reform the offence of reckless driving (and therefore causing death by reckless driving) by replacing it with the offence of dangerous driving—see the Road Traffic Act 1991. The effect of this was to make clear that the offence could now be committed without any form of *mens rea* that required reference to the defendant's state of mind. Recklessness was replaced, as a fault element, by the term 'dangerous'. Whilst it could and was argued that recklessness implied some conscious risk-taking by the accused, there was no doubt that 'dangerousness' as a fault element rested entirely upon an objective assessment of the defendant's conduct. In other words a defendant could drive dangerously because he had a badly secured load on the back of his trailer—there was no need for him to be aware of this. In summary this suggests that Parliament liked the idea of criminal liability based on failure to think about risk, but was not comfortable with the idea that 'traditional' *mens rea* terms like 'recklessness' might be used to describe it.

As far as recklessness is concerned the argument has, for the time being at least, been decided in favour of the traditional, subjective, approach. In *R v G* [2003] 4 All ER 765, the House of Lords held that a defendant could not be properly convicted under s. 1 of the Criminal Damage Act 1971 on the basis that he was reckless as to whether property was destroyed or damaged when he gave no thought to the risk and, by reason of his age and/or personal characteristics, the risk would not have been obvious to him, even if he had thought about it. Lord Bingham observed that recklessness should at least require a knowing disregard of an appreciated and unacceptable risk of, or a deliberate closing of the mind to, such risk. In his view it was not clearly blameworthy to do something involving a risk of injury to another if one genuinely did not perceive the risk.

R v G reflects a general judicial trend in favour of subjectivity, as evidenced in decisions such as *B v DPP* [2000] 1 All ER WLR 833. Indeed, the high watermark of this approach to fault was the House of Lords' decision in *DPP v Morgan* [1976] AC 182, where it was held that if a defendant made a genuine mistake of fact—such as wrongly believing that a woman was consenting to sexual intercourse, he had to be judged on the facts as he believed them to be, not as the reasonable person would have believed them to be. Lord Hailsham made it clear that there was no room either for a 'defence' of honest belief or mistake, or of a defence of honest and reasonable belief or mistake. The reasonableness of the defendant's honest belief was simply a factor relating to its credibility. The mental element in the offence of rape has now been modified by the Sexual Offences Act 2003, so that rape is effectively now an offence with a fault element based on negligence. The rationale of *DPP v Morgan* survives, however, at common law to the extent that a defendant should normally be judged on the facts as he honestly believes them to be.

As has been noted above in the case of dangerous driving, fault elements that do not require reference to the defendant's state of mind are used. At common law this can be seen in the offence of killing by gross negligence. In *R v Adomako* [1994] 3 WLR 288, Lord Mackay LC explained that liability would be established if the prosecution could prove that the defendant's conduct departed from the proper standard of care incumbent upon him, thereby creating a risk of death, and involved such a departure from acceptable standards of care as to deserve the stigma of criminalization. As was made clear in *Attorney-General's Reference (No. 2 of 1999)* [2000] 3 All ER 182, evidence of the defendant's state of mind might be useful in guiding a jury as to whether or not the negligence was gross, but this fault element can be made out without any direct evidence as to the defendant's state of mind. Whilst this may seem to run counter to the trend in favour of subjectivity it should be remembered that it serves a useful social purpose in making it easier to impose criminal liability on companies that kill.

In summary, therefore, it is undoubtedly true to say that *mens rea* normally does involve an examination of the defendant's state of mind to ascertain a degree of awareness of the consequences of his actions. The law will, however, allow departures from this where the social utility of doing so outweighs the need to ensure the fairness to the defendant that ensues from adopting a subjective approach to fault.

Question 3

You are told that the (fictitious) Ancient Book Act 2009 has just received the Royal Assent and that s. 1 provides, 'It shall be an offence to destroy any book printed before 1800'.

Discuss the criminal liability of each party (in relation to the 2009 Act) in the following situation.

Arthur owns 200 books, which he thinks are worthless. He is concerned in case any of the books were printed before 1800 and consults Ben, an expert on old books, who assures him that all the books were printed long after 1800. Arthur destroys the books and is now horrified to discover that three of them were printed in 1750.

Commentary

This is an unusual question which has caused students difficulties, with many writing about the offence of criminal damage. This is a mistake as the question requires a detailed analysis of the *mens rea* requirement of the Ancient Book Act 2009, and in particular analysis of the concept of strict liability.

In a survey by Justice referred to in an article by A. Ashworth and M. Blake, 'The Presumption of Innocence in English Criminal Law' [1996] Crim LR 306, it is estimated that in over one half of criminal offences either strict liability is imposed, or the prosecution have the benefit of a presumption. It is obviously an important topic, and popular with examiners!

A good answer will require a detailed consideration of the possibility of this offence being one of strict liability and the effect of this. Candidates should also consider the position if the courts decide that intention or recklessness is the appropriate mental state.

Answer plan

- Strict liability—*Sweet v Parsley* [1969]
- Presumption of *mens rea*—*B v DPP* [2000]
- The exceptions
- Recklessness
- Mistake—*Morgan* [1976]
- Ben's liability under the **Serious Crime Act 2007**

Suggested answer

The first point to note is that s. 1 of the Ancient Book Act 2009 is silent as to the *mens rea* requirement of the offence. This could mean that the offence is one of absolute liability (i.e., strict liability in the sense that no *mens rea* whatsoever is required). Alternatively it could be a strict liability offence in the sense that intention, recklessness or negligence is only required as regards one or more elements of the *actus reus*. The imposition of absolute liability may be very harsh on the defendant. For example, in *Pharmaceutical Society of Great Britain v Storkwain* [1986] 2 All ER 635, the House of Lords upheld the conviction of a pharmacist who had given drugs to a patient with a forged doctor's prescription, although the court found the pharmacist blameless. Whilst the decision demonstrates the inherent unfairness of strict liability, it can be justified on the basis that the misuse of drugs is a grave social evil and therefore should be prevented at all costs.

The first case of statutory strict liability was *R v Woodrow* (1846) 15 M & W 404, where the accused was found guilty of being in possession of adulterated tobacco, even though he did not know that it was adulterated. Many early decisions revealed an inconsistent approach as the courts were trying to interpret old statutes in ascertaining the will of Parliament. However, Lord Reid in the House of Lords' decision in *Sweet v Parsley* [1969] 1 All ER 347 laid down the following guidelines:

(a) Wherever a section is silent as to *mens rea* there is a presumption that, in order to give effect to the will of Parliament, words importing *mens rea* must be read into the provision.

(b) It is a universal principle that if a penal provision is reasonably capable of two interpretations, that interpretation which is most favourable to the accused must be adopted.

(c) The fact that other sections of the Act expressly require *mens rea* is not in itself sufficient to justify a decision that a section which is silent as to *mens rea* creates an absolute offence. It is necessary to go outside the Act and examine all relevant circumstances in order to establish that this must have been the intention of Parliament. So in *Cundy v Le Coq* (1884) 13 QB 207, a publican was found guilty of selling intoxicating liquor to a drunken person under s. 13 of the Licensing Act 1872, even though the publican did not know and had no reason to know that the customer was drunk; whereas in *Sherras v De Rutzen* [1895] 1 QB 918, a publican was not guilty under s. 16(2) of the Licensing Act 1872 of serving alcohol to a police constable while on duty when the accused did not know or have reason to know that the police constable was on duty. The former case was held to be an offence of strict liability, whereas in the latter, in order to obtain a conviction, the prosecution had to prove *mens rea* on behalf of the publican, which they were unable to do.

Despite the fact that there is a presumption in favour of *mens rea* when a statute is silent, the courts have been prepared to rebut this presumption on many occasions. The leading case on this point is *Gammon v Attorney-General for Hong Kong* [1985] AC 1, where Lord Scarman set out the applicable principles. If the offence is truly criminal in character the presumption is particularly strong, but it can be displaced where the statute is concerned with an issue of social concern. Thus, in *Gammon*, as the accused's activities involved public safety, the Privy Council were prepared to hold that the legislature intended the offence to be one of strict liability.

On analysis these principles appear inconsistent. It could be argued that all crimes by definition are grave social evils, yet if the offence is truly criminal in character, strict liability does not apply. In practice, the courts have adopted a flexible approach, but it is recognized that certain spheres of activity are always likely to attract the conclusion that this is an offence of strict liability. Thus inflation (*R v St Margaret's Trust Ltd* [1958] 2 All ER 289), pollution (*Alphacell Ltd v Woodward* [1972] 2 All ER 475), and dangerous drugs (Pharmaceutical Society of Great Britain v Storkwain, above) are traditional areas where strict liability has been imposed. However, it does seem in recent years that the category of grave social concern is expanding to encompass new social activity to include acting as a director whilst disqualified (*R v Brockley* [1994] Crim LR 671) and unauthorized possession of a dangerous dog (*R v Bezzina* [1994] 1 WLR 1057).

However, the House of Lords have again emphasized the need for the prosecution to prove *mens rea* in *B (A minor) v DPP* [2000] 1 All ER 833, where Lord Hutton stated (at p. 855), 'the test is not whether it is a reasonable implication that the statute rules out *mens rea* as a constituent part of the crime—the test is whether it is a necessary implication'. Further in *R v Lambert* [2001] 3 All ER 577, the House held that although s. 28 of the Misuse of Drugs Act 1971 required the defence to prove a defence, this only meant introduce evidence of, rather than establish a defence on the balance of probabilities.

In view of these developments, it is submitted that it would be most unlikely for s. 1 of the Ancient Book Act 2009 to be an offence of strict liability, and therefore Arthur will only be guilty if the prosecution can establish that he had the necessary *mens rea*.

If the court were to decide that the offence required the prosecution to prove intention, it is submitted that Arthur would not be convicted. He obtained the opinion of Ben, an expert and clearly did not desire or even foresee the consequence that protected books would be destroyed. Arthur has made a mistake, and even if an accused makes an un-reasonable mistake, in accordance with the House of Lords' decision in *DPP v Morgan* [1976] AC 182, he is, in the absence of any clear statutory intent to the contrary, entitled to be judged on the facts as he believed them to be.

If the court decides that the offence could be committed recklessly, it would still be very difficult for the prosecution to establish the appropriate *mens rea*. It is almost certainly the case that subjective recklessness would have to be proved—i.e., the prosecution must show that the accused foresaw the consequence and took an unjustified risk (*R v Cunningham* [1957] 2 All ER 412 and *R v G* [2003] 4 All ER 765) (although technically the latter only deals with the issue of recklessness in relation to criminal damage). As Arthur sought the opinion of an expert it is difficult to see how it could be argued that he was consciously taking an unjustified risk.

It is therefore submitted that Arthur could be guilty of the offence only if the court decides that s. 1 of the Ancient Book Act 2009 creates an offence of strict liability.

Turning to Ben's liability, if he genuinely believed the books to be of post-1800 vintage and the courts interpret the offence as requiring at least recklessness on this issue, he could not be convicted as an accomplice as he would lack the necessary *mens rea*. If the offence were held to be one of strict or absolute liability Ben could only be convicted as an accomplice if he knew of the facts that constituted the offence—i.e. he knew the books dated from before 1800—see *Johnson v Youden* [1950] 1 KB 544.

Alternatively, if Ben knew or believed the books to date from before 1800 he could be charged with either:

(i) doing an act capable of encouraging or assisting the commission of an offence intending to encourage or assist its commission contrary to s. 44 of the Serious Crime Act 2007; or

(ii) doing an act capable of encouraging or assisting the commission of an offence believing that the offence will be committed and that his act will encourage or assist its commission contrary to s. 45 of the Serious Crime Act 2007.

The act in question would be giving advice to Arthur he knew to be wrong. The fact that Arthur, in destroying the books, might have acted without *mens rea* will not absolve Ben. If the offence under the Ancient Book Act 2009 is construed as requiring fault it will be sufficient for the prosecution to prove that Ben's state of mind was such that, had he destroyed the books, he would have acted with the degree of fault required for the full offence; see s. 47(5) (a) (iii) of the 2007 Act. If the 2009 Act is a strict liability offence, Ben can be convicted under the Serious Crime Act 2007, provided he believed that the books dated from before 1800 or was reckless as to whether or not they did.

Question 4

Gloria, Wood's eccentric aunt, aged 57, was invited to stay with Wood and his girlfriend Mary at their property on the coast. It was agreed that Gloria would stay for three weeks and would occupy 'the lodge' in the garden of the Wood's house some 30 yards away. Gloria also agreed to pay £40 to cover the electricity she would use in the lodge.

Everything went well for two weeks, with all three sharing meals at the house. However, a change of mood then came over Gloria who decided that she no longer wanted to have meals with Wood and Mary. Gloria spent more and more time by herself at the lodge.

After 20 days of the holiday Gloria, whose physical condition had visibly deteriorated, announced that she refused to leave the lodge and was going to stay there the rest of the winter. This so enraged Wood and Mary that the next day they told her to leave immediately, which she did.

Six hours later, at 11 pm, Gloria rang their bell pleading to be let in as she was cold and hungry and had nowhere else to go. Wood and Mary refused, and during that night Gloria was taken to hospital suffering from hypothermia.

While in hospital, Gloria fell unconscious and was placed on a life support machine. After five days she was correctly diagnosed by Dr Spock as being in a persistent vegetative state with no hope of recovery. He accordingly disconnected the machine.

Discuss the criminal responsibility (if any) of Wood and Mary.

 Commentary

The sensible way to tackle this question is to start with an examination of failure to act as a basis for liability. The key aspect of this will be the comparison of the given cases with earlier decisions such as *R v Instan* and *R v Stone and Dobinson*. Care must be taken to distinguish between the facts of those cases and the current problem. The facts of the question require an examination of at least three bases for liability: blood relationship, reliance, and creating a dangerous situation.

Do not fall into the trap of thinking that the discussion of omission is all that is required. Candidates must establish a causal link between the omission and the death—in fact and in law.

Finally, candidates will need to consider the most appropriate form of homicide. Candidates are advised not to waste valuable time considering murder or unlawful act manslaughter—they are clearly not relevant on the facts. In relation to killing by gross negligence, candidates need to devote some time to the issue of duty of care—note that this covers very similar ground to the discussion relating to liability for omission—but the decision in *R v Evans* is particularly helpful and relevant here. *Note*: Candidates are not required to consider the responsibility of Dr Spock.

 Answer plan

- Is there a causative omission?
- Examine the bases for liability for failing to act—statutory, contractual, and common law
- Distinguish *R v Instan* and *R v Stone & Dobinson*
- Consider *R v Miller* and *R v Evans*
- Consider killing by gross negligence
- Can a duty of care be established?
- Is the degree of fault required made out on the facts?

Suggested answer

The first issue to be resolved is whether or not Wood and Mary can be said to have caused the death of Gloria. As there is no positive act by either of them that causes death, the court would need to investigate whether or not liability can be based on the failure of either or both of them to prevent Gloria's death.

The question as to whether an omission, as opposed to an act, can actually cause a consequence is a moot point. Traditionally, the criminal law has always drawn a clear distinction between acts and omissions, being loath to punish the latter. Other European countries—e.g., Greece, France and Germany—do not exhibit the same reluctance, and there is dispute as to whether the English approach is correct. See in particular the different views of Professors A. Ashworth (1989) 105 LQR 424 and G. Williams (1991) 107 LQR 109. However, apart from the numerous statutes that impose a duty to act, e.g., s. 170 of the Road Traffic Act 1988, it appears that the common law will impose a duty to act only in very limited circumstances.

There can be no criminal liability imposed on Wood and Mary in respect of their failing to care for Gloria unless the prosecution can establish that they were under a positive legal duty to care for her. Such a duty can be imposed by statute, but that is clearly not the case here. Similarly a legal duty to act can arise from a contract between the parties. For example in *R v Pittwood* (1902) 19 TLR 37, where the defendant, a railway gate operator, was found guilty of manslaughter when a person was killed crossing a railway line as a result of the defendant leaving the gate open when a train was coming. In the present case it could be argued that there was a contractual relationship, in that Gloria agreed to pay for her electricity and was in occupation of the lodge, but it is hard to see how any positive duty to care for Gloria can be implied—and in any event it would be argued that the contract was only for the initial three-week period, and that it was a purely domestic arrangement not intended to give rise to legally enforceable obligations.

In respect of Wood it could be argued that he was under a common law duty to care for Gloria because she was a relative. Where the relationship is that of parent and child the common law has had little difficulty in identifying a positive legal duty of care so that failing to act can result in liability where it causes harm; see *R v Gibbins and Proctor* (1918) 13 Cr App R 134. In *R v Instan* [1893] 1 QB 450, liability for manslaughter was imposed upon a niece who failed to care for her aunt with whom she was living, having been given money by the aunt to supply groceries. Liability in *Instan* was largely based on the existence of a blood relationship between the parties. This would seem to suggest that, at least in the case of Wood, there might be a common law duty to act. It is submitted that the present case can be distinguished from *Instan*. In *Instan* the defendant actually occupied the same house as the deceased, and had expressly undertaken the task of purchasing food for her, which she subsequently failed to do, knowing well that her aunt could not fend for herself. In the present case Gloria decided for herself that she wanted to stay in the lodge alone, thus raising the question of whether Wood was obliged to do anything more for her than he had been doing during the first two weeks of her stay. Furthermore the evidence suggests that it was refusing to readmit Gloria after she had been told to leave that led to her death—raising the question of whether Wood was under any obligation to readmit Gloria.

The much more promising argument for the prosecution is that a positive legal duty to act at common law arose in respect of both Wood and Mary because they had allowed a relationship of reliance to develop between themselves and Gloria. The key authority here is *R v Stone and Dobinson* [1977] QB 354. In that case the Court of Appeal upheld convictions for killing by gross negligence on the basis that the defendants had admitted the deceased to their house and had attempted to care for her. They then failed to discharge their duty adequately and failed to summon any assistance in discharging that duty. The court stressed that the duty to act arose not simply because of a blood relationship between one of the defendants and the deceased, but because of the reliance relationship.

It could be argued that in allowing Gloria to stay Wood and Mary allowed a relationship of reliance to develop—but the present case can be distinguished from *Stone and Dobinson* on the grounds that Wood and Mary placed a time limit on Gloria's stay, and Gloria left of her own volition. Thus the argument as to whether or not there is any liability for failing to act is finely balanced.

The prosecution could run an alternative argument on the basis that when Gloria begs to be readmitted to the house Wood and Mary are aware that their expulsion of Gloria has created a dangerous situation. There is evidence that Gloria's physical condition had visibly deteriorated. Gloria was cold, hungry, and had nowhere to go. There was evidence that Gloria was eccentric. Applying *R v Miller* [1983] 1 All ER 978, where the House of Lords upheld the accused's conviction for criminal damage where he had inadvertently started a fire and then, when he realized what he had done, simply left the building without making any attempt to prevent the fire spreading or to call the fire brigade, it could be argued that by failing to offer Gloria shelter, Wood and Mary committed culpable omission that caused Gloria's death. For the *Miller* principle to apply, the prosecution would have to show that the defendants were both aware that their expulsion of Gloria had created a dangerous situation. On the facts this should not be too difficult.

Assuming that the failure to care for Gloria, or the refusal to readmit her to the house, can form the basis of liability, the prosecution will have to show that this omission caused Gloria's death. It is not necessary for the prosecution to prove that the omission was the sole or main cause, merely that it contributed significantly to the victim's death (*R v Cheshire* [1991] 3 All ER 670). The accused could argue that the doctor's turning off the life support system constituted a *novus actus interveniens,* breaking the chain of causation; but this argument was rejected by the House of Lords in *R v Malcherek; R v Steel* [1981] 2 All ER 422, where Lord Lane CJ stated that 'the fact that the victim has died, despite or because of medical treatment for the initial injury given by careful and skilled medical practitioners, will not exonerate the original assailant from responsibility for the death'.

It is therefore clear that the medical treatment, of itself, will not be held to have broken the chain of causation in law.

Wood and Mary could be charged with manslaughter on the basis of killing by gross negligence (they could not be charged with constructive manslaughter as the prosecution would not be able to establish an unlawful act causing Gloria's death). Killing by gross negligence, by contrast, can be based on an omission; see *R v Lowe* [1973] 1 All ER 805.

The key authority regarding killing by gross negligence is the House of Lords' ruling in *R v Adomako* [1994] 3 All ER 79, where their Lordships held that an accused would be guilty of manslaughter if the following four conditions were satisfied:

(1) the accused owed a duty of care to the victim;

(2) that duty was broken;

(3) the conduct of the accused was grossly negligent;

(4) that conduct caused the victim's death.

In some cases the existence of a duty of care will be self-evident, for example doctor and patient, parent and child etc. It may not be the case that all familial relationships give rise to a duty of care in themselves. Helpful guidance on this point is to be found in the Court of Appeal decision in *R v Evans* [2009] EWCA Crim 650, where Judge LCJ explained that the duty necessary to found gross negligence manslaughter is likely to arise where a person has created or contributed to the creation of a state of affairs which he knows, or ought reasonably to know, has become life-threatening. In such cases the defendant will be under a legal duty to take reasonable steps to mitigate the harm threatened.

The trial judge in the present case should direct that they can conclude that a duty of care existed provided they find certain facts established—and the trial judge should make clear to the jury what those key facts are. It is submitted that there is sufficient evidence for the jury to conclude that a duty of care existed.

The breach of the duty of care is evident in their not helping Gloria and not attempting to obtain any alternative assistance for her—they did not even call the police to advise them of the problem. The issue of whether this breach of the duty of care can be said to have caused the death of Gloria has already been considered above.

The remaining live issue, therefore, is that of gross negligence. Following the House of Lords' decision in *R v Adomako* the jury will have to determine whether or not the accused's conduct:

(a) departed from the proper standard of care incumbent upon them;

(b) involved a risk of death to the victim;

(c) was so grossly negligent that it ought to be regarded as criminal.

As later cases such as *R v Mark and another* [2004] All ER (D) 35 (Oct) indicate, actual foresight of risk of death by the accused is not required. The test for *mens rea* is objective—does the jury regard the act or omission leading to the breach of duty as being so culpable that it should be labelled as 'criminal'? Evidence that the defendants knew they would cause harm by not acting is admissible to establish the required fault, but is not essential. Similarly, evidence that Mary and Wood had never thought about what might happen to Gloria could be admissible to show that they should not be labelled as criminals, but such evidence would not preclude a finding by the jury that they had acted, or failed to act, in a manner that was grossly negligent.

Question 5

Critically analyse with reference to decided cases, the reasons why the development and application of the criminal law is often unpredictable and inconsistent.

 Commentary

Occasionally an exam will contain a question that requires candidates to take a wider view of the criminal law. This is such a question. Candidates cannot simply home in on a specific area and cover it in detail. Candidates must try to think of instances throughout the syllabus that can be used in your arguments to answer the question. Avoid the common mistake of interpreting the question to read 'Choose one area of the criminal law where there are difficulties and write all about them'! This question has been included as it enables candidates to think more widely about the role of the criminal law within the legal system and society as a whole. Providing a good answer requires the ability to take a broad view of the syllabus—something candidates who revise topics in isolation are not always able to do.

 Answer plan

- Constant change–*R v R* [1991]
- Lack of code—*Caldwell* [1981], *Morgan* [1975]
- Logic v policy
- Role of House of Lords–*Clegg* [1995]

Suggested answer

The development of many areas of law follows a consistent and logical course. The basic foundations, their concepts and application are accepted by the vast majority, and only fine tuning or adjustments of these principles are required to meet new situations. Unfortunately this cannot be said about criminal law, where the debate about fundamental concepts—such as whether recklessness should be interpreted subjectively or objectively; whether a mistake of fact relied upon by a defendant should have to be one that a reasonable person would have made; whether duress should be a defence to a charge of murder—is still ongoing.

One of the problems is that the criminal law is subject to constant change. It has to adapt to cover new phenomena, such as stalking, drug abuse, and internet fraud and to reflect society's changing social and moral standards. As the House of Lords stated in *R v R* [1991] 4 All ER 481, abolishing the husband's marital rape exemption, the common law is capable of evolving in the light of social, economic and cultural developments. In that case the recognition that the status of women had changed out of all recognition from the time (*Hale's Pleas of the Crown 1736*) when the husband's marital rape exemption was initially recognized was long overdue. Similarly, the criminal law once reflected the moral position that it was a crime to take one's own life. Failure in such an enterprise was prosecuted as attempted suicide and could be punished. However, attitudes softened and it was recognized that such a person needed help, not a criminal trial; the law was consequently amended by the Suicide Act 1961. The 1960s saw similar changes in respect of the law relating to homosexuality and abortion. Changes in the law can also result from a shift in ideology on the part of an elected government, or as a response to new threats to the safety and stability of society—for example legislation to combat terrorism.

There is no doubt that the development and application of the criminal law would be more consistent and predictable if the courts exhibited a more uniform approach to its development. The problem is illustrated by two House of Lords' decisions: *Metropolitan Police Commissioner v Caldwell* [1981] 1 All ER 961, where an objective approach to recklessness was used, and *DPP v Morgan* [1975] 2 All ER 347, where a subjective approach to mistake was applied. Why was it that liability for recklessness was imposed on an objective basis, but where a defendant made a mistake of fact he was entitled (subject to any statutory provision to the contrary) to be judged on the facts as he honestly believed them to be? Commentators may argue that two different areas of the criminal law were being considered, criminal damage and rape (note that the law has since been changed as regards rape by the Sexual Offences Act 2003), but the inconsistency is still stark. At least in so far as recklessness is concerned, the House of Lords has now embraced the notion of subjectivity again in *R v G* [2003] 4 All ER 765, but the very fact that the legal definition of such a basic concept can change so much in the space of 20 years is itself startling.

The Law Commission has long argued that the solution lies in codifying the law (see Law Com. No. 143) on the basis that: 'the criminal law could then exhibit a uniform approach to all crimes and defences'.

All other major European countries (France, Germany, and Spain) have a detailed criminal code, with a uniform approach providing a starting point for interpreting the law. The criminal law in England and Wales has developed in a piecemeal fashion, with one offence's development showing little consistency with another's. So often it is difficult to say what our law actually is, even before lawyers start to debate how it should be applied, e.g., *R v Savage*; *R v Parmenter* [1992] 1 AC 699, interpreting (after over 130 years of use) the provisions of the Offences Against the Person Act 1861. A code could be expressed in clear language with definitions of fundamental concepts such as intention and recklessness, as suggested by the Law Commission's Draft Criminal Code; although, as the former chairman of the Law Commission Justice Henry Brooke stated ([1995] Crim LR 911): 'Nobody in their right mind would want to put the existing criminal law into a codified form'.

Often the criminal law follows a logical approach in its application; but as it does not exist in a vacuum and is not simply the application of academic principles, policy considerations sometimes have to prevail. As Lord Salmon stated in *DPP v Majewski* [1976] 2 All ER 142, regarding the defence of intoxication, 'the answer is that in strict logic the view [intoxication is no defence to crimes of basic intent] cannot be justified. But this is the view that has been adopted by the common law which is founded on common sense and experience rather than strict logic'. Policy considerations are also behind s. 1(3) of the Criminal Attempts Act 1981, whereby in the offence of attempt, the facts are to be as the accused believes them to be. Thus an accused, objectively viewed, may appear not to be committing a criminal act but because they believe they are, they can be guilty of attempting to commit that criminal act, as in *R v Shivpuri* [1986] 2 All ER 334.

There is often no means of predicting which approach will prevail. In *Jaggard v Dickinson* [1980] 3 All ER 716, the accused, who had been informed by her friend X that she could break into X's house to shelter, while drunk mistakenly broke into V's house. She was charged with criminal damage under s. 1(1) of the Criminal Damage Act 1971, but argued that she had a lawful excuse under s. 5(2) of the Act as she honestly believed that she had the owner's consent. Although the prosecution contended that this was a crime of basic intent and therefore drunkenness was no defence (citing the House of Lords' decisions of *Metropolitan Police Commissioner v Caldwell* and *DPP v Majewski* in support), the Court of Appeal quashed her conviction, giving priority to the statutory provision of s. 5(2) of the 1971 Act.

One important aspect of the criminal law process in recent years, which has caused uncertainty, is the role of the House of Lords in changing the criminal law. Clearly judges are there to say what the law is, not what it should be; but Lord Simon in *DPP for Northern Ireland v Lynch* [1975] 1 All ER 913 said: 'I am all for recognising that judges do make law. And I am all for judges exercising their responsibilities boldly at the proper time and place...where matters of social policy are not involved which the collective wisdom of Parliament is better suited to resolve'. Thus in *R v R*, the House of Lords changed the law of rape, by abolishing the husband's defence of marital rape immunity without waiting for Parliament to implement the Law Commission's recommendations. However, their Lordships took the opposite view in *R v Clegg* [1995] 1 All ER 334, where they refused to follow the Law Commission's suggestion that a person who was entitled to use force in self-defence but who used unreasonable force, thereby killing the victim, would be guilty of manslaughter, not murder. Lord Lloyd stated:

> I am not adverse to judges developing law, or indeed making new law, when they can see their way clearly, even where questions of social policy are involved. [A good example is *R v R*.] But in the present case I am in no doubt that your Lordships should abstain from law making. The reduction of what would otherwise be murder to manslaughter in a particular class of case seems to me essentially a matter for decision by the legislature.

It is difficult to appreciate the essential difference in issues in these two cases, despite Lord Lowry's justifications in *R v Clegg* that '*R v R* dealt with a specific act and not with a general principle governing criminal liability'. Clearly there is a difference in opinion amongst the Law Lords as to the correct application of these principles. This is well illustrated by the House of Lords' decision in *R v Gotts* [1992] 1 All ER 832. The majority decision not to allow duress as a defence to attempted murder was on the basis that duress was no defence to murder. The minority view to the contrary revealed a different analysis. They argued that duress is a general defence throughout the criminal law with the exceptions of the offences of murder and treason. It is for Parliament, and not the courts, to limit the ambit of a defence; and as attempted murder is a different offence to murder, duress must therefore be available.

It is submitted that these are the main reasons why the development and application of the criminal law is often uncertain and unpredictable. There are other factors, such as whether an issue is a question of law for the judge or fact for the jury, e.g., the meaning of 'administer' (*R v Gillard* (1988) 87 Cr App R 189); the difficulty in ascertaining the *ratio decidendi* of many cases, e.g., *R v Brown* [1993] 2 All ER 75 (consent); and the possible effect of the decisions of the European Court of Human Rights. But it is the lack of a code and uniform principles which are the main factors causing the inherent uncertainty.

Question 6

Critically assess the grounds upon which liability for failing to act will be imposed in English criminal law.

 Commentary

Liability for omissions is a popular topic with examiners, either as an element of a problem question—typically linked to killing by gross negligence to bring out the duty of care issues—or as an essay topic in its own right. To deal comfortably with essay-style questions on omissions it is necessary to have a good knowledge of the basic cases. For degree level examinations, however, it is likely that some element of analysis will be necessary. The extent to which this is the case will vary according to the level at which the paper is set. Second and third year undergraduates and CPE students would be expected to display more developed skills of critical evaluation. Try to avoid simply describing the law—ensure that some comment is provided on the examples given. There is not a great deal of material on law reform in this area—the Law Commission has not explored it in great detail, but it should not be difficult to identify some of the anomalies that the case law throws up.

 Answer plan

- Basic rule on liability for omissions
- Legal duty based on statute
- Legal duty based on contract
- Legal duty based on office
- Common law duty to act
- Where a duty ceases to exist
- Possible reforms

Suggested answer

Every offence in criminal law requires proof of an *actus reus* on the part of the accused. In the vast majority of cases statute or common law defines this *actus reus* in terms of a positive act. Indeed, the expression *actus reus* literally translates as 'guilty act'. A moment's thought reveals, however, that a defendant can commit an offence by failing to act, just as readily as he can by positive action. If the parents of a newly born baby administer a lethal dose of poison to the child no one would seriously suggest that there would be a problem in establishing *actus reus*. Why should it be any different where the defendants decide not to feed the child, with the result that the child dies of starvation? The answer is that there is no difference in criminal law, but the method by which liability is established may differ where it is based on an omission as opposed to a positive act.

The basic rule in English criminal law is that there is no general positive duty to act to prevent the commission of criminal offences or to limit the effect of harm caused by the actions of others. This position reflects what is sometimes referred to as the individualistic approach to liability. If D is at a swimming pool, and he sees P (a young child with whom he has no connection) drowning in the deep end, why should D be required to go to P's aid? D has no special responsibility for P, and did not cause the risk to arise. It is pure chance that D is in a position to help. Why should fate be the basis for imposing a liability for failing to prevent P's death? Critics of the current position at common law argue for a 'social responsibility' approach. This view proposes that liability should arise for failing to attend those in peril partly because of the moral obligation to do so, but also because it reflects a more complex social pact. A positive duty to aid others would impose a responsibility but would also confer a corresponding benefit. D might one day find himself compelled to help P, but the next day he might be the beneficiary of the duty on P to aid D where D is in peril. At a macro level society benefits because less harm is suffered by individuals.

In reality English criminal law does impose criminal liability for failing to act, but it does so on the basis of exceptions. Thus D will not incur liability for failing to act unless the prosecution can point to a positive legal duty to act.

The most obvious source of such legal duties will be statute. Parliament creates liability for failing to act in two ways. At a very simple level it creates offences of omission. It is an offence for the owner of a vehicle to fail to display a valid tax disc. It is an offence to fail to submit a tax return, or to provide company accounts, etc. In these cases the omission itself is the crime. In many cases they are offences of strict or absolute liability. Alternatively Parliament may enact legislation that places a category of person under a duty to act in a particular way. A failure to comply with this duty may result in liability where the failure causes the commission of some prohibited consequence. Perhaps the best known example of this is provided by the Children and Young Persons Act 1933, which places parents and guardians under a legal duty to care for children. Suppose that parents go out for the evening leaving a four-year-old child alone. Whilst they are out he falls onto a fire and is killed. It is likely that the court would find that there was a culpable omission based on the breach of statutory duty, and liability could be imposed if causation and fault are also established.

An alternative basis for establishing a legal duty to act is where D is subject to a contractual duty or holds an office that suggests the imposition of a duty. In the case of employees the court will look at the express or implied terms of the contract to determine the extent and nature of the duties imposed on D. In *R v Pittwood* (1902) 19 TLR 37, a railway crossing gatekeeper opened the gate to let a cart pass, but then went off to lunch, forgetting to close the gate. A hay cart crossed the line and was hit by a train. The defendant was convicted of manslaughter. He argued that the only duty he owed was to his employers, with whom he had a contract. It was held, however, that his contract imposed a wider duty upon him to users of the crossing. Thus the duty arising under a contract inures to the benefit of those who are not privy to the contract—i.e., the passengers on the train. In *R v Dytham* [1979] 3 All ER 641, D was a police constable on duty. He witnessed V being ejected from a nightclub and beaten up by a doorman. D did not intervene. V died from his injuries. D was convicted of the common law offence of misfeasance in public office and his appeal against conviction was dismissed. The case begs the question—why was D not charged with causing the death of V by his failure to intervene? The answer may be that in cases of failing to act, proof of causation may be problematic. D obviously failed in his duty as a police officer—but would his intervention have prevented V's death? The mere fact that there is an agreement between parties does not necessarily mean that there will be a contractual duty to act. In *R v Instan* [1893] 1 QB 450, D was given money by her aunt to buy groceries. D failed to care for her aunt who subsequently died. It is unlikely that any contractual duty existed in this case, as the agreement was a domestic one—hence there would have been no intention to create legal relations.

Inevitably there are situations where, despite the absence of any statutory or contractual duty to act, it is felt that liability ought to be imposed. In such cases it falls to the common law to perform its residual function of supplying the omission. Judges 'discover' new common law duties to act because it is felt they ought to exist. *R v Instan* is a case in point. For the last 12 days of her life the aunt was suffering from gangrene in her leg and was unable to look after herself. Only D knew this. D did not provide her aunt with food nor did she obtain medical attention. This omission accelerated the aunt's death. D's conviction for manslaughter was upheld, the court proceeding on the basis that a common law duty was simply a moral duty so fundamental the courts had to enforce it. As Lord Coleridge CJ observed, a legal common law duty is nothing else than the enforcing by law of that which is a moral obligation without legal enforcement.

The problem with the common law is that it is reactive—it only develops because cases come to the courts on appeal. A narrow reading of *R v Instan* suggests that a common law duty is owed to one's blood relatives, but clearly the scope should be wider than that. The court in *R v Gibbins and Proctor* (1918) 13 Cr App R 134, accepted that a duty could be imposed upon a common law wife to care for her partner's child because, although the child was not hers, she had assumed a duty towards the child by choosing to live with the child's father and accept housekeeping money to buy food for them all. The problem with such rulings is that the limits of liability are left vague—what if D had lived with the child's father only on weekends?

Imposing liability for omissions where D undertakes to care for P and P becomes reliant on D may even be counter-productive. In *R v Stone and Dobinson* [1977] QB 354, the defendants were convicted of the manslaughter of Stone's sister Fanny because they took her in but failed to care for her adequately. With hindsight they might have been advised not to help her in the first place. The law therefore sends mixed messages. One ought to care for others, but one should not start to do so unless one is able to discharge that duty properly.

The common law duty to act was developed further by the important House of Lords' decision in *R v Miller* [1983] 1 All ER 978. D, who was squatting in an empty house, fell asleep whilst smoking a cigarette. Whilst he was asleep the cigarette set fire to the mattress. D woke, realized the mattress was on fire, but took no steps to dose the fire. The house was damaged in the ensuing blaze. He was obviously not under a statutory duty to put the fire out, nor was he under a contractual duty to do so. At the time the common law duties to act were based on duties owed to blood relatives, or arising from reliance. The House of Lords had little choice but to 'discover' a new legal duty at common law. Such a duty arises where D accidentally causes harm, realizes that he has done so, and it lies within his power to take steps, either himself or by calling for the assistance to prevent or minimize the harm. The omission itself is not, of course, the offence. For criminal damage it must be shown that the omission caused the harm, and that D had the requisite *mens rea* at the time of the *actus reus*. Whilst the ruling in *R v Miller* is socially desirable—there is great social utility in D being required to limit the effect of his careless actions—there are many uncertainties. What is it that D is required to do once he realizes he has caused harm? Is the test objective or subjective? Must he act as the reasonable person would have done, or does he simply have to do his best? The latter would certainly accord with the general trend towards subjectivity in criminal law.

Even where a positive legal duty to act can be identified, uncertainties may arise as to whether D has been or can be absolved from that duty. In *R v Smith* [1979] Crim LR 251, D's wife was seriously ill. She asked D not to seek help. Her condition worsened and she eventually asked D to get help, which he did, but it was too late to save her. D was charged with manslaughter and the trial judge directed the jury that D was under a duty by virtue of being the victim's husband, but he could be released from that duty if she so indicated and she was of sound mind at the time. This places the husband in a difficult legal position. At what point must he ignore his wife's wishes and obtain medical help? Some clarification is provided by the House of Lords' decision in *Airedale NHS Trust v Bland* [1993] AC 789, where it was held that doctors were under a duty to treat a patient where it was in the patient's best interests to do so. Where, however, all hope of the patient recovering had disappeared, the duty to nourish and maintain the patient would also cease.

To date the Law Commission has done little more than suggest a codification of the common law position as outlined above. It is submitted that a more radical approach would be to adopt the French model of creating a general statutory duty of 'easy rescue'. Essentially there would be liability for failing to prevent harm where such prevention would not be too onerous or difficult for D to achieve. The accident that led to the death of Princess Diana in the Paris underpass illustrates the point. French photographers were charged with manslaughter based on their failure to help because they allegedly photographed the crash scene when they could have been offering aid to the injured. Such a prosecution would not have been possible under English law.

Liability for failing to act

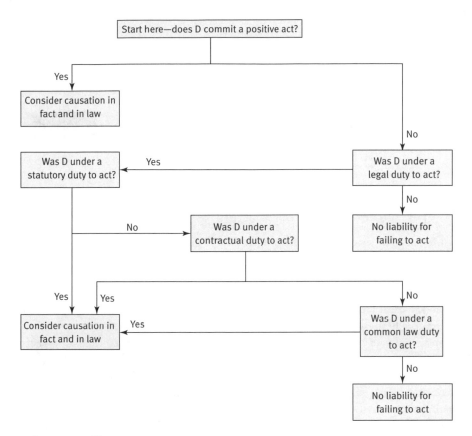

Further reading

Amirthalingam, K., '*Caldwell* Recklessness is Dead, Long Live *Mens Rea*'s Fecklessness' [2004] MLR 491.

Ashworth, A., 'Interpreting Criminal Statutes' [1991] LQR 419.

Ashworth, A. and Blake, M., 'The Presumption of Innocence in English Criminal Law' [1996] Crim LR 306.

Kaveny, C.M., 'Inferring Intention from Foresight' (2004) LQR 120.

Keating, H., 'Reckless Children?' [2007] Crim LR 546.

Norrie, A., 'Oblique Intent and Legal Politics' [1989] Crim LR 793.

Pedain, A., 'Intention and the Terrorist Example' [2003] Crim LR 549.

Smith, J.C., '*R v Woollin*' [1998] Crim LR 890.

3

Unlawful homicide

Introduction

One of the themes of this book, and of the substantive criminal law itself, is the constant pressure for change and consequent uncertainty. This is aptly illustrated by the offences of murder and manslaughter, aspects of which have been considered and reconsidered by the House of Lords in its judicial capacity and which have also been the subject of Law Commission reports (in particular Involuntary Manslaughter (Law Com. No. 237), Partial Defences to Murder (Law Com. No. 290) and Murder, Manslaughter and Infanticide (Law Com. No. 304)).

Despite the fact that Parliament has intervened in the past to amend aspects of homicide, e.g., in the Homicide Act 1957 and the Law Reform (Year and a Day Rule) Act 1996, the offence of murder is still governed by a common law definition. The *actus reus* of the offence is essentially causing the death of a human being. The *mens rea* is sometimes referred to as 'malice aforethought'—but it is suggested that this term should be avoided as it is likely to mislead. Murder does not require any proof of malice towards the victim on the part of the defendant, and there is no requirement that the killing should have been in any way premeditated. *R v Moloney* [1985] 1 All ER 1025, reaffirms that the *mens rea* is intention to kill or cause grievous bodily harm. *R v Woollin* [1998] 4 All ER 103 provides a gloss on this by providing that in cases where there may be some doubt as to intention the jury can have regard to the extent to which the defendant foresaw death or grievous bodily harm resulting from his actions. Intention should only be inferred where the defendant foresees a consequence as virtually certain to result from his actions.

The debate as to whether intention to kill or do grievous bodily harm should be the *mens rea* has been fuelled by Lord Mustill's *obiter dicta* in *Attorney-General's Reference (No. 3 of 1994)* [1997] 3 All ER 936. He was critical of the conspicuous anomaly that intention to cause grievous bodily harm of itself could be sufficient *mens rea* for murder. This anomaly has also been recognized by the Law Commission, whose Draft Code (cl. 54) provides that the definition of *mens rea* for murder should be restricted to require at least an intention to cause serious personal harm *being aware that death may occur*. However, this suggestion, together with those abolishing the mandatory life sentence for murder, is likely to go unheeded on the basis that such changes would send the wrong message to society. Public opinion seems to favour a wide definition for the *mens rea* for murder. The problem is that a wide definition coupled with a mandatory life sentence results in a lack of differentiation between killings that are deliberate, and those that result from behaviour that borders on the reckless.

The need for legislation in this area was also recognized by the Law Lords in *Airedale NHS Trust v Bland* [1993] 1 All ER 821, concerning the criminal responsibility of doctors regarding euthanasia. This was another example of the problems caused by the absence of a criminal code, highlighting the fact that sometimes we do not actually know what the law is until it is formulated in a House of Lords' decision. It is certainly most unsatisfactory that their Lordships had to resort to the distinction between acts and omissions, in deciding that disconnecting the naso-gastric tube was an omission (to give further treatment), in order to hold that a doctor in these circumstances would not be committing murder or manslaughter.

Question 1

Mary, intending to give her neighbours Jill and Stan a fright, lit a fire in their letterbox not knowing whether anybody was in the house. In fact, Jill and Stan had gone out for the evening, but their aged parents, Meg and Hugh, who were staying at their home, were overcome by fumes. Due to an administrative error, two ambulances arrived to take the victims to hospital; and the ambulance in which Hugh was transported was driven so negligently that it was involved in an accident and by the time it arrived at hospital Hugh had died.

Meg arrived at hospital and was informed that a blood transfusion would save her life. However, because of religious beliefs, she refused and died two days later.

Discuss the criminal liability of Mary.

 ## Commentary

Most criminal law exams will contain a question on murder, and this question is typical. When dealing with the offence of murder candidates should always consider the possibility of involuntary manslaughter as an alternative (unless expressly excluded by the rubric) as examiners often leave the issue of *mens rea* for murder in doubt. In this answer the constructive basis of involuntary manslaughter is dealt with in detail.

The other major area that must be covered in detail is causation. Again this is a topic that candidates will often find included in questions based on unlawful homicide, and in this answer the cases concerning medical treatment as a *novus actus interveniens* must be analysed. In terms of construction of your answer, it generally aids clarity to deal with causation at the outset, as it is a common factor whatever form of homicide is involved.

Although there are difficulties surrounding these topics a well-prepared student would be confident of obtaining a high mark on a question of this nature.

Answer plan

- Causation
- Murder—whether or not *mens rea* is made out
- Transferred malice
- Constructive manslaughter
- Causation
- **Criminal Damage Act 1971**

Suggested answer

The most serious offences that Mary may be charged with are murder and manslaughter. Murder comprises causing the death of a human being within the Queen's peace with intention to kill or intention to do grievous bodily harm. It has not been necessary since the coming into force of the Law Reform (Year and a Day Rule) Act 1996, that the death takes place within a year and a day of the unlawful act or omission.

The first issue to consider is that of causation. But for Mary starting the fire neither death would have occurred—hence causation in fact is established. As to causation in law, the prosecution does not have to prove that Mary's actions were the main cause or even a substantial cause of the victims' deaths, merely that they made a significant contribution to the consequence (*R v Cheshire* [1991] 3 All ER 670). Mary would argue in respect of Meg's death that her decision to refuse a blood transfusion was unreasonable and thus constituted a *novus actus interveniens* that broke the chain of causation. This point was resolved in *R v Blaue* [1975] 1 WLR 1411 where, on similar facts, the court applied the 'egg-shell skull' principle that you take your victim as you find him. Thus an accused will not be exonerated merely because the consequences of the accused's act are exacerbated by the susceptibilities of the victim. As Lawton LJ stated in *Blaue*: 'It has been the policy of the law that those who use violence on other people must take their victims as they find them. This in our judgement means the whole man, not just the physical man.' In *Blaue* the court refused to say that the victim's decision was unreasonable, but even if it were, on the authority of *R v Holland* (1841) 2 Mood and R 351, it would still not exonerate Mary. In this case the accused severely cut the victim's hand with an iron sword. The victim refused to have his fingers amputated although he was given medical advice that failure to do so would result in lockjaw and his death. Unfortunately, the diagnosis proved correct and the victim died. Nevertheless the accused was convicted of murder.

The position regarding Hugh's death is more complicated. Mary would argue the authority of *R v Jordan* (1956) 40 Cr App R 152, which decided that if the medical treatment received was the sole cause of death and was also grossly negligent, the chain of causation will be broken. However, later cases have isolated *Jordan*, demonstrating that it is very difficult to succeed with this argument. Thus in *R v Smith* [1959] 2 All ER 193, the accused stabbed the victim in a barrack room brawl. The victim was dropped twice while being taken to the medical orderly, who failed to diagnose the full extent of his wounds. Not surprisingly the victim died, but the accused's conviction for murder was upheld as the court held that as the original wound was still an operating cause of death the chain of causation was not broken. Similarly in *R v Cheshire* (above), on facts similar to *R v Jordan*, the Court of Appeal upheld the accused's conviction for murder, Beldam LJ stating: 'it will only be in the most extraordinary and unusual case that such treatment can be said to be so independent of the acts of the accused that it could be regarded in law as the cause of the victim's death to the exclusion of the accused's act'.

So even if the evidence was capable of showing that the injuries sustained by Hugh in the ambulance accident were the sole cause of death, the court might still conclude that this was not 'so independent of the acts of the accused' and therefore not sufficient to break the chain of causation.

The *mens rea* for murder is satisfied by the prosecution establishing that the accused intended to kill or cause grievous bodily harm. This was stated in *R v Moloney* [1985] 1 All ER 1025 and confirmed by the House of Lords in *R v Hancock and Shankland* [1986] 1 All ER 641 and *R v Woollin* [1998] 4 All ER 103. This is a question of fact for the jury, and in *Moloney* the House of Lords stated that unless intention was a very complicated issue because of the facts of the case the trial judge should avoid any elaboration or paraphrasing of what is meant by intention, but simply leave it to the jury's good sense as intention is a word in common use and easily understood by the public.

If the issue is complex the trial judge might follow the guidelines laid down by the House of Lords in *Woollin*, where it was stated that if the simple direction was not enough, the jury should be further directed that they were not entitled to find the necessary intention unless they felt sure that death or serious bodily harm was a virtually certain result of D's actions (barring some unforeseen intervention) and that D had appreciated that fact.

However, Lord Scarman in *Hancock and Shankland* did emphasize that there is no magic formula that the trial judge must follow, although he should point out to the jury that the more probable the consequence the more likely the accused foresaw it and intended it. Nevertheless, foresight of consequence is not conclusive proof of intention, although it is evidence from which the jury may infer intention.

Mary may argue that she intended only to frighten the occupants of the house and not to cause death or grievous bodily harm. She may also argue that she did not intend to harm Hugh and Meg, but this argument will fail because of the doctrine of transferred malice, i.e., if Mary has the *mens rea* for a particular offence against a particular victim but she actually commits that crime against a different victim, the *mens rea* will be transferred to the actual victim and Mary will be guilty of that offence. Thus in *R v Mitchell* [1983] 2 All ER 427, the accused was found guilty of manslaughter when he deliberately hit a 72-year-old man who fell against an 89-year-old woman, knocking her over and causing her to break a femur. This required an operation and she died as a result of complications arising from it. The Court of Appeal rejected the accused's argument that the doctrine could only apply if the actual victim and the intended victim were identical; and more recently in *Attorney-General's Reference (No. 3 of 1994)* [1996] 1 Cr App R 351, the court held that the doctrine could apply to convict an accused of murder who stabbed a pregnant woman with the result that the baby was born alive but later died as a result of injuries inflicted by the accused (although this decision was reversed by the House of Lords: [1997] 3 All ER 936).

As intention is a question of fact for the jury, it is not possible to be certain that they would conclude that Mary had the necessary *mens rea*. A jury might accept that her action was directed at simply damaging the house or simply frightening the occupants. If this were the case, Mary could still be convicted of involuntary manslaughter, which is unlawful homicide without intention to kill or do grievous bodily harm. There are two broad categories of involuntary manslaughter. First, manslaughter by an unlawful and dangerous act (constructive manslaughter), where the prosecution must prove that the accused committed a criminal and dangerous act that caused the victim's death. Secondly, manslaughter by gross negligence (*R v Adomako* [1994] 3 All ER 79).

To establish liability for constructive manslaughter the prosecution would need to establish that Mary had committed a criminal act—in this case the evidence of criminal damage being at least reckless as to whether life is endangered is pretty much evident from the facts.

It is not necessary for the prosecution to prove that Mary knew the act was unlawful or dangerous, simply that she intended to do that act—i.e., set fire to the house. Whether the act is unlawful is clearly a question for the judge and jury. It is clear that Mary has committed the *actus reus* of criminal damage, and although the jury must be satisfied that Mary had the necessary *mens rea* for this offence (*R v Jennings* [1990] Crim LR 588), she clearly intended to start the fire.

Mary may argue that she did not realize that this was dangerous, but this contention will not succeed as the House of Lords in *DPP v Newbury and Jones* [1976] 2 All ER 365 confirmed that this is a question of fact for the jury and the prosecution does not have to prove that the accused recognized the risk of danger. Following *R v Dawson* (1985) 81 Cr App R 150, the jury can conclude that the criminal act is 'dangerous' for these purposes if a sober and reasonable person, at the scene of the crime, watching the unlawful act being performed, knowing what the defendant knows of the circumstances, and seeing what the defendant sees, would have foreseen the risk of some physical harm resulting therefrom. A key issue here would be Mary's knowledge of whether the house was occupied. The facts indicate that she is not certain of this, but is willing to take the risk that the house may be occupied. On this basis her awareness of the risk that the house might be occupied can be attributed to the hypothetical reasonable bystander for the purposes of the test in *R v Dawson*. It is submitted that, on these facts, the jury would be likely to conclude that the criminal damage was dangerous.

In *R v Dalby* [1982] 1 All ER 916, the Court of Appeal appeared to introduce a third condition into constructive manslaughter—i.e., the act must be directed at the victim and likely to cause immediate injury. This was quickly amended by *R v Mitchell* to an act directed at another (not necessarily the victim). However, in *R v Goodfellow* (1986) 83 Cr App R 23, where the accused, intending to be re-housed by the council, set fire to his house, thereby causing the death of some of his family, the 'aimed-at doctrine' was rejected and the accused was convicted of constructive and reckless manslaughter. Thus it appears that as long as there is no intervening act, this condition is satisfied.

There has always been uncertainty as to what the appropriate *mens rea* for manslaughter should be, and indeed actually is. As Lord Aitkin stated in *Andrews v DPP* [1937] 2 All ER 552 at pp. 554–5, 'of all crimes manslaughter appears to afford most difficulties of definition, for it concerns homicide in so many and so varying conditions'. It is submitted that the *mens rea* for the unlawful act of criminal damage should suffice—thus following the decision of the House of Lords in *R v G* [2003] 4 All ER 765, Mary must be shown to have at least been aware of the risk of criminal damage and to have (unreasonably) taken that risk.

Given that the elements of unlawful act manslaughter seem to be established it is unlikely that the prosecution would have to resort to arguments based on killing by gross negligence. In any event, this form of liability for manslaughter is normally used in 'duty' situations where no criminal act can be identified.

In the unlikely event of Mary's arguments on causation succeeding, she would still be guilty of offences under the Criminal Damage Act 1971. In particular, arson under s. 1(3) and intentionally or recklessly endangering life under s. 1(2).

Homicide causation flowchart

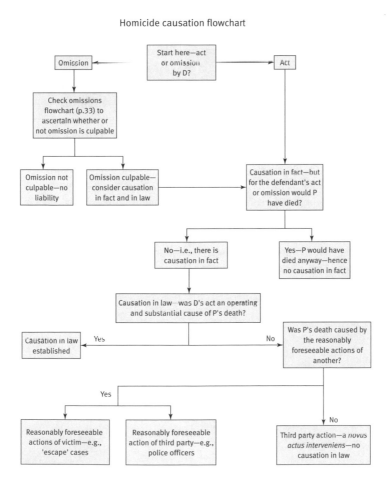

Question 2

On a very cold winter's night, Don, accompanied by Mrs X, is driving along a lonely country road. Don's attention is distracted by his talking with Mrs X and he knocks down Tim, a pedestrian. Don is worried that Mrs X's husband may somehow learn of their relationship and therefore drives on although he can clearly see that Tim is injured and unconscious. Tim's body is not discovered until the following morning, by which time he has died from exposure to the exceptional cold. If he had received proper medical treatment the previous night, he would not have died.
Discuss Don's criminal liability for murder and manslaughter.

Commentary

Even a cursory examination of this question should reveal that it raises issues of liability for failing to act, causation and manslaughter. The key to writing a good answer lies in getting the structure right and then calculating what emphasis to place on the various facets of the problem.

Note that the rubric requires candidates to address liability for homicide, hence avoiding getting side-tracked into a consideration of offences against the person. Candidates should recognize that there are two possible routes to liability based on the given facts. One relates to the positive act of colliding with Tim, the other relates to the consequences of Don's liability for failing to act.

In most answers candidates have to make decisions about how much material to include on specific elements. In this answer, as a conviction for murder is most unlikely, there is very little to suggest the necessary *mens rea*. (By contrast with the answer to the previous question, where this issue was in some doubt, and therefore required extensive coverage of the issue of intention.) Here, on the other hand, manslaughter is analysed in great detail, with an emphasis on applying the law to the facts of this problem.

Note that candidates are not required to consider the criminal responsibility of Mrs X, or offences other than murder or manslaughter, although clearly Don would be guilty of offences under the **Road Traffic Acts 1988 and 1991** (as amended).

Answer plan

- Act or omission
- Causation
- Murder
- Manslaughter
- Constructive manslaughter
- Manslaughter by gross negligence
- Duty of care

Suggested answer

Don's liability for the death of Tim could be based on his positive act of colliding with him. But for the collision Tim would not have died—hence Don in fact caused Tim's death. As to causation in law, the operating and substantial cause of death is hypothermia—in effect Tim being left out all night in the cold. He does not actually die from his injuries, although these obviously played a part. For this reason the prosecution would be advised to base Don's liability on his failure to care for Tim immediately following the collision.

There is no general liability for failing to act, but the law recognizes exceptions where D is under a positive legal duty to act. Don would have been under a positive legal duty to report a road accident involving injury to another person, but this is an offence in its own right and is not the ideal basis for an allegation that he has committed homicide. More promising is the contention that Don accidentally caused harm to Tim, realized that he had done so, and thereby came under a common law duty to limit the extent of that harm so far as it was in his power to do so. The prosecution would argue that the facts satisfy the requirements for culpable omission laid down by the House of Lords in *R v Miller* [1983] 1 All ER 978. The House of Lords stated that a duty owed by someone who had created a danger was broken when that person deliberately failed to take steps to minimize that danger. Lord Diplock said:

> I see no rational ground for excluding from conduct capable of giving rise to criminal liability conduct which consists of failing to take measures that lie within one's power to counteract a danger that one has oneself created, if at the time of such conduct one's state of mind is such as constitutes a necessary ingredient of the offence.

This principle would apply to impose a duty on Don to summon medical assistance.

Although Don might argue that the weather operated as a *novus actus interveniens,* the prosecution has to establish only that Don's conduct was a significantly contributing cause (*R v Cheshire* [1991] 3 All ER 670). The courts are also traditionally reluctant to accept the argument that a *novus actus interveniens* has broken the chain of causation and it cannot be envisaged that the extreme cold weather could be deemed the sole cause of death thereby exonerating Don.

Assuming causation can be established, attention turns to consideration of the type of homicide Don might be charged with. Murder seems most unlikely. In *R v Moloney* [1985] 1 All ER 1025, the House of Lords stated that only an intention to kill or cause grievous bodily harm would be sufficient to constitute the *mens rea* for murder. Their Lordships in *Moloney* also held that as intention is a word in common use, easily understood by the public, it should be left to the jury by the trial judge without any elaborate definition or direction. It is submitted that as Don was simply inadvertent when initially knocking Tim over, there is no question of the requisite intent being made out and accordingly this issue should not be left to the jury.

Manslaughter is divided into two categories: voluntary and involuntary. Voluntary manslaughter occurs when the accused causes the victim's death with intent to kill or do some grievous bodily harm, but successfully relies on one of the four partial defences arising under the Homicide Act 1957. These defences are: provocation; diminished responsibility; infanticide; or death arising as a result of a suicide pact. On the facts of this question there is no evidence of these elements and voluntary manslaughter would not be considered by the court.

Involuntary manslaughter is unlawful homicide without intent to kill or do some grievous bodily harm. The prosecution must prove that the accused caused the victim's death and committed a criminal and dangerous act with the *mens rea* required for that criminal act (constructive manslaughter), or that he was grossly negligent in causing the death (*R v Adomako* [1994] 3 All ER 79).

A manslaughter charge alleging constructive manslaughter could be problematic, as there is doubt as to whether an omission can constitute an unlawful and dangerous act for this purpose. The uncertainty stems from the Court of Appeal decision in *R v Lowe* [1973] 1 All ER 805; and in *R v Shepperd* [1980] 3 All ER 899, the House of Lords distinguished between omissions and commission stating:

> If I strike a child in a manner likely to cause harm it is right that if that child dies I may be charged with manslaughter. If, however, I omit to do something with the result that it suffers injury to its health which results in its death, we think that a charge of manslaughter should not be an inevitable consequence even if the omission is deliberate.

The prosecution would, therefore, be advised to concentrate on the allegation of killing by gross negligence, a form of manslaughter that can be based on a failure to act. The elements of the offence were established by the House of Lords in *R v Adomako*, where their Lordships decided that in cases of death resulting from a duty of care situation, the prosecution must prove the following conditions:

(a) the accused owed a duty of care to the victim;

(b) the accused acted in breach of that duty;

(c) the accused's conduct was grossly negligent; and

(d) that conduct caused the victim's death.

Whether or not conduct is grossly negligent is a question of fact for the jury and will depend on the seriousness of the breach in all the circumstances in which the accused was placed when it occurred. 'The jury will have to consider whether the extent to which the accused's conduct departed from the proper standard of care incumbent upon him involving as it must have done a risk of death to the victim was such that it should be judged criminal' (*per* Lord Mackay in *R v Adomako*).

As regards the collision, if Don had been only momentarily distracted while driving and the incident took place on a lonely country road where there was little possibility of other traffic or pedestrians, it is unlikely that the jury would find him grossly negligent as to the risk of death. However, Don's liability will be based on the fact that he realized that he had knocked Tim over and then deliberately left him. In such circumstances there seems little doubt that Don owed Tim a duty of care—see *R v Evans* [2009] EWCA Crim 650. Don has created or contributed to the creation of a state of affairs which he knew, or ought reasonably to known, had become life-threatening—hence he was under a duty to take reasonable steps to save Tim's life.

The issue will be as to whether or not Don's breach of that duty was grossly negligent. It is a question for the jury as to whether Don's negligence was so gross it deserves to be labelled as 'criminal'. Persuasive factors will be that Tim was unconscious; it was a lonely country road, and there was therefore little possibility of a passer-by coming to his assistance; and it was an extremely cold night, which meant that Tim's condition would rapidly deteriorate. Establishing the fault element for killing by gross negligence does not require any direct evidence of Don's state of mind. Liability is established objectively by the jury coming to a conclusion regarding Don's actions or failure to act. There is no need to prove that Don even thought about the possibility of death or serious harm occurring; see *Attorney-General's Reference (No. 2 of 1999)* [2000] 3 All ER 182, and *R v Mark and another* [2004] All ER (D) 35 (Oct). It is therefore submitted that the prosecution should now be able to establish all the ingredients of killing by gross negligence and that Don would be found guilty of involuntary manslaughter.

Question 3

John is a keen gardener who specializes in growing prize-winning fruit and vegetables in his garden. Over the years John has been the victim of vandalism carried out by local children trespassing in his garden. One afternoon Mike, an eleven-year-old schoolboy, enters John's garden and smashes the windows of his greenhouse. John spots Mike and chases after him. Mike, who has special educational needs and is of low intelligence, tries to escape by climbing over a wall into the next garden. Mike fails to realize that the ground on the other side of the wall is much lower and he falls onto a pile of broken glass, suffering extensive and severe cuts to his body. John climbs the wall and sees Mike lying injured on the other side. John realizes that Mike is bleeding but is unaware of the extent of his injuries. John shouts at Mike 'Serves you right, you hooligan!' and goes back into his house. Mike bleeds to death from his injuries.

Advise John who has been charged with the manslaughter of Mike.

 Commentary

For most candidates this should be a fairly straightforward homicide question. It should be noted that the rubric specifically precludes consideration of liability for murder, hence the issues are essentially omission, causation, and involuntary manslaughter. Failure to comply with the rubric will result in much wasted time contemplating murder and possibly provocation—neither of which are required here. The question does require candidates to consider alternative routes to liability, the positive acts linked to unlawful act manslaughter and the omission linked to killing by gross negligence. Care is needed to ensure these two issues are dealt with clearly. Note that there is no need to consider self-defence here. The offence has already been committed by the time John chases after the victim. There is no clear evidence that he is using reasonable force to prevent further harm.

Answer plan

- Liability for omission
- Causation in fact and in law
- Elements of unlawful act manslaughter
- Killing by gross negligence as an alternative basis for liability

Suggested answer

The facts indicate two possible bases for establishing the *actus reus* of manslaughter. The first possibility is that John's liability could be based on his positive act of chasing after Mike. The alternative is that liability could be based on his failure to assist Mike once he had fallen over the wall and sustained injuries. The difficulty with basing liability on John's failure to assist Mike lies in the fact that an omission can only give rise to criminal liability where the defendant is under a legal duty to act. On these facts it is hard to ascertain any statutory or contractual duty to act. The prosecution would proceed on the basis that John was under a common law duty to act arising from the fact that he 'accidentally' caused the harm, and realized that he had caused the harm; see *R v Miller* [1983] 1 All ER 978, as applied in *DPP v Santana-Bermudez* [2003] All ER (D) 168 (Nov). A key factor here will be evidence as to whether or not it lay within John's power to take steps, either himself or by calling for assistance, to prevent or minimize the harm to Mike. The facts clearly indicate an awareness of harm, albeit not the degree of harm. It also seems clear that John could have assisted Mike. Hence it is submitted that there is a culpable omission on these facts.

Regardless of whether the case proceeds on the basis of a culpable omission or positive act, the prosecution will have to establish that John's act or omission caused the death of Mike both in fact and in law. Causation in fact should be unproblematic. In relation to his positive acts the test will be: but for John chasing Mike would Mike have died?; see *R v White* [1910] 2 KB 124. The answer is clearly 'no', hence causation in fact would be made out. Causation in law is likely to be more contentious. Mike does not die as a direct result of John's acts. John's chasing of Mike is not the operating and substantial cause of Mike's death; see *R v Smith* [1959] 2 QB 35. John will argue that in making such a foolhardy escape Mike effectively broke the chain of causation in law between his being chased by Mike and falling to his death (i.e. the escape was a *novus actus interveniens*). Cases such as *R v Roberts* (1971) 56 Cr App R 95, provide that the jury should be directed to consider the extent to which Mike's reaction was something that could reasonably have been foreseen as the consequence of what John was saying or doing. This is an objective test, hence it is for the jury to determine the issue. But the court in *R v Roberts* accepted that the chain of causation in law could be broken by evidence that the victim, in the course of escaping, had done something so 'daft', or unexpected that no reasonable person could have been expected to foresee it. John will therefore argue that jumping over the wall onto the broken glass was a stupid thing to do, and that Mike's actions amounted to a *novus actus interveniens*.

There are a number of reasons why John's argument is likely to fail. First, on the basis of *R v Williams* [1992] 2 All ER 183, the jury will be directed to bear in mind the fact that, in making his escape, Mike may have simply made a bad decision. The jury will be directed to have regard to Mike's age and his intellectual capacity. Further, in *R v Corbett* [1996] Crim LR 594, despite the fact that the victim, who was intoxicated and suffering from mental illness, ran into a road and was killed in a collision with a vehicle, the court upheld the jury's finding that the defendant had caused the victim's death. The jury had been entitled to conclude that the victim's actions were reasonably foreseeable. The case law thus reflects the approach in *R v Blaue* [1975] 1 WLR 1411, to the effect that John must take his victim as he finds him. The fact that Mike made an error of judgement in jumping over the wall, possibly arising from his having special educational needs and being of low intelligence, is unlikely to be a factor that John can rely on.

As regards the omission causing death, there is evidence to suggest that Mike could have been saved if he had received some first aid when John first became aware that Mike had been injured. This would be compelling evidence that John's failure to act hastened Mike's death, and that there was no *novus actus interveniens*.

Assuming that the issues of omission and causation are established by the prosecution, there are two forms of common law manslaughter that may be charged in respect of Mike's death. The first, unlawful act manslaughter, requires proof that John committed a dangerous criminal act causing Mike's death, and that he had the *mens rea* for the criminal act. The second is killing by gross negligence.

Regarding unlawful act manslaughter, the prosecution could be in some difficulty, as it will have to establish that John committed a criminal act in chasing after Mike. This form of manslaughter cannot be based on liability for failing to act; see *R v Lowe* [1973] QB 702.

The evidence suggests that the criminal act would be assault—i.e., Mike apprehended immediate physical violence because he was frightened of what John would do if he caught him; see *R v Savage; R v Parmenter* [1992] 1 AC 699. *R v Arobieke* [1988] Crim LR 314 illustrates the fact that evidence that John was chasing Mike will not, on its own, suffice. Assuming the prosecution can prove an assault by John, the question will then be whether or not the assault was dangerous. For the purposes of unlawful act manslaughter the test will be whether or not a sober and reasonable person, present at the scene and watching the unlawful act being performed, knowing what the defendant knows, would have foreseen the risk of some physical harm occurring to the victim; see *R v Church* [1965] 2 All ER 72 and *R v Dawson* (1985) 81 Cr App R 150.

Crucial questions will arise as to whether or not John knew that the ground on the other side of the wall that Mike was climbing was lower. Was John aware of the hazard of broken glass on the other side of the wall? All this is conjecture that would have to be resolved by looking at the evidence of John's state of mind. If John merely foresaw Mike being frightened (i.e. psychic disturbance) that would not suffice to make the unlawful act dangerous. What is required is an objectively assessable risk of physical harm occurring to the victim.

The *mens rea* for unlawful act manslaughter is essentially the *mens rea* for the unlawful (i.e., criminal) act that causes death. As Lord Hope explained in *Attorney-General's*

Reference (No. 3 of 1994) [1998] AC 245, the prosecution will only have to prove that John 'intended to do what he did'. It is submitted that an intention to assault Mike (in the narrow sense) or recklessness as to whether Mike would apprehend immediate physical violence would suffice.

If any of the constituent elements of unlawful act manslaughter cannot be established, or liability is to be based on John's failure to act (see *R v Lowe*, above) the prosecution could alternatively rely on killing by gross negligence. On the basis of *R v Adomako* [1994] 3 WLR 288, the prosecution would have to prove that John owed Mike a duty of care; that he breached the duty of care to such an extent that he created a risk of death; and that the breach of the duty of care was sufficiently gross to warrant it being regarded as 'criminal'. *Attorney-General's Reference (No. 2 of 1999)* [2000] 3 All ER 182, further states that the offence of killing by gross negligence can be established without proof of *mens rea* on the part of John, although evidence of his state of mind might be relevant in assisting a jury in determining the extent to which his negligence was gross.

The difficulty for the prosecution here is that killing by gross negligence is normally charged in so-called reliance situations, such as that arising between doctor and patient, or business and client. Does a householder chasing after a vandal owe a duty of care? Significantly, in *R v Khan (Rungzabe)* [1998] Crim LR 830, the Court of Appeal declined to find that a defendant who had supplied drugs to a teenage girl owed her a duty of care in circumstances where she proceeded to overdose on the drugs with fatal results. Against this, in the later case of *R v Evans* [2009] EWCA Crim 650 the Court of Appeal held that a defendant who supplied heroin to the deceased and who knew that the deceased had overdosed, did owe the deceased a duty of care because the defendant had created or contributed to the creation of a state of affairs which she knew, or ought reasonably to have known, had become life-threatening. The evidence in the present case is that John knows Mike is injured, but not how badly injured he is. The key point for the jury, therefore, will be as to whether or not John, having chased Mike, ought reasonably to have known that Mike's life was in danger if he (John) did nothing to help.

Hence it is submitted that the prosecution should proceed with an unlawful act manslaughter charge, but it should be noted that this may founder on the issue of 'criminal' act and 'dangerousness'.

Question 4

Nick is married to Judith. Their marriage has been going through a difficult period because of Nick's prolonged impotence and violent mood swings. Nick has known for some time that Judith has been unfaithful to him but has said nothing to her. On a number of occasions he has lost his temper and assaulted Judith. A psychiatrist has examined Nick and advised that he suffers from a behavioural disorder that manifests itself in aggression towards women. Recently Nick has also become depressed because he has been made redundant and cannot find another job. One afternoon Nick returns home unexpectedly from work and finds Judith in bed having sex with David, his best friend. As he happens to be in an exceptionally phlegmatic mood, Nick calmly opens his wallet, takes out a £50 note and gives it to David, telling him to '...go and find a real whore...'. As Nick turns to leave the room Judith shouts 'At least he satisfies me, which is more than you can do!' Nick picks up a heavy hand-held mirror from Judith's dressing table and deals her a series of savage blows about the head, killing her. The glass from the mirror is dislodged by the impact with Judith's head and flies across the bed, hitting David in the neck. Nick sees what has happened but runs off in panic. David dies within minutes through loss of blood. Nick is apprehended by the police shortly afterwards.

Advise the Crown Prosecution Service as to the liability of Nick for the deaths of Judith and David.

 ## Commentary

Given the twists and turns in the development of the defence of provocation since 1957 it would be surprising indeed to find a criminal law examination paper that did not require candidates to deal with the subject at some point. If presented with an essay question on provocation candidates might be expected to go into the way in which the law has 'flip-flopped' between an objective approach and a subjective approach. Some reference to the Law Commission Report on Partial Defences to Murder (Law Com. No. 290) would also be in order. For the purposes of a problem question, however, candidates should apply the law based on the most recent case law decisions. As the law stands there is a clear contradiction between the House of Lords' decision in *R v Smith* [2000] 3 WLR 654, and the later Privy Council decision in *Attorney-General for Jersey v Holley* [2005] UKPC 23. Normally the Privy Council decision would be merely persuasive but, as detailed in the suggested solution, because of the composition of the Privy Council in the *Holley* case, the Court of Appeal, in *R v James; R v Karimi* [2006] EWCA Crim 140, has taken the unusual step of regarding *Holley* as effectively overturning the decision in *Smith*. Beyond the complication of the defence of provocation the question is a fairly standard test of the student's grasp of homicide. A logical structure is key, dealing with the victims separately, starting with causation and working through *mens rea* and defences. Note the way in which liability for omission arises in relation to the death of David. Note, too, the limitations imposed by the rubric. There is no need to consider criminal damage as a free-standing offence, although it could play a part in the examination of unlawful act manslaughter.

 ## Answer plan

- Causation
- *Mens rea*
- s. 3, Homicide Act 1957
- Subjective test for provocation
- Objective test for provocation—*Holley* [2005]
- Issues related to transferred malice

Suggested answer

In relation to the death of Judith it would appear that Nick has caused the death in fact and in law. Nick commits a positive voluntary act that does cause her death. But for his actions she would not have died: *R v White* [1910] 2 KB 124. Nick's act is also the cause in law of Judith's death. His act is the 'operating and substantial cause' of her death: see *R v Smith* [1959] 2 QB 35. There is no evidence of any *novus actus interveniens*. In order for him to be found guilty of murder the prosecution must prove that Nick had either the intention to kill or to do grievous bodily harm; *R v Woollin* [1998] 4 All ER 103. Intent can be based on 'purpose/desire' or on evidence of foresight. It would appear to have been Nick's purpose to do some grievous bodily harm—this would suffice for the *mens rea* of murder. If necessary the trial judge could give a '*Woollin*' direction. This would involve asking the jury to consider whether or not there was evidence that Nick foresaw death or grievous bodily harm as virtually certain to result from his action. Foresight here is to be determined in accordance with s. 8 Criminal Justice Act 1967. Only if there was evidence that Nick foresaw death or grievous bodily harm as virtually certain to result from his actions would a jury be entitled to infer that he intended death or grievous bodily harm. Assuming that Nick has the *mens rea* for murder, attention will turn to possible defences.

The most obvious defence on the facts is provocation. This defence is only available to a defendant charged with murder, and if successfully pleaded will reduce his liability to manslaughter. The first stage in establishing the defence of provocation is the subjective test—was Nick provoked? It should be noted that anything, including words alone, can be provocation: see *R v Doughty* (1986) 83 Cr App R 319. There is no bar on provocation being induced by the actions of the defendant; see *R v Johnson* [1989] 2 All ER 859. The basic ingredients of this common law defence are to be found in the judgment of Devlin J in *R v Duffy* [1949] 1 All ER 932, coupled with s. 3 Homicide Act 1957. The first issue is whether or not there is evidence that Nick was provoked. If there is, as certainly seems to be the case here, the trial judge should leave the defence to the jury, with a suitable direction by way of guidance. There does not appear to be any problem with 'cooling time'—Nick's actions in respect of Judith seem to have been an immediate response to her comments. The fact that he was initially phlegmatic about the incident is not really material here. It is submitted that on the evidence presented in this question the subjective stage will be made out.

As to the objective stage the key decision is now that of the Privy Council in *Attorney-General for Jersey v Holley* [2005] UKPC 23, where it was confirmed that, for the purposes of the defence of provocation, a defendant had to be judged by the standard of a person having ordinary powers of control. This standard is a constant, objective standard in all cases. The role of the jury is two-fold. First the jury will have to assess the gravity of the provocation to the defendant. In doing so the jury has to take the defendant as they find him. On the given facts, this would involve taking into account that Nick was suffering from impotence, had been made redundant and could not find another job and had an unhappy marriage. It is submitted that the evidence of Nick suffering from a behavioural disorder that manifests itself in aggression towards women would not be taken into account for these purposes as it is evidence of a mental abnormality that should be relied upon for the purposes of advancing the defence of diminished responsibility, not provocation.

Secondly, having assessed the gravity of the provocation to the defendant, the jury will have to assess the degree of self-control shown by Nick. The test to be applied is whether or not, given the degree of provocation experienced, Nick displayed the self-control to be expected of a person having and exercising ordinary powers of self-control. The Privy Council's ruling in *Holley* makes clear that the issue of whether or not the provocation was enough to make a reasonable man do as the defendant did is to be judged by one objective standard not, as was decided in the earlier House of Lords' decision of *R v Smith* [2000] 4 All ER 289, according to the standards to be expected from each individual defendant. The decision in *Holley* has subsequently been endorsed by the Court of Appeal in *R v Mohammed* [2005] EWCA Crim 1880, and in *R v James; R v Karimi* [2006] EWCA Crim 14.

Assuming, as suggested above, that characteristics indicating mental illness will now be excluded from the defence of provocation, Nick would be advised to consider reliance on diminished responsibility as an alternative defence. Under the Homicide Act 1957 s. 2(1) Nick would have to provide evidence that he was: '...suffering from such abnormality of mind (whether arising from a condition of arrested or retarded development of mind or any inherent causes or induced by disease or injury) as substantially impaired his mental responsibility for his acts and omissions in doing...the killing.' An abnormality of the mind would be a state of mind that the normal person would regard as abnormal—'...not only the perception of physical acts and matters and the ability to form rational judgement...but also the ability to exercise will-power to control physical acts in accordance with that rational judgement'—see *Byrne* [1960] 2 QB 396. Nick would appear to have the evidence to support this defence. His mental abnormality does not have to amount to borderline insanity: see *Seers* (1984) 79 Cr App R 261. Ultimately the jury will decide: see *Walton v R* [1978] 1 All ER 542. On the facts this may be a more appropriate defence than provocation.

In the unlikely event that the *mens rea* for murder cannot be established Nick could be charged with constructive manslaughter based on the unlawful act of maliciously inflicting grievous bodily harm contrary to s. 20 of the Offences Against the Person Act 1861. The act is clearly 'dangerous' (see below where this issue is considered in more depth regarding the death of David) and Nick would have had the *mens rea* for the unlawful act.

Turning to Nick's liability for the death of David, the first issue to consider is that of causation. There are two ways of approaching this. On the one hand Nick commits a positive act that causes David's death—i.e., smashing the mirror. Alternatively the prosecution could base liability on his failure to summon help—on the basis that he accidentally caused the shards of glass to pierce David's skin, realized what he had done, came under a responsibility to act and failed to discharge that responsibility: see

R v Miller [1983] 1 All ER 978. His act, or failure to act, is the cause in fact of David's death: see *White* (above); and the cause in law, see *R v Smith* (above).

To be guilty of murder Nick must be shown to have had intention to kill or do grievous bodily harm: see *Woollin* (1998)—considered above. Nick does not appear to have had 'purpose' type intent, but in any event there seems to be evidence of his having foreseen death or grievous bodily harm to an extent that would enable a jury to infer intent. One moot point is whether the prosecution could invoke the principle of transferred malice, whereby the *mens rea* directed at Judith can be used in relation to David: see *Latimer* (1886) 17 QBD 359. It may be easier for the prosecution to base liability for murder on Nick's failure to act—his knowledge of the injury to David, the loss of blood etc. and his failure to act is strongly suggestive of someone who foresees death as 'virtually certain'.

If Nick is charged with the murder of David he may seek to rely on the defences of provocation and diminished responsibility as outlined above.

Alternatively the prosecution could charge Nick with constructive manslaughter—this would have to be on the basis of the positive act of smashing the mirror, as opposed to an omission—see *Lowe* (1973). The positive act must be a crime—here this could be grievous bodily harm to Judith or criminal damage to her mirror. The criminal act must be dangerous as determined by the objective test laid down in *Church* [1965] 2 All ER 72, and *R v Dawson* (1985) 81 Cr App R 150. Would a sober and reasonable person at the scene of the crime, with the knowledge of the accused, have foreseen the risk of some physical harm? This is a question to be determined by the jury. Note that the unlawful act does not have to be directed at the actual victim: see *Mitchell* [1983] QB 741, and *R v Goodfellow* (1986) 83 Cr App R 23. Assuming the unlawful act is seen as dangerous, Nick must have the *mens rea* for the unlawful act—in the case of the grievous bodily harm. It would be enough that he was 'malicious' as in s. 20 of the Offences Against the Person Act 1861—i.e. did he foresee the possibility of some physical harm (albeit slight) occurring to another person. Alternatively criminal damage could be used as the unlawful act. Following the decision of the House of Lords in *R v G* [2003] 4 All ER 765, the prosecution would have to show that Nick was aware of the risk of criminal damage and that it was, in the circumstances known to him, unreasonable for him to take the risk.

In theory Nick could be charged with killing David by gross negligence—see *R v Adomako* [1994] 3 WLR 288—especially if liability is to be based on his failure to summon help. This type of manslaughter tends to be charged in 'duty' situations, such as that arising between doctor and patient; householder and tradesman; landlord and tenant. The prosecution would presumably allege that having injured David, Nick came under a duty to care for him: see *R v Miller* (above). Assuming a duty of care did arise, the steps to liability, as set out in *R v Adomako,* would involve an examination of: (i) the extent to which Nick's conduct departed from the proper standard of care incumbent upon him; (ii) whether this involved a risk of death to David; and (iii) whether the breach of duty was so serious that it should be judged criminal.

Question 5

Kathleen, Fareed, and Jimmy are all homeless, and at night they sleep rough near the railway station. Kathleen, a chronic alcoholic, has also been diagnosed as suffering from paranoid schizophrenia. One night, after a heavy drinking session, Kathleen beds down in her usual spot. Once she is asleep Jimmy decides that it would be funny to urinate on Kathleen, something he has done several times before, to her great annoyance. Kathleen wakes to find Jimmy and Fareed laughing, and also notices Fareed drinking from a bottle of gin that she had hidden under her bedclothes. Kathleen flies into a rage, picks up a large piece of wood and chases after Fareed and Jimmy. Fareed, who is partially sighted, runs into the road and is hit by an oncoming bus. On admission to hospital the medical attendants fail to administer sufficient oxygen and he dies. In the course of running away Jimmy trips over a kerbstone and falls heavily. The bottle of cider in his coat pocket is smashed in the fall and he suffers severe cuts. Jimmy does not receive treatment for these cuts, which heal badly. Jimmy keeps picking at the wounds as they cause him discomfort and in due course he dies from blood poisoning caused by the resultant infection.

 Advise the Crown Prosecution Service as to the criminal liability of Kathleen for both of these deaths.

Commentary

A fairly standard homicide question combining issues relating to causation, provocation and diminished responsibility, and constructive manslaughter. In terms of structure candidates would be advised to follow two simple rules. The first is to deal with each victim separately. It may be thought that this will involve a degree of duplication in that, for example, causation will have to be considered twice. In practice it is acceptable to go through an issue once in detail in relation to one incident, and then simply use the 'see above' approach if the same issue arises later on, although care must be taken to ensure that any distinguishing factors are raised and dealt with. The second rule is to deal with causation first. As a matter of logic, if the defendant has not caused the death of the victim there is little point in considering other aspects of liability for homicide—different offences would need to be considered instead.

Answer plan

- Causation
- *Mens rea* for murder
- Provocation and diminished responsibility
- Intoxication
- Constructive manslaughter
- Killing by gross negligence

Suggested answer

Kathleen's liability for the death of Fareed

Did Kathleen cause the death of Fareed? On the facts one can assume that there was causation in fact. But for Kathleen chasing Fareed into the road would he have died? The obvious answer is no. Turning to causation in law, Kathleen will argue that Fareed is the author of his own misfortune. In legal terms this means her asserting that his actions in running into the road amounted to a *novus actus interveniens,* or a break in the chain of causation in law. The common law has been reluctant to recognise instances where the actions of the victim can be seen as amounting to a *novus actus,* but Kathleen might argue that this should be seen as an 'escape' case. Following *Roberts* (1971) 56 Cr App R 95, where the victim was injured after jumping from a moving car to escape from the defend- ant, the test for the jury will be to consider whether Fareed's escape was the natural result of what Kathleen said and did, in the sense that it was something that could reasonably have been foreseen as the consequence of what she was doing. In particular the jury would have to be directed that if Fareed had done something 'daft' or unexpected that no reasonable man could be expected to foresee, the harm he suffered could rightly be regarded as self-in- flicted—i.e., the escape would be a *novus actus.* At this level running into the road into the path of an oncoming bus would be seen as 'daft', but the situation is complicated by other factors. The facts indicate that Fareed's judgement may have been impaired by alcohol con- sumption and that he was partially sighted. The Court of Appeal decision in *Blaue* [1975] 1 WLR 1411 states that you must take your victim as you find him; *Williams* [1992] 2 All ER 183 provides that it should be borne in mind that a victim may in the agony of the moment do the wrong thing, and that the jury should bear in mind particular characteris- tics of the victim and the fact that in the agony of the moment he may act without thought or deliberation. *Corbett* [1996] Crim LR 594, suggests that this type of escape is within the range of foreseeable responses—even where the victim has been drinking. On balance, it is submitted that the chain of causation in law will not be broken by the escape attempt.

Medical treatment will not normally break the chain of causation. Although the medical treatment may be incompetent, the operating and substantial cause of death is still the injury inflicted by the defendant. In *R v Mellor* [1996] 2 Cr App R 245, the appellant contended that a substantial cause of the victim's death was the failure of the medical attendants at the hospital to administer sufficient oxygen to the victim. The appeal was dismissed, Schiemann LJ, observing that there was no onus on the Crown to prove that any supervening cause, such as medical treatment, was not a substantial cause of death. As he explained it is a question of fact and degree in each case for the jury to decide, having regard to the gravity of the supervening event, however caused, as to whether or not the injuries inflicted by the defendant were a significant cause of death.

Assuming causation in respect of the death of Fareed is made out, can Kathleen be guilty of murder? Given that she is chasing after Fareed with a weapon there is evidence that she intended some grievous bodily harm at least—consider the direction to the jury on intent in *R v Woollin* [1998] 4 All ER 103. The greater the probability of a consequence the more likely it is that the consequence was foreseen and that if that consequence was foreseen the greater the probability that that consequence was also intended. The jury will have to be reminded that the decision is theirs to be reached upon a consideration of all the evidence. In a case such as this the simple direction on intent may not suffice. The jury will need to be directed that they are not entitled to infer the necessary intention unless they feel sure that death or serious bodily harm was virtually certain (barring some unforeseen intervention) to result from Kathleen's actions and that she appreciated that such was the case.

Assuming she is charged with murder Kathleen could raise a number of defences. The most obvious of these is provocation. Following *R v Duffy* [1949] 1 All ER 932, and the provisions of s. 3 of the Homicide Act 1957, there is evidence that she lost her self-control. There is no obvious issue as to 'cooling time' and there is effectively no bar on what can amount to provocation: see *R v Doughty* (1986) 83 Cr App R 319. Section 3 of the 1957 Act sets out the role of the judge and jury. The question whether the provocation was enough to make a reasonable man do as he did will be left to be determined by the jury, and in determining that question the jury will take into account everything both done and said according to the effect which, in their opinion, it would have on a reasonable man. Note that the provocation can be cumulative. *R v Dryden* [1995] 4 All ER 987, endorses the 'last straw' approach; as does *Humphreys* [1995] 4 All ER 889. On these facts it means that the jury should be directed to consider the history of events between the parties. This direction is important as the final act of provocation, if looked at in isolation, may not seem sufficiently grave to warrant the defence being allowed.

The correct approach to the objective stage of the test for provocation is now that endorsed by the Privy Council in *Attorney-General for Jersey v Holley* [2005] UKPC 23. The jury must first consider all the relevant evidence relating to the defendant's characteristics to the extent that they have a bearing on the gravity of the provocation. On the given facts this will include the fact that Kathleen is sleeping rough and has no ready access to sanitary facilities, and the fact that she is alcohol dependent, thus more likely to be angered by the theft of her alcohol. Having assessed the extent of the provocation, the jury would then have to consider the effect of the provocation on a reasonable person (woman for these purposes, although gender is not really material on the facts). The key point to consider here is the extent to which the jury can take into account the fact that Kathleen is a chronic alcoholic, diagnosed as suffering from paranoid schizophrenia. Following *Holley*, it is now clear that the reasonable person, for the purposes of the defence of provocation, is assumed to be both sane and sober. The standard of self-control by which Kathleen's conduct is to be evaluated for the purpose of the defence of provocation is the external standard of a person having and exercising ordinary powers of self-control. Kathleen's intoxicated state is not a matter to be taken into account by the jury when considering whether she exercised ordinary self-control. Given that there is sufficient evidence of provocation for the matter to be left to the jury, it will be a question of fact for the jury as to whether the defence is made out.

Intoxication could be raised as a separate substantive defence to murder, reducing Kathleen's liability to manslaughter if successful. Murder is regarded at common law as a specific intent crime: see *DPP v Majewski* [1976] 2 All ER 142. There would have to be evidence that Kathleen did not form the specific intent because of the intoxication. It is submitted that it is far from clear on the given facts whether or not this was the case.

Arguably the more appropriate defence, given the medical evidence, would be diminished responsibility. Under s. 2 of the Homicide Act 1957 the burden would be on Kathleen to establish on the balance of probabilities, that she was suffering from such abnormality of mind (whether arising from a condition of arrested or retarded development of mind or any inherent causes or induced by disease or injury) as substantially impaired her mental responsibility for her acts. Note that her schizophrenia would probably satisfy this, but intoxication confuses the matter somewhat. Where substance abuse has resulted in a condition that has caused permanent harm to a defendant's mental health such that it affects her responsibility for her actions even when she is sober, it can be taken into account for the purposes of establishing diminished responsibility; see *Tandy* [1989] 1 All ER 267. If there is no evidence of brain damage caused by substance abuse the court will follow the guidance offered in *R v Stewart* [2009] EWCA Crim 593 (relaxing the approach of the House of Lords in *R v Dietschmann* [2003] 1 All ER 897) to the effect that diminished responsibility could still be available as a defence if the defendant can show that the dependency on alcohol amounted to a recognized medical condition (such as alcohol dependency syndrome) caused by disease (the effect of alcohol abuse) and that it substantially impaired Kathleen's responsibility for her actions. A key issue here will be the need for evidence that her alcohol dependency meant that she could not resist her impulses, as opposed to her simply choosing not to resist them. On this basis Kathleen should have a good basis for establishing diminished responsibility.

An involuntary manslaughter charge against Kathleen in respect of the death of Fareed will be problematic. What was the unlawful act? If regard is had to *R v Arobieke* [1988] Crim LR 314, it will be seen that simply chasing someone is not enough. Even if the prosecution relies on assault (i.e., on the basis that the victim apprehended immediate physical harm), was the assault 'dangerous', when viewed objectively? On the basis of *R v Watson* [1989] 1 WLR 684, it must be an act that the reasonable sober bystander, equipped with the knowledge of the defendant, would see as likely to cause some *physical* harm. In theory Kathleen could be charged with killing by gross negligence, but establishing the necessary duty of care that is a cornerstone of liability would be problematic. Does D owe P a duty of care where D is the victim of a theft and D chases P who is suspected of having committed that theft? On the basis of *R v Evans* [2009] EWCA Crim 650, the prosecution would have to prove that Kathleen created, or contributed to the creation of, a state of affairs which she knew, or ought reasonably to known, had become life-threatening. Simply chasing after Fareed may not be sufficient here. His running into a road makes it life-threatening, but it then begs the question what she could have done to stop him from doing that—other than not chasing him in the first place. It will be for the trial judge to direct the jury as to whether there are facts here which, if found, would justify a conclusion that a duty of care existed.

Kathleen's liability for the death of Jimmy

The prosecution would have little difficulty in establishing causation in fact—but for Kathleen's actions Jimmy would not have died. As to causation in law, the points raised above in respect of Fareed's escape would apply equally here. The argument would be as to whether or not the *R v Blaue* principle of 'take your victim as you find him' would cover the bottle in the pocket. It is submitted that there is no reason in principle why it should not. Hence the only remaining argument on *novus actus* and Jimmy's death relates to the consequent self-neglect. On the basis of *R v Dear* [1996] Crim LR 595, deliberately picking at wounds will not amount to a *novus actus interveniens*, provided they are the wounds inflicted by the defendant.

If causation is established the prosecution may charge Kathleen with murder, as outlined above, and she may raise the defences of provocation, diminished responsibility and even intoxication.

If the *mens rea* for murder is not made out, the prosecution could be in difficulties with unlawful act manslaughter. The unlawful act would presumably be the assault apprehended by Jimmy, but there may be doubts as to whether or not it satisfies the tests for dangerousness—see above. In particular, the reasonable sober person at the scene of the crime is imbued with the knowledge of the defendant. If Kathleen did not know Jimmy had a bottle in his pocket, the reasonable man does not have that knowledge. This makes establishing a dangerous unlawful act less likely. Killing by gross negligence remains a possibility, but as with Fareed's case it is not an obvious duty of care situation; see *R v Evans*, considered above. Even if it were, could it be said that Kathleen's negligence in chasing Jimmy was so bad as to warrant being labelled criminal? This seems doubtful.

Question 6

Clive is a drug dealer. Clive injected Malcolm, at Malcolm's request, with a prohibited drug. Malcolm was aware of the nature of the drug being used by Clive. Later that same day Malcolm died from the effects of the drug as he had a weak heart.

Clive then met Emma, aged 18, in the park. At her request, he gave her a syringe filled with prohibited drugs and encouraged her to inject herself. Emma, who had not taken drugs before, did this and then began to cough and shake uncontrollably. However, Clive simply left her and she died shortly after. Finally, Clive gave a packet of prohibited drugs to Dennis, an experienced drug user. Dennis, aware of the contents of the packet, took the drugs to his house and, whilst alone in his house, injected himself and subsequently died of a drug overdose.

Advise Clive as to his criminal liability in respect of these deaths. Do not consider Clive's liability under the Misuse of Drugs Act 1971.

 Commentary

This is an interesting homicide question focusing on a number of important decisions: *R v Khan* [1998] Crim LR 830, *R v Kennedy* [2007] UKHL 38, *R v Dias* [2002] Crim LR 490, and *R v Rogers* [2003] 1 WLR 1374.

The key to dealing with the problem proficiently lies in dealing with each victim separately. Malcolm's case is fairly straightforward, involving as it does a consideration of causation and the unlawful act in constructive manslaughter—see *R v Cato* [1976] 1 All ER 260, and *R v Dalby* [1982] 1 All ER 916. Emma's case may look similar, but candidates are required to display a good knowledge of the impact of *R v Kennedy* [2007] UKHL 38, in particular the significance of the victim having knowledge and an informed choice. There is also the complicating factor of liability for omissions. Dennis's case offers a further twist as it can be distinguished on its facts from the situation arising in Emma's case, the problem for candidates being the extent to which that distinction actually leads to a different conclusion.

Note: There is no need to consider Clive's substantive liability under the Misuse of Drugs Act 1971.

 ## Answer plan

- Causation in each case
- Whether voluntary consumption breaks the chain of causation
- 'Thin skull' rule
- *Mens rea* for murder unlikely
- Involuntary manslaughter
- Whether any unlawful act
- Dangerousness
- *Mens rea* for the unlawful act
- Killing by gross negligence
- Omission in respect of Emma

Suggested answer

Clive's liability in respect of Malcolm

Clive causes Malcolm's death in fact—but for his actions Malcolm would not have died. As to causation in law, any contention by Clive that it was Malcolm's weak heart that was the main cause of death would fail. *R v Cheshire* [1991] 3 All ER 670, states that the prosecution, to satisfy causation in law, only needs to prove that Clive's act was a significant contribution to Malcolm's death, and *R v Blaue* [1975] 1 WLR 1411 demonstrates the principle that you take your victim as you find him (the 'egg-shell skull' or 'thin skull' principle). Thus, the fact that Malcolm is exceptionally vulnerable because he has a weak heart does not mean that Clive did not cause his death.

It is unlikely that Clive would be charged with murder in respect of Malcolm's death. In *R v Moloney* [1985] 1 All ER 1025, the House of Lords confirmed the *mens rea* as intention to kill or cause grievous bodily harm. It is submitted that the prosecution would find it very difficult to establish beyond reasonable doubt that Clive had the necessary intention. It is therefore much more likely that Clive will be charged with constructive manslaughter. The prosecution must prove that Clive committed a dangerous criminal act that caused the death of Malcolm, and that Clive has the *mens rea* for that criminal act.

The circumstances in this question are very similar to those considered by the Court of Appeal in *R v Cato* [1976] 1 All ER 260. As in that case, there may be some dispute as to what constitutes the unlawful (criminal) act. Even though Malcolm consented to Clive injecting him, this could still constitute aggravated assault under s. 47 of the Offences Against the Person Act 1861. This is because consent is not a defence to the deliberate infliction of actual bodily harm or more serious harm, unless it is in the course of a lawful activity (*R v Brown* [1993] 2 WLR 556). Clearly the injecting of drugs in these circumstances would not amount to a lawful activity and therefore is an unlawful act. The alternative unlawful act could be administration of a noxious substance contrary to either s. 23 or s. 24 of the Offences Against the Person Act 1861.

Whichever unlawful act is relied upon by the prosecution, Clive may argue that, as he did not know that Malcolm had a weak heart, his act was not dangerous. The test is essentially whether or not a reasonable bystander would have foreseen the risk of physical harm occurring to the victim. In *R v Watson* [1989] 2 All ER 865, the Court of Appeal held that for the purpose of ascertaining whether there was an obvious risk of some physical harm, the reasonable man had to be put in the same circumstances as the accused. The reasonable person does not have the benefit of hindsight. Hence in assessing the dangerousness of the act of injecting Malcolm, the jury must ignore the fact that Malcolm had a weak heart, as this fact was not known to Clive. The jury may still resolve, however, that any injection of prohibited drugs carries with it a risk of physical harm—thus the test for dangerousness would be satisfied regardless.

Clive's action in injecting Malcolm with the drugs is clearly intentional, hence Clive would have the *mens rea* for the unlawful act causing death, see *Attorney-General's Reference (No. 3 of 1994)* [1997] 3 All ER 936. It is likely, therefore, that Clive will incur liability for the manslaughter of Malcolm.

Clive's liability in respect of Emma

Clive's liability in respect of the death of Emma could be based on his supply of the prepared syringe, or on his failure to help her once she became distressed. Regarding his supply of the syringe, Clive clearly causes Emma's death in fact—but for supplying the syringe she would not have died. As with Dennis, however, Clive will argue that Emma broke the chain of causation by injecting herself. Both *R v Dalby* [1982] 1 All ER 916, and *R v Dias* [2002] Crim LR 490, support the argument that where drugs are supplied to the victim by the defendant and self-administered by the victim, the victim's voluntary consumption of the drugs can amount to a *novus actus interveniens*. More recently, in *R v Kennedy* [2007] UKHL 38, the House of Lords held that there could be no liability for manslaughter where D, having prepared a dose of heroin for P in the form of a syringe ready for injection, then left P to self-inject the heroin, resulting in P's death from an overdose. Their Lordships confirmed that, provided P was a fully informed and responsible adult, it was never appropriate to find the supplier of the prepared syringe guilty of manslaughter. The self-administration of the heroin was to be seen as a free and voluntarily act by the deceased that was an independent and operating cause of death. In short the self-administration would be regarded as a *novus actus interveniens*. The problem for Clive, however, is that Emma is not an experienced drug user. Was her self-administration a fully informed and responsible act? For these purposes fully informed should mean that Emma has the information she needs to assess the risk—including the potency of the drug she is being offered. In Clive's case the prosecution will seek to distinguish *R v Kennedy* on this point. Looking at it another way it could be argued that it was reasonably foreseeable that an inexperienced drug user would rely on Clive for guidance and consume what he supplied and for that reason her self-administration would not be regarded as a *novus actus*. In the final analysis it is a matter of fact and degree for the jury to determine. If Emma had been 12 there would be no argument about causation—at 18 she is more mature. The fact remains, however, that she lacked knowledge about drugs. On this basis it seems clear that Clive will be held to have caused Emma's death in fact and in law.

Assuming causation is established, liability for murder is most unlikely, given the facts—see above. As to unlawful act manslaughter, the prosecution might be in some difficulty establishing an unlawful act. The supply of drugs is an offence, but it is the self-administration of the drugs that causes the death. Self-administration of drugs is not criminal, beyond the technical offence of possession at the moment of administration, see again, *R v Kennedy*. The heroin was self-administered by Emma, not jointly administered with Clive. Clive did not administer the drug, nor did he cause the drug to be administered to or taken by Emma. Even assuming there is a criminal act here its dangerousness would be assessed according to the principles set out in relation to Clive's liability for the death of Malcolm, see above. *Mens rea* for this unlawful act would appear to be evident.

As an alternative, the prosecution can proceed with a manslaughter prosecution based on Clive's liability for his failure to care for Emma. His liability for failing to act could be based on a common law duty arising from her reliance on him: see *R v Stone and Dobinson* [1977] QB 354. Alternatively, and more promisingly, the prosecution could rely on *R v Miller* [1983] 1 All ER 978, where the House of Lords decided that if a defendant created a dangerous situation and realized this, he was under a legal duty to take steps to minimize the danger. So, Miller, who inadvertently set fire to property, was guilty of criminal damage when, realizing what he had done, failed to call the fire brigade. The same principle should be applied to Clive. He has created the dangerous situation, and it would be easy for him to summon medical attention to minimize the danger he has caused Emma. This would tie in with the prosecution charging him with killing by gross negligence which, unlike constructive manslaughter, does not require proof of a positive criminal act on the part of the defendant.

Following the House of Lords' decision in *R v Adomako* [1995] 1 AC 171, in order to prove gross negligence manslaughter the prosecution would have to establish the following four conditions:

(a) Clive owed Emma a duty of care;

(b) Clive was in breach of that duty;

(c) Clive's conduct was grossly negligent, i.e., having regard to the risk of death, Clive's conduct fell so far beneath the required standard, and was so bad as to amount to criminal negligence;

(d) Clive's conduct caused Emma's death.

Notwithstanding the earlier decision of the Court of Appeal in *R v Khan* [1998] Crim LR 830, the prosecution should be able to establish the necessary duty of care by citing the more recent decision in *R v Evans* [2009] EWCA Crim 650, where it was held that a duty of care, for the purposes of killing by gross negligence, could arise where the defendant had created, or contributed to the creation of, a state of affairs which he knew, or ought reasonably to have known, had become life-threatening. In such cases the defendant comes under a duty to act, by taking reasonable steps, to save the other person's life. Clive is clearly aware that Emma is in difficulties having taken the drugs and he does nothing to help. This would seem to establish both the duty of care and the required breach. Further, the extent of the breach is likely to be regarded as criminal, although this is ultimately a matter for the jury to resolve.

Clive's liability in respect of Dennis

But for Clive supplying Dennis with the drugs Dennis would not have died—hence causation in fact is made out. The first real problem for the prosecution relates to causation in law. Dennis is an experienced drug user, and is aware of the contents of the packet. Hence Clive will contend that Dennis's voluntary and informed consumption of the drugs amounted to a *novus actus interveniens*. It is submitted that this argument will succeed, as it is a view reflected in the Court of Appeal's decision in *R v Dalby* [1982] 1 All ER 916. On similar facts it was held that the unlawful act of the supply of the dangerous drug by the defendant to the deceased did not constitute the *actus reus* of manslaughter. This was on the basis that the unlawful act of supplying drugs was not an act directed against the person of the victim, and did not cause any direct injury to him. This controversial decision appeared to add a new ingredient to constructive manslaughter in that the act had to be directed at the victim. However, in *R v Goodfellow* [1986] 83 Cr App R 23, the Court of Appeal rejected this submission and explained the decision in *R v Dalby* on the basis that the victim's actions had broken the chain of causation.

Although, in order to satisfy the causation in law element, the prosecution has only to prove that Clive's acts were a significant contribution to Dennis's death (*R v Cheshire* [1991] 3 All ER 670), there is a powerful argument that a voluntary act by the victim operates as an intervening act. This view is stated by Professor Glanville Williams in *Textbook on Criminal Law* (2nd edition), at p. 39: 'what a person does (if he had reached adult years, is of sound mind and is not acting under mistake, intimidation or similar pressure) is his own responsibility and is not regarded as having been caused by other people. An intervening act of this kind, therefore, breaks the causal connection that would otherwise have been perceived between previous acts and the forbidden consequence'.

Against this the prosecution might seek to rely on *R v Blaue* [1975] 1 WLR 1411, which demonstrates the principle that you take your victim as you find him (the 'egg-shell skull' or 'thin skull' principle). In effect the argument will be that if Dennis chose to be foolhardy and consume an excessive amount of the drug, so much the worse for Clive. It is submitted that the courts ought not to accept this argument no matter how reprehensible the supply of drugs might be. Dennis is responsible for his own welfare. If Clive had unlawfully supplied Dennis with a knife that Dennis had in turn stabbed himself to death with, there is no serious argument that Clive would be regarded as having been the legal cause of Dennis's death.

The decision in *R v Kennedy* [2007] UKHL 38, discussed above in relation to Emma, certainly supports the contention that Dennis' voluntary and informed act of self-administration amounts to a *novus actus interveniens*. It is clear from the facts that Dennis was alone when he decided to consume the drugs—it is submitted that this is the basis for a rational distinction. Dennis's consumption of the drugs is not part and parcel of the transaction of supply. If there is no *novus actus* on these facts it begs the question as to how far Clive's potential liability might extend. What if Dennis decided to consume the drugs three weeks later? Would the chain of causation still be unbroken?

If for any reason the argument as to the *novus actus interveniens* were to fail, Clive might be charged with unlawful act manslaughter (constructive manslaughter) in respect of Dennis's death, but there could be serious problems in identifying any criminal act by Clive that causes death. Supply is obviously an unlawful act under the Misuse of Drugs Act 1971, but it is not the supply that causes Dennis's death. It is the self-administration. Self-administration of drugs is not a crime.

Charging Clive with killing by gross negligence would also be problematic. Did Clive owe Dennis any duty of care? He contributed to the dangerous state of affairs by supplying the drugs but had no way of knowing that the supply had led to a life-threatening situation—hence there would seem no scope for invoking the decision in *R v Evans* (above) regarding the duty of care owed by suppliers of narcotics.

Question 7

Critically assess the factors prompting the enactment of the Corporate Manslaughter and Corporate Homicide Act 2007, and the extent to which it provides a coherent framework for liability.

 Commentary

The Corporate Manslaughter and Corporate Homicide Act 2007 came into force in April 2008, hence it is safe to assume that if examiners set questions on this topic candidates will now have to have a sound knowledge of the broad principles of the legislation. Given that there is a new statutory framework, with little in the way of case law to provide any gloss, essay questions are perhaps more likely than problem questions in this area for the time being. Candidates will need to have some understanding of what the position was at common law to be able to contextualize the changes introduced by the **2007 Act**, as the question under consideration here demonstrates. Much of the Act is devoted to consideration of the special position of public bodies in respect of corporate manslaughter. Interesting as this is, it is arguably more an aspect of public law than criminal law as such, hence the solution concentrates on those changes in the law that seek to remedy the failings of the common law in imposing liability on private companies, such as those involved in major rail and shipping disasters.

Answer plan

- Set out general principles of criminal liability
- Particular issues in imposing criminal liability on corporate bodies
- Disasters prompting reform of the law
- New offence under the **2007 Act**
- Meaning of gross breach of duty
- Change from identification to aggregation of fault
- New sanctions

Suggested answer

The general principles of criminal law in England and Wales have developed essentially to deal with the imposition of criminal liability on individual wrongdoers. The principles of *actus reus* and *mens rea* concern themselves with what the defendant did (or failed to do) and what he may, or may not, have been thinking at that time. The law has struggled to some extent to deal with the issue of accessorial liability, in the sense that the liability of an accomplice at common law has to be derived from that of the principal offender who actually commits the offence (although see Part 2 of the Serious Crime Act 2007 which introduces a number offences of encouraging or assisting crime where liability is independent of any action subsequently taken by the principal offender). The imposition of criminal liability on corporations has, at common law at least, presented yet further challenges. A company has legal identity just as a real person has, but can a company 'do' things? Can a company have *mens rea*?

The answer to the problem of imposing criminal liability on companies has been addressed, to some extent at least, by the creation of strict (i.e. absolute) liability offences—offences that do not require any proof of *mens rea*. Hence companies can easily be convicted of offences where the prosecution merely has to prove a particular state of affairs, or that the company (through its servants and agents) permitted a particular activity, or caused a particular consequence.

The problem in relation to homicide is that offences such as murder and manslaughter require proof of fault (to varying degrees). If a company is to be convicted of such an offence (as distinct from the employees or directors being charged with homicide offences as private individuals) it is necessary to establish that a non-human legal entity possessed the requisite fault.

Before turning to the technicalities of this problem, and the solution now provided by Parliament, it is useful to reflect on why the issue of imposing liability for homicide on companies arises at all. Where companies permit dangerous practices that result in the death of their employees, the prosecution will often resort to charges under the Health and Safety at Work etc. Act 1974. Typically the offences charged under that Act will not have required proof of fault, and the company concerned would, upon conviction, have been sanctioned through the imposition of a fine. So far so good, but in cases of particularly flagrant breaches of health and safety requirements there may be public pressure for what the layman might regard as 'properly criminal' charges to be brought, such as murder and manslaughter, with appropriate custodial sentences imposed upon those managing or directing the company for allowing such dangerous practices to prevail. Where lax safety practices result in the death of a company's customers, such as rail passengers, or ferry passengers, the clamour for the prosecution to use the more serious homicide offences, and for senior managers to be punished as manifestations of the companies they direct becomes even greater. Examples include the Herald of Free Enterprise disaster in 1987; the King's Cross fire in 1987; the Clapham rail crash in 1988; and the Southall rail crash in 1997.

In all these well-known cases of corporate failure resulting in the deaths of members of the travelling public the problem for the prosecution lay in establishing that a sufficiently senior manager—one who could be described as a 'controlling mind' of the company in question—had had the necessary degree of fault so as to enable the jury to attribute that manager's fault to the company itself; see *Tesco Supermarkets v Nattrass* [1972] AC 153. In practical terms the problem was:

(a) that one had to go fairly high into the management hierarchy of a company to find a manager or director who could be said to have the level of authority justifying his or her being described as a controlling mind of the company; and

(b) once such a senior person was identified, the likelihood was that they would be so senior as not to have day to day knowledge of the operational factors that had caused the danger that led to the deaths in question.

Perhaps unsurprisingly the relatively few successful prosecutions for corporate manslaughter at common law (i.e. companies being convicted of killing by gross negligence) involved very small companies where the directors and/or managers could be closely identified with the day to day running of the company; see *R v OLL Ltd, Kite and Stoddart* (the Lyme Bay canoeing disaster—(1994), unreported), where a company and its managing director were convicted of manslaughter at Winchester Crown Court after the jury had found that they were grossly negligent in allowing schoolchildren to go canoeing on the sea without proper supervision, thereby causing their deaths.

Parliament's response to this problem was the enactment of the Corporate Manslaughter and Corporate Homicide Act 2007, based on the Law Commission's 1996 report Legislating the Criminal Code: Involuntary Manslaughter (Law Com. No. 237).

Section 1 of the 2007 Act creates an offence whereby a company or other organization can incur criminal liability (subject to the DPP consenting to proceedings being brought) if the way in which its activities are managed or organized causes a person's death, and the resultant practices amount to a gross breach of the duty of care owed by the organization to the deceased.

The offence replaces killing by gross negligence, s. 20 of the 2007 Act making it clear that the common law offence is abolished in so far as corporations and other organizations covered by the 2007 Act are concerned.

Whether or not a duty of care was owed to the deceased in any given case is, by virtue of s. 2(5), a question of law. Essentially a duty of care will exist for the purposes of the s. 1 offence in situations where a duty of care would exist under common law negligence principles, but s. 2(1) goes on to provide a considerably extended definition that goes beyond the typical duty of care owed to employees, customers, and 'neighbours in law'.

A breach of a duty of care is to be regarded as 'gross' for the purposes of s. 1 of the 2007 Act if the conduct alleged to amount to a breach of that duty falls far below what could reasonably be expected of the organization in the circumstances; see s. 1(4)(b). Under s. 8(1), in determining this question the jury must consider whether the evidence shows that the organization failed to comply with any health and safety legislation that relates to the alleged breach, and if so: (a) how serious that failure was; and (b) how much of a risk of death it posed. The jury may also consider the extent to which the evidence shows that there were attitudes, policies, systems or accepted practices within the organization that were likely to have encouraged, or produced tolerance of, the failings amounting to or giving rise to the breach of duty (s. 8(3)). The jury may also have regard to any other matters they consider relevant; see s. 8(4). It may be that this could extend to examining the failings of employees outside the scope of those in senior management positions. The failings of senior management must be a substantial cause of the breach of duty, but evidence of what other employees were doing will also be material in determining whether the breach was gross. The ability of the jury to take a more holistic view of an organization's attitudes to health and safety is a considerable advance on the previous position at common law.

By contrast, it is rightly most unlikely that an organization would incur liability under s. 1 for the rogue activities of a maverick employee. Evidence of an employee disobeying safety procedures and causing death is not consistent with the requirement under s. 1 that the prosecution establish that the death was caused by a breach of duty resulting from the way in which the organization's activities were *managed or organized*.

Once the duty of care is established, and the prosecution has proved that the breach of the duty was gross, the prosecution has to establish that the way in which the organization's activities were managed or organized by its senior management was a substantial element in the breach of the duty of care that caused the victim's death.

Liability still depends on identifying those who could be regarded as the senior management of the organization, and for these purposes s. 1(4)(c) provides that this means those who play significant roles in making of decisions about how the whole or a substantial part of the organization's activities are managed or organized, or those who play a significant role in the actual managing or organizing of the whole or a substantial part of those activities. The key difference between the statutory offence and the common law provision it replaces is that under the 2007 Act the fault of a number of senior managers can be aggregated to provide evidence that the breach of duty was gross—as opposed to the identification of an individual with sufficient fault as was the requirement at common law; see *A-G's Ref (No. 2 of 1999)* [2000] QB 796.

It should be noted that although there might be strong evidence that individual directors or managers may have been at fault in causing the breach of duty, s. 18 of the 2007 prohibits any individual from being charged as an accomplice to a corporate manslaughter offence. Similarly, s. 62 of the Serious Crime Act 2007 prevents an individual from being charged with an offence, under Part 2 of that Act, of encouraging or assisting the offence of corporate manslaughter.

This evidence could be used, however, to prosecute a manager, director, or indeed any employee in an individual capacity for killing by gross negligence at common law.

If an organization is convicted of corporate manslaughter the court can impose an unlimited fine—see s. 1(6). Whilst a heavy fine might be an effective way of registering the public disapproval of the harm caused by a company, as a punishment it is not particularly effective in ensuring that such events do not recur, other than through the rather drastic consequence of pushing the company into insolvency. Further, heavy fines simply reduce profits, reducing the funds available for distribution to shareholders as dividends. It might be asked why shareholders should be punished in this way.

In recognition of this the 2007 Act introduces the concept of remedial orders and publicity orders. Under s. 9, following conviction under s. 1, the court can make a remedial order requiring the convicted organization to take specified steps to remedy the relevant breach and any matter that appears to the court to have resulted from the relevant breach and to have been a cause of the death. The court can also issue a remedial order in respect of any deficiency, as regards health and safety matters, in the organization's policies, systems, or practices of which the relevant breach appears to the court to be an indication.

Under s. 10 a publicity order can be made by a court, following a conviction under s. 1, requiring the convicted organization to publicize in a specified manner the fact that it has been convicted of the offence; the details of the offence; the amount of any fine imposed; and the terms of any remedial order made.

How effective the 2007 Act proves to be in dealing with cases of corporate manslaughter remains to be seen. The key changes that are to be welcomed are:

(i) The shift to the concept of aggregated fault, meaning that the prosecution does not have to find a senior manager with sufficient fault to warrant a prosecution. The court can now examine the much wider concept of how a company was run.

(ii) The introduction of sanctions that may serve to prevent a recurrence of the breach of duty—principally the remedial order, but also the publicity order.

The notion that large fines were a meaningful sanction was always somewhat suspect. Fines do not compensate the victims of the breach of duty—civil actions can be brought to seek compensation as appropriate. The shift to prevention of harm is a far more imaginative and appropriate way to deal with badly run companies.

Further reading

Edwards, S. 'Descent into murder—provocation's stricture—the prognosis for women who kill men who abuse them' (2007) J Crim L 342.

Griew, E., 'The Future of Diminished Responsibility' [1988] Crim LR 75.

Herring J., and Palser, E., 'The Duty of Care in Gross Negligence Manslaughter' [2007] Crim LR 24.

Holton, R. and Shute, S., 'Self-Control in the Modern Provocation Defence' (2007) 27 Oxford JLS 1.

Horder, J. and McGowan, L., 'Manslaughter by Causing Another's Suicide' [2006] Crim LR 1035.

Mackay, R.D., 'The Abnormality of Mind Factor in Diminished Responsibility' [1999] Crim LR 117.

Mackay, R.D. and Mitchell, B.J., 'Replacing Provocation: More on a Combined Plea' [2004] Crim LR 219.

Mitchell, B., 'More Thoughts about Unlawful and Dangerous Act Manslaughter and the One-punch Killer' [2009] Crim LR 502.

O'Doherty, J.P.S., 'Involuntary Manslaughter: Where to Now?' [2004] JP 168.

Ormerod, D. and Fortson, R., 'Drug Suppliers as Manslaughterers (Again)' [2004] Crim LR 819.

Ormerod, D. and Taylor, R., 'The Corporate Manslaughter and Corporate Homicide Act 2007' [2008] Crim LR 589.

Phippen, L. and Radlett, D., 'Drugs and Manslaughter' (2005) 155 NLJ 1054.

Power, H., 'Provocation and Culture' [2006] Crim LR 871.

Tadros, V., 'The Homicide Ladder' (2006) 69 MLR 601.

Homicide—murder or unlawful act manslaughter?

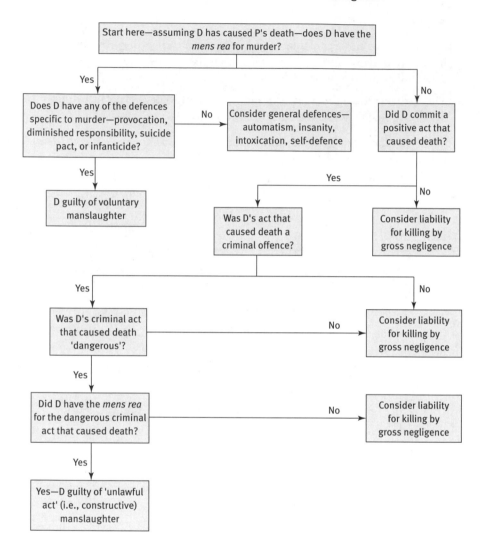

4

Non-fatal offences against the person

Introduction

Apart from motoring and theft-related offences, criminal assaults, batteries, and woundings are the staple diet of the criminal courts, with more than 100,000 prosecutions a year. Because of the historical increase in crime there has been an increase in the number of Crown Court judges, recorders, and assistant recorders, many of whom have been recruited from outside the ranks of specialist criminal practitioners. It is therefore imperative that the offences are clear, fair, and easily applied. However, as the Law Commission has pointed out (Law Com. No. 177):

> the existing interface between common law and statutory provisions undoubtedly contributes to make the law obscure and difficult to understand for everyone concerned. This may lead to inefficiency, the cost and length of trials may be increased, because the law has to be extracted and clarified and there is greater scope for appeals on misdirections on points of law.

Sir Henry Brooke, the former head of the Law Commission, in announcing the Law Commission's proposals for reform of offences against the person (Law Com. No. 122) stated that it was intolerable that the courts were still wrestling with the intricacies and inconsistencies of the Offences Against the Person Act 1861, which is full of antique and obscure language and which has been the subject of many appeals that displayed serious disagreement as to the basic content of the law. Even after the House of Lords' decisions in *R v Savage*; *R v Parmenter* [1992] 1 AC 699, *R v Brown* [1993] 2 All ER 75 and *R v Burstow* and *R v Ireland* [1997] 4 All ER 225, many aspects of the law are unsatisfactory and its application erratic (for example, see *R v Wilson* [1996] 3 WLR 125 where the Court of Appeal in quashing a conviction decided that the trial judge was wrong to apply *Brown* on the facts of the case).

The Law Commission's work on this topic has taken many years and has massive support amongst judges, magistrates, the police, and solicitors and barristers. If implemented, the recommendations would save the waste of enormous amounts of valuable court, lawyers', and citizens' time and money simply on attempts to find out what the law is, and in correcting errors where the administration of justice has gone wrong when obscure law has been wrongly applied. The report was published in 1994, but no Draft Bill has been placed before Parliament, and with the passage of time prospects for legislative reform seem increasingly bleak.

The questions included in this chapter cover all the typical offences against the person one would expect to find on a standard criminal law syllabus. There is no specific coverage of the Public Order Act 1986, or indeed terrorism offences, as these will normally be covered in a Constitutional Law, Public Law, or Civil Liberties syllabus. The emphasis is, therefore, on the Offences Against the Person Act 1861, in particular ss. 18, 20 and 47. Candidates will normally be expected to show an awareness of the Protection from Harassment Act 1997, although it is likely that the more serious incidents will be prosecuted under the 1861 Act. This again demonstrates the need for a code as the present development of principles depends on the accidents of litigation and piecemeal legislation. The common law method of resolving uncertainty by retrospective declaration of the law is objectionable in principle as it may lead to the conviction of a defendant on the basis of criminal liability not known to exist in that form before he acted. Examiners often link assault questions with the defence of self-defence—hence a good knowledge of the common law principles as clarified in s. 76 of the Criminal Justice and Immigration Act 2008 is required.

The one area of non-fatal offences against the person that has been thoroughly overhauled by Parliament is sexual offences. The Sexual Offences Act 2003 sweeps away the Sexual Offences Act 1956 to create, *inter alia*, a revised offence of rape, and a new offence of serious sexual assault. A completely new approach to consent in relation to sexual offences is introduced, one that puts the onus firmly on the defendant to ascertain free and informed consent prior to engaging in sexual activity.

Question 1

Femi is driving his car through central London. At a point where the road narrows from two lanes down to one, a car driven by Roy cuts in front of Femi's car. Femi is infuriated. As the traffic is at a standstill Femi gets out of his car, pulls open Roy's car door, and shouts abuse at him. Roy is very frightened by this. Louise, a passenger in Roy's car, gets out to remonstrate with Femi, whereupon Femi head-butts her. Louise is wearing steel-rimmed glasses and, as a result of this attack, both she and Femi suffer deep cuts to their foreheads, the frame of the glasses having caused the lacerations. Chiquitta, an elderly woman, sees this disturbance and tries to intervene. Femi pushes her away, causing Chiquitta to lose her balance and fall heavily. Chiquitta suffers a fractured hip and receives hospital treatment. Complications set in and Chiquitta dies a few weeks later from a blood clot on the brain. Louise becomes increasingly ill in the weeks following the attack, and tests reveal that she has become HIV+. Subsequent tests prove that she contracted the condition from Femi who, it transpires, is a drug addict. As a result of sharing needles, he became HIV+ some months prior to his attack on Louise.

Advise the Crown Prosecution Service as to the criminal liability of Femi.

Commentary

Most assaults problems are designed to take candidates through the range of mainstream offences under the **Offences Against the Person Act 1861**, namely **s. 18, s. 20**, and **s. 47**. As a matter of technique it is advisable to start by looking at the harm suffered by the victim. That will lead candidates into consideration of the most suitable offence. Hence if the harm suffered was a bruise, it would be foolish to start with **s. 18** as this requires either grievous bodily harm or wounding. Once the harm done has been identified, it makes sense to start with the most serious offence that might have been committed in causing the harm, and then work down to the less serious offences. In short, 'start high and work down'. Be prepared to argue in the alternative—it may look as though a particular offence has been committed, but if a particular element cannot be proved it may be necessary to consider a lesser offence. In this particular question it makes sense to take the incidents in the order in which they occur. The point about words alone constituting an assault is a very popular one with examiners so it pays to be prepared to deal with this. Avoid the common mistake of assuming that offensive or threatening words amount to an assault. Look at the effect on the victim—did he apprehend immediate physical violence? Candidates should also avoid unwarranted assumptions. On the given facts it might be tempting to discuss Femi's liability for the inevitable death of Louise. As far as the question is concerned, however, she is still alive and the answer given should be limited to Femi's liability for non-fatal offences. Although candidates are told that Femi is a drug addict there is no evidence that he acts under the influence of drugs at the time of the assaults outlined in the question. The defence of intoxication should not, therefore, be considered in any depth.

 Answer plan

- Femi's attack on Roy—possible liability for assault
- Whether Roy suffers psychological harm
- Injuries to Louise—**s. 18** and **s. 20**
- Death of Chiquitta—causation and constructive manslaughter
- Louise becoming HIV+—liability for grievous bodily harm

Suggested answer

The facts state that Femi shouted abuse at Roy, frightening him. Femi may have incurred liability for common assault. The *actus reus* requires proof that Roy apprehended immediate physical violence. The events will be viewed from the perspective of the victim, not the reasonable person: see *Smith v Chief Supt Woking Police Station* (1983) 76 Cr App R 234. It is possible to commit a 'narrow' assault by words alone. The authority for this is the House of Lords' decision in *R v Burstow; R v Ireland* [1998] AC 147. Overturning earlier decisions such as *R v Meade & Belt* (1823) 1 Lew CC 184, Lord

Steyn described the proposition that a gesture may amount to an assault but that words can never suffice as unrealistic and indefensible. The *mens rea* for assault is intention to cause the victim to apprehend immediate physical harm, or recklessness as to whether the victim apprehends such harm: see *R v Savage*; *R v Parmenter* [1992] 1 AC 699. The recklessness is subjective—Femi must at least be aware of the risk that Roy will fear immediate physical violence. It is submitted that Femi could be guilty of common assault on these facts and should be charged under s. 39 of the Criminal Justice Act 1988; see further *DPP v Little*; *DPP v Taylor* [1992] 1 QB 645.

Reference to Roy being very frightened raises the possibility that Roy may have suffered some psychological harm as a result of the abuse from Femi. Both *R v Chan-Fook* [1994] 2 All ER 552, and *R v Burstow*; *R v Ireland* (above), make it clear that psychological disturbance can amount to actual bodily harm, or even grievous bodily harm, provided there is medical evidence to substantiate this. Merely being upset will not suffice. As Lord Steyn explained, in *R v Burstow*; *R v Ireland*: '...neuroses must be distinguished from simple states of fear, or problems in coping with everyday life. Where the line is to be drawn must be a matter of psychiatric judgment.' If Roy's fright amounts to actual bodily harm Femi could be charged under s. 47 of the Offences Against the Person Act 1861 with assault occasioning actual bodily harm. The assault is apparent, as explained above. It would be for the prosecution to establish that this assault caused the actual bodily harm. The *mens rea* would be as for common assault—outlined above. It is not necessary to prove that Femi foresaw the risk of actual bodily harm: see further *R v Savage*; *R v Parmenter* (above).

Femi then head-butts Louise, causing her to suffer deep cuts to her forehead because of the contact with the frame of her glasses. The harm done could amount to grievous bodily harm, if the lacerations are categorized as 'serious harm': *see R v Saunders* [1985] Crim LR 230. Femi could therefore be charged with an offence under s. 18 Offences Against the Person Act 1861. The difficulty with a s. 18 charge would be proof of the necessary intent. Did Femi intend grievous bodily harm? The prosecution would have to prove that it was either his purpose to do some grievous bodily harm, or that in attacking Louise he foresaw such harm as at least virtually certain—thus permitting a jury to infer intent, as per *R v Woollin* [1998] 4 All ER 103.

The more likely charge is under s. 20 of the Offences Against the Person Act 1861. The lacerations would clearly amount to 'wounding'—see *JCC v Eisenhower* [1983] 3 WLR 537. There has been a break in the surface of the skin. The *mens rea* requires proof that Femi acted maliciously. On the basis of *R v Mowatt* [1967] 3 All ER 47, the prosecution must prove that Femi foresaw that some physical harm to some person, albeit of a minor character, might result from his actions. This direction was subsequently endorsed by the House of Lords in *R v Savage*; *R v Parmenter* [1992] 1 AC 699. On the facts there appears to be little doubt that the *mens rea* for s. 20 will be established. There is overwhelming evidence that Femi foresaw at least some physical harm being caused to Louise. The fact that he may not have foreseen lacerations being caused by contact with the frame of her glasses is neither here nor there.

It should be noted that, if the lacerations are seen as amounting to grievous bodily harm, as discussed above, Femi might also be guilty of maliciously inflicting grievous bodily harm contrary to s. 20 of the 1861 Act. Femi could also be charged with criminal damage in relation to the spectacles worn by Louise, provided he was aware of the risk that property might be damaged: see the decision of the House of Lords in *R v G* [2003] 4 All ER 765, where the subjective approach to recklessness was approved in preference to the objective approach previously dictated by *Metropolitan Police Commissioner v Caldwell* [1981] 1 All ER 961.

Femi may incur liability in respect of the death of Chiquitta. But for his actions she would not have died—hence causation in fact is established. As to causation in law, Femi will argue that Chiquitta dies from a blood clot, not the injuries he caused. The question that arises, therefore, is whether or not the blood clot amounts to a *novus actus interveniens*. Medical evidence will be required as to the likelihood of Chiquitta having suffered the blood clot in any event. It is submitted that unless the blood clot can be identified as an independent and potent cause of death the chain of causation will be intact. The blood clot will be seen as 'part and parcel' of the injuries caused by Femi. He clearly commits a battery. *R v Blaue* (1975) 61 Cr App R 271, makes it clear that a defendant must take his victim as he finds him. The 'thin skull' rule would extend to cover the victim's propensity to complications following an attack by the defendant. Assuming Femi is found to have caused Chiquitta's death, it is unlikely he would be charged with murder. There is little evidence that it was his intention to kill or do grievous bodily harm: see *R v Woollin* (above).

Liability for constructive, or unlawful act, manslaughter could be based on his assault. This is obviously a criminal act, but there may be difficulties in establishing that it is objectively dangerous.

On the basis of *R v Church* [1965] 2 All ER 72, and *R v Dawson* (1985) 81 Cr App R 150, the jury would be directed to consider whether a sober and reasonable person, present at the scene of and watching the unlawful act being performed, knowing what the defendant knows, and seeing what the defendant sees, would have foreseen the risk of some physical harm. Given Chiquitta's age, the reasonable person might have foreseen physical harm as a result of her being pushed away by Femi—this would accord with the reasoning in *R v Watson* [1989] 2 All ER 865. The *mens rea* for constructive manslaughter would be the *mens rea* for the assault—as to which see above. There seems little doubt that the prosecution could establish this.

Can Femi incur further liability in respect of Louise becoming HIV+? The condition itself would undoubtedly amount to grievous bodily harm—see above. The most straight-forward charge would be under s. 18 of the 1861 Act. The prosecution would have to prove that Femi caused grievous bodily harm (evident) and intended to do so. The complication would be the *mens rea*. There is no evidence that Femi knew he was HIV+, although it might be tempting to infer this from his having shared needles.

As an alternative the prosecution might consider liability under s. 23 of the Offences Against the Person Act 1861. Section 23 requires proof that Femi unlawfully and maliciously administered to Louise any poison or other destructive or noxious thing, so as thereby to endanger her life, or inflict grievous bodily harm on her. It is submitted that the term 'administration' is liberally interpreted. The AIDS virus could be the 'noxious substance'. Causing Louise to become HIV+ would amount to endangering her life. Again the problem would be whether or not Femi was aware of his condition. If not there could be difficulties in establishing that he foresaw the risk of the harm specified in s. 23, assuming the courts apply *R v Mowatt* (above).

Question 2

Wayne, aged 15, calls at houses in his neighbourhood on Halloween night for 'trick or treat'. He knocks at the door of John, a visibly frail old age pensioner, who offers Wayne some bars of chocolate. Wayne indicates that he expects to be given money, but John tells him that he can have the bars of chocolate or nothing. Wayne spits in John's face and leaves empty-handed. He later decides to punish John by telephoning him repeatedly in the middle of the night, ringing off when the receiver is lifted. John's wife Trudy becomes very distressed by these calls and has to receive treatment from her doctor for palpitations, sweating, and breathlessness as a result.

The following week Wayne goes to a party where he consumes large quantities of alcohol. On the way home he takes a small bronze statue from John's front garden and throws it, causing the statue to hit the living room window at the front of John's house. The window shatters. John, who was watching television in the room at the time, is blinded in one eye when he is hit by flying glass.

Advise the Crown Prosecution Service as to the offences committed by Wayne.

 Commentary

This is a mixed question in that candidates have to consider a number of **Theft Act** and assault offences, but it does raise some typical points relating to the latter. In terms of structure it is sensible to take the incidents in the order in which they come. As regards the blackmail issue, note the significance of the defendant's age in respect of the subjective test as to whether the demands were warranted. Words as an assault, and assaults by telephone are often popular issues with examiners, hence a good knowledge of *Burstow; Ireland* [1997] 4 All ER 225 is essential. Avoid the common error of assuming that the phone calls cause an assault. Remember that the victim must actually apprehend immediate physical violence for the *actus reus* to be made out. Simply being upset will not suffice. Note the change to criminal damage following the abandoning of '*Caldwell*' recklessness—*R v G* establishes that subjective fault now prevails, but the decisions in *R v Caldwell* regarding intoxication and criminal damage still hold good.

Answer plan

- Possible liability for blackmail
- Wayne assaulting John by spitting
- Trudy's neuroses as a result of the telephone calls
- Criminal damage to the window
- GBH suffered by John
- Intoxication as a defence to criminal damage and the assault offences

Suggested answer

Although 'trick or treat' is seen by some as a harmless prank, there is evidence to suggest that many older people find the behaviour of youths who indulge in the practice to be quite intimidating. There is obviously a fear that if something is not provided to those playing 'trick or treat' there may be unpleasant consequences. This raises the possibility that Wayne may have committed the offence of blackmail, especially where Wayne indicates that he was expecting money. Under s. 21 of the Theft Act 1968, blackmail requires proof that the defendant made a demand, although this can be implied—see *R v Collister and Warhurst* (1955) 39 Cr App R 100. The trick or treat game would be the demand in this case. The demand must be menacing. On the basis of *Thorne v MTA* [1937] AC 797, it would suffice that the demand was accompanied by a threat that would have unpleasant consequences (i.e., the 'trick' element of trick or treat).

The basic objective test for menaces is that laid down in *R v Clear* [1968] 1 QB 670; and *Garwood* [1987] 1 WLR 319. However, in the latter case Lord Lane CJ observed that: '…where the threats in fact affected the mind of the victim, although they would not have affected the mind of a person of normal stability…the existence of menaces is proved providing that the accused…was aware of the likely effect of his actions upon the victim.' The fact that Wayne knows the victim to be elderly and frail may assist the prosecution here. Hence the demand may be menacing even though a reasonable person would not have been concerned. Wayne may have deliberately picked on John believing an old-aged pensioner to be more likely to accede to his demands.

Although he clearly makes the demand with a view to gain, Wayne might be able to argue that the demand was warranted—see s. 21(1), Theft Act 1968. For these purposes a demand with 'menaces' is unwarranted unless the person making it does so in the belief: '(a) that he has reasonable grounds for making the demand; and (b) that the use of the menaces is a proper means of reinforcing the demand.' Wayne, being 15 years of age, may honestly believe that the custom of 'trick or treat' gives him reasonable grounds for making the demand, and he may also believe that relying on 'trick or treat' is a reasonable way of enforcing the demand. There is no intimation here that he is suggesting that he will commit a serious offence if not given the money.

In spitting at John it is likely that Wayne will have committed the offence of battery. The *actus reus* of common battery simply requires proof of unlawful physical contact; see *Cole v Turner* (1705) 6 Mod Rep 149, and *Coward v Baddeley* (1859) 28 LJ Ex 260. There is little doubt that spitting would constitute the *actus reus* for these purposes. The action appears to be entirely intentional, hence the *mens rea* would also appear to be evident (intention or subjective recklessness): see *R v Savage; R v Parmenter* [1992] 1 AC 699. Common assault could be considered as an alternative charge if John apprehended immediate physical violence, but the facts do not suggest this. Neither is there evidence that the spitting caused what could be regarded as actual bodily harm—thus a charge under s. 47 of the Offences Against the Person Act 1861 of assault occasioning actual bodily harm would not be appropriate.

Wayne's subsequent nuisance telephone calls cause John's wife Trudy to become very distressed, culminating in her receiving medical treatment for palpitations, sweating, and breathlessness. The issue for the prosecution will be whether or not these conditions can amount to actual bodily harm. On the basis of *R v Burstow; R v Ireland* [1997] 4 All ER 225, approving *R v Chan-Fook* (1994) 99 Cr App R 147, psychiatric harm can be grievous bodily harm or actual bodily harm, depending on its severity. In either case there must be expert medical evidence as to the extent of the harm. In *R v Burstow; R v Ireland* (above) Lord Steyn observed that neuroses should be '...distinguished from simple states of fear, or problems in coping with everyday life. Where the line is to be drawn must be a matter of psychiatric judgment.' It is a moot point, therefore, as to whether or not Trudy has suffered actual bodily harm. In any event, a charge under s. 47 would require proof that Wayne had committed an assault, at least in the narrow sense of causing his victim to apprehend immediate physical violence. That this can be caused by means of a telephone call, even a silent call, was clearly established in *R v Burstow; R v Ireland* (above). The difficulty lies in establishing the assault itself. Trudy is distressed by the calls, but that does not necessarily mean that the calls caused her to apprehend physical violence, let alone immediate physical violence. Causing her to feel generally uneasy will not suffice for these purposes. If the *actus reus* of assault is not made out, not only does the charge under s. 47 of the 1861 Act fail, but also the common assault charge.

Even if Trudy did apprehend immediate physical violence, Wayne must be shown to have intended this, or to have at least been aware of the risk that his victim might suffer such harm; see *R v Savage; R v Parmenter* (above). The fact that the intended victim of his calls might have been John, not Trudy, is immaterial. Under the principles of transferred malice the identity of the victim is irrelevant; see *R v Latimer* (1886) 17 QBD 359.

There is no likelihood of Wayne incurring liability for theft of the statue, under s. 1 of the Theft Act 1968. The statue is property belonging to another, and he does appropriate it. Assuming he was dishonest, the problem for the prosecution would be in establishing intention to permanently deprive John—this is not made out on the facts.

Wayne does commit criminal damage in smashing the window. Contrary to s. 1 of the Criminal Damage Act 1971 he damages or destroys property belonging to another.

There is evidence that his actions were intentional, but recklessness would suffice. Following the House of Lords' decision in *R v Caldwell* [1982] AC 341, it would have sufficed to show that Wayne gave no thought to an obvious risk of property being damaged. This formulation of recklessness has now been abandoned, however, and the decision of the House of Lords in *R v G* [2003] 4 All ER 765, makes clear that the prosecution will have to prove that Wayne was at least aware of the risk of criminal damage, and that it was, in the circumstances known to him, unreasonable for him to take the risk, in order to have the necessary *mens rea*. On the facts it is submitted that this will be established. Wayne may seek to rely on his self-induced intoxication as a defence. The mere fact that he has been drinking does not necessarily mean that he will succeed with the defence. There must be evidence that, as a result of the alcohol consumption, he could not and did not form the necessary *mens rea*; *R v Cole and ors* [1993] Crim LR 300. Further, 'simple' criminal damage contrary to s. 1(1) of the Criminal Damage Act 1971 is a basic intent crime—i.e., one where the *actus reus* does not go beyond the *mens rea*. Hence self-induced intoxication will not provide a defence unless Wayne was not reckless in consuming the alcohol (not likely on the facts), or if the risk of harm would not have occurred to him even if he had been sober (again, no evidence of this).

On the basis of the leading authority, *DPP v Majewski* [1976] 2 All ER 142, therefore, Wayne would not have a defence of self-induced intoxication as regards a s. 1(1) charge. A charge of aggravated criminal damage could be brought if Wayne was at least reckless as to whether the damaging of the property would endanger life: see *R v Steer* [1988] AC 111. This means that Wayne would have to be reckless as to whether the smashing of the window would endanger life. Recklessness here would be subjective: see *R v G* (above). Given that John is injured by the broken glass the prosecution has the evidential basis for charging the aggravated offence under s. 1(2). In *R v Caldwell* (above) the House of Lords held that aggravated criminal damage, where the defendant was reckless as to whether or not life would be endangered, was to be regarded as a basic intent crime, on the basis that the recklessness in becoming intoxicated provides the necessary fault. Hence again, Wayne would not be able to plead intoxication as a defence.

John losing the sight in one eye would amount to grievous bodily harm. Wayne clearly causes this harm, hence the *actus reus* of the offence under s. 18 of the Offences Against the Person Act 1861 would be made out. *Mens rea* would be the problem—especially as Wayne had been drinking. The prosecution would have to prove an intent to do some grievous bodily harm. It is submitted that this is most unlikely on the facts. In any event, s. 18 is a specific intent crime. On the basis of *DPP v Majewski* (above) Wayne would be able to plead self-induced intoxication as a result and if successful this would reduce his liability to s. 20 of the Offences Against the Person Act 1861. The blinding constitutes the required harm. Wayne will be malicious if he foresaw the risk of some physical harm, albeit slight; see *R v Mowatt* [1967] 3 All ER 47 and *DPP v W* [2006] All ER (D) 76.

One argument he might raise is that he foresaw someone being frightened by his actions, but it did not occur to him that anyone would be hurt. *R v Sullivan* [1981]

Crim LR 46, confirms that an intention to frighten will not suffice under s. 20 unless it encompasses foresight of some physical harm. If this is the case the prosecution may have to pursue a s. 47 charge instead. Self-induced intoxication is normally no defence to a charge under s. 20 as the crime is one of basic intent: see *DPP v Majewski* (above). Regarding a s. 47 charge, the harm done to John clearly amounts to actual bodily harm. Assault for the purposes of s. 47 encompasses battery, hence the indirect physical contact with the glass will supply the 'assault' element. There are no causation issues. Wayne will therefore have committed the *actus reus* of the s. 47 offence. On the basis of *R v Savage*; *R v Parmenter* (above), Wayne can be shown to have had the *mens rea* for assault provided he was aware of the risk that he would commit a battery, or cause another to apprehend immediate physical violence. Only if this never crossed his mind would he be able to deny *mens rea*. There is no need to show he foresaw the harm done, or even actual bodily harm. Again, self-induced intoxication would not normally be a defence to a charge under s. 47 as it is a basic intent crime.

Question 3

Mike and Karen are both lecturers at Crammershire University. Karen is a member of the university's karate club and she persuades Mike to join. The day of the next karate club meeting is Karen's birthday. Before the club meeting she spends a few hours in the bar drinking with friends. By the time she leaves the bar to go to the training sessions Karen has drunk six pints of lager and several vodka 'shots'. During the training session Karen hits Mike in the face with her forearm. Mike falls awkwardly hitting his head on a nearby bench. Mike's girlfriend Gaye, who had come along to watch the session, witnesses the attack on Mike and runs towards Karen screaming abuse. Karen, who is intensely jealous of Gaye's relationship with Mike, throws Gaye to the ground and kicks her in the head. Gaye suffers minor bruising and grazes. Karen, who is distressed, runs off to the changing rooms without bothering to attend to Mike. Other club members call for medical help. It later transpires that Mike has a broken leg and has lost the hearing in one ear.

The following week Mike sees Karen coming towards him in the corridor at the university. As she approaches Karen raises her arm intending to give Mike a hug and apologize for what she has done. Mike fears that she is about to hit him again. He pulls his mobile telephone out of his pocket and thrusts it towards Karen's face with the result that Karen suffers several broken teeth and her glasses are smashed.

In the weeks following these incidents Gaye becomes increasingly depressed and neurotic and has to seek professional psychological help to cope with the trauma caused by Karen's attack.

Advise the Crown Prosecution Service as to the respective criminal liabilities of Karen, Gaye and Mike.

Commentary

This question brings together issues one would normally expect to see in a problem question concerned with non-fatal assaults. The link between violence and intoxication is well known, hence candidates can expect examiners to use the framework of the 1861 Act to test their knowledge of the basic intent/specific intent dichotomy. Consent is also an issue that arises in questions involving assaults, and here it has to be explored in the context of sporting activities. It is natural for victims who are attacked to seek to defend themselves in some way if they can. Hence candidates should also expect to see issues relating to self-defence arise in the context of assaults questions. The basic test for self-defence is fairly simple, hence examiners often add a 'twist' by including an issue of mistake relating to self-defence; **s. 76 of the Criminal Justice and Immigration Act 2008** needs to be referred to here. Note also that the question contains a trap for the unwary in respect of omissions. It is not enough to identify a duty and a corresponding failure to act. Where the defendant is charged with a 'result' crime it has to be proved that the omission was one of the causes of that result if the omission is to be used as the basis for liability.

Answer plan

- Grievous bodily harm suffered by Mike—possibility of **s. 18 or s. 20, 1861 Act**
- **Section 47** and common law offences as residual basis for liability
- Karen's defences—consent and intoxication
- Assaults on Gaye and possible self-defence raised by Karen—intoxication and self-defence
- Gaye's liability for verbal assault and possible self-defence arguments
- Mike's liability for actual bodily harm to Karen, and criminal damage to her glasses
- Mike's self-defence argument

Suggested answer

Turning first to incidents arising out of the karate session, Mike suffers a broken leg and loss of hearing as a result of the fall. The broken leg and loss of hearing could each be classified as 'grievous bodily harm'—i.e., serious harm: see *R v Saunders* [1985] Crim LR 230. This opens up the possibility of charges under s. 18 and s. 20 of the Offences Against the Person Act 1861. Section 18 requires proof that Karen caused grievous bodily harm—but for her actions Mike would not have suffered the harm. Causation in law requires proof that the harm was a reasonably foreseeable consequence of her actions. The fact that Mike falls and hits his head etc. will not break the chain of causation. In any event *R v Blaue* [1975] 1 WLR 1411 makes it clear that Karen must take Mike as she finds him—including his propensity to fall over when hit! The *mens rea* for s. 18 is intent—although there is no clear authority at the moment as to what intent means in the context of s. 18 it would be intolerable if the courts adopted any approach other than that in *R v Woollin* [1998] 4 All ER 103. If intention to do grievous bodily harm is sufficient for murder, the intent must be the same under a s. 18 charge. On the facts it may be difficult to establish that Karen intended to do grievous bodily harm—in any event intoxication will be a complicating factor as explained below.

A charge under s. 20 Offences Against the Person Act could be brought as an alternative. The harm required is either grievous bodily harm (see above) or wounding. The injuries suggest that he has suffered a wound. On the basis of *JCC v Eisenhower* [1984] QB 331 this requires proof of a rupture of the dermis and the epidermis. Under s. 20 the grievous bodily harm must be inflicted—but for these purposes this would be satisfied by proof of causation: see *R v Burstow; R v Ireland* [1997] 4 All ER 225. The *mens rea* under s. 20 is satisfied by proof that Karen was malicious: see *R v Mowatt* [1968] 1 QB 421. Karen must at least have been aware of the possibility of causing some physical harm— see further *DPP v W* [2006] All ER (D) 76. She does not need to have foreseen the harm actually caused. It should be possible to establish this on the facts.

In the unlikely event that the *mens rea* for s. 20 cannot be established a charge under s. 47 Offences Against the Person Act 1861 could be sustained on the basis that Karen committed an assault (see below) and the assault caused actual bodily harm—see below. Note that under s. 47 Karen need not have any *mens rea* in respect of the actual bodily harm—she only needs the *mens rea* for the assault (either broad or narrow): see *R v Savage; R v Parmenter* [1992] 1 AC 699.

As to lesser offences, hitting Mike in the face would constitute a battery. Any unlawful touching will suffice: see *Cole v Turner* (1705) 6 Mod Rep 149. The *mens rea* is intention or (subjective) recklessness: see *R v Savage; R v Parmenter* (above). There is *prima facie* evidence of *mens rea*, subject to what is said below regarding intoxication. If Mike sees the blow coming and apprehends immediate physical violence Karen may also have committed an assault in the 'narrow' sense—the *mens rea* is as for battery.

Karen's failure to help Mike once she has injured him may not be significant. In theory she has caused harm and comes under a responsibility to limit the effect of that harm: see *R v Miller* [1983] 2 AC 161. Note, however, that there is no liability for the omission *per se*—the omission must cause some harm. If the facts are that her failure to act has only a *de minimis* effect in terms of making the harm worse it should be ignored as a basis for liability.

Turning to consider the defences that Karen might raise in respect of the harm done to Mike, she may seek to rely on his consent to harm. On the basis of *R v Donovan* [1934] 2 KB 498, a victim cannot validly consent to physical harm if it amounts to actual bodily harm or worse unless the activity comes within a range of policy-based exceptions. The obvious one here is 'manly diversion' or sport. The issue would be whether or not karate classes come within this exception. Even if they do, a further issue would be the extent of the harm or risk of harm consented to by participants. Conduct that went beyond what a player might reasonably be regarded as having accepted by taking part was not covered by the defence of consent. What was accepted in one sport, such as the physical contact inevitable in martial arts, would not necessarily be covered by the defence of consent in another, for example lawn tennis.

In *R v Barnes* [2004] EWCA Crim 3246, Lord Woolf CJ observed that if the defendant's actions are within the rules and practice of the game and do not go beyond it, that will be a firm indication that what has happened is not criminal. He went on to observe that, with highly competitive sports, conduct outside the rules could be expected to occur in the heat of the moment. Even if that conduct resulted in a player being disciplined or excluded from the game, it did not necessarily mean that the line had been crossed whereby the actions became unlawful, warranting the intervention of the criminal law. The jury would have to be directed to consider the type of sport, the level at which it was being played, the nature of the act, the degree of force used, the extent of the risk of injury and the state of mind of the defendant. Karen is, on the facts, a more experienced martial arts exponent and it could be argued that Mike consented to a restricted range of risks—i.e., that he did not expect to be hit by her. The key point will be as to whether or not her actions are regarded as having been so obviously late or violent as not to be seen as an instinctive reaction, error or misjudgement in the heat of the contest. This is a moot point that can only be determined by a trial. On the facts it is submitted that Mike will probably be regarded as having validly consented to the risk of being hit.

In addition to the common law exception permitting consent as a defence to harm greater than actual bodily harm where this occurs in the course of a legitimate sporting activity, the common law also permits the defence of consent where parties engage in mutual 'horseplay' and practical jokes: see *R v Aitken* [1992] 1 WLR 1066, and *R v Richardson and Irwin* [1999] Crim LR 494. This could be relevant if the court rejects the argument that the contact between Karen and Mike occurred in the course of a legitimate sporting contest. If the defence succeeds on either basis Karen will have a complete defence to charges under s. 18, s. 20, and s. 47 of the Offences Against the Person Act 1861.

The alternative defence would be self-induced intoxication. If Karen was merely drunk she has no defence as such—intoxication requires evidence that she was incapable of forming, and did not form, the necessary intent. On the basis of *DPP v Majewski* [1977] AC 142, her voluntary intoxication could be a defence to crimes of specific intent but not crimes of basic intent. Section 18 of the Offences Against the Person Act 1861 is a specific intent crime because the *mens rea* goes beyond the *actus reus*. If Karen was charged under s. 18 and successfully pleads intoxication her liability will be reduced to the 'lesser included' offence of s. 20 Offences Against the Person Act 1861—a basic intent crime. Hence if she is charged under s. 20 or s. 47 Offences Against the Person Act 1861 or charged with common assault or battery she will not escape liability on the grounds of self-induced intoxication, as these are all basic intent crimes. She cannot claim that her consumption of the alcohol was anything other than reckless: see *R v Hardie* [1984] 3 All ER 848. The only possible escape route would be an argument that she would not have been aware of the risk of harm even if she had been sober. There is no evidence to suggest this. Her liability will, therefore, be imposed on the basis that she was reckless in becoming intoxicated and recklessness is sufficient *mens rea* in respect of any one of the basic intent offences.

Karen may also have incurred liability in respect of the harm caused to Gaye. Psychological harm can amount to grievous bodily harm or actual bodily harm depending on its seriousness: see *R v Burstow*; *R v Ireland* (above). The prosecution will have to produce medical evidence to show that the harm is not transient and minor. On the facts, bearing in mind the *mens rea* requirements outlined above, a charge under s. 47 of the Offences Against the Person Act 1861 seems the most likely here.

Minor bruising and grazes would most likely constitute actual bodily harm contrary to s. 47 of the Offences Against the Person Act 1861: see *R v Miller* [1954] 2 QB 282. Grazing would not amount to a wound unless the definition in *JCC v Eisenhower* (above) was satisfied. As indicated above the *mens rea* for s. 47 would be intention or subjective recklessness. Provided Karen intended to assault Gaye it does not matter that she might not have foreseen the actual bodily harm that actually transpired; see *R v Savage*; *R v Parmenter* (above)

Karen may raise the defence of self-defence in respect of Gaye. Karen is entitled to use reasonable force to protect herself—see e.g., *R v Julien* [1969] 1 WLR 839. The question will be whether or not the force she used was reasonable in the circumstances; see s. 76 of the Criminal Justice and Immigration Act 2008, which largely reproduces the common law on this point. Karen cannot avail herself of the fact that she misjudged the amount of force required due to her being intoxicated: see *R v O'Grady* [1987] 3 WLR 321, confirmed in *R v Hatton* [2005] All ER (D) 308 (Oct), and now enshrined in s. 76(5) of the 2008 Act.

As to Gaye's possible liability, she makes no physical contact with Karen, hence the only possible charge could be in relation to 'narrow' assault based on her threats. The House of Lords has made it clear that words can constitute an assault—see *R v Burstow*; *R v Ireland* (above). The problem for the prosecution would be in establishing that Karen actually apprehended any immediate physical harm. She may not have been perturbed by Gaye's threats. Gaye would need to have the *mens rea* for assault—see above. Gaye could rely on self-defence (i.e., reasonable force used in defence of another), on the basis that she was acting to protect Mike. Alternatively she could invoke the statutory defence under s. 3 of the Criminal Law Act 1967—using reasonable force to prevent the commission of a criminal offence. Section 76 of the 2008 Act applies equally to the common law and the statutory defence under s. 3 of the 1967 Act regarding how the court should approach the question of whether or not the force used was reasonable. Assuming Gaye did believe the facts were such as to warrant her acting in self-defence, sub-section 76(7) provides that the court dealing with the issue should have regard to the fact that she may not have been able to weigh to a nicety the exact measure of any necessary action; and that her evidence of having only done what she honestly and instinctively thought was necessary for a legitimate purpose constitutes strong evidence that only reasonable action was taken by her for that purpose.

In breaking Karen's teeth Mike may have caused actual bodily harm contrary to s. 47 of the Offences Against the Person Act 1861. He appears to have caused the harm with the necessary *mens rea*—i.e., he was at least aware of the risk of harm: see *R v Savage*;

R v Parmenter (above). The obvious defence would be self-defence at common law—considered above. The issue to note here is that Mike is mistaken—there is in fact no need for him to defend himself. Following *Beckford v R* [1987] 3 WLR 611, and now s. 76(3) of the 2008 Act, Mike will be judged on the facts as he honestly believed them to be—hence if he honestly believed he was about to be attacked again by Karen he could use force that would have been reasonable to defend himself in such circumstances.

In damaging Karen's glasses Mike may have committed the offence of criminal damage contrary to s. 1(1) Criminal Damage Act 1971. Mike has committed the *actus reus* by damaging property belonging to another—the main issue for argument would be *mens rea*. He does not appear to have intended the harm, hence the prosecution will have to establish that he was at least reckless. *MPC v Caldwell* [1982] AC 341 no longer applies here, following the decision of the House of Lords in *R v G* [2003] 4 All ER 765. Hence the prosecution will have to show that Mike was at least aware of the risk that property might be damaged by his actions. If he gave no thought to the risk he might escape liability. Again Mike could argue that he was using reasonable force to prevent harm to himself (e.g., where D destroys a gun that X is about to use to shoot D).

Question 4

Critically assess the position taken in English criminal law in respect of consent to:

(a) the deliberate infliction of harm;

(b) participation in activities carrying a risk of serious harm.

Commentary

This is a challenging question on a difficult issue. Consent as a defence in criminal law has always caused problems, and since *R v Brown* [1993] 2 All ER 75, where the House of Lords attempted to clarify the law in relation to consent and the deliberate infliction of physical harm, there have been two very detailed Law Commission reports on the subject. It is always likely, therefore, to be the subject of an exam question.

The topic raises issues as to the legitimate aims and functions of the criminal law. As English criminal law is not codified, there is no statute that sets out the law's aims and functions, so it is necessary to consider case law, Law Commission reports, and the views of commentators to ascertain these. In this answer, candidates must attempt to cover all aspects of this issue, as the question is not simply an invitation to candidates to write all they know about *R v Brown*. Decisions since *R v Brown* have sought to develop the common law position in respect of consent to the risk of harm and the nature of informed consent. A good answer will incorporate these points. The conclusion on this topic could therefore be totally different from this author's; but provided it is logically developed from earlier analysis, it would not mean that the answer given would necessarily obtain a lower mark. Indeed, it might result in a higher one!

 Answer plan

- Aims of the criminal law
- House of Lords' decision in *Brown* [1993]
- Lord Templeman's rationale
- Law and morals
- *R v Dica* and informed consent
- Conclusion

Suggested answer

Consent as a defence to the deliberate infliction of harm

There will never be complete agreement as to the correct aims and functions of the criminal law and, in the absence of a criminal code setting out a rationale containing fundamental principles, this issue will remain a topic of debate. However, the aims and functions of English criminal law, it is submitted, are similar to those stated in the American Law Institute Model Penal Code, i.e.:

(a) To forbid and prevent conduct that unjustifiably and inexcusably inflicts or threatens substantial harm to individual or public interests.

(b) To subject to public control persons whose conduct indicates that they are disposed to commit crime.

(c) To safeguard conduct that is without fault from condemnation as criminal.

(d) To give fair warning of the nature of the conduct declared to be an offence.

(e) To differentiate on reasonable grounds between serious and minor offences.

In addition to protecting the public from harmful activity, we also expect the criminal law to respect certain individual liberties such as freedom from coercion, fraud or fear; the right to protest, demonstrate etc. Individual freedom of choice is also a liberty that we place high on our list of priorities, and it is this conflict between individual freedoms and collective interests which was one of the major issues in *R v Brown* [1993] 2 All ER 75.

In *Brown*, a group of middle-aged men willingly participated in sado-masochistic activities that involved the deliberate infliction of wounds. Videos were made of their activities and circulated to members of the group, but not to outsiders. The men were charged with various offences including assault occasioning actual bodily harm (Offences Against the Person Act 1861, s. 47) and malicious wounding (Offences Against the Person Act 1861, s. 20) and pleaded guilty when the trial judge ruled against their defence of consent. The Court of Appeal upheld their conviction but certified the following point of law of general public importance: 'Where A wounds or assaults B occasioning him actual bodily harm in the course of a sado-masochistic encounter, does the prosecution have to prove lack of consent on the part of B before they can establish A's guilt under section 20 or section 47 Offences Against the Person Act 1861?'. The House of Lords answered this question in the negative and dismissed the appeal. Lord Templeman, who gave the majority judgment, decided the issue using a mixture of precedent and public policy. He stated that consent is not a general defence where actual bodily harm or wounding has been caused. There are exceptions to this rule, and violence intentionally inflicted will not be a criminal offence if it occurs in the course of a lawful activity, such as contact sports, surgical operations, rough horseplay or tattooing. For some of these exceptions at least, such as sport and surgical treatment, there is a clearly identified public policy advantage in permitting a wider scope for the defence of consent—promoting fitness through sport, and saving lives through surgery. Permitting consent as a defence to activities such as tattooing and horseplay has more to do with drawing the line between what is the legitimate concern of the state (anti-social behaviour, or the exploitation of vulnerable persons) and personal autonomy.

The question for the House therefore was whether or not sado-masochistic behaviour as occurred in *Brown* could be regarded as positively beneficial or as falling within the domain of private activities that were of no concern to the state provided vulnerable persons were not being exploited.

Lord Templeman concluded that the criminal law had to provide sufficient safeguards against exploitation and corruption of others, particularly those who are young, weak in body or mind, inexperienced or in a state of special physical, official or economic dependence. He referred to three reasons leading to the conclusion that sado-masochistic behaviour was not in the public interest:

(a) It glorified the cult of violence ('pleasure derived from the infliction of pain is an evil thing').

(b) It increased the risk of AIDS and the spread of other sexually transmitted diseases.

(c) It could lead to the corruption of youth.

Lord Templeman concluded: 'I am not prepared to invent a defence of consent for sado-masochistic encounters which breed and glorify cruelty and result in offences under section 47 and section 20 of the Act of 1861.'

The minority (Lords Mustill and Slynn) interpreted the relevant cases (*R v Coney* (1882) 8 QBD 534; *R v Donovan* [1934] 2 KB 498; and *Attorney-General's Reference*

(No. 6 of 1980) [1981] QB 715) and the public interest requirements differently. Lord Mustill decided that the decks were clear for the House to tackle completely anew the question of whether the public interest required s. 47 to be interpreted as penalizing the conduct in question. He concluded that:

> the state should interfere with the rights of the individual to live his or her life as he or she may choose no more than is necessary to ensure a proper balance between the special interests of the individual and the general interests of the individuals who together comprise the populace at large.

In relating the majority decision to aims and functions, many questions arise. First, in ascertaining public interest, how far should the Law Lords take into account society's morals? This involves reference to the Hart–Devlin debate (see Lord Devlin, *The Enforcement of Morals*) as to whether conduct should be criminalized simply because it is a moral wrong, and whether the criminal law should simply reflect society's moral standards or try to improve them. This is virtually impossible to answer briefly, but it is submitted that if it is not morally right to encourage deliberate injury through sado-masochistic activity, the majority decision does not conflict with this objective. If the majority had not declared it unlawful, their decision could have been interpreted as condoning or even encouraging such activities.

Secondly, was the House of Lords' decision in *Brown* creating new law, or was it giving effect to the will of Parliament expressed in the 1861 Act? Again, this is difficult to answer, but the application of the defence of consent is probably correct as there has been traditionally a reluctance to extend its boundaries, partially because of the difficulties in deciding whether consent was freely given by a victim capable of understanding the nature of the act (see *Burrell v Harmer* [1967] Crim LR 169—consent to tattooing given by boys aged 12 and 13 held invalid). It is submitted that their Lordships were not abolishing an existing defence (as they did when they removed the husband's marital rape immunity in *R v R* [1991] 4 All ER 481) but were simply declaring the boundaries of an existing offence.

Thirdly, was this a situation where respect for individual freedom should have been outweighed by the need to protect society from such conduct? The participants were middle-aged men who were in control of the activities, but the Law Lords considered that because of the risk of future, younger, inexperienced participants, the accused's individual liberty had to be sacrificed. This aspect of the decision has been criticized (e.g., N. Bamforth, 'Sado-Masochism and Consent' [1994] Crim LR 661), and rather misses the point that the question ought to have been whether or not the victims did validly consent. The fact that others might not in different circumstances is not a compelling reason to limit the defence on these facts. The muddled thinking in this area was compounded by the Court of Appeal in *R v Wilson* [1996] 3 WLR 125, where the defendant had his conviction for actual bodily harm contrary to s. 47 of the 1861 Act quashed. He had agreed to his wife's request that he should brand his initials on her buttocks with a hot knife. The court took the view that the husband's activities could be regarded as coming within the tattooing exception, and that, in any event, as explained by Russell LJ:

> it is not in the public interest that activities such as the appellant's in this appeal should amount to criminal behaviour. Consensual activity between husband and wife, in the privacy of the matrimonial home, is not, in our judgement, normally a proper matter for criminal investigation, let alone criminal prosecution.

In *Wilson*, therefore, individual autonomy overrode the public morality argument, whereas in *Brown*, the deciding factor was protection of the public. Both decisions were based to some extent on the concept of public policy, which has been described as an 'unruly horse'. Both cases demonstrate the difficulties of applying the criminal law and in deciding whether a judgment is right or wrong.

Consent to the risk of harm

The law distinguishes between situations where a victim consents to inevitable and deliberate harm, and those where the victim consents to the risk of harm. As outlined above, consent to inevitable harm can only operate as a defence within certain limits dictated by public policy. Hence deliberate harm of a minor nature can be incurred without criminal liability as this falls within the permissible scope of individual autonomy. More serious deliberate harm may be permitted if it is in the course of justifiable surgical interference. Many other activities, however, carry only the risk of harm, such as engagement in sports, or dangerous exhibitions, such as where a member of the audience volunteers to stand in front of a knife thrower's target as part of a show. The audience member is not consenting to being stabbed; indeed it is doubtful any such consent would be recognized as valid. What he or she is consenting to is the risk of harm, as the stunt cannot be conducted without some risk. The distinction between consent to harm and the consent to activities carrying a risk of harm was made clear by the Court of Appeal in *R v Dica* [2004] 3 All ER 593. Judge J gave as an example the case of a husband and wife who have sexual intercourse because they desperately want a family, notwithstanding medical advice that carrying a child to full term could result in serious harm to the health of the wife. As he explained, if the serious harm resulted, the law would not deny the husband the defence of consent. In his view interference of this kind with personal autonomy, and its level and extent, could only be authorized by Parliament.

It follows that if consent to risk of harm is to be a more general defence than consent to inevitable harm, issues will arise as to the extent to which the victim's consent has to be fully informed. In *R v Konzani* [2005] EWCA Crim 706, the Court of Appeal held that the doctrine of informed consent should form part of the criminal law, hence the fact that a woman consented to sexual intercourse with a man, unaware that he was HIV+ did not mean that she consented to the risk that she might herself become HIV+.

Applying this to the knife thrower example above, the volunteer from the audience assumes the knife thrower is a professional who can perform the stunt without causing harm. If in fact the knife thrower is an amateur who has never successfully performed the stunt it would be difficult to argue that the volunteer had genuinely consented to the risk of harm, should the stunt go wrong. Were the knife thrower to reveal this fact before asking for a volunteer, then anyone volunteering would do so with the necessary knowledge, although this might still throw up the question of whether any adult should be permitted to run such risks just for the sake of public entertainment.

As Lord Woolf CJ explained in *R v Barnes* [2004] EWCA Crim 3246, participants in sports certainly consent to the risk of quite serious harm—the more competitive the sport and the more it involves physical contact, the higher the level of risk. Rugby union is probably a good example of this. Players can suffer horrific injuries resulting in permanent paralysis but it does not mean a criminal prosecution must follow. Such injuries are a foreseeable risk arising from participation, even where they result from action that is in breach of the rules. What players do not consent to is the risk of deliberate harm being caused outside the normal run of play—such incidents can and have led to criminal prosecutions as the defence of consent does not extend that far. This brief analysis perhaps explains why the legality of boxing has been questioned as that is a sport where the object is to beat one's opponent into submission. With boxing it appears that a participant can validly consent to a very real risk of death. Whether this is in the public interest is questionable, and throws into stark relief the need for more physical sports to be properly organized, licensed and refereed if they are to be protected by the defence of consent.

In conclusion it can be said that the contours of the defence of consent, whether to the deliberate infliction of harm or the risk of harm being caused, are tolerably clear. Where the law gets into difficulties, and runs the risk of looking both ridiculous and partial, is where it strays from a utilitarian approach based on 'greater good' and attempts to moralize on what consenting adults should do in private.

Question 5

Akerman becomes involved in an argument with Beck about who should sit at a particular desk in the examination hall. Beck is sitting where Akerman wants to sit and Beck warns Akerman that he will '...get his head kicked in...' if he continues to argue about the seat. Akerman eventually decides to let the matter go, tapping Beck under the chin with his pen and laughing at Beck, commenting on his sexual inadequacy.

Beck becomes enraged by this and picks up a nearby chair and breaks it over Akerman's head. Akerman suffers bruising and a graze to his scalp. Carlton, another student waiting to sit the exam, is alarmed at what is happening. Carlton punches Beck repeatedly in the stomach to stop him attacking Akerman. Beck falls to the floor with a ruptured spleen.

Advise the Crown Prosecution Service as to the criminal liability of Akerman, Beck and Carlton.

Commentary

For most candidates this should be a very attractive question as it essentially involves a consideration of the main offences under the 1861 Act and an evaluation of the defence of self-defence. As ever with assault questions candidates should consider the harm suffered by the victim first and use this as a guide to the relevant offence to be considered. It normally makes sense to start with the most serious possible offence arising out of each incident and work down by a process of elimination to the less serious offences until an offence is identified where proof of the *actus reus* and *mens rea* looks fairly certain.

 Answer plan

- Common assault and battery—Criminal Justice Act 1988, s. 39
- Offences Against the Person Act 1861, s. 47
- Offences Against the Person Act 1861, s. 20
- Offences Against the Person Act 1861, s. 18
- *R v Savage*; *R v Parmenter* [1992]
- Self-defence

Suggested answer

Criminal liability of Akerman

Akerman's only liability is in respect of his tapping Beck under the chin with his pen. On the basis of *Cole v Turner* (1705) 6 Mod Rep 149, and *Coward v Baddeley* (1859) 28 LJ Ex 260, the merest touching can be enough to constitute a battery. It is clear that there is no element of implied consent on the part of Beck. On the basis of *R v Savage*; *R v Parmenter* [1992] 1 AC 699, the *mens rea* required is either an intention to commit battery or recklessness that battery will occur. On the facts intention would appear to be evident. Hence Akerman could be charged with common battery contrary to s. 39 of the Criminal Justice Act 1988.

Criminal liability of Beck

(i) When Beck warns Akerman that he will '…get his head kicked in…' if he continues to argue about the seat, Beck may have committed a common assault, contrary to s. 39 of the Criminal Justice Act 1988. The prosecution will have to prove that Beck caused Akerman to apprehend immediate physical violence as a result of the words used; see *Fagan v Metropolitan Police Commissioner* [1969] 1 QB 439, and *R v Lynsey* [1995] 3 All ER 654. In establishing this *actus reus* regard should be had to the victim's perceptions; see *Smith v Chief Superintendent of Woking Police*

Station (1983) 76 Cr App R 234. There is no need to prove exactly what Beck was frightened of—it is sufficient that he thought the physical violence was immediate. Since the House of Lords' decision in *R v Burstow; R v Ireland* [1997] 4 All ER 225, it has been settled that an assault in the narrow sense can be committed by means of words alone. Again, the crucial issue will be the effect of the words used on the victim. As with the offence of common battery, *R v Savage; R v Parmenter* (above), confirms that the *mens rea* required is either an intention to commit an assault or recklessness that the victim will apprehend immediate physical violence. Beck may argue that he had no intention of carrying out the threat, but a conviction can be secured provided Beck was at least aware of the risk that the victim would apprehend immediate physical violence.

 (ii) When Beck becomes enraged and hits Akerman over the head with a chair he may have committed offences contrary to ss. 47, 20 and 18 of the Offences Against the Person Act 1861. If the graze to Akerman's head resulted in a rupturing of the surface of the skin (dermis and epidermis), the injury could constitute a wound, thereby opening up the possibility of a charge under either s. 18 or s. 20 of the 1861 Act; see *JCC v Eisenhower* [1983] 3 WLR 537. In either case, provided the injury was regarded by the court as amounting to a wound, there would be no issues as to causation. For liability under s. 18 the prosecution would have to establish that Beck had intended to do some grievous bodily harm when he broke the chair over Akerman's head. Adopting the direction on intent approved in *R v Woollin* [1998] 4 All ER 103, the prosecution would have to provide evidence that Beck foresaw the grievous bodily harm as virtually certain to result from his actions. It would then be for the jury to find, if appropriate, that this provided enough evidence of Beck's having intended the grievous bodily harm. It is submitted that liability under s. 18 is unlikely unless there is evidence, for example, that Beck hit Akerman intending to fracture his skull. Assuming that liability under s. 18 cannot be established, the prosecution may charge Beck with malicious wounding contrary to s. 20 of the 1861 Act. The 'wounding' element of the offence is as discussed above. Beck will be found to have had the requisite *mens rea* provided he was aware that, by his actions, there was a risk that the victim might suffer some physical harm, albeit slight; see *R v Mowatt* [1967] 3 All ER 47, as approved in *R v Savage; R v Parmenter* (above). On the facts this *mens rea* would appear to be evident, hence, provided the harm done constitutes a wound, a s. 20 conviction seems sustainable.

Regarding s. 47, the bruising or the graze could constitute actual bodily harm. This term is not defined in the 1861 Act but is widely accepted as requiring proof that the victim suffered some interference with his health or comfort; see *R v Miller* [1954] 2 QB 282, and *R (on the application of T) v DPP* [2003] Crim LR 622. It is submitted that bruising that is more than superficial would be enough evidence of actual bodily harm to leave to a jury. There are no issues of causation on these facts, Beck's actions clearly result in the harm suffered by the victim. The assault element of the s. 47 offence can be satisfied either by evidence that Akerman apprehended immediate physical violence—

i.e. he was aware of the attack, or by evidence of a battery; see *Fagan v Metropolitan Police Commissioner* [1969] 1 QB 439; and *R v Lynsey* [1995] 3 All ER 654. At least one of these two alternatives will be satisfied on the given facts. Following the House of Lords' decision in *R v Savage*; *R v Parmenter* (above), the prosecution will only need to establish *mens rea* in relation to the 'assault' element of the s. 47 offence—i.e. intention to assault or recklessness as to whether the victim would be assaulted. This should be evident on the given facts. There is no need to establish any *mens rea* in relation to the actual bodily harm that results from the assault.

Criminal liability of Carlton

When Carlton punches Beck repeatedly in the stomach to stop him attacking Akerman, Beck suffers a ruptured spleen. The harm done here would undoubtedly satisfy the requirements of grievous bodily harm for the purposes of both s. 18 and s. 20 of the 1861 Act; see *R v Saunders* [1985] Crim LR 230—it would be regarded as serious harm. As outlined above in relation to Beck's liability, under s. 18 the prosecution would have to establish that Carlton foresaw the grievous bodily harm as virtually certain to result from his actions. Applying *R v Woollin* (above), the jury could then decide whether this justified a conclusion that Carlton intended the grievous bodily harm. The facts suggest this will be made out. The alternative charge would be maliciously inflicting grievous bodily harm. There is no doubt that Carlton inflicted such harm, and the *mens rea* requirement for s. 20, discussed above in relation to Beck, would clearly be made out.

Carlton will presumably seek to rely on the common law defence of self-defence, and possibly the statutory defence under s. 3(1) of the Criminal Law Act 1967. The common law defence of self-defence extends to permitting a defendant to use reasonable force in the protection of others; see *R v Rose* (1884) 15 Cox CC 540, and *R v Duffy* [1967] 1 QB 63. Usually there will be some connection between the defendant and those whom he seeks to protect, but the courts seem willing to accept that the defence extends, at common law, to situations where no such relationship exists; see *Re A (Children) (Conjoined Twins: Surgical Separation)* [2000] 4 All ER 961.

The evidence indicates that Carlton was alarmed, and was motivated in his actions by a desire to stop Beck attacking Akerman—hence he was not 'spoiling for a fight' or motivated by any desire for revenge.

The issue for the jury will be as to whether the force used in the circumstances was reasonable. The test is objective, although the jury will be directed to bear in mind that Carlton may have been acting in a moment of crisis, unable to weigh to a nicety the exact measure of necessary defensive action; see s. 76(7) of the Criminal Justice and Immigration Act 2008, which largely restates the common law on this issue. Evidence that Carlton had only done what he honestly and instinctively thought was necessary would be potent evidence that his actions and the force used had been reasonable; see *Palmer v R* [1971] AC 814, and now s. 76(7) of the 2008 Act. It may be the case that Carlton was mistaken as to the amount of force required to prevent further harm to Akerman. If this is the case the jury should be directed in the light of s. 76 of the 2008 Act. This would involve consideration of two questions: (i) did Carlton honestly believe that it was necessary to defend Akerman?; if so, (ii) on the basis of the facts and the danger perceived by Carlton, was the force used reasonable?

If self-defence is accepted by the jury Carlton must be acquitted. If, however, the jury accept that Carlton was acting to protect another, but went beyond the use of reasonable force, he will have no defence; see *R v Clegg* [1995] 2 WLR 80.

As noted above, Carlton could also rely on the statutory defence created by s. 3(1) of the Criminal Law Act 1967, which permits the use of reasonable force to prevent the commission of a criminal offence. The attack on Akerman clearly involved the commission of an offence. Under s. 3 there is no requirement for there to be any link or connection between the defendant and those whom he seeks to protect. The issue of the reasonableness of the force used will be approached on the same basis as is the case in relation to the common law defence considered above—both are now governed by the guidelines established in s. 76 of the 2008 Act.

Question 6

Enrico is owed £1,000 by Alonzo in respect of some unpaid gambling debts. Enrico has told Alonzo that if the money is not repaid within 48 hours Alonzo will have his legs chopped off by Enrico's associates.

In desperation Alonzo visits his former partner Katya who lives with their child Gloria. Alonzo finds the front door to Katya's house has been left open and he walks in uninvited. On finding Katya in bed Alonzo says he wants to have sex with her and that he will take Gloria abroad with him if she refuses. Katya allows Alonzo to have sex with her. As he is leaving Alonzo takes £500 in cash from Katya's handbag.

Alonzo then visits Claudia who is working as a prostitute for Serpico. When Alonzo and Claudia are alone in the room she uses for sex with her clients, she explains to Alonzo that she is an illegal immigrant being held captive by Serpico and pleads with Alonzo to help her escape. Alonzo, having paid Serpico £25 for sex with Claudia, proceeds to have sexual intercourse with her anyway. As he leaves Alonzo takes £500 in cash that Claudia had hidden under her mattress.

Alonzo uses the money to repay his debt to Enrico.

Advise the Crown Prosecution Service as to the criminal liability of Alonzo.

Commentary

This question has been included in this chapter because it provides a useful opportunity to consider the operation of the **Sexual Offences Act 2003**. It will be noted, however, that it also throws up quite diverse topics such as theft and duress. Given developments in respect of duress it is likely to be a popular topic with examiners for the foreseeable future. Given that this is a factually complex question it makes sense to break up the answer under headings and sub-headings. Structurally, compulsion should be left to the end as it can then be considered in relation to all the offences considered. In dealing with the duress points a good knowledge of *R v Hasan* [2005] UKHL 22, is essential as the House of Lords addressed several aspects of the defence in that decision. Note that as no crime is nominated by Enrico, duress *per minas* does not actually arise as a defence, however there is a basis for considering duress of circumstances. Similarly, candidates should have a clear understanding of the relationship between **ss. 74 to 76 of the Sexual Offences Act 2003** which is *vital* in order to explain the various possibilities in relation to consent, both as regards *actus reus* and the defendant's *mens rea*. The facts of the question provide an opportunity to demonstrate that the provisions of the **2003 Act** regarding consent do not necessarily solve all the problems that existed before its enactment.

 Answer plan

- Burglary in Katya's house
- Rape of Katya and consent issues
- Theft of money from Katya
- Rape of Claudia and consent issues
- Theft of money from Claudia
- No duress *per minas*
- Duress of circumstances
- Extent to which duress is self-induced
- Test to be applied for duress

Suggested answer

Entering Katya's house

Does Alonzo commit burglary when, finding the front door to Katya's house has been left open, he walks in uninvited? He clearly enters a building. Whether or not he does so as a trespasser depends on whether or not he has permission to enter the house. Given that it is no longer the matrimonial home, and there is no evidence that he has a key, it would appear that he did not have express permission to enter, but he may argue that he had some residual implied permission, given that his daughter lives there. In any event there can be no liability under s. 9(1)(a) of the Theft Act 1968 unless the prosecution can prove that, at the time he entered as a trespasser Alonzo had one of the specified ulterior intents (i.e. intent to steal, do grievous bodily harm, or criminal damage). The facts indicate that he stole £500 before leaving the house, but there is no clear evidence that there was intention to steal at the time he entered the house.

Katya allows Alonzo to have sex with her

The prosecution may consider charging Alonzo with rape contrary to s. 1 of the Sexual Offences Act 2003. The offence, on these facts, requires proof that Alonzo intentionally penetrated Katya's vagina; that Katya did not consent to the penetration; and that Alonzo did not reasonably believe that Katya was consenting to the penetration. The facts indicate that Katya 'allowed' Alonzo to have sexual intercourse with her—is this synonymous with consent? The scheme created by the 2003 Act provides for a number of situations where the complainant is irrebuttably presumed not to have consented to sexual intercourse—such as where the defendant intentionally deceives the complainant as to the nature or purpose of the relevant act, or induces the complainant to consent by impersonating a person known personally to them. None of these provisions apply on the given facts.

Section 75 of the 2003 Act sets out a number of scenarios where the complainant is presumed not to have consented unless the defendant produces evidence to rebut the presumption. The only one of these that might be relevant is s. 75(b)(ii)—that Katya feared that immediate violence would be used against another person (i.e. Gloria). The difficulty here is that there is no evidence that the removal of Gloria would have involved violence, and even if this was the case, there is no evidence that, at the time of the sexual intercourse, the threat of violence was immediate.

Assuming the provisions of s. 75 do not apply the jury will be directed to consider the basic direction on consent under s. 74 of the 2003 Act, i.e. '...a person consents if she agrees by choice, and has the freedom and capacity to make that choice'. Clearly Katya has the capacity to consent, but there could be some dispute here as to the extent to which a woman being threatened with the removal of her daughter from the country actually has the 'freedom' to make real choices.

If the jury concludes that Katya did not consent, the next issue will be whether or not Alonzo had the necessary *mens rea*. In particular, whether he had any reasonable belief that Katya was consenting. There are no grounds for applying any of the conclusive presumptions under s. 76 to the effect that he had no such reasonable belief, and as indicated above, unless s. 75(b)(ii) applies, there is no basis for any presumption that Alonzo had no reasonable belief that Katya was consenting. The matter will simply be one for the jury to decide—they can convict if the prosecution can prove beyond all reasonable doubt that Alonzo had no reasonable belief that Katya was consenting. Under s. 1(2) whether Alonzo's belief that Katya was consenting was reasonable will be determined having regard to all the circumstances, including any steps Alonzo took to ascertain whether Katya was consenting. The evidence suggests very strongly that he realized her consent was not freely given, but obtained by duress.

As an alternative to rape the prosecution ought to consider a charge under s. 63 of the 2003 Act, which provides that a person commits an offence if he is a trespasser on any premises, and intends to commit (*inter alia*) rape, and he knows or is reckless as to whether he is a trespasser. The point to note in relation to this offence is that there is no requirement that the defendant entered the property as a trespasser. It could be argued that Alonzo became a trespasser when he decided to threaten Katya intending to have sex with her, inasmuch as she would have wanted him to leave at that point. The prosecution would still, however, have to prove that Alonzo intended to commit rape, as to which, see above in relation to whether he had any reasonable belief that Katya would have been consenting to the sexual intercourse.

Alonzo takes £500 in cash from Katya's handbag

In taking the £500 cash from Katya's bag Alonzo almost certainly commits theft contrary to s. 1(1) of the Theft Act 1968. The cash is property belonging to another, and he appropriates it with the intention of permanently depriving Katya of it. There is no evidence to suggest that he is not dishonest—see s. 2(1)(a)–(c) of the Theft Act 1968. He does not appear to believe he has any legal right to the money, nor does he believe that Katya consents to his taking it. It should be noted that if he is found to have entered Katya's house as a trespasser (see above), this theft could result in his being charged with burglary contrary to s. 9(1)(b) of the Theft Act 1968—that he entered as a trespasser and stole.

Alonzo has sexual intercourse with Claudia

Alonzo could be charged with raping Claudia contrary to s. 1 of the Sexual Offences Act 2003—the elements of the offence are outlined above as regards Katya. Although Claudia was working as a prostitute, and therefore might be assumed to be consenting to the sexual intercourse, the prosecution might argue that there is a presumption that she was not consenting as she was (and Alonzo was not), unlawfully detained at the time of the sexual intercourse, and Alonzo was aware of this—see s. 75(b)(iii) of the Sexual Offences Act 2003. The jury will be entitled to presume that Claudia did not consent unless sufficient evidence is adduced to raise an issue as to whether she consented.

Assuming the absence of consent is made out, the issue will then be as to whether or not Alonzo had any reasonable belief that Claudia was consenting. Given the evidence about Claudia being held captive, the jury can presume that Alonzo did not reasonably believe that Claudia consented to sex, unless sufficient evidence is adduced by Alonzo to raise an issue as to whether he reasonably believed she was consenting. Beyond the fact that she was being forced to work as a prostitute it is not clear what evidence Alonzo could adduce to rebut the presumption that he had no reasonable belief that Claudia was consenting. As with Katya, if s. 75 cannot be used to create a presumption that Alonzo realized Claudia was not consenting the issue of *mens rea* will fall to be determined under s. 1(2)— was Alonzo's belief that Claudia was consenting reasonable, taking into account all the circumstances. These circumstances could include the fact that she is being held captive and that she is being forced to work as a prostitute. Alonzo did not specifically ask if Claudia was consenting. On the scope of 'circumstances' see further the discussion in *Attorney-General's Reference (No. 79 of 2006); R v Whitta* [2006] EWCA Crim 2626.

Taking the £500 from under the mattress

Alonzo will be guilty of theft of the £500, as outlined above in relation to the theft of money from Katya.

Compulsion defences

Duress *per minas* will not be available as a defence to Alonzo as the facts indicate that Enrico did not 'nominate' a crime that Alonzo had to commit in order to prevent the threat from being carried out. Enrico simply indicated what would happen to Alonzo if the debt was not repaid; see *R v Cole* [1994] Crim LR 582. Although the issue requires further clarification in the appeal courts, it may be possible for Alonzo to plead the defence of duress of circumstance cases—see *R v Martin* [1989] 1 All ER 652, on the basis that he acted reasonably and proportionately in order to avoid a threat of death or serious injury. The jury would have to be satisfied that: (i) Alonzo was impelled to act as he did because as a result of what he believed to be the situation he had good cause to fear that otherwise death or serious physical injury would result; and (ii) that a sober person of reasonable firmness, sharing Alonzo's characteristics, would have responded to the situation by acting as Alonzo did.

There is no doubt that Alonzo feared death or grievous bodily harm, but he faces a number of significant difficulties in raising a 'duress' based defence. Following *R v Abdul-Hussain and others* [1999] Crim LR 570, the jury should be asked to consider whether or not the threat was operating on Alonzo's mind at the time when he committed the crimes in question. It is hard to see how the threats could be relevant to anything other than the thefts committed by Alonzo as the threats related to the unpaid debts. He would, therefore, have no duress-based defence to the sexual offences outlined above.

The second issue is that of immediacy. As Lord Bingham explained in *R v Hasan* [2005] UKHL 22, if the retribution threatened against the defendant is not such as he reasonably expects to follow immediately or almost immediately on his failure to comply with the threat there may be: '...little room for doubt that he could have taken evasive action, whether by going to the police or in some other way, to avoid committing the crime with which he is charged.' The question for the court is whether or not the 48 hours in which Alonzo had to comply with the demand constituted an opportunity to obtain police protection.

The third problem faced by Alonzo relates to the extent to which his problems were self-induced. Gambling debts are unenforceable in a court of law, hence a creditor may resort to threats, possibly threats of violence, in order to recover the sums due. In *R v Hasan* (above), Lord Bingham expressed the view that if a person voluntarily becomes or remains associated with others engaged in criminal activity in a situation where he knows or ought reasonably to know that he may be the subject of compulsion by them or their associates, he cannot rely on the defence of duress to excuse any act which he is thereafter compelled to do by them. Although this decision, if interpreted strictly, relates to duress *per minas* (i.e. where the defendant is ordered to commit a particular crime or face the consequences) it is submitted that the rationale could be extended to the situation where a defendant, through his own voluntary actions, places himself in a situation where he is exposed to such threats. If applicable, the ruling in *R v Hasan* (above) would militate strongly against Alonzo being permitted to rely on a duress-based defence, but he might try to distinguish his situation on the basis that he was a 'client' of Enrico rather than a member of Enrico's criminal gang. If the defence of duress succeeds, Alonzo would have a complete defence to the theft and burglary charges.

Actus reus of rape—s. 1 Sexual Offences Act 2003 ('SOA')

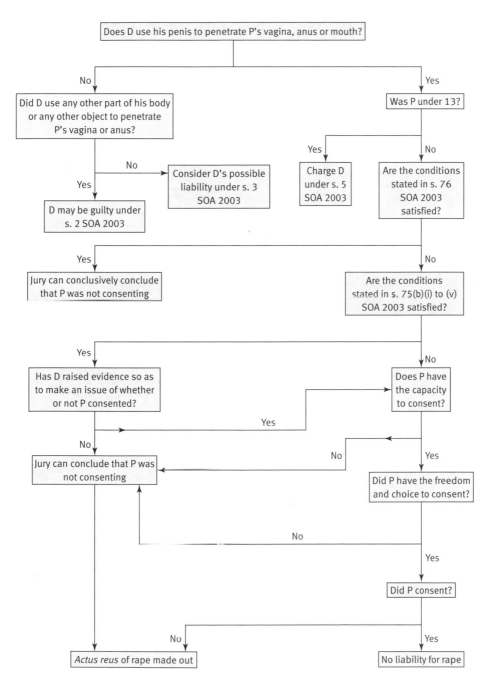

Mens rea of rape—s. 1 Sexual Offences Act 2003 ('SOA')

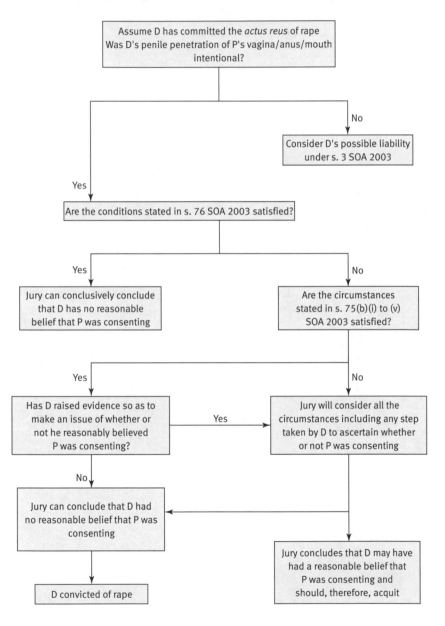

Question 7

Answer both parts (a) and (b).

(a) Steve is having a coffee with his friends Dave and Barry. They discuss women's attitudes to sex and Dave expresses the view that all women really mean 'yes' when they say 'no' to sexual intercourse. Steve invites Dave and Barry back to his house where Linda, Steve's wife, is asleep. Steve tells Barry that Linda loves to have sex with men other than her husband, but also likes to pretend that she is being raped. Steve reassures Barry that any resistance on the part of Linda will be part of her 'play-acting'. Dave visits the bathroom and, in error, enters the bedroom where Linda is asleep in bed. He goes into her bedroom and starts to have sexual intercourse with Linda who is still asleep. On waking, Linda tries to fight Dave off but he continues to have sex with her.

Linda runs downstairs in distress. Barry takes this as his cue to have sexual intercourse with her on the sofa in the living room. Linda begs Barry to leave her alone but he persists. Steve stands by watching the events unfold.

Discuss the criminal liability of Dave and Barry.

(b) One evening Rory walks past Lizzie's house and notices that the front door is not fully closed. He pushes the door open and has a look around inside the house. He discovers Lizzie asleep in her bed. Without waking Lizzie he pulls her bedclothes aside and raises her nightclothes enabling him to see her naked body.

The next day Rory, seeking to impress, tells his friend Kasra how he went out on a blind date the previous evening with Lizzie. He tells Kasra that the evening culminated in them having sexual intercourse at her house. Rory concludes by telling Kasra that Lizzie is 'always dead keen for it'.

The following day Kasra visits Lizzie's house posing as a double-glazing salesman. Lizzie agrees to let Kasra in so that he can give her an estimate. Whilst they are in her bedroom Kasra suggests that she might like to have sex with him there and then. Lizzie is shocked and frightened but she remains calm, suggesting that Kasra gets himself ready whilst she visits the bathroom. Lizzie leaves the bedroom intending to call the police. Kasra, encouraged by her response, runs after Lizzie and, pushing her onto the hallway floor, proceeds to have sexual intercourse with her, despite her protestations that he should stop. Once Kasra leaves, Lizzie calls the police.

Advise the Crown Prosecution Service as to the criminal liability of Rory and Kasra. Do not consider Rory's liability as an accomplice to Kasra, or any potential liability Rory may have under Part 2 of the Serious Crime Act 2007.

 Commentary

Although the Sexual Offences Act 2003 came into force in May 2004, there is still, at the time of writing, very little indication through reported decisions of how its provisions are being interpreted by the courts. This creates uncertainty for candidates as to the type of question that will be set in an examination. For the purposes of this chapter some problem questions have been selected to attempt an examination of how the law might now apply to situations that proved problematic under the pre-2004 law.

It should be stressed that factual problems involving sexual offences often, of necessity, refer to unpleasant attitudes and activities. Simply because the facts of the question reflect reprehensible attitudes or offensive behaviour, do not assume that these in any way reflect the views of the examiner! Chauvinistic attitudes towards consent do exist in real life and can cause problems when cases come to trial. Note the rubric to part (a) does not require consideration of Steve's liability, hence the answer does not cover issues relating to his accessorial liability. Similarly there is an injunction against considering Roy's accessorial liability in part (b). Examiners will attach such limitation where necessary to keep the candidate's task within reasonable bounds, given the time constraints imposed by the examination format, or the word limits imposed on coursework.

 ## Answer plan

(a) Steve, Dave, and Barry

- Dave and *actus reus* of rape
- Rebuttable assumptions concerning consent under the **2003 Act**
- *Mens rea* for rape—objective test
- Dave and offence of trespass with intent to commit a sexual offence

(b) Rory and Kasra

- Rory's liability, **s. 4, Sexual Offences Act 2003**
- Rory's liability, **s. 3, Sexual Offences Act 2003**
- Rory's liability, **s. 63, Sexual Offences Act 2003**
- Kasra's liability, **s. 63, Sexual Offences Act 2003**
- Kasra's liability, **s. 1, Sexual Offences Act 2003**

Suggested answer

Part (a)

On the given facts it is likely that Dave would be convicted of rape contrary to s. 1 of the Sexual Offences Act 2003. In terms of *actus reus* the prosecution would first have to prove that Dave had penetrated the vagina, anus, or mouth of another person with his penis. The fact that he started to have sexual intercourse with Linda would appear to satisfy this. There is no need to prove ejaculation. Section 79(2) of the 2003 Act specifies that penetration '...is a continuing act from entry to withdrawal...'. The prosecution would have to establish that, at some time during the penetration Dave had the necessary *mens rea*.

The second element of *actus reus* to be established is that Linda did not consent to the penetration. The issue of consent is now governed by the rather complex provisions of sections 74 to 76 of the 2003 Act.

Under s. 76 the jury will be entitled to conclusively presume that Linda was not consenting if the prosecution can prove that, in order to have sexual intercourse with Linda, he intentionally deceived her as to the nature or purpose of what he was doing, or that he induced her to consent to sexual intercourse by impersonating a person known personally to her. There is no evidence to support either assertion.

The prosecution may be able to rely on s. 75, which goes on to establish certain rebuttable assumptions as to consent. Where the defendant has:

(i) committed the *actus reus* of rape as defined in s. 1(1)(a) (i.e., has penetrated the vagina, anus, or mouth of another person), and;

(ii) the complainant was asleep at the time of the penetration, and;

(iii) the defendant knew that this was the case

the complainant will be taken not to have consented to the sexual intercourse unless sufficient evidence is adduced to raise an issue as to whether the complainant consented. This effectively places Dave under a burden to provide evidence that Linda was consenting even though she was asleep—on the facts there would appear to be no such evidence.

In the event that the absence of consent cannot be resolved by reliance on s. 75, s. 74 provides that a person consents if she agrees by choice, and has the freedom and capacity to make that choice. This on its own would appear to be enough to establish that Linda could not have been consenting at the time Dave started to have sexual intercourse with her. A person who is asleep does not have the capacity to make decisions.

Turning to *mens rea*, Dave's penetration of Linda is clearly intentional, hence the only live issue will be as to whether or not he reasonably believed that Linda was consenting.

Under s. 75 of the 2003 Act, given that Dave has:

(i) committed the *actus reus* of rape as defined in s. 1(1)(a) (i.e., has penetrated the vagina, anus, or mouth of Linda); and

(ii) she was asleep at the time of the penetration; and

(iii) Dave knew that this was the case

the jury can *presume* that Dave did not reasonably believe that Linda consented to the relevant act, unless sufficient evidence is adduced by Dave to raise an issue as to whether he reasonably believed Linda was consenting.

If s. 75 does not lead the jury to a conclusion that Dave had the necessary *mens rea*, they would be directed that, in any event, s. 1(2) of the 2003 Act provides that whether or not a belief is reasonable is to be determined having regard to all the circumstances, including any steps the defendant took to ascertain whether the complainant was consenting. There is no evidence of Dave having taken such steps, hence he will be guilty of raping Linda. Note that Steve has said nothing to Dave about Linda enjoying 'rape fantasies'.

It should be noted that Dave may also have committed the offence of trespass with intent to commit a sexual offence, contrary to s. 63 of the Sexual Offences Act 2003. The offence is made out where he is a trespasser on any premises; he intends to commit rape; and he knows that, or is reckless as to whether, he is a trespasser. Being in Linda's bedroom intending to have sexual intercourse with her could make him a trespasser in premises. Intention to have sexual intercourse whilst she is asleep would be evidence of his intention to rape her. This offence replaces the offence under s. 9(1)(a) of the Theft Act 1968—entry as a trespasser with intent to commit rape.

Barry's situation is very similar, except that Linda was clearly conscious at the time of the sexual intercourse. Again the prosecution would have to prove that Barry penetrated the vagina, anus, or mouth of Linda with his penis, and that at the time she was not consenting. Given that the preconditions for the application of s. 76 of the 2003 Act are not apparent on the facts, the starting point again is s. 75. Under s. 75, if it can be proved that:

(i) Barry had sexual intercourse with Linda;

(ii) Barry was, immediately before the sexual intercourse, using violence against Linda, or causing her to fear that immediate violence would be used against her; and

(iii) Barry knew that those circumstances existed,

Linda will be presumed not to have consented to the sexual intercourse unless sufficient evidence is adduced to raise an issue as to whether she consented. The problem here for the prosecution is the absence of any direct evidence that Barry used force on Linda, although if she did not want sexual intercourse with him it may be implied that he would have had to physically overpower her for this to have happened. If s. 75 cannot be relied upon to establish the absence of consent, the prosecution will turn to s. 74 which provides that Linda consents if she agrees to the sexual intercourse by choice, and has the freedom and capacity to make that choice. The facts indicate that there was no free choice on her part.

As outlined above in relation to Dave's liability, the absence of any reasonable belief by Barry as to whether or not Linda was consenting could be resolved under s. 75 if it can be shown that, immediately before the sexual intercourse, Barry was using violence against Linda, or causing her to fear that immediate violence would be used against her; and he knew that those circumstances existed. If this was the case the jury can presume that Barry did not reasonably believe that Linda consented to the relevant act, unless sufficient evidence is adduced by Barry to raise an issue as to whether he reasonably believed Linda was consenting.

If s. 75 does not, of itself, dispose of the *mens rea* issue, the issue of whether Barry's belief in Linda's consent was reasonable is to be determined having regard to all the circumstances, including any steps Barry took to ascertain whether the complainant was consenting. Under the pre-Sexual Offences Act 2003 law, *DPP v Morgan* [1975] 2 All ER 347, would have required Barry to be judged on the facts as he honestly believed them to be. Hence he could have relied on Steve's assurances as to Linda's consent. Under the 2003 Act the onus instead is on Barry to obtain Linda's consent. On the one hand Barry will contend that he acted on Steve's reassurances. On the other hand the prosecution will argue that the 2003 Act requires the jury to have regard to the steps taken by Barry to ask Linda if she was consenting. In the absence of any case law it is unclear how the courts will interpret these provisions. The test is now objective, but the reassurances by Steve may be seen as making Barry's assumptions as to consent reasonable. Much may depend on how the courts interpret s. 1(2) of the 2003 Act where it provides that whether a belief is reasonable is to be determined having regard '…to all the circumstances…' If a wide view is taken of circumstances it will include the assurances given to Barry by Steve. The narrow view is that the circumstances will be limited to the encounter between Barry and Linda. In *Attorney-General's Reference (No. 79 of 2006)*; *R v Whitta* [2006] EWCA Crim 2626 the Court of Appeal, *obiter*, seemed to be indicating that the wider view of circumstances was preferable.

Part (b)

When Rory enters Lizzie's house he does so as a trespasser as he has no permission to be there. He does not commit an offence under s. 9(1)(a) of the Theft Act 1968, however, as he does not enter with intent to steal, do grievous bodily harm, or criminal damage. Where he subsequently pulls her bedclothes aside and raises her nightclothes to see her naked body, he probably does commit an offence contrary to s. 4 of the Sexual Offences Act 2003—causing a person to engage in sexual activity without consent. The prosecution would have to prove that the activity was 'sexual' in nature. For these purposes this is defined by s. 78 as penetration, touching or any other activity that, whatever its circumstances or any person's purpose in relation to it, a reasonable person would consider of a sexual nature. Alternatively it can be penetration, touching, or any other activity that, because of its nature, may be sexual and, because of its circumstances or the purpose of any person in relation to it (or both), is sexual. The test is clearly objective, although the court can take into account the defendant's purpose.

That Lizzie was not consenting to the activity is presumed from the fact that she was asleep—see s. 75(2)(d) of the 2003 Act, and the fact that Rory was aware of this. In terms of *mens rea*, Rory's actions are intentional in lifting the nightclothes. There is no need to prove that he was aware that the actions were sexual. The only argument he could raise would be as regards consent. Given the facts there appears to be no basis on which he could argue that he reasonably believed Lizzie to be consenting.

The facts also raise the possibility of a charge of sexual assault contrary to s. 3 of the 2003 Act. This provides that a person commits an offence if he intentionally touches another person, the touching is sexual, the complainant does not consent to the touching, and the defendant does not reasonably believe that the complainant consents.

The technical difficulty for the prosecution with a s. 3 charge lies in proving that Rory touched Lizzie. Section 79(8) defines 'touching' as including touching with any part of the body, with anything else, through anything, and in particular includes touching amounting to penetration. There is no evidence that Rory actually touches Lizzie, although he may have done so 'through' her nightclothes. Note that in *R v H* [2005] All ER (D) 16 (Feb), it was held that where a person was wearing clothing, touching of that clothing constituted 'touching' for the purposes of the offence contrary to s. 3 of the 2003 Act. If this technicality can be overcome, a s. 3 charge is possible.

Assuming the *actus reus* is made out, the prosecution must prove the absence of any reasonable belief that the victim was consenting. Again regard would be had to s. 75(2)(d) of the 2003 Act—as Lizzie was asleep the jury would be able to presume that there was no reasonable belief on Rory's part that she was consenting. Beyond s. 75, whether Rory's belief in Lizzie's consent is reasonable is to be determined having regard to all the circumstances, including any steps he took to ascertain whether she was consenting. On the facts the *mens rea* seems evident.

Rory might also have incurred liability for trespassing with intent to commit a sexual offence, contrary to s. 63 of the Sexual Offences Act 2003. The offence is made out where he is a trespasser on any premises and intends to commit a 'relevant offence'—for these purposes 'relevant offence' encompasses both sexual assault and causing sexual activity without consent. One assumes that the prosecution can prove that Rory knew he was, or was reckless as to whether he was, a trespasser.

When Kasra deceives Lizzie into letting him enter her house he may also have committed the offence of trespass with intent to commit a sexual offence, contrary to s. 63 of the Sexual Offences Act 2003. Liability would require proof that he was present intending to have sexual intercourse regardless of whether or not Lizzie consented. If he believed that, having tricked her into letting him in, he would be able to have consensual intercourse, there may not be any liability under s. 63.

Does Kasra commit rape when he has sexual intercourse with Lizzie? The facts make it quite clear that the *actus reus* of the offence under s. 1 of the 2003 Act is made out. Kasra commits the act of penile penetration in respect of Lizzie and she was not consenting. If necessary resort could be had to s. 75 of the 2003 Act:

(i) Kasra had sexual intercourse with Lizzie;

(ii) Kasra was, immediately before the sexual intercourse, using violence against Lizzie, or causing her to fear that immediate violence would be used against her; and

(iii) Kasra knew that those circumstances existed.

On this basis the jury could presume Lizzie was not consenting unless Kasra can raise evidence to rebut the assumption.

The problem area for the prosecution will be *mens rea*. Kasra will contend that he honestly believed Lizzie was consenting. The absence of any reasonable belief on the part of Kasra as to whether or not Lizzie was consenting could be resolved under s. 75 if it can be shown that, immediately before the sexual intercourse, Kasra was using violence against Lizzie, or causing her to fear that immediate violence would be used against her; and he knew that those circumstances existed. If this was the case the jury can presume that Kasra did not reasonably believe that Lizzie consented to the relevant act, unless sufficient evidence is adduced by Kasra to rebut that presumption and raise the question as to whether he reasonably believed Lizzie was consenting. Kasra will rely upon the fact that he did ask Lizzie if she would like to have sex. As a ploy to buy time to telephone the police she gave him the impression that she would be willing. All of this is evidence that Kasra will rely on to contend that a reasonable person would have thought Lizzie was consenting, and that he checked to make sure that she was. More difficult for Kasra is the fact that Lizzie subsequently makes it plain that she does not want to have sex with him and that he nevertheless persists.

Question 8

On Thursday night James (aged 21), meets Carly (aged 19) in a night club. He falsely claims to be a footballer with Chelsea FC. Carly is impressed by this and agrees to go to James' flat that night, where they have sex. The following morning James confesses to Carly that he lied about being a professional footballer. Carly is angry with James, but subsequently agrees to meet him in a bar the following Saturday night.

When they next meet, James introduces Carly to his friend Didier (aged 23). James then leaves to drink with friends at a nearby bar. Didier and Carly chat for a while and Didier buys Carly several rounds of drinks, always ordering a double measure of spirits instead of a single for Carly's drinks. Didier drinks mineral water. As the evening progresses Carly becomes increasingly giggly as the alcohol takes effect, but she remains lucid. Didier leaves the club with Carly and they walk to her flat which is nearby. Carly opens the door and Didier follows her inside, whereupon she slumps against the hallway wall and, laughing and giggling, falls to the floor. Didier picks Carly up and takes her to her bedroom where he proceeds to have sex with her. Carly is aware of what Didier is doing but she does not try to physically prevent him from having sex with her. Having had sex with Carly, Didier leaves her asleep in her bed and goes home.

The following morning Carly reports James and Didier to the police claiming that she has been raped by both of them. Under questioning James says that he took some pills before leaving the night club to go back to his flat with Carly, and that he cannot remember anything else about what happened that evening. Didier, who confirms that he was sober throughout the evening, says he thought Carly was consenting to having sex with him.

Advise the Crown Prosecution Service as to the criminal liability of James and Didier.

Commentary

This question requires a good knowledge of the offence of rape under the Sexual Offences Act 2003, in particular the provisions dealing with proof that the complainant did not consent and those dealing with whether or not the accused was aware that the complainant was not consenting. It is not uncommon for examiners to introduce intoxication as an element that might vitiate the complainant's consent, but care needs to be taken as, on the given facts, this may only be an issue in relation to the sexual intercourse with Didier. Particular points to note here are: fact management issues—the evidence about James taking pills needs to be linked to what occurs in his flat; and the fact that the automatism and/or in-toxication on the part of James may be irrelevant if Carly was in fact consenting to sexual intercourse with him. There is no clear authority on Didier's deception point so all sensible arguments need to be canvassed. Note that the uncertainty regarding Didier's permission to be in Carly's flat raises issues regarding trespass-based offences. The plying with alcohol by Didier requires an examination of the 'old' law (i.e., **s. 23/s. 24** administering a noxious substance, **Offences Against the Person Act 1861**) and the new (**s. 61 of the Sexual Offences Act 2003**). Be prepared to leave open issues regarding Didier's liability for rape. The question is meant to be finely balanced on whether Carly could consent and whether Didier had the *mens rea* for rape—the candidate's task in such cases is to point out the questions of fact that can only be determined by a properly directed jury.

Answer plan

- James' liability for rape—consent issues—effect of deception—no significant vitiating factors
- Significance of James taking the pills—automatism—self-induced—absence of *mens rea* for rape
- Didier's liability for administering the alcohol—**s. 23/s. 24** administering a noxious substance
- Didier's liability under **s. 61 of the Sexual Offences Act 2003**
- Didier's liability under **s. 63 of the Sexual Offences Act 2003**
- Didier's liability for rape—consent issues under **s. 75**—Carly intoxicated
- Didier's *mens rea*—did he reasonably believe Carly was able to and did consent?

Suggested answer

James' liability

The prosecution may decide to charge James with rape contrary to s. 1 of the Sexual Offences Act 2003. Under the provisions of s. 1 James commits rape if: (i) he intentionally penetrates Carly's vagina with his penis; (ii) Carly does not consent to the penetration; and (iii) James does not reasonably believe that Carly consents. Clearly, on the facts, sexual intercourse takes place. The live issues relate to consent. Was Carly consenting?

Ostensibly yes, but the facts raise an issue of deception. Does James' lie regarding his status as a professional footballer vitiate her apparent consent? Under s. 76 of the 2003 Act, if James is found to have intentionally deceived Carly as to the nature or purpose of the sexual intercourse, or to have induced Carly to have sexual intercourse with him by impersonating a person known personally to Carly, the jury will be entitled to conclusively presume that Carly did not consent to the relevant act. As to the latter point, there is no evidence that James claimed to be someone he was not—indeed he did not claim to be any particular person. His lies related to his profession or occupation. This deception is not caught by the second limb of s. 76. There was no deception on his part as to the nature of the act being performed, he did not claim to be doing anything but having sexual intercourse—compare with *R v Williams* [1923] 1 KB 340. Hence the only basis on which the prosecution could argue that consent was vitiated under s. 76 is that his lies in some way related to the quality of the act; James claimed Carly would be having sex with a professional footballer, when this was not the case. The matter is not directly governed by the 2003 Act. There is no authority under the pre-2003 Act law to suggest that deception as to attributes of this nature would be enough to vitiate consent to sexual intercourse.

Section 75 of the 2003 Act has no application on these facts. Under s. 74 Carly will be held to have consented to the sexual intercourse if she had the choice of whether or not to consent, and had the freedom and capacity to make that choice. There is no evidence on the facts that Carly's judgement had been clouded by the effects of alcohol or any other drug. On this basis it is submitted that Carly was consenting to sexual intercourse, thus rendering a conviction under the 2003 Act unlikely.

If this submission is not correct attention would shift to James' state of mind at the time of the sexual intercourse. The evidence suggests that he was unaware of his actions at the time because of the effect of the pills that he had taken. This could amount to the defence of automatism—which if successful would be a complete defence—arguably a denial of not only *mens rea* but also *actus reus*. There are a number of issues James would need to address in order to establish the defence. First, on the basis of *Attorney-General's Reference (No. 2 of 1992)* [1993] 3 WLR 982, the defence of automatism requires that there was a total destruction of voluntary control on James' part. Impaired, reduced or partial control is not enough. Medical evidence will be required as to the type of drug taken by James and its likely and actual effect on his consciousness. *Bratty v Attorney-General for Northern Ireland* [1963] AC 386, emphasizes that James' own say so as to the effect of the pills will not suffice. Even if the expert evidence suggests that he was in a state of automatism, there will be an inquiry into what the pills were and why he took them. If they were medically prescribed and James was unaware of the side effects, the defence might succeed. If however, as the facts suggest, James simply took the pills of his own accord, the prosecution may argue that he was at fault in causing the state of automatism to arise, and thus he should not be permitted the defence on policy grounds—see *R v Bailey* [1983] 2 All ER 503. If James knew that his taking of the pills was likely to make him aggressive, unpredictable or uncontrolled the jury will be entitled to find that he was reckless, thus providing the fault element required in relation to rape.

Similarly if he tries to argue that he was intoxicated at the time of the sexual intercourse. Rape is a basic intent crime and his recklessness in taking the drugs would provide the necessary fault element for the offence; see *DPP v Majewski* [1976] 2 All ER 142, and *R v Heard* [2007] EWCA Crim 125 (in relation to the s. 3 offence but applicable also, it is submitted, to s. 1). Only if he can show that he would have been unaware of the risk of Carly not consenting even if he had been sober will he be able to raise intoxication as a defence.

Didier's liability

By plying Carly with drinks Didier may have committed an offence contrary to ss. 23 and 24 of the Offences Against the Person Act 1861, or possibly s. 61 of the Sexual Offences Act 2003. If Didier caused Carly to consume more alcohol than she had wanted to he could be charged with maliciously administering a noxious substance contrary to either s. 23 or s. 24 of the 1861 Act. The s. 23 offence requires proof that the administration endangered Carly's life, or inflicted grievous bodily harm on her. There is no evidence to support this—hence a charge under s. 24 seems more appropriate. For s. 24 the prosecution would have to prove that Didier unlawfully and maliciously administered to, or caused to be administered to or taken by Carly, any poison or other destructive or noxious thing, with intent to injure, aggrieve or annoy Carly. The alcohol would constitute the poisonous or noxious thing (given the quantities involved—see *R v Marcus* [1981] 1 WLR 774), and Didier clearly causes Carly to consume it. The only other issue under s. 24 is as to whether or not he intended to injure, aggrieve or annoy. It is submitted that if it was his intention to lower her inhibitions in order to make it easier to have sexual intercourse with her the prosecution would have a case—see *R v Hill* (1986) 83 Cr App R 386. Proof, however, would be problematic, and the jury may (rightly or wrongly) regard Carly as to some extent the author of her own misfortune.

The offence under s. 61 of the Sexual Offences Act 2003—administering a substance with intent to have sexual intercourse—may be a more appropriate charge. The prosecution would have to prove that Didier caused Carly to consume additional amounts of alcohol without her consent, knowing she did not consent, intending to stupefy or overpower her so as to enable him (or indeed any other person) to engage in sexual activity with Carly. In general terms the facts may appear to support such a charge but there are two evidential difficulties. First, can the prosecution prove that at the time Didier bought Carly the drinks he knew she was not consenting to drinking larger measures of alcohol? Secondly, can the prosecution prove that, at the time he purchased the drinks with the larger measures of spirits, Didier intended to have sex with Carly (there being no evidence to suggest he intends anyone else to have sex with her whilst she is stupefied by drink)?

Didier may also be charged with the offence of entering Carly's flat as a trespasser with intent to commit a sexual offence, contrary to s. 63 of the 2003 Act. The facts are silent as to whether Carly actually asked Didier to enter her flat—thus raising the possibility that he may have been a trespasser there (i.e., to have been there without, or in excess of, any express or implied permission granted by Carly). Thus the possibility arises that, even if Carly did invite Didier in, she may not have been inviting him in for sexual purposes. If, therefore, Didier either entered without any permission, or entered for a purpose in excess of any implied permission (see further *R v Jones and Smith* [1976] 3 All ER 54), he could have been trespassing. Under s. 63 of the 2003 Act, Didier will have committed an offence if he was a trespassing in Carly's flat and at the time he intended to commit a 'relevant sexual offence' on the premises—for these purposes rape would be a relevant offence. The prosecution would additionally have to prove that Didier knew or had been reckless as to whether or not he was a trespasser.

Everything, therefore, turns on Didier's state of mind. If he thought Carly was inviting him back for sexual intercourse it will be hard to establish that he knew he was trespassing or was even aware of the risk that he might be. If trespass is not established no liability under s. 63 can be established. Even if Carly was not inviting Didier back to her flat for sex, he may have believed that she was, and there is nothing in the construction of s. 63 to suggest he should not be judged on the facts as he honestly believed them to be. The only basis for liability is if there is evidence that, at some point in time whilst in her flat, Didier intended to have non-consensual intercourse with Carly (or at least sexual intercourse whether she consented or not). The problem with this basis for liability is that it would be virtually impossible to establish without evidence from Didier that this had been his state of mind. Unless he obliges the prosecution with a confession the evidence is unlikely to emerge.

As to Didier's liability for rape—sexual intercourse took place and Carly is clearly alleging that it was non-consensual. Turning first to the issue of whether or not Carly was consenting, s. 76 of the 2003 Act has no application—there is no evidence of any deception. Under s. 75, however, the jury is entitled to presume that Carly did not consent if satisfied that (*inter alia*), Didier had administered to or caused to be taken by Carly (without Carly's consent), a substance which, having regard to when it was administered or taken, was capable of causing or enabling Carly to be stupefied or overpowered at the time of the sexual intercourse. The jury must also be satisfied that Didier knew that Carly had consumed a substance that was capable of having these effects. The prosecution will presumably argue that the extra alcohol purchased by Didier as Carly's drinks was the stupefying substance, and he clearly would have known that the alcohol had been consumed as he purchased it. There is a moot point here as to whether or not Carly consented to the consumption of the alcohol. She knew she was drinking some alcohol, but did she realize how much? Was it her choice to continue drinking even though she felt increasingly intoxicated? Assuming the prosecution can establish these points, the burden will shift to Didier to show that, notwithstanding the above, he still had reasonable grounds for believing that Carly had been consenting to the sexual intercourse. Even if the conditions required for the application of s. 75 in relation to his *mens rea* are not made out, the prosecution could still invoke s. 74 to the effect that Carly cannot have been consenting to the sexual intercourse unless she had the freedom and capacity to make that choice. Her intoxicated state would militate against her having had the requisite capacity—although this is very much a matter of fact and degree. In *R v Bree* [2007] EWCA Crim 256, the Court of Appeal observed that if, through drink, a complainant in a rape case temporarily loses her capacity to choose whether or not to have intercourse she is not consenting. On the other hand, if she has voluntarily consumed even substantial quantities of alcohol, but nevertheless remains capable of choosing whether or not to have intercourse, and in drink agrees to do so, the defendant would not be guilty of rape. Hence it will be a fine question of fact for the jury.

Assuming the prosecution can establish the absence of consent on Carly's part, it will still be necessary to prove that Didier had the necessary *mens rea* for rape. He obviously intended to have sexual intercourse, but did he believe Carly was consenting (and that she was able to do so?). Again, s. 76 of the 2003 Act has no application here. Under s. 75 the jury can presume that Didier had no reasonable belief that Carly was consenting if there is evidence of her having consumed a substance that could cause her to be stupefied or overpowered at the time of the sexual intercourse and that Didier knew of this. As indicated above, if the jury believe this to be the case, Didier will have to produce evidence as to why, notwithstanding these circumstances, he still reasonably believed Carly to have been consenting. Even if the conditions for the application of s. 75 are not made out, the prosecution can still direct the jury to consider all the circumstances, including any steps Didier took to ascertain whether Carly was consenting, in determining whether he had any reasonable belief that she was consenting.

There is no evidence of Didier taking positive steps to check with Carly that she was consenting to sexual intercourse. The spirit of the 2003 Act is that this onus rests upon the defendant. If it appears that Didier took advantage of Carly's intoxicated state the jury may determine against him.

Further reading

Anderson, J., 'No Licence for Thuggery: Violence, Sport and the Criminal Law' [2008] Crim LR 751.

Clarkson, C., 'Law Commission Report No. 218' [1994] Crim LR 324.

Elliott, C. and De Than, C., 'The Case for a Rational Reconstruction of Consent in Criminal Law' (2007) 70 Mod LR 225.

Gillespie, A., 'Muddying the Waters—Indecent or Sexual Assault?' [2006] 156 NLJ 50.

Gross, H., 'Rape, Moralism and Human Rights' [2007] Crim LR 220.

Herring, J., 'Mistaken Sex' [2005] Crim LR 511.

Herring, J., 'Human Rights and Rape: a Reply to Hyman Gross' [2007] Crim LR 228.

Lacey, N., 'Beset by Boundaries: The Home Office Review of Sex Offences' [2001] Crim LR 3.

Temkin, J. and Ashworth, A., 'Rape, Sexual Assaults and the Problem of Consent' [2004] Crim LR 328.

Weait, M., 'Knowledge, Autonomy and Consent: *R v Konzani*' [2005] Crim LR 763.

Williams, R., 'Deception, Mistake and Vitiation of the Victim's Consent' (2007) 124 (Jan) LQR 132.

Non-fatal non-sexual offences against the person—flowchart (a)

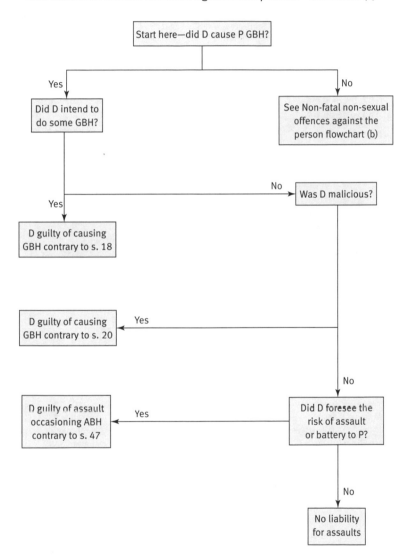

Non-fatal non-sexual offences against the person—flowchart (b)

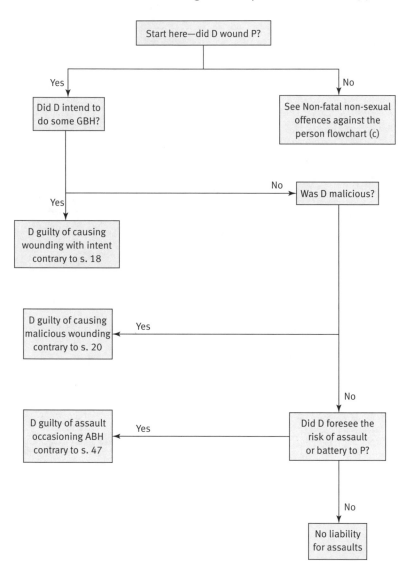

Non-fatal non-sexual offences against the person—flowchart (c)

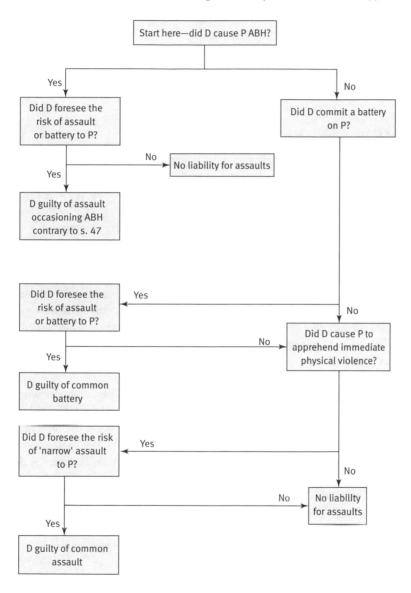

5

The defences I

Introduction

The general defences to criminal responsibility are a large and important part of the criminal law syllabus. An exam paper may well contain two questions on the general defences, or one full question with an additional one involving the specific defences that reduce murder to manslaughter. Therefore it is an area that candidates must know comprehensively, and because it contains a vast array of diverse material this is no easy task.

For the purposes of this book the defences have been divided between two chapters, chapter 5 dealing with the defences of automatism, insanity, diminished responsibility, and intoxication; and chapter 6 covering duress, necessity, mistake, and self-defence. In some textbooks candidates will find the material relating to automatism and mistake in chapters covering *actus reus* and *mens rea,* but as questions on insanity usually involve consideration of automatism (and often diminished responsibility) and questions on self-defence generally involve mistake, the questions in this chapter have been formed accordingly.

It must be appreciated that many people suffering from mental disorder who commit crimes never actually stand trial but will be detained under the Mental Health Act 1983 provisions. If they are tried and are deemed fit to plead, they have the difficult decision of whether to put their mental incapacity before the court. The risk in so doing is being found not guilty by reason of insanity on application of the *M'Naghten* Rules 1843, which (despite constant criticism) remain the test for insanity in the eyes of the law. That the concept of 'disease of the mind' (which underpins the legal test for insanity) is no longer a medical concept has long been recognized by the Butler Committee (1975) and the Law Commission, who recommended (Draft Code, cl. 35) that the concept of mental disorder was more appropriate (thus a mental disorder verdict would be returned if the defendant was suffering from severe mental illness or severe mental handicap).

It is clear that such a change is required, if only because many defendants are loath to risk the defence being put to the jury. So in *R v Sullivan* [1983] 2 All ER 673, the accused preferred to plead guilty to assault occasioning actual bodily harm, a crime which carries a maximum sentence of five years' imprisonment, when the trial judge suggested that his epilepsy constituted a disease of the mind and his relevant defence was therefore not automatism but insanity. This problem has to some extent been alleviated as far as murder is concerned by the Homicide Act 1957, which introduced the partial defence of diminished responsibility; most mentally disordered defendants charged with murder would now plead this defence in the knowledge that it has succeeded in a wide variety of situations not covered by insanity.

As *Sullivan* indicates, the defences of insanity and automatism are closely linked, as for both defences the accused has acted while not in control of his or her mental faculties. If automatism succeeds the accused is found not guilty with no custodial repercussions; but although since the passing of the Criminal Procedure (Insanity and Unfitness to Plead) Act 1991, an accused found not guilty by reason of insanity will not inevitably be detained there is still the stigma of being labelled criminally insane. Identifying a clear boundary between the two defences, is not easy, as is aptly illustrated by the cases of *R v Quick* [1973] 3 All ER 347 and *R v Hennessy* [1989] 2 All ER 9, both involving defendants suffering from diabetes. In the first case, it was held by the Court of Appeal that a diabetic who was in a state of hypoglycaemia as a result of taking insulin and alcohol could not be deemed insane (within the *M'Naghten* Rules). In the second case, an accused in a state of hyperglycaemia because he hadn't taken his insulin was found to be insane! Only a criminal lawyer could explain the reasoning for this outcome.

The defence of intoxication has also undergone review by both the Law Commission (Consultation Paper No. 127 'Intoxication and Criminal Liability', 1993; Law Com. No. 229, 1995) and the House of Lords (*R v Kingston* [1994] 3 All ER 353). It can be a defence to certain crimes (those where the prosecution must prove intention) and it is also a factor in considering the availability of other defences. Accordingly two questions have been set on this important topic.

Question 1

Albert and John attend a party where they have some non-alcoholic drinks. It is known that Albert has recently been experiencing dizzy spells and fainting fits, but he has not sought medical treatment. At the party Albert becomes dizzy and is given six Valium tablets by an unknown person in an attempt to calm him down. Very shortly after taking the tablets Albert leaves the party with John. On the way home Albert repeatedly hits John over the head with a bottle, thereby killing him.

When arrested and charged with murder, Albert says:' I cannot remember hitting him. I must have had a blackout.'

Discuss Albert's possible defences.

 Commentary

Questions on mental abnormality are quite common in examinations. They are often in essay form, but this problem does require the student to take into account the alternative reasons why Albert acted as he did. If a murder has taken place and insanity is an obvious issue, a consideration of the related defences of automatism and diminished responsibility is required. The ingredients of all three defences must therefore be covered in detail with a clear demonstration of the differences between them. Sometimes voluntary intoxication must also be considered, as it is easy to link relevant facts giving rise to this issue in a question of this nature.

For the sake of completeness, the non-availability of the defence of provocation is referred to briefly. However, this author would not deduct marks if this was not contained in a student's answer. Note that candidates are not asked to consider the liability of whoever supplied the drugs to Albert.

Answer plan

- Diminished responsibility—s. 2, Homicide Act 1957
- Automatism—*Bratty* [1963]
- Insanity—*M'Naghten* Rules 1843
- Intoxication
- Provocation

Suggested answer

Albert has caused the death of John in fact and in law. There is no evidence of anything that would suggest a *novus actus interveniens*. In order to support a charge of murder the prosecution will have to establish that Albert intended to kill John, or intended to do him some grievous bodily harm: see *R v Moloney* [1985] 1 All ER 1025 and *R v Woollin* [1998] 4 All ER 103. If Albert's evidence is plausible it may be that he will successfully defend a murder charge by relying on one of a number of defences involving a partial or complete denial of *mens rea*, such as automatism, insanity and diminished responsibility.

Diminished responsibility is only a partial defence that reduces murder to manslaughter. The defence was introduced by s. 2(1) of the Homicide Act 1957, which places a legal burden on the defendant to show that, at the time of the killing, he was suffering from such abnormality of mind (whether arising from a condition of arrested or retarded development of mind or any inherent causes or induced by disease or injury) as substantially impaired his mental responsibility for his acts or omissions.

Defendants charged with murder tend to rely on diminished responsibility rather than insanity, and it has succeeded in a wide variety of circumstances, including mercy killings, crimes of passion and killings as a result of irresistible impulse. Professor Andrew Ashworth has pointed out that in 80 per cent of cases where it is raised the prosecution are prepared to accept the plea. In two cases involving 'battered women's syndrome'— *R v Ahluwalia* [1992] 4 All ER 889 and *R v Thornton (No. 2)* [1996]

1 WLR 1174—although the juries had convicted the accused of murder, in the retrials different juries found that the accused had established the defence of diminished responsibility on the balance of probability and were guilty of manslaughter.

Is there evidence of an abnormality of the mind? Albert would have to provide expert medical evidence establishing on the balance of probabilities that he was suffering from such a condition. Simply having dizzy spells will not, of itself, discharge the legal burden of proof on Albert as regards establishing the defence. Neither will the transient effect caused by the taking of Valium suffice. The jury would have to be satisfied that, setting aside the consumption of the Valium, Albert suffered from an underlying abnormality of mind that had substantially impaired his responsibility for the actions that caused the death. In the absence of more expert medical evidence this defence is unlikely to succeed. There is no evidence of any underlying dependency on drugs that could amount to a disease of the mind, hence the issues considered in *R v Stewart* [2009] EWCA Crim 593, do not pertain here.

Prima facie, the most attractive defence to Albert is automatism, as this is a complete defence to murder and the burden of proof is on the prosecution to disprove the existence of the defence. Albert simply has to provide an evidential basis for reliance on the defence. Automatism was defined by Lord Denning in *Bratty v Attorney-General for Northern Ireland* [1963] AC 386, as 'an act which is done by the muscles without any control by the mind such as a spasm, a reflex or a convulsion, or an act done by a person who is not conscious of what he is doing such as an act done whilst suffering from concussion or whilst sleep-walking'.

Albert will argue that he did not know what he was doing and therefore his act was involuntary. The prosecution must prove that the act was voluntary, but they are entitled to rely on the presumption that every man has sufficient mental capacity to be responsible for his act; and if the defence wishes to displace this presumption they must give some evidence from which the contrary may reasonably be inferred. Much will therefore depend on the expert medical evidence.

For automatism to succeed the court must accept that there was a total loss of control. In *Attorney-General's Reference (No. 2 of 1992)* [1993] 4 All ER 683, the Court of Appeal ruled that the trial judge was wrong to direct the jury that a syndrome known as 'driving without awareness' could amount to automatism. Impaired, reduced or partial control is not enough. So the prosecution could argue that as Albert had enough control to pick up a bottle and repeatedly hit John over the head, automatism should not apply.

A second problem concerns the fact that Albert had not sought medical treatment for his condition. The prosecution could argue that the automatism was therefore self-induced and that Albert was blameworthy in not seeking treatment. Further, if Albert had taken alcohol or non-prescribed hallucinatory drugs, automatism will not succeed (*R v Lipman* [1969] 3 All ER 410)—but see intoxication, below. Notwithstanding these two issues, if the Valium had the effect of completely destroying Albert's self-control, and he was unaware that this would be the consequence of taking the drug, he may succeed with the defence of automatism.

Where, however, there is evidence that Albert actually suffered from some inherent medical condition that, in conjunction with the Valium, had the effect of causing him to lose his self-control, the prosecution may seek to lead evidence suggesting that insanity is a more appropriate defence. Under the *M'Naghten* Rules 1843, everyone is presumed sane until the contrary is proved. However, it is a defence for the accused to show that he was labouring under such defect of reason due to disease of the mind as either:

(a) not to know the nature and quality of his act; or

(b) if he did know this, not to know that what he was doing was wrong (in the sense of contrary to law, as opposed to morally wrong—see *R v Johnson* [2007] EWCA Crim 1978).

The trial judge must first decide if Albert was suffering from a disease of the mind, and if so, the jury will then decide if the other ingredients of the defence have been satisfied. The judicial pronouncements on insanity are certainly at variance with medical practice, and the question of public safety is a factor that the judiciary obviously takes into account. In *Bratty,* Lord Denning stated that 'any mental disorder which has manifested itself in violence and is prone to recur is a disease of the mind' and this was reiterated by Lord Diplock in *R v Sullivan,* where the House of Lords upheld the trial judge's decision to label epilepsy 'a disease of the mind', when he stated:

> if the effect of a disease is to impair these facilities [of reason, memory and understanding] so severely as to have either of these consequences referred to in the latter part of the rules, it matters not whether the aetiology of the impairment is organic, as in epilepsy, or functional, or whether the impairment itself is permanent or is transient and intermittent, provided that it subsisted at the time of the commission of the act.

Thus arteriosclerosis (*R v Kemp* [1956] 3 All ER 249); diabetes (*R v Hennessy* (1989) 89 Cr App R 10); and violent sleepwalking (*R v Burgess* [1991] 2 All ER 769) have all been deemed diseases of the mind. In the latter case the Court of Appeal held that many people sleepwalk, but that if an accused uses violence while sleepwalking, the condition would have to be regarded as being due to a disease of the mind. So the accused, who while sleepwalking violently assaulted the victim, was found 'not guilty by reason of insanity' as he was plainly suffering from a defect of reason from some sort of failure of the mind causing him to act as he did without conscious motivation. The Court of Appeal upheld the trial judge's decision to label the condition as a disease of the mind, on the basis that it was due to an internal factor that manifested itself in violence.

If Albert is found 'not guilty by reason of insanity', he has the right to appeal under s. 1 of the Criminal Procedure (Insanity) Act 1964; and if the appeal succeeds because the judge wrongly directed the jury, the accused will be entitled to a 'not guilty' verdict with no custodial repercussions or attached conditions for treatment (Criminal Procedure (Insanity and Unfitness to Plead) Act 1991).

Albert may seek to rely on the common law defence of intoxication. There is little doubt that, if his loss of awareness was caused by the consumption of the Valium tablets, he could be regarded as having been in a state of intoxication; see *R v Cole and others* [1993] Crim LR 300. Murder is a specific intent crime, hence on the basis of *DPP v Majewski* [1976] 2 All ER 142, self-induced intoxication can be raised as a defence. If it succeeds it will reduce Albert's liability to manslaughter.

There may be an argument that Albert might escape liability altogether on the basis of the intoxication. Even in respect of basic intent crimes such as manslaughter there must be evidence that the defendant was reckless in consuming the intoxicant. In the case of alcohol or Class A drugs this is rarely an issue. In the case of Valium there may be some debate as to whether Albert was aware of the risk of what side effects there might be. *R v Hardie* [1984] 3 All ER 848 provides that if there is evidence that the self-administration of drugs may not have been reckless, the issue ought to be left to the jury. In short, if it was not Albert's fault that he lost consciousness he should be acquitted.

Finally, it is submitted that on the facts, as there is no evidence of it, provocation could not succeed as a partial defence. This has been illustrated by *R v Acott* [1997] 1 All ER 706, where the House of Lords confirmed that some evidence of provocation had to be raised for the judge to be under an obligation to put it to the jury.

Question 2

Mark lives with Anita and James, Anita's two-year-old son from a previous relationship. Mark hates James and wishes the boy was dead. One day Anita loses her temper with James when he wets his bed. She attacks James with a poker, striking him on the head. Mark, who is downstairs watching television when this happens, rushes upstairs to investigate the disturbance. He finds James bleeding profusely from a head wound. Mark tells Anita it is all her fault and goes out to the pub without summoning any help. By the time Anita calls an ambulance James has bled to death.

Advise the Crown Prosecution Service as to the possible criminal liability of Anita and Mark in respect of the death of James. Do not consider liability for non-fatal offences.

After fully considering the above, go on to consider how the answer would differ in each of these scenarios:

(i) Anita had had an epileptic fit immediately prior to attacking James, the evidence being that she cannot recall attacking him.

(ii) Anita had been a diabetic who had taken insulin but had not eaten prior to the attack, the evidence being that the attack occurred whilst she was unaware of her actions because she had been in a hypoglycaemic state.

(iii) Anita had been a diabetic who had failed to take insulin prior to the attack, the evidence being that the attack occurred whilst she was unaware of her actions because she had been in a hyperglycaemic state.

(iv) When attacking James, Anita had honestly believed she was fighting off a nest of vipers because she voluntarily consumed LSD shortly beforehand.

Commentary

This rather bleak question provides a very effective run through of defences to murder based on provocation, automatism, insanity, and intoxication. In particular it seeks to identify the borderline between sane and non-insane automatism, hence a good knowledge of the relevant authorities in that area is essential. Mark's liability also requires an effective examination of liability for failing to act where liability is based on membership of a household, rather than a clear duty relationship. It remains to be seen to what extent criminal law syllabuses are extended to encompass the offence of permitting the death of a child or vulnerable adult contrary to **s. 5 of the Domestic Violence, Crime and Victims Act 2004**. However, the answer to this question also provides an opportunity to consider the main element of what is a rather convoluted offence.

Answer plan

- Anita causes death—*mens rea*—provocation
- Mark's liability based on his failure to act
- Consideration of the applicability of **s. 5 of the Domestic Violence, Crime and Victims Act 2004**
- Anita's liability and insanity
- Anita's liability and automatism—internal cause
- Anita's liability and automatism—external cause
- Anita's liability and intoxication

Suggested answer

Anita's liability for the death of James

Anita causes the death of James in fact and in law. But for the attack James would not have died. There is no evidence of a *novus actus interveniens*. The evidence suggests that Anita acted with foresight as to the consequences of her actions. For murder the prosecution will have to show that she intended to kill or do some grievous bodily harm. On the basis of *R v Woollin* [1998] 4 All ER 103, the jury will be entitled to infer intent if there is evidence that Anita foresaw death or grievous bodily harm as virtually certain to result from her actions. It is hard to see how this evidence would not be present given that she has hit a young child on the head with a heavy metal object.

There is evidence that Anita lost her temper with the child, hence the defence of provocation ought to be left to the jury should she choose to raise it. *R v Doughty* (1986) 83 Cr App R 319 makes clear that anything can be provocation, even the actions of a small child. There are no issues here regarding 'cooling time' or cumulative provocation. Assuming that there is evidence that Anita was provoked to lose her self-control, the question will then arise as to whether she acted in a manner that was reasonable. Following *Attorney-General for Jersey v Holley* [2005] UKPC 23, the jury will be directed to consider all the relevant evidence that would indicate the gravity of the provocation to Anita. This could include her domestic circumstances and the history of problems with her son. Once the 'quantity' of provocation has been assessed, the jury will then be directed to consider whether or not Anita displayed the degree of self-control to be expected from the average reasonable woman. For these purposes no account would be taken of any characteristics of Anita's, other than age and gender. She will be judged by the standard of a person having ordinary powers of control, a constant, objective standard in all cases. See further *R v Mohammed* [2005] EWCA Crim 1880, and *R v James; R v Karimi* [2006] EWCA Crim 14, where the Court of Appeal accepted that the Privy Council decision in *Holley* now established the correct approach to provocation in domestic law.

If Anita did not have the *mens rea* for murder, she would be convicted of manslaughter based on her unlawful attack upon James. There are no contentious issues in this regard.

Mark's liability for the death of James

The prosecution could seek to impose liability on Mark in respect of the death of James based on his failure to help when he realized the harm that had been done to the child. Mark does not encourage or help in the attack, hence he cannot be an accomplice. At common law his failure to act to help the child cannot raise any criminal liability unless he was under a legal duty to act at the time. A possible basis for that duty could be found under the Children and Young Persons Act 1933 if it is successfully argued that Mark has the role of parent or guardian in respect of James. Failing that, at common law, he may have incurred a duty towards James if he has chosen to live with the child's mother as a family unit; see *R v Gibbins and Proctor* (1918) 13 Cr App R 134. The court will examine the permanency and stability of the relationship, the involvement of Mark in the child's upbringing, and the degree of reliance on Mark. *R v Stone and Dobinson* [1977] QB 354, also stresses that a relationship of reliance can give rise to a positive legal duty of care. *R v Miller* [1983] 1 All ER 978 would not be relevant because the harm to James is not caused by Mark's accidental act.

Assuming Mark was under a common law duty to act, the prosecution would have to prove that his failure to act contributed to the death of James. Medical evidence would clearly show that James' condition worsened after Mark became aware of the injury. If Mark's omission was causative, he could be charged with murder if he had the necessary *mens rea*—see above. The evidence of his animosity towards the child, if available, would be cogent here. If Mark cannot be shown to have had the *mens rea* for murder it should be noted that he cannot be convicted of constructive manslaughter (unlawful act manslaughter) as this cannot be committed by omission: see *R v Lowe* [1973] 1 All ER 805. The prosecution would have to charge Mark with killing by gross negligence. Following *R v Adomako* [1994] 3 WLR 288, the jury would have to consider whether the extent to which Mark's conduct departed from the proper standard of care incumbent upon him (involving a risk of death to James) was such that it should be judged criminal. It is submitted that this would be made out on the facts.

An alternative charge that might be considered by the prosecution is under s. 5 of the Domestic Violence, Crime and Victims Act 2004. Mark will be guilty of the offence if it is proved that:

(i) James died as a result of the unlawful act of a person who was a member of the same household as James, and had frequent contact with her. Clearly Anita's causing the death of James would satisfy these elements.

(ii) Mark was a member of the household, there was a significant risk of serious physical harm being caused to James by the unlawful act of Anita, and that Mark ought to have been aware of the risk that she would cause James harm. Under s. 5(4) Mark will be regarded as a member of the household on the basis that he visits it often enough to be reasonably regarded as a member of it.

(iii) Mark failed to take such steps as he could reasonably have been expected to take to protect James from the risk, and Anita's acts occurred in circumstances of the kind that Mark foresaw or ought to have foreseen.

It is submitted that the prosecution might, on the given facts, struggle to establish the necessary evidence that Mark foresaw, or ought to have foreseen, any significant risk of serious physical harm being caused to James by the unlawful act of Anita. There is no direct evidence of any history of abuse, notwithstanding Mark's antipathy towards James. As a consequence it becomes difficult to prove his failure to take steps to prevent abuse unless the specific incident where Anita attacks James is relied upon.

Variations on Anita's liability

(i) Anita had had an epileptic fit immediately prior to attacking James, the evidence being that she cannot recall attacking him

Anita would presumably argue that she had been in a state of automatism— *Attorney-General's Reference (No. 2 of 1992)* [1993] 3 WLR 982—a total destruction of voluntary control on her part. Lord Denning in *Bratty v Attorney-General for Northern Ireland* [1963] AC 386 suggested that automatism could arise from a fit or spasm. If Anita succeeds with this argument she will be acquitted. Her problem is that the courts will look at what gave rise to the lack of awareness. In her case it is her epilepsy—an internal condition; a defect of the nervous system that affects the working of the brain. Her condition has the effect that she is unaware of her actions—the *M'Naghten Rules* (1843) 10 C & F 200, clearly provide that a defendant can be regarded as criminally insane if she is (was) labouring under a defect of reason, from disease of the mind, as not to know the nature and quality of the act she was doing. Further, epilepsy is a condition that manifests itself in violence and is likely to recur. As such the courts will not allow her to plead automatism.

She can either plead guilty, or plead not guilty on the grounds of insanity; see the explanation of this in *R v Sullivan* [1983] 1 All ER 577. Rather than run the risk of the insanity defence, Anita might be better advised to rely on the defence of diminished responsibility under s. 2(1) of the Homicide Act 1957. She would have little difficulty in establishing medical evidence that she had been suffering from an abnormality of mind arising from a disease or injury such as substantially impaired her mental responsibility for her acts. If successful the defence would reduce her liability to manslaughter.

(ii) Anita had been a diabetic who had taken insulin but had not eaten prior to the attack, the evidence being that the attack occurred whilst she was unaware of her actions because she had been in a hypoglycaemic state

On the basis of *R v Quick* [1973] QB 910, diabetes resulting in hypoglycaemia is not regarded in law as a mental condition. As Lawton LJ observed, Quick's mental condition was not caused by his diabetes but by his use of the insulin prescribed by his doctor. The malfunctioning of Quick's mind was caused by an external factor and not a bodily disorder in the nature of a disease that disturbed the working of his mind. This would suggest that Anita would be permitted the defence of automatism, but it should be noted that in *R v Bailey* [1983] 2 All ER 503, the court ruled that the defence would not be available in cases where the state of automatism could be regarded as 'self-induced', i.e., there was evidence that the defendant was at fault in lapsing into the state of automatism. The test is whether or not Anita was aware of the consequences of taking insulin and not eating. If she was reckless in taking the insulin and not eating this will provide the basic intent for any offence she commits whilst in the subsequent state of automatism. On these facts that would mean she might incur liability for manslaughter (a basic intent crime), but not murder (a specific intent crime).

(iii) Anita had been a diabetic who had failed to take insulin prior to the attack, the evidence being that the attack occurred whilst she was unaware of her actions because she had been in a hyperglycaemic state

On the basis of *R v Hennessy* [1989] 1 WLR 287 (diabetic failing to take insulin resulting in hyperglycaemic state), the defence of automatism will not be available. The hyperglycaemia (high blood sugar), will be regarded as having been caused by an inherent defect (the diabetes), i.e., a disease. If that disease causes a malfunction of the mind that manifests itself in violence the courts will only allow Anita the defence of insanity.

(iv) When attacking James, Anita had honestly believed she was fighting off a nest of vipers because she voluntarily consumed LSD shortly beforehand

Anita might wish to raise the defence of automatism but, for reasons outlined above, she will be regarded as having brought about the condition through her own fault, hence the defence will not be available (*R v Bailey*). Intoxication can be raised as a defence to murder: *DPP v Majewski* [1976]—as murder is a regarded as a specific intent crime. Anita will thus be convicted of manslaughter on the grounds of intoxication. *R v Lipman* [1970] 1 QB 152 confirms this.

Mental illness—flowchart (a)

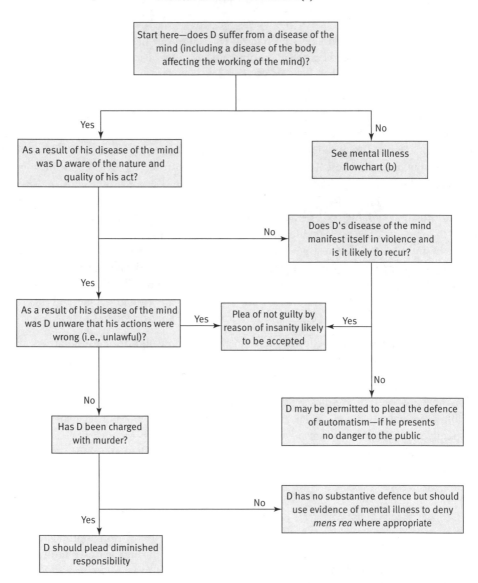

Mental illness—flowchart (b)

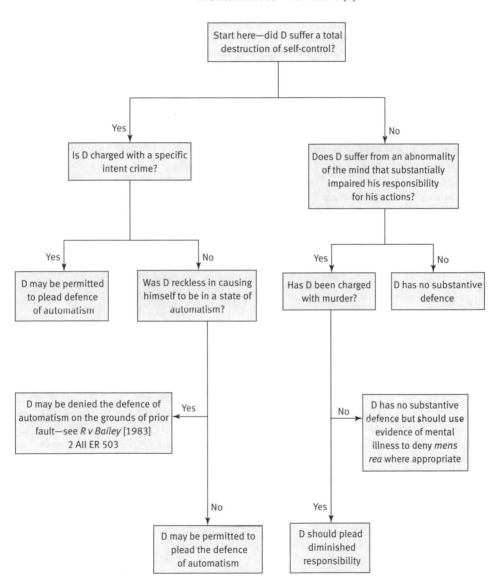

Question 3

Quentin is an ex-soldier who left the army because he suffered from severe post-traumatic stress disorder following his experiences fighting in combat zones overseas. He has to take regular medication to control his condition, a side effect of which is that he has periods where he acts as an automaton, unaware of what he is doing.

Walking home one evening, Quentin sets fire to a pile of rubbish that someone has dumped near the front of his house. Shortly after this, Ronaldo—a vagrant who has made the pile of rubbish his shelter for the night and whose presence asleep beneath it would not have been obvious to a passer-by suddenly leaps from beneath the pile of rubbish with his clothes on fire. Quentin does nothing to put out the fire and Ronaldo suffers severe burns as a result.

Sacha, a neighbour, rushes out to remonstrate with Quentin. Quentin pulls out a sharp knife and threatens Sacha, who falls backwards, cutting his head on the pavement.

Quentin is arrested and taken into custody. Under questioning Quentin states that he believed Sacha was an enemy soldier who was trying to kill him. He also claims that he cannot recall setting fire to Ronaldo and that he must, at the time, have been acting during one of his periodic bouts of unconscious automatism.

Advise the Crown Prosecution Service as to the criminal liability, if any, of Quentin. Ignore liability for offences of possessing offensive weapons.

Commentary

Candidates attempting this question have been known to get things horribly wrong by assuming that Ronaldo dies of his injuries, when in fact there is no evidence that this is the case. Hence the need to read questions carefully! Candidates need to take the two victims separately although there is inevitably some overlap in terms of the discussion of defences. Set out the various possibilities, including criminal damage, before considering relevant defences. Where a possible defence is automatism, and there is evidence to support this, candidates may feel it a little artificial to go through the *mens rea* elements of the offence knowing that the defendant may not have been aware of his actions. It is better to approach the problem this way, however. It follows the logical order of *actus reus, mens rea,* defences, and ensures that the mental element to be established is clearly identified in the event that one of the defences is not made out. Reference to self-defence must now include the statutory basis for the defence, and note the difficult point in this question regarding the relationship between self-defence and insanity.

Answer plan

- Quentin's liability for 'basic' criminal damage—consideration of recklessness
- Quentin's liability for aggravated criminal damage—query whether ulterior intent made out
- Quentin's liability for non-fatal offences against Ronaldo—from **s. 18** down

- Whether failure to act actually caused any further harm
- Defences—non-insane automatism—need for evidence
- Defences—insane automatism
- Quentin's liability for injuries suffered by Sacha
- Self-defence re Sacha and role played by mistake
- Link between mistake and insanity

Suggested answer

Quentin's liability in respect of Ronaldo

By setting fire to the pile of rubbish Quentin could be charged with criminal damage contrary to s. 1(1) of the Criminal Damage Act 1971. Even though it is rubbish that is damaged and destroyed it can still be 'property' for the purposes of the offence; see s. 10(1). There may, however, be an issue as to whether or not the property belongs to another. Arguing by analogy with the offence of theft, if the property is 'lost' it can still be regarded as belonging to another. If it has been abandoned Quentin could argue that it ceases to be property belonging to another and hence the *actus reus* of the offence is not made out. The *mens rea* for the offence would be intention to damage or destroy property belonging to another, or at least recklessness as to whether this would result. Recklessness for these purposes being subjective, as decided in *R v G* [2003] 4 All ER 765—a defendant must at least be aware of the risk and the risk must be such that, in the circumstances known to the defendant, it was unreasonable for him to take the risk. Subject to proof of sane or insane automatism, as to which see below, Quentin appears to have intended the damage and destruction, but he may have reasonably assumed that there was no risk of the property belonging to another.

Given that Ronaldo is asleep under the pile of rubbish and is set on fire by Quentin's actions, the prosecution might opt to charge the aggravated form of criminal damage contrary to s. 1(2) of the 1971 Act, namely that Quentin damaged or destroyed property being at least reckless as to whether life would be endangered thereby. Note that with the aggravated offence there is no issue as to the ownership of the property. What the prosecution would have to establish, however, is that Quentin was reckless as to whether setting fire to the pile of rubbish would endanger life. The prosecution cannot simply base its case on the assertion that starting a fire might endanger life *per se*; see *R v Steer* [1988] AC 111. Given that Quentin's evidence is that he cannot recall setting fire to Ronaldo, establishing subjective recklessness in respect of the aggravated offence looks unlikely but the recklessness required would be as in *R v G* (above).

Quentin could be charged with a range of non-fatal offences against the person in respect of the harm suffered by Ronaldo. Severe burns can be regarded as grievous bodily harm (see *R v Doyle* [2004] EWCA Crim 2714), opening up the prospect of liability under s. 18 and s. 20 of the Offences Against the Person Act 1861. For the purposes of s. 18 Quentin clearly causes the grievous bodily harm. Liability will depend upon proof that he intended to cause the harm. Again, his non-recollection of the event would militate against this. Similarly with a charge under s. 20. Quentin inflicts grievous bodily harm by setting fire to Ronaldo (there being no need to prove a direct assault for the purposes of proving infliction—see *R v Burstow; R v Ireland* [1998] AC 147), but proof that he acted maliciously in doing so (which requires proof that he foresaw the possibility of some physical harm albeit slight—*R v Mowatt* [1967] 3 All ER 47) seems unlikely. Even if he could recollect the events, if Quentin genuinely thought he was burning rubbish there would be no basis for this *mens rea*. Even assault and battery charges would fail, as he does not, on this evidence, foresee the risk of causing another to apprehend immediate physical violence, or the risk of unlawful contact with another person.

A further possibility is that Quentin's liability could be based on his failure to aid Ronaldo and limit the harm done. On the basis of *R v Miller* [1983] 1 All ER 978, Quentin would have had a responsibility to limit the scope of the harm if he had accidentally caused it and realized that he had accidentally caused it. There would need to be evidence that there was something Quentin could have reasonably done to prevent further harm. Assuming the *R v Miller* elements of liability for failing to act are made out, the prosecution would still need to prove that the omission actually caused further harm—a question of fact for the jury. Once the *actus reus* is made out, based on omission, Quentin could be charged under s. 18 or s. 20 as detailed above.

Whether he is charged with criminal damage or assault offences Quentin has, on the facts, a number of possible defences he could raise. The most promising of these is non-insane automatism. The question will be as to whether Quentin was aware of the nature and quality of his act (i.e. omission to help)—if not he may have a complete defence based on automatism. Quentin will need to provide medical evidence that he suffered a complete destruction of his ability to consciously direct his actions. Impaired, reduced or partial control is not enough for the defence to be made out; see *Attorney-General's Reference (No. 2 of 1992)* [1993] 3 WLR 982.

The need for medical evidence was stressed in *Bratty v Attorney-General for Northern Ireland* [1963] AC 386, where Lord Denning stressed that it was not sufficient for a man to say that he had simply had a black-out. In his view a court would need some medical or scientific evidence to distinguish the genuine cases from the fraudulent.

There is no doubt that properly evidenced post-traumatic stress disorder could form the basis of a defence of automatism in principle—see, for example, *R v T* [1990] Crim LR 256. The issue of public policy is whether or not it is desirable to allow a defendant suffering from such a condition to receive a complete acquittal. If this is the outcome the court loses all jurisdiction over the defendant and the public might be at further risk; see further *R v Sandie Smith* [1982] Crim LR 531, where automatism based on severe pre-menstrual tension was refused for this very reason. Quentin will argue that his periodic loss of consciousness is not the result of any 'fault' or recklessness on his part, and that his mental health problems are caused by an 'external' factor. This is of course true, but if he cannot be treated with any other form of medication the courts are rightly to take the view that he needs to be detained for the better protection of the public.

The more likely view is that Quentin in fact falls within the *M'Naghten* Rules on insane automatism. He suffers from a disease of the mind—severe post-traumatic stress disorder—which, despite the medication, still manifests itself in violence. In short, he is a danger to others, hence public policy would dictate that he should only be allowed the defence of insanity—see *R v Sullivan* [1981] Crim LR 46. Quentin should be advised therefore to plead automatism, but to expect the court to rule that only insanity will be accepted as a defence.

It is worth observing that there is no point in advising Quentin simply to rely on mistake of fact as a denial of *mens rea* in relation to the assault charges (i.e. he honestly believed he was only setting fire to rubbish, not a human being). For one thing his evidence is that he cannot recall what he was doing. For another, if he puts his state of mind in issue by relying on mistake of fact the prosecution will be entitled to lead evidence that he made the mistake of fact because of his insanity.

Quentin's liability in relation to Sacha

The cut to Sacha's head will satisfy the definition of a wound for the purposes of both s. 18 and s. 20 of the Offences Against the Person Act 1861—as confirmed in *JCC v Eisenhower* [1983] 3 WLR 537. The offence under s. 18 requires proof that Quentin caused the wound with intent to do some grievous bodily harm. Although there is no clear authority at the moment as to what intent means in the context of s. 18 it would be odd indeed if the courts adopted any approach other than that in *R v Woollin* [1998] 4 All ER 103. If intention to do grievous bodily harm is sufficient for murder, the intent must be the same under a s. 18 charge. The issue will be whether there is evidence that Quentin foresaw grievous bodily harm as virtually certain to result from his actions. Given that Quentin only threatened Sacha this seems very unlikely. Malicious wounding contrary to s. 20 of the 1861 Act requires proof that Quentin was malicious, i.e. that he at least had foresight of the risk of some physical harm albeit slight. Again this is problematic as Quentin only intended to frighten. *R v Sullivan* (above) makes it clear that foreseeing fright is not enough to satisfy a charge under s. 20. The more appropriate charge therefore is likely to be one of assault occasioning actual bodily harm contrary to s. 47 of the 1861 Act. The threat with the knife is an assault in the narrow sense, and the cut to the head is actual bodily harm (ABH)—causation is evident. Quentin only needs to have *mens rea* for the assault, not the causing of ABH—*R v Savage; R v Parmenter* [1992] 1 AC 699. Subjective recklessness would suffice—was Quentin aware of the risk that Sacha would apprehend immediate physical violence?

Looking at the defences that Quentin might be entitled to rely on, perhaps self-defence is the most attractive (because if successful it would provide a complete defence to any charge). Normally self-defence would require evidence that the force used was no more than was reasonable in the circumstances; see *R v Julien* [1969] 1 WLR 839, as confirmed in s. 76 of the Criminal Justice and Immigration Act 2008. On an objective basis the defence would therefore fail. Applying s. 76(3) of the Criminal Justice and Immigration Act 2008, which consolidates the position at common law, Quentin will argue that he is entitled to be judged on the facts as he honestly believed them to be—

i.e. that he believed Sacha was an enemy soldier, who was trying to kill him. Following s. 76(6) the defence should be available to Quentin provided the degree of force used was not disproportionate in the circumstances as he believed them to be.

Two further complications arise here. The first is that there is evidence that Quentin's mental condition may have adversely affected his ability to judge the nature of threats posed by other people. In *R v Martin* [2001] EWCA Crim 2245 the Court of Appeal held that evidence of D's mental state, which might show him to believe threats to be more serious than they actually were, was not to be taken into account in assessing the reasonableness of the force used by D in self-defence. This decision is hard to reconcile with the notion that D is to be judged on the facts as he honestly believed them to be. If, because of his mental state (not arising from voluntary intoxication), D mistakenly but honestly believes V to be presenting a serious threat to him and in consequence uses what he believes to be reasonable force to protect himself, he should be able to rely on the defence of self-defence. Section 76(8) creates room for challenging the decision in *R v Martin* [2001] EWCA 2245, where it provides that 'other matters' can be taken into account by the jury in determining whether the force used by D was reasonable in the circumstances as he believed them to be. It could be argued that these 'other matters' might extend to evidence of D's mental instability; see further *R v Martin (Paul)* [2000] 2 Cr App R 42, and *Shaw (Norman) v The Queen* [2001] UKPC 26.

The second issue, and one that might render recourse to self-defence an entirely academic exercise, is that, as indicated above, by raising mistake of fact Quentin puts his state of mind in issue—thus allowing the prosecution to lead evidence of insanity if they wish to—in effect agreeing that Quentin made the mistake of fact but arguing that he did so because he is insane. If the prosecution argue this point successfully, Quentin could be found not guilty by reason of insanity—see above. A further point to note on this is that the insanity, if established, may fall under the second limb of the *M'Naghten* Rules—i.e. that although Quentin was aware of his actions, he was suffering from a disease of the mind that resulted in him not realizing that his actions were 'wrong' (he does not say that he cannot recall threatening Sacha). Following *R v Windle* [1952] 2 QB 826, for this argument to succeed Quentin would have to prove that did not realize his actions were contrary to law. Given that he believed he was defending himself he could well argue that he believed his actions were justified, and therefore lawful. Note that this narrow interpretation of *Windle* was unsuccessfully challenged in *R v Johnson* [2007] EWCA Crim 1978, and thus stands for the time being.

Question 4

Alfred is an alcoholic. Alfred's girlfriend Marti leaves Alfred to move in with Alfred's work colleague Victor. Alfred becomes very jealous of Victor. One evening Albert visits the pub and drinks nine pints of strong beer to give himself the courage to confront Victor. On his way home whilst in a drunken stupor, Alfred encounters Victor and Marti kissing in the street. Alfred shouts abuse at Victor who waves Alfred away. Alfred, mistakenly believing that Victor is about to attack him, stabs Victor with a knife causing his death.

Discuss Alfred's possible defences to a charge of murder.

Commentary

At first sight this might seem to be a very simple and straightforward question, but consideration of all the possible defences takes considerable time, and requires a good knowledge of the interrelationship between those defences. The rubric asks candidates to deal only with liability for murder, hence there is no need to go into detail on involuntary manslaughter. Candidates should still, however, consider the elements of murder before considering the defences in detail. A knowledge of developments in self-defence and provocation is essential, as is an understanding of the relevance or irrelevance of intoxication in respect of self-defence, provocation, and diminished responsibility. Less space should be devoted to insane automatism in this answer, given the likelihood that other defences are going to be more appropriate.

Answer plan

- Mistake and self-defence—effect of **s. 76 of the Criminal Justice and Immigration Act 2008**
- Provocation—*Attorney-General for Jersey v Holley* [2005]
- Diminished responsibility—*Tandy* [1987] and *R v Stewart* [2009]
- Intoxication
  - *Majewski* [1977]
  - *Gallagher* [1963]
- Automatism—*Lipman* [1969]
- Insanity—*M'Naghten* Rules 1843

Suggested answer

The elements of liability

Alfred clearly causes Victor's death both in fact and in law. Alfred's actions are an operating and substantial cause of Victor's death. *Mens rea* also seems evident i.e., that Albert intended to kill Victor or to cause him grievous bodily harm, subject to what is said below regarding the availability of any defences that effectively denies the existence of the necessary *mens rea*.

Defences—self-defence

Assuming *actus reus* and *mens rea* for murder are made out, there are a number of defences that may be available to Alfred, but *prima facie* the most favourable would be self-defence, as this is a complete defence to a murder charge. Alfred has the evidential duty to raise self-defence, but the burden of proof remains on the prosecution to prove that the force used was not necessary or reasonable; see further *R v Julien* [1969] 1 WLR 839, as consolidated in s. 76 of the Criminal Justice and Immigration Act 2008. The fact that an accused has made a mistake of fact leading him to wrongly believe that it is necessary for him to act in self-defence will not necessarily rule out the defence; see *R v Williams* (1983) 78 Cr App R 276 and s. 76 of the 2008 Act. Alfred is to be judged on the facts as he honestly believed them to be. Therefore, if an unreasonable mistake as to the facts has been made, this will not in itself cause the defence to fail, provided the mistake was honestly made. The amount of force used, however, must still be within the bounds of what would have been reasonable had the facts actually been as the accused believed them to be. The complicating fact here is intoxication. It is one thing for a sober defendant to rely on self-defence because he genuinely, but erroneously, believes he is being attacked. It is quite another for a defendant who, of his own volition has become intoxicated, to seek to rely on such a mistake. At common law the courts refused to allows defendants to rely on a mistaken belief caused by voluntary intoxication; see *R v O'Grady* [1987] 3 All ER 420 and more recently *R v Hatton* [2005] All ER (D) 308 (Oct). The matter has now been settled by Parliament in s. 76(5) of the 2008 Act which provides that any mistaken belief on the part of a defendant attributable to his voluntary induced intoxication cannot be relied upon as the basis for his mistaken belief as to the need to defend himself or the extent of the force required. The sub-section sweeps over any distinction between crimes of basic intent and crimes of specific intent in this respect—hence the prohibition applies to a charge of murder, even though the defence of intoxication itself would still be available (see below).

However, the court there did agree to certify a point of law of general public importance, namely whether a defendant who raised the issue of self-defence was entitled to be judged on the basis of what he had mistakenly believed to be the situation, when that mistaken belief was brought about by self-induced intoxication by alcohol or other drugs. Thus Alfred may wish to pursue this argument, depending on how the House of Lords resolve the issue raised in *R v Hatton*.

Defences—provocation

Alfred might next turn to provocation which (if successful) would reduce murder to manslaughter. Under s. 3 of the Homicide Act 1957, Albert has to provide some evidence that he was provoked at the time of the killing. On the facts there may be an issue here in terms of Alfred convincing the trial judge that he did lose his self-control and that this is a case of provocation. Despite cases such as *R v Ahluwalia* [1992] 4 All ER 889 and *R v Thornton* [1996] 2 Cr App R 108 recognizing the fact that women suffering from 'battered women's syndrome' may react on a slower fuse, the courts still insist that there must be a sudden and temporary loss of self-control. As Alfred is jealous of Victor, it may be the case that his conduct will be regarded as a cold-blooded act of revenge, rather than retaliation in the heat of the moment to provocation. Alfred will doubtless argue that it was the sight of Marti and Victor together which reignited his anger.

Assuming there is evidence of provocation to put before the jury, there will be further difficulties. Under s. 3 of the 1957 Act, the question of whether the provocation was enough to make a reasonable man do as Alfred did will be left to be determined by the jury. In determining that question the jury shall take into account everything both done and said according to the effect which, in their opinion, it would have on a reasonable man.

Whilst the jury could take into account the fact that Alfred was an alcoholic when assessing the gravity of the provocation (i.e. how much provocation he was subjected to) it is questionable whether there is any basis for doing so on the given facts, as Alfred is not taunted about his alcoholism; see further *R v Morhall* [1995] 3 All ER 659. The history of the relationship between Marti and Alfred will be relevant on this point as it explains why the sight of her and Victor together was provoking. Having assessed the gravity of the provocation, the jury following the Privy Council decision in *Attorney-General for Jersey v Holley* [2005] UKPC 23, will assess Alfred's reaction according to the standards of the person having ordinary powers of control. That standard is a constant, objective standard in all cases. Under the 1957 Act the sufficiency of the provocation (whether the provocation was enough to make a reasonable man do as Alfred did) has to be judged by one standard, not a standard that varies from defendant to defendant. In assessing whether the reasonable person would have lost his self-control so as to kill as Alfred did will be assessed without regard to the issue of intoxication as the reasonable person is irrebuttably presumed to be sober for these purposes. Intoxication, if established by the evidence has to be the basis of a separate defence, as to which see below. On the facts it is hard to see how a defence of provocation could succeed, given the return to the more restrictive view of the defence as evidenced in *Attorney-General for Jersey v Holley*.

Defences—diminished responsibility

Alfred might have more chance of success with the defence of diminished responsibility, which was created by virtue of s. 2 of the Homicide Act 1957. This defence, which is only available to a defendant charged with murder, will reduce the defendant's liability to manslaughter if successfully pleaded.

It will be for Alfred to prove, on the balance of probabilities, that when he killed Victor he was suffering from an abnormality of mind (whether arising from a condition of arrested or retarded development of mind or any inherent causes or induced by disease or injury) that had the effect of substantially impairing his mental responsibility for his acts in carrying out the killing. If Alfred killed Victor because he was drunk, this in itself would not amount to an abnormality of the mind for the purposes of the defence. On the other hand, several cases (including *R v Tandy* (1987) 87 Cr App R 45) make it clear that the damage caused by prolonged alcohol abuse can constitute such an abnormality. The key issue is for the jury to consider the defendant's state of mind at the time of the killing. In *R v Dietschmann* [2003] 1 All ER 897 it was held that if a defendant could show that, notwithstanding his voluntary alcohol consumption, his abnormality of mind (i.e., the brain damage caused by his alcoholism) substantially impaired his mental responsibility for his acts, the jury should find him not guilty of murder but guilty of manslaughter; see further *R v Swan* [2006] All ER (D) 208 (Dec). The difficulty for the jury in carrying out this assessment, with its rigid dichotomy between voluntary consumption of alcohol, and consumption of alcohol caused by an irresistible craving for alcohol, was recognized by the Court of Appeal in *R v Stewart* [2009] EWCA Crim 593. If there is no evidence of Albert having suffered damage to his brain as a result of his alcoholism, the court should consider whether or not there is evidence that he suffers from alcohol dependency syndrome. If the evidence is sufficiently compelling this could amount to an abnormality of the mind caused by disease. The issue of fact for the jury will then be the extent to which this disease impaired Albert's responsibility for his actions. Evidence of his having voluntarily consumed alcohol is not fatal to the defence succeeding. The jury will be directed to reflect on the extent to which the alcohol dependency led to Albert choosing not to resist his impulses (defence fails) and the extent to which it led to him not being able to resist his impulses (defence should succeed).

Defences—intoxication

The evidence strongly suggests that Alfred was intoxicated at the time of the killing and this probably provides the strongest of the defences upon which he might choose to rely. He will have to provide evidence that, as a result of his voluntary consumption of alcohol he was rendered incapable of forming the necessary intent for the offence, in this case the specific intent to kill or do grievous bodily harm; see *DPP v Beard* [1920] AC 479.

DPP v Majewski [1976] 2 All ER 142 provides that, as murder is a specific intent crime (i.e. one for which evidence of recklessness cannot suffice as the *mens rea*) self-induced intoxication can operate as a partial defence reducing the defendant's liability to that of the lesser-included basic intent offence, namely manslaughter. The recklessness in becoming intoxicated provides the fault element for the basic intent crime in respect of which the defendant is convicted—in this case manslaughter.

What should be noted, however, is that Alfred may still fall foul of the principle established in *Attorney-General for Northern Ireland v Gallagher* [1963] AC 349, to the effect that if a defendant forms the *mens rea* of the offence (i.e., decides to kill) and then deliberately get drunk to give himself 'Dutch courage', the defence may not be permitted. It is submitted that this decision is open to criticism. If the defendant, despite getting himself drunk, still knows what he is doing at the time of the killing, he is not intoxicated in the sense that the word was used in *DPP v Beard*. Conversely, if he is intoxicated at the time of the killing, the fact that he deliberately reduced himself to such a condition should really have no relevance.

Defences—sane and insane automatism

Alfred might argue that as he was drunk and did not know what he was doing, he was in a state of automatism at the time of the killing and should be acquitted. Lord Denning in *Bratty v Attorney-General for Northern Ireland* [1963] AC 386 described automatism as 'an act which is done by the muscles without any control by the mind such as a spasm, a reflex or a convulsion; or an act done by a person who is not conscious of what he is doing such as an act done whilst suffering from concussion or whilst sleep-walking'. Alfred's condition might sound as though it meets these requirements, however in *R v Lipman* [1969] 3 All ER 410, the court made it quite clear that this defence cannot succeed if the automatism has been induced by the accused voluntarily taking alcohol or non-prescribed hallucinatory drugs. The legal position is driven by public policy. It is one thing to allow a defendant who voluntarily intoxicates himself to have his liability reduced from murder to manslaughter. It is another thing altogether to allow such a defendant an acquittal—the result of successfully pleading the defence of sane automatism.

Assuming sane automatism is not available, it is unlikely that Alfred would actively seek a defence based on insane automatism under the *M'Naghten* Rules (see *M'Naghten's* case (1843) 10 C & F 200). Alfred would have to show that, at the time of committing the act, he was labouring under such a defect of reason, from disease of the mind, as not to know the nature and quality of the act he was doing or, if he did know it, he did not know that what he was doing was wrong.

In *R v Quick and Paddison* [1973] QB 910, the Court of Appeal stated that a condition produced by the application of extraneous substances such as alcohol or drugs, could not be regarded as a disease of the mind if it was only a temporary or transient state. However, in *R v Inseal* [1992] Crim LR 35, it was recognized that heavy drinking over a long period of time could have had such an effect on the mind as to amount to a disease of the mind within the meaning of the *M'Naghten* Rules. Surprisingly, this is a question of law for the trial judge, and if the judge resolves that a disease of the mind exists then the jury must decide if the other elements of the defence have been made out.

Given the availability of the defence of diminished responsibility (considered above), it is submitted that Alfred would not raise the defence of insanity; and if the trial judge threatened to leave it to the jury, he might do the same thing as many accused in this position and change his plea to guilty, in the hope that the judge's conduct might be sufficient for a successful appeal.

Further reading

Child, J., 'Drink, Drugs and Law Reform: A Review of Law Commission Report No. 314' [2009] Crim LR 488.

Gough, S., 'Surviving without Majewski' [2000] Crim LR 719.

Loughman, A., '"Manifest Madness": Towards A New Understanding of the Insanity Defence' (2007) 70 Mod LR 379.

Mackay, R.D. and Mitchell, B.J., 'Sleepwalking, Automatism and Insanity' [2006] Crim LR 901.

Mackay, R.D. and Reuber, M., 'Epilepsy and the Defence of Insanity—Time for a Change?' [2007] Crim LR 782.

Mackay, R.D., 'Righting the Wrong?—Some Observations on the Second Limb of the M'Naghten Rules' [2009] Crim LR 80.

Samiloff, J., 'Time to Change the Voluntary Intoxication Rule?' [2004] NLJ 154.

Simester, A.P, 'Intoxication is Never a Defence' [2009] Crim LR 3.

Virgo, G., 'The Law Commission Consultation Paper on Intoxication' [1993] Crim LR 415.

Ward, T., 'Magistrates, Insanity and the Common Law' [1997] Crim LR 796.

Voluntary intoxication

6

The defences II

Introduction

The questions in this chapter focus on the defences of compulsion—duress by threats (sometimes referred to as duress *per minas*), duress of circumstances, necessity, and self-defence. Mistake is also considered in so far as a mistake of fact may lead a defendant to wrongly believe in the existence of circumstances (either the existence of a compelling threat, or the need to use force for self-protection) that would give rise to a substantive defence. Candidates need to be prepared to tackle both essay questions that focus primarily on compulsion defences and problem questions where compulsion arises as a defence—typically in relation to non-sexual offences against the person.

Although duress by threats has existed as a defence for many years, uncertainty regarding the correct principles to be applied was highlighted by the Law Commission's Consultation Paper No. 122, which identified the following five questions as requiring discussion:

(a) Against whom must the threat be directed?

(b) If the actor might resort to police or other official protection, is it relevant that such resort is likely to prove, or that the actor thinks it is likely to prove, ineffective?

(c) Must the actor's belief in the existence or nature or seriousness of the threat, or in the impossibility of avoiding the threatened harm, be reasonably held?

(d) Is the defence to be denied to one who is incapable of mounting the resistance to the threat that would be put up by a person of 'reasonable firmness' or steadfastness?

(e) Should the defence be available on a charge of murder or attempted murder?

It is, of course, this last question that has demonstrated the difference of opinion between the Law Commission and the Law Lords. On two occasions the Law Commission have recommended that duress should be available as a defence to murder, but in both *R v Howe* [1987] 1 All ER 771 and *R v Gotts* [1992] 1 All ER 832, the House of Lords refused to so recognize it. This issue is fully explored in Question 4. Indications that the courts are becoming increasingly concerned at the regularity with which defendants are raising the defence of duress are to be found in the speech of Lord Bingham in *R v Hasan*

[2005] UKHL 22. Candidates need to be well acquainted with the effect of this decision and the extent to which it addresses the Law Commission's queries at (a) to (c) above. In summary the ruling changes the defence of duress in three important respects:

(a) the defendant's belief in the duressor's threats of death or serious harm must be genuine and reasonable;

(b) a defendant who has a genuine opportunity to negate the effect of the threats, for example by going to the police, and fails to do so, will not be allowed to rely on the defence;

(c) the defence will no longer be available to a defendant who voluntarily associates with others whom he realized (or ought to have realized) would put him under pressure of any sort to commit a criminal act.

The conventional wisdom is that the development of the defence of necessity has been hampered by the ruling in *R v Dudley and Stephens* [1881–5] All ER Rep 61 that the defence was not available on a murder charge. The effect of this case for many years was that when a defendant chose the lesser of two evils, the defence would not be considered. The restrictive approach was seen in decisions such as *R v Kitson* (1955) 39 Cr App R 66. The defendant had fallen asleep whilst travelling as a passenger in a car. When he awoke he found that he had to suddenly take control of the car because the driver was no longer in control. Although the defendant was drunk he managed to steer the car to safety. The defence of necessity was not permitted and the conviction for driving under the influence of alcohol was upheld. The courts have now recognized that the defence of duress of circumstances may be available in the same way as duress by threats, see e.g., *R v Pommell* [1995] 2 Cr App R 607.

Many commentators believed that duress of circumstances was the defence of necessity in disguise, but the Law Commission have recognized that there is a difference between the two concepts, by recommending that, whereas duress by circumstances should be defined by statute, necessity should be allowed to develop through judicial decision (see cl. 43 of the Draft Code, and the Draft Criminal Law Bill). Necessity was recognized as a defence by the House of Lords in *F v West Berkshire Health Authority* [1989] 2 All ER 545, where Lord Brandon said that 'it will not only be lawful for doctors, on the ground of necessity to operate on or give other medical treatment to adult patients disabled from giving their consent, it will also be their common law duty to do so'.

Further recognition of the defence of necessity was made by the Court of Appeal in *Re A (Children) (Conjoined Twins: Surgical Separation)* [2000] 4 All ER 961, when the court authorized an operation to separate conjoined twins, which was necessary to save the life of the stronger twin, although it would inevitably cause the death of the weaker twin. Brooke LJ stated that the three necessary requirements for the application of the defence of necessity were satisfied, namely:

(a) the act was needed to avoid inevitable and irreparable evil;

(b) no more should be done than was reasonably necessary for the purpose to be achieved; and

(c) the evil inflicted was not disproportionate to the evil avoided.

Dudley and Stephens was distinguished, and although *Re A* is a civil case, it is clear that the defence of necessity could, potentially, be developed to apply to all offences. An issue that often affects the defences of duress and self-defence is mistake. There may be situations where, in fact the conditions for the defence may not be in place but the defendant nevertheless honestly believes that they are. Should the defendant's liability be assessed on the facts as he honestly believed them to be, or should the law only permit reliance on reasonable mistakes of fact?

Regarding self-defence, candidates' answers should reflect the fact that much of the common law related to the defence has been placed on a statutory footing by s. 76 of the Criminal Justice and Immigration Act 2008, which came into force in July 2008. Hence the subjective approach illustrated in *R v Williams* (1983) 78 Cr App R 276 applies. With duress the approach currently favoured by the House of Lords in *R v Hasan* [2005] UKHL 22 supports an objective test based on what he reasonably believed the threat to be.

The other major controversy relating to self-defence is the House of Lords' decision in *R v Clegg* [1995] 1 All ER 334, where their Lordships concluded (against the recommendations of the Law Commission, 14th Report, Cmnd 7844) that a defendant who is entitled to use force in self-defence but who kills an attacker by using force that goes beyond what is reasonable, will be guilty of murder instead of manslaughter. Perhaps the defendant in these circumstances lacks the culpability of a murderer, but as Australia recognized (*Zecevic v DPP (Victoria)* (1987) 162 CLR 645), in practical terms the defendant is generally in a better position if the prosecution's case is weak and the jury only have the options of murder or acquittal (as opposed to a third option of manslaughter). The problem of course for Clegg was that he was tried by a 'Diplock court' with no jury; but even if there is a jury, it is often difficult to predict the outcome.

Question 1

Mary, an unmarried mother aged 17, suffers from anxiety and panic attacks. She is a member of a protest group, 'Free West Country TV from Welsh Influence', and is told by Alan, the leader of the group, that unless she takes part in an attack on the local TV station her young daughter will be killed.

As a result, Mary takes part in the raid. She accosts Sid, a motorist, takes his car and causes him slight injuries. Then she collects Alan and drives him to the TV station where he murders a night-watchman, Bill.

Discuss the criminal liability of Mary.

 Commentary

Candidates should start by considering Mary's liability in respect of taking the car. There is clearly an assault, either in the broad or narrow sense, but there are complications regarding theft, robbery, and taking without consent. The question does not make clear what Mary's intentions are once she has taken the car. If she intends to treat it as her own to dispose of, she may have committed theft. If so, the use of force in order to steal could turn that theft into a robbery. On the other hand, if she was simply using the car and then abandoning it, the theft charge cannot be sustained, neither can the robbery. Candidates will need to consider **s. 12** *of the Theft Act* **1968** as an alternative.

The bulk of the question is concerned with Mary's accessorial liability and the defence of duress. One of the difficulties here, and one that is common in many exam questions (whether intended by the examiner or not!) is the absence of evidence on key issues. It is not clear, for example, where Mary is when Alan commits the murder—this has a key bearing on how her accessorial liability is assessed. Neither is any evidence provided regarding what crimes Mary contemplates Alan committing. Regarding duress, candidates must be familiar with the House of Lords' decision in *R v Hasan* **[2005] UKHL 22** and the clarification resulting therefrom of issues regarding the scope and definition of the defence of duress. There are various aspects of the defence that are likely to be problematic for Mary, such as her failure to go to the police, whether it was reasonable to believe in Alan's threats, and whether she is barred on policy grounds from raising the defence because she voluntarily joined the pressure group.

Note: Candidates are not required to discuss Alan's criminal responsibility.

Answer plan

- Consider offences
  - assault; aggravated assault
  - possible theft and robbery : **s. 12, Theft Act 1968**
  - aiding and abetting murder
- Duress—definition
- Conditions for the defence of duress
- Duress and murder

Suggested answer

Mary could be charged with a number of offences in connection with this event. When she accosts Sid, the motorist, she could be guilty of common assault under s. 39 of the Criminal Justice Act 1988. However, as she has caused him slight injuries the charge is more likely to be the more serious offence of assault occasioning actual bodily harm under s. 47 of the Offences Against the Person Act 1861. Actual bodily harm covers slight injuries such as bruising, or even psychiatric injury, which is established by expert evidence (*R v Mike Chan-Fook* [1994] 2 All ER 552). The *mens rea* for the s. 47 offence is the same as for assault and battery. There is no requirement for the prosecution to prove that Mary intended or foresaw the risk of actual bodily harm (*R v Savage;*

R v Parmenter [1992] 1 AC 699). It will suffice that she either intended to assault Sid (in the narrow sense of frightening him or touching him) or that she was reckless as to whether she did so. The recklessness would be subjective, meaning she would, at the very least, have to be shown to have been aware of the risk of assaulting Sid.

Further, when Mary takes Sid's car she could be committing theft under s. 1 of the Theft Act 1968, i.e., she 'dishonestly appropriates property belonging to another with the intention of permanently depriving the other of it'. Given that she used force in order to take the car, a charge of robbery contrary to s. 8 of the Theft Act 1968 might be possible. The problem for the prosecution will be in establishing that, when she appropriated Sid's car, Mary had an intention permanently to deprive him of it. The facts given do not indicate what happens to the car after it is taken. If Mary merely abandoned it, intention to permanently deprive will not be made out. Abandoned cars can be traced back to their owners fairly easily; see *R v Mitchell* [2008] EWCA Crim 850. Alternatively, if the evidence was that, having taken the car, Mary destroyed it, or sold it on, there would be much stronger evidence of intention to permanently deprive —(treating the car as her own to dispose of within the wording of s. 6(1) of the Theft Act 1968). If the theft is made out it could in turn support a charge of robbery in relation to the car under s. 8. The prosecution case would be that Mary used force in order to steal the car.

If theft of the car cannot be established the prosecution will rely instead on a charge under s. 12 of the Theft Act 1968, 'taking a conveyance without the owner's authority'. For this offence temporary deprivation is sufficient. All the elements of the s. 12 offence appear to have been made out.

The most serious offence that Mary might face is that of aiding and abetting murder. An unlawful homicide has occurred and Alan is the principal offender. The extent of Mary's accessorial liability may depend on whether she was present at the scene when Alan carried out the murder. On the facts it is clear that Mary at least drove Alan to the scene of the crime. Confirmation that this can constitute the *actus reus* of being an accomplice to the offence subsequently committed by the principal offender is provided by *DPP for Northern Ireland v Lynch* [1975] AC 653.

Turning to the *mens rea* that has to be established in cases where the accomplice is involved in the preliminary stages of the commission of the offence by the principal offender, the prosecution must show that an accomplice at least contemplated the type of crime actually committed by the principal offender; see *R v Bainbridge* [1959] 3 All ER 200. Given that the protest group she joins is dedicated to addressing the influence of Welsh TV in the West Country Mary will argue that violence against the person was clearly outside the scope of the offences she expected Alan to commit—hence Mary should argue that murder was not the type of crime she contemplated Alan committing and that he was acting alone when he murdered Bill. The decision in *R v Bryce* [2004] EWCA Crim 1231, arguably makes the prosecution's task in this regard yet more demanding by providing that establishing the *mens rea* involves proving that Mary drove Alan to the TV station realizing that her actions were capable of assisting the offence Alan committed, and that she contemplated his commission of the offence as a real possibility. It is uncertain from the facts whether this can be made out. It would not be wise for Mary to argue that she knew Alan was a violent and dangerous man but did not know quite what he planned to do. If she does pursue such a strategy the prosecution might seek to rely on the argument in *DPP for Northern Ireland v Maxwell* [1978] 3 All ER 1140, to the effect that when Mary drove Alan to the TV station she did so on the basis that she realized he might commit any one of a number of serious offences, and hence she was effectively giving him *carte blanche* to do as he saw fit. Whether this is the case or not will depend entirely on the evidence that emerges from questions put to Mary and Alan. The further point supporting the prosecution's case regarding Mary's having contemplated violence on Alan's part is the fact that he had already threatened to kill her daughter if she did not comply—hardly the actions of a man reluctant to commit serious offences against the person.

If Mary was present at the scene of Bill's murder the prosecution might seek to establish her accessorial liability on the basis that she was engaged in a joint enterprise with Alan. For these purposes a joint enterprise is to be distinguished from other forms of accessorial liability on the basis that the accomplice is at the scene of the crime acting in concert with the principal offender; see further *R v Petters and Parfitt* [1995] Crim LR 501. Establishing this form of accessorial liability will, therefore, require evidence of Mary having been present whilst Bill was murdered, offering some form of assistance (which could be her mere presence).

On the basis of *R v Powell and English* [1997] 4 All ER 545, Mary can be guilty as an accomplice to the murder of Bill if it is proved that she foresaw that Alan might kill or cause grievous bodily harm and she foresaw him acting with intent to kill or cause grievous bodily harm. Whether or not this is the case will, of course, depend on the evidence emerging in the course of the investigation and trial. If it never occurred to Mary that Alan would kill or cause grievous bodily harm then she should be acquitted. If she contemplated it as a possibility, albeit one that she did not welcome, she has sufficient *mens rea*. If there is evidence that, by his actions in killing the night-watchman, Alan deliberately exceeded the scope of the joint enterprise, for example by engaging in conduct that was fundamentally different and more dangerous than that contemplated by Mary, she could escape liability. Much depends on what she contemplated. If she contemplated Alan killing the night-watchman then it matters not how he did it. If however, she contemplated Alan causing grievous bodily harm, albeit that he might kill as a result, then she can benefit from the 'fundamentally different' rule: see *R v Rahman and others* [2007] EWCA Crim 342, as confirmed in *R v Yemoh* [2009] EWCA Crim 930. For example, in *Gamble* [1989] NI 268 the accomplice contemplated that the principal offender would cause grievous bodily harm by kneecapping the victim by shooting him in the back of the knee joint. The accomplice contemplated the possibility that the victim might die as a result, but the joint enterprise was to do grievous bodily harm. In fact the principal offender slit the victim's throat with a knife. The court held that this was a fundamentally more dangerous act than that contemplated by the accomplice and as a result he was not a party to the killing, even though he had contemplated the death of the victim as a possible outcome of the joint enterprise.

More evidence is needed here to determine Mary's liability in respect of this issue. A further possibility is that Mary could be an accomplice to manslaughter, notwithstanding that Alan commits murder, if it can be shown that: (i) the acts committed by Alan were of the type she contemplated as part of the joint enterprise (for example beating up the victim); (ii) she contemplated Alan inflicting unlawful violence on a victim falling short of grievous bodily harm (i.e. she did not have enough *mens rea* to be an accomplice to murder); and (iii) Alan committed the acts she contemplated, but did so with more *mens rea* than she contemplated. Authority to support this conclusion can be found in *R v Stewart and Schofield* [1995] 1 Cr App R 441, and *R v Gilmour* [2000] 2 Cr App R 407. The logic here is that Mary was willing to be a party to an unlawful act which in fact caused death, and Alan does not deliberately commit any *act* beyond that contemplated by Mary. Only if Mary can show that she did not foresee any harm occurring to the night-watchman (or perhaps nothing more than his suffering a fright not amounting to actual bodily harm) can she escape liability as an accomplice to manslaughter altogether—support for this submission is to be found in *Attorney-General's Reference (No. 3 of 2004)* [2005] EWCA Crim 1882.

Mary will seek to raise the defence of duress *per minas* (duress by threats) in respect of the above charges: assault, possible theft and robbery, s. 12 TDA, accomplice to murder, and accomplice to manslaughter.

Duress is a long-established general defence available when there have been 'threats of immediate death or serious personal violence so great as to overbear the ordinary powers of human resistance' (*Attorney-General v Whelan* [1934] IR 518). Threats of lesser harm, such as false imprisonment or damage to property, are not sufficient (*R v Howe*)—the threat must be of immediate death or grievous bodily harm.

If the prosecution can show that Mary had an opportunity to nullify the threat from Alan by seeking police protection and that she unreasonably failed to do so, the defence will probably fail. Following the House of Lords' decision in *R v Hasan* [2005] UKHL 22, Mary should be advised that if Alan's threat to her daughter was not such as she reasonably expected to follow immediately or almost immediately on her failure to comply with the threat, there will be little room for doubt that she could have taken evasive action, whether by going to the police or in some other way, to avoid committing the crime with which she is charged. If this is the conclusion that the jury comes to, the defence will not be available.

The fact that the threats were to harm Mary's child, and not Mary herself, will not cause the defence to fail. The Australian case of *Hurley and Murray* [1967] VR 526, decided that threats to kill the accused's *de facto* wife amounted to duress. In *R v Hasan* Lord Bingham observed that the threats could be to the defendant or her family or a person for whom she reasonably feels responsible. Thus threats against the life or safety of a defendant's family and others to whom she owes a duty almost certainly will, and threats to a stranger possibly will, be sufficient evidence of duress.

It is arguable whether there should be an objective requirement that the will of a reasonable person would have been overborne for the defence to succeed, since if the accused was too frightened to resist, then this should be sufficient. However, the relevance of the objective criterion was confirmed in *R v Graham* [1982] 1 All ER 801, where the House of Lords approved the following jury direction formulated by Lord Lane CJ:

> was (D) or may he have been, impelled to act as he did because, as a result of what he reasonably believed (E) had said or done, he had good cause to fear that if he did not so act (E) would kill him or...cause him serious physical injury?...If so, have the prosecution made the jury sure that a sober person of reasonable firmness, sharing the characteristics of (D), would not have responded to whatever he reasonably believed (E) said or did by taking part in the killing?

Note that the *R v Graham* formulation requires Mary's belief in the circumstances giving rise to the duress to have been reasonable. The objective nature of this part of the direction to the jury was reaffirmed by the House of Lords in *R v Hasan*.

Notwithstanding the broadly objective nature of the test for duress Mary can argue that the jury should take into account her age and medical condition when applying the test in *R v Graham* above. Thus, the fact that Mary is aged 17 and arguably less resilient than an adult, and consequently less able to resist the threat, may be taken into account. However, the fact that she suffers from anxiety and panic attacks is less certain of being admitted. In *R v Hegarty* [1994] Crim LR 353, expert evidence to show that the accused was 'emotionally unstable or in a grossly elevated state' was held inadmissible; whereas in *R v Emery* (1993) 14 Cr App R (S) 394, the Court of Appeal stated *obiter* that it would be correct to allow expert evidence as to the causes and effects of learned helplessness. The traditional approach has always been that, as it is within the jury's experience as to how a reasonable person should react, there is no need to hear from experts. However, as Beldam LJ pointed out in *R v Hurst* [1995] 1 Cr App R 82: 'we find it hard to see how the person of reasonable firmness can be invested with the characteristics of a personality which lacks reasonable firmness'. It is therefore submitted that, unless there is expert psychiatric evidence to the effect that this is a recognized psychiatric illness (in which case, in accordance with *R v Bowen* [1996] 4 All ER 837, the jury should consider it), the anxiety and panic should not be taken into account when considering the objective condition.

A further difficulty that Mary faces regarding the availability of duress as a defence is the fact that she is an existing member of the protest group. In *R v Sharp* [1987] QB 853, Lord Lane CJ stated:

> Where a person has voluntarily, and with knowledge of its nature, joined a criminal organization or gang which he knew might bring pressure on him to commit an offence and was an active member when he was put under such pressure, he cannot avail himself of the defence of duress.

Because the protection of society demands that people do not easily capitulate to the threat of violence, this principle has been strictly enforced in a number of cases, and in *R v Heath* [2000] Crim LR 109 the Court of Appeal held that the accused, a heroin user, could not rely on duress, because although he was not a member of any criminal organization, he had voluntarily exposed himself to unlawful violence. The leading authority on this point is now the House of Lords' decision in *R v Hasan*, where it was held that if a person voluntarily becomes or remains associated with others engaged in criminal activity in a situation where she knows or ought reasonably to know that she may be the subject of compulsion by them or their associates, she cannot rely on the defence of duress to excuse any act which she is thereafter compelled to do by them. A key issue, therefore, will be what Mary should reasonably have been expected to know about the nature of the 'Free West Country TV from Welsh Influence' pressure group. Was there any history of violence and criminality? Without more evidence on this point it is impossible to advise on the likelihood of duress being excluded on the grounds of prior criminal association.

Finally, regarding the availability of duress, the courts have recognized it as a general, and complete, defence to all crimes except treason and murder. Thus, if Mary is able to overcome the difficulties outlined above, she could be acquitted in respect of the assault on Sid, the Theft Act 1968 offences in respect of the car, and in respect of her being an accomplice to manslaughter. Following *R v Howe*, Mary would not be able to raise the defence in respect of a charge of murder as an accomplice.

Question 2

Anne, who was of a nervous disposition and routinely carried a gun because she feared being attacked, was walking home alone late at night. The street along which she was walking was deserted apart from John who was approaching Anne because he wanted to kiss her. Anne had been the victim of sexual abuse as a child and there was medical evidence to the effect that she suffered from psychiatric disorders that manifested themselves in violence as a result. Anne recognized John and remembered him as someone with a reputation for violence. As John approached, Anne noticed that he was reaching into the inside pocket of his jacket. Anne wrongly believed that John was reaching for a knife that he intended to use to threaten her into having sex with him. Anne panicked, took out her gun and repeatedly shot John in the face. John, who was unarmed, died later in hospital as a result of his injuries.

   Discuss Anne's liability in respect of a charge of murder (ignoring liability for firearms offences).

 ## Commentary

This is a relatively straightforward question. Even though the rubric limits the answer to murder, candidates will need to consider the elements of the offence, as there could be an issue as to *mens rea*. Regarding defences, the major topic is obviously self-defence, but note the need to consider diminished responsibility and to touch upon insanity. Regarding self-defence, candidates must incorporate the statutory provisions in **s. 76 of the Criminal Justice and Immigration Act 2008**. There are issues to consider here such as the extent to which Anne's characteristics might be relevant, her mistake of fact (see *DPP v Morgan* [1976] AC 182; *R v Williams* [1987] 3 All ER 411), and the significance of her exceeding the use of reasonable force (*R v Clegg* [1995] 1 All ER 334).

Answer plan

- Murder—definition—*mens rea*

- Diminished responsibility and insanity

- Self-defence—definition—effect of **s. 76 of the Criminal Justice and Immigration Act 2008**

    - reasonable force

    - mistake—*Williams* [1987]

    - relevance of defendant's characteristics

    - excessive force—*Clegg* [1995], *Martin* [2002]

Suggested answer

The facts provide that Anne has been charged with murder. There is no doubt that she has caused John's death in fact and there is no evidence of any *novus actus interveniens*. The prosecution will be required to establish that Anne had the necessary *mens rea*, namely intention to kill or cause grievous bodily harm: see R v Moloney [1985] 1 All ER 1025. Unless this is regarded as a case where the intention to kill is deemed to be evident from the facts (the fact that she fires at John's face may be seen as conclusive on this point), the jury may need to be directed on the issue of indirect intent. Even if Anne's purpose was to fend off a sexual assault, she can still be regarded as having had the *mens rea* for murder if there is evidence that she foresaw death or grievous bodily harm as virtually certain to be the result of her actions; see R v Woollin [1998] 4 All ER 103.

Although Anne would be advised to run self-defence as her preferred defence (see below), a murder charge would give her the option of raising the defence of diminished responsibility as defined in s. 2 of the Homicide Act 1957. The statute places the legal burden of proof on Anne to establish on the balance of probabilities that, at the time of the killing, she was suffering from an abnormality of the mind such that it substantially impaired her responsibility for her actions. It is clear from the facts that she has access to the necessary medical evidence to support such a claim. The courts have made clear that the term 'abnormality of the mind' is to be construed in a broad non-specialist way to encompass any state of mind that the normal person would regard as abnormal;

see *R v Byrne* [1960] 2 QB 396. The determination of these issues is largely a matter of fact for the jury, even if the medical evidence all points towards a mental abnormality; see *Walton v R* [1978] 1 All ER 542, and *R v Sanders* (1991) 93 Cr App R 245. If the defence succeeds Anne's liability will be reduced to manslaughter.

As they are complete defences, self-defence at common law (i.e., the use of reasonable force), and the statutory version of self-defence under s. 3 of the Criminal Law Act 1967 are much more attractive propositions for Anne. Section 3 provides that a person may use such force as is reasonable in the circumstances in the prevention of crime, thus both defences allow persons to use reasonable force to defend themselves or others from an attack.

Section 76 of the Criminal Justice and Immigration Act 2008 was enacted to clarify certain issues relating to the common law defence of self-defence and the use of force in order to prevent the commission of an offence under s. 3 of the Criminal Law Act 1967. For the provisions of s. 76 to be engaged two questions must be in issue:

(i) whether or not the defendant ('D') was entitled to rely on self-defence (or its statutory equivalent); and

(ii) whether the degree of force used by D against the complainant ('V') person was reasonable in the circumstances.

In many respects the 'clarification' given in s. 76 on these issues involves a straightforward restatement of the common law. Hence sub-section (3) provides that: 'The question whether the degree of force used by D was reasonable in the circumstances is to be decided by reference to the circumstances as D believed them to be...'. Thus, assuming Anne did believe the facts were such as to warrant her acting in self-defence, sub-section (7) provides that the court dealing with the issue should have regard to the following considerations: (a) that she may not have been able to weigh to a nicety the exact measure of any necessary action; and (b) that evidence of her having only done what she honestly and instinctively thought was necessary for a legitimate purpose constitutes strong evidence that only reasonable action was taken by her for that purpose.

Where, as in Anne's case, the evidence is that the defendant was mistaken as to the need to act in self-defence the jury can have regard to the reasonableness of Anne's belief in determining whether she genuinely held that belief. Once the jury determines that Anne did genuinely have a particular belief, she is to be judged on the facts as she believed them to be regardless of the fact that her belief was mistaken, and regardless of the fact that the mistake may not have been one made by a reasonable person.

On this basis, provided Anne honestly believed she was about to be attacked by a violent man wielding a knife, the jury would confine itself to considering the reasonableness of her action in opening fire with a gun. It is difficult to predict how this issue would play with a jury. They may well frown upon an individual routinely arming herself with a loaded gun, but alternatively they may think it reasonable for a woman to react in this way if she really believed that only firing a gun could stop a man about to wield a knife.

Matters are complicated by the evidence that Anne was of a nervous disposition and had suffered child abuse. The defendant is to be judged on the facts as she believed them to be, but what if that belief stems from mental characteristics that would not normally be attributed to the reasonable person? In *R v Martin* [2001] EWCA Crim 2245 the Court of Appeal held that evidence of D's mental state, that might show him to believe threats to be more serious than they actually were, was not to be taken into account in assessing the reasonableness of the force used by D in self-defence. This decision is hard to reconcile with the notion that D is to be judged on the facts as he honestly believed them to be. If, because of his mental state (not arising from voluntary intoxication) D mistakenly but honestly believes V to be presenting a serious threat to him, and in consequence uses what he believes to be reasonable force to protect himself, D should be allowed the protection of the defence. By leading such evidence D will, of course, be putting his state of mind in issue and thus allowing the prosecution to lead evidence of insanity if they have it. That alone should provide sufficient protection in cases where it is felt that to acquit D might result in putting members of the public at risk.

There is support for the more subjective approach in both *R v Martin (Paul)* [2000] 2 Cr App R 42, and *Shaw (Norman) v The Queen* [2001] UKPC 26, and now s. 76(8) creates room for further challenge to the decision in *R v Martin* [2001] EWCA Crim 2245, where it provides that 'other matters' can be taken into account where they are relevant to deciding whether the use of force by way of self-defence was necessary and whether the force used was reasonable. Anne should argue that these 'other matters' could include evidence of her mental instability. It is submitted that she will need expert medical evidence of a recognized condition for this argument to succeed.

If the jury conclude that Anne was entitled to use force in self-defence but had used unreasonable force, it would appear, following the House of Lords' decision in *R v Clegg* [1995] 1 All ER 334, that she would be convicted of murder. The Law Commission (cl. 59 of the Draft Code) has accepted the argument that a person in this situation lacks the culpability of a murderer. However, although the House of Lords agreed with this approach, their Lordships felt that it was for Parliament and not them to change the law, and Clegg's conviction for murder (as opposed to manslaughter) was upheld.

In conclusion it is submitted that the courts will be reluctant to permit a defendant with mental abnormalities to rely on self-defence with the possibility of a complete acquittal. If this were to be the result the court would have no jurisdiction over Anne, who clearly presents a danger to the public. If she only pleads self-defence the prosecution could lead evidence of insanity, as her claim to self-defence involves her in putting her state of mind in issue (her mistaken belief that she was about to be raped). Hence the better course of action for Anne might be to lead evidence of self-defence, but also lead evidence of diminished responsibility as an alternative defence.

Question 3

James was driving on a narrow mountain road. He came to a hairpin bend where he saw Norma sitting in her parked car. Because the road was narrow he could not go back or forward, or around the car. He saw a sign by the side of the road 'Danger—serious risk of avalanche' and noticed small rocks coming down the mountainside. Fearing an impending avalanche and believing he had no alternative, he drove into the car in front, knocking it over the mountainside. He realized that this course of action was dangerous, and it resulted in Norma (the occupant of the car) being killed and the car being badly damaged. There was in fact no avalanche.

Discuss the criminal liability (if any) of James.

Commentary

This question involves a detailed consideration of the defence of necessity/duress of circumstances. There are many uncertainties concerning the defence and this question should be attempted only by candidates confident of dealing with these issues.

In answering the question candidates must, however, guard against the risk of dealing only with this defence, as due consideration must be given to the ingredients of the offences with which James could be charged. Thus a full discussion of the concepts of intention and recklessness must be given in relation to murder, manslaughter and criminal damage.

Note: Road traffic offences have not been considered in detail.

Answer plan

- Murder—definition
- Intention—*Moloney* [1985], *Woollin* [1998]
- Involuntary manslaughter
- Criminal damage—s. 1(1) and s. 1(2), Criminal Damage Act 1971
- Necessity/duress of circumstances

    - conditions—*Graham* [1982]
    - availability—*Pommell* [1995]

Suggested answer

James could face charges involving unlawful homicide and criminal damage, but he may be able to raise the defence of necessity and/or duress of circumstances. The most serious offence to consider is murder. James has clearly caused Norma's death in fact—but for his actions she would not have died. There is no evidence to suggest that there has been any break in the chain of causation. The *mens rea* of murder is satisfied by the prosecution proving that James intended to kill or cause grievous bodily harm (*R v Moloney* [1985] 1 All ER 1025). This is a question of fact for the jury. Although the general rule is that intention is a word in common use, easily understood by the public, and therefore there is no need for the trial judge to embark on a detailed explanation of the concept, this case might require a further direction.

Whereas it is clear that foresight of consequence is evidence that can be used to prove intention, it is not in itself conclusive evidence. Similarly, a judge cannot direct the jury that if James foresaw the consequence and the result was a natural consequence, James intended it. The trial judge would now use the direction suggested by the House of Lords in *R v Woollin* [1998] 4 All ER 103 that the jury would not be entitled to find the necessary intention unless they felt sure that death or serious bodily harm was a virtually certain result of D's actions (barring some unforeseen intervention), and that D had foreseen death or grievous bodily harm as virtually certain.

James could argue that although he foresaw this possible consequence, death or grievous bodily harm was not his purpose as his motive was to save himself. Although this argument succeeded in *R v Steane* [1947] 1 All ER 813, this was not a murder case, and it is recognized that motive is not the same as intention. Motive is the reason why one acts, whereas intention is the state of mind present when the act is committed. In short, indirect intention will suffice.

If the jury decided that James lacked the *mens rea* for murder, he could still be found guilty of involuntary (constructive) manslaughter, i.e., unlawful killing without intention to kill or do grievous bodily harm. For constructive manslaughter the prosecution must prove that James committed a dangerous criminal act that caused the victim's death. Traditionally there has been a reluctance to use a driving offence as the unlawful act in constructive manslaughter. Thus in *Andrews v DPP* [1937] AC 576, the House of Lords held that an accused would not automatically be guilty of manslaughter when he killed the victim as a result of careless driving. Lord Aitkin said: 'There is an obvious difference in the law of manslaughter between doing an unlawful act and doing a lawful act with a degree of carelessness which the legislature makes criminal'.

Alternatively the prosecution could rely on offences under the Criminal Damage Act 1971 as the basis for an unlawful act manslaughter charge. It appears that James committed criminal damage under s. 1(1) of the Act when he damaged Norma's car. Liability could be based on 'simple' criminal damage contrary to s. 1(1) of the 1971 Act, or on aggravated criminal damage contrary to s. 1(2), i.e., damaging or destroying property either intending that or being reckless that the life of another would thereby be endangered.

The second ingredient of constructive manslaughter is that the act must be dangerous. It is enough that a sober and reasonable person at the scene of the unlawful act would have been aware of the possibility of some physical harm occurring as a result of James' actions: see *R v Church* [1965] 2 All ER 72, and *R v Dawson* (1985) 81 Cr App R 150. Given the facts, it is submitted that the prosecution would have no difficulty in satisfying this condition.

There has always been uncertainty as to how the *mens rea* requirement for unlawful act manslaughter should be expressed. As Lord Hope explained in *Attorney-General's Reference (No. 3 of 1994)* [1997] 3 All ER 936, the prosecution must prove that the defendant intended to do what he did. It is not necessary to prove that he knew that his act was unlawful or dangerous. It is unnecessary to prove that he knew that his act was likely to injure the person who died as a result of it. All that need be proved is that he intentionally did what he did—in practice it will suffice if James was at least reckless as to whether property would be damaged or destroyed; see *R v G* [2003] 4 All ER 765.

On this basis, liability for constructive manslaughter should be made out.

It is worth noting that James could also incur liability for causing death by dangerous driving contrary to s. 1 of the Road Traffic Act 1991. The fault element is 'dangerousness', and this is assessed objectively.

What defences might be available to James?

For many years the development of the defence of necessity (duress of circumstances) was hindered by the decision in *R v Dudley and Stephens* [1881–5] All ER Rep 61, in which two shipwrecked seaman killed and ate a cabin boy in order to survive. The court ruled that necessity could be no defence to murder and the accused were found guilty, and many commentators believed that the case was authority for the principle that necessity was not available as a general defence to other charges. It was not until the mid-1980s that the argument was renewed in a number of cases involving road traffic offences (*R v Willer* (1987) 83 Cr App R 225; *R v Conway* [1988] 3 WLR 1338; and *R v Martin* [1989] 1 All ER 652) and the related defence of duress of circumstances was developed.

If the defence is raised the prosecution retains the burden of proof, and according to the Court of Appeal in *R v Martin* (1988) 88 Cr App R 343, the jury will be directed to consider whether James acted reasonably and proportionately, in order to avoid a threat of death or serious injury. The direction should be in these terms:

(i) Was James, or may he have been, impelled to act as he did because as a result of what he reasonably believed to be the situation he had good cause to fear that otherwise death or serious physical injury would result? If so;

(ii) Might a sober person of reasonable firmness, sharing the characteristics of James, have responded to that situation by acting as James did?

If both questions are answered affirmatively James should be acquitted.

Note that the test applied to the defendant's belief in the reality of the threat is objective. This could be a problem for James as, although he believed there was an impending avalanche, this was not in fact the case. Although in *R v Williams* [1987] 3 All ER 411 it was recognized that for the defence of self-defence, the accused should be judged on the facts as he believed them to be, and an honest but unreasonable mistake would not prevent the defence succeeding, the objective basis for compulsion defences, such as duress, was confirmed by the House of Lords in *R v Hasan* [2005] UKHL 22.

Assuming duress of circumstances is established according to the tests outlined above, are there policy reasons that would prevent the defence being available to James? Duress *per minas* (by threats) is not a defence to murder—that much is clear from *R v Howe* [1987] 1 All ER 771. *R v Dudley and Stephens* (above) provides that necessity is not a defence to murder, but *R v Dudley and Stephens* is actually a case involving duress of circumstance, hence directly applicable to James' case. James would have no duress-based defence to a charge of murder. *Re A (Children) (Conjoined Twins: Surgical Separation)* [2000] 4 All ER 961, does envisage necessity being available as a defence to murder, but the key distinguishing point is that there the Court of Appeal was concerned with a situation where the doctors causing the death of one of the conjoined twins would not have been acting to save their own lives at the expense of another. James is clearly acting to save his own life at the expense of Norma's, hence *Re A (Children) (Conjoined Twins: Surgical Separation)* is not applicable.

If James is charged with unlawful act manslaughter duress of circumstances could be available as a defence—success will depend upon the extent to which the jury conclude that he acted as the reasonable person would have done.

Question 4

Critically assess the development of the defence of duress by threats.

 ## Commentary

This is one of the most controversial topics within the criminal law, the Law Commission's views being the opposite of two House of Lords' decisions.

The question requires an analysis of the defence of duress with reference to the uncertainties concerning its ingredients. There are many arguments justifying an extension of the defence to murder and these must be covered in detail, together with the counter-arguments of the House of Lords found mainly in *R v Howe* [1987] 1 All ER 771.

Because there is so much to cover candidates must avoid the pitfall of covering the facts of the key cases in detail. They are not important and there will not be enough time to do this.

 ## Answer plan

• Duress—definition

• Threats against whom?

- Types of threats
- Subjective and objective tests—*Hasan* [2005]
- Availability of *Howe* [1987]
- Gang membership—*Hasan* [2005]
- Law Commission No. 122

Suggested answer

The defence of duress *per minas* is available when the accused has been forced to commit a crime against his will. This is because 'threats of immediate death or serious personal violence so great as to overbear the ordinary power of human resistance should be accepted as a justification for acts which would otherwise be criminal' (*Attorney-General v Whelan* [1934] IR 518, *per* Murnaghan J). However, despite the fact that the defence has been recognized for many years, Lord Keith stated in *R v Gotts* [1992] 1 All ER 832, that 'the complexities and anomalies involved in the whole matter of the defence of duress seem to me to be such that the issue is much better left to Parliament to deal with in the light of broad considerations of policy'.

Lord Mackay also referred to these uncertainties in the leading House of Lords' decision in *R v Howe* [1987] 1 All ER 771, and used this argument in refusing to extend this defence to murder: 'I question whether the law has reached a sufficiently precise definition of that defence to make it right for us sitting in our judicial capacity to introduce it as a defence for an actual killer for the first time in the law of England.' There are many such uncertainties as was recently demonstrated in *R v Abdul Hussain and others* [1999] Crim LR 570 where the Court of Appeal decided that if the threat of death or grievous bodily harm was imminent (as opposed to immediate) duress could still be established. Nevertheless it is submitted that they could have been easily clarified by the House of Lords.

1. Who must be threatened?

Must the threat be against the accused, or is it sufficient if it is directed against a third party? In *Hurley v Murray* [1967] VR 526, the Supreme Court of Victoria held that threats to kill or seriously injure D's *de facto* wife amounted to duress. This was followed in *R v Hasan* [2005] UKHL 22, where Lord Bingham observed that the defence would be available where threats were made against the defendant or his family or a person for whom he reasonably feels responsible. It could be argued that there should not be any need for any connection between the defendant and the person threatened. A defendant can act in self-defence (i.e. use reasonable force) to protect a complete stranger against unlawful violence—see *R v Duffy* [1966] 1 All ER 62—hence the present limit on the scope of duress seems unprincipled.

2. The nature of the threat

A second question is whether or not threats of harm less than death or grievous bodily harm would be sufficient. In *R v Graham* [1982] 1 All ER 801 and in *R v Conway* [1988] 3 All ER 1025, the Court of Appeal required death or grievous bodily harm to be threatened; and more recently in *R v Baker and Wilkins* [1997] Crim LR 497, the Court of Appeal rejected serious psychological injury as being sufficient for duress of circumstances. The defence will not succeed if the threats are to damage property or cause financial loss. This seems to reflect a correct balancing of two evils where the defendant tries to rely on duress when charged with an offence against the person, but why not allow threats to property as the basis for the defence where the offence that the defendant is charged with is also an offence against property? If the duressor threatened to destroy the Mona Lisa unless D killed P's dog, why should D not have a duress defence to any subsequent charge of criminal damage arising from the destruction of the dog?

3. An avoidable threat

It is good public policy that a defendant should not be permitted to have the defence of duress put before the jury if he could in fact have negatived the threat by seeking protection from it. In the House of Lords in *R v Hasan* [2005] UKHL 22, Lord Bingham confirmed that juries should be directed that: 'if the retribution threatened against the defendant or his family or a person for whom he reasonably feels responsible is not such as he reasonably expects to follow immediately or almost immediately on his failure to comply with the threat, there may be little if any room for doubt that he could have taken evasive action, whether by going to the police or in some other way, to avoid committing the crime with which he is charged.'

Note the objective nature of the test. The defendant's failure to avail himself of protection must be based on a reasonable belief that this cannot be achieved. Again this could be open to criticism where the test takes insufficient account of the age, or frailty, of the defendant in any given case.

4. Defendant's belief in the efficacy of the threat

Again in *R v Hasan* [2005] UKHL 22, the House of Lords was asked to clarify whether or not a defendant's belief in the efficacy of the threats made by the duressor had to be reasonable. Lord Bingham noted that the model direction on duress as formulated in *R v Graham* and approved in *R v Howe* was 'he [the defendant] reasonably believed'. His Lordship saw no warrant for relaxing the requirement that the belief must be reasonable as well as genuine.

The issue of balancing public policy and fairness to the defendant arises again here. Restricting the scope of a defence that it is easy to raise and difficult to disprove is sound public policy, but the adoption of the subjective test runs largely counter to the trend in the common law development of individual liability, which concentrates on the defendant's fault, not what the reasonable person would have done or believed.

5. Extent to which the characteristics of the accused can be taken into account

As was recognized in *R v Graham*, the defence of duress fails if the prosecution prove that a person of reasonable firmness sharing the characteristics of the defendant would not have given way to the threats as did the defendant. This begs the question as to what characteristics of the accused the jury can take into account. In *R v Hegarty* [1994] Crim LR 353, the Court of Appeal stated that 'as the test predicted a sober person of reasonable firmness, there was no scope for attributing to that hypothetical person as one of the characteristics of the accused a pre-existing mental condition of being emotionally unstable or in a grossly elevated neurotic state'. Further, as Beldam LJ pointed out in *R v Hurst* [1995] 1 Cr App R 82, 'we find it hard to see how the person of reasonable firmness can be invested with the characteristics of a personality which lacks reasonable firmness'. Against this, however, the Court of Appeal in *R v Bowen* [1996] 4 All ER 837, has stated that if the accused was suffering from a recognized psychiatric illness, this characteristic could be taken into account. Curiously we now have a situation where the objective test for duress may be more favourable to the accused than the objective test for provocation. With the latter defence, *Attorney-General for Jersey v Holley* [2005] UKPC 23, takes the law on provocation back to the position whereby the defendant is judged according to the degree of self-control to be expected of the reasonable person—only the characteristics of age and sex being taken into account for these purposes. Unless there is some clearly articulated difference between duress and defence it could be argued that they ought to adopt the same position on the relevance of the defendant's characteristics. At the moment duress is a complete defence but has a more restrictive approach. Provocation, on the other hand, is a defence to murder, whereas duress is not— is this the basis for the difference in approach? It is all a bit of a muddle at present.

6. Voluntarily associating with criminals

The courts have long taken the view that a defendant who joins a violent criminal gang and subsequently finds himself forced by fellow gang members to commit offences should not be permitted to raise the defence of duress; see *R v Fitzpatrick* [1977] NI 20. The public policy is clear—any other rule would grant the greatest immunity to the defendant who joins the most violent and ruthless organization. Whilst this limitation was restricted to membership of terrorist organizations it was largely unobjectionable. Given the huge increase in the number of trials where duress is now raised, the courts have sought to extend the scope of this public policy rule, so that in *R v Hasan* [2005] UKHL 22, it was held that if a person voluntarily becomes or remains associated with others engaged in criminal activity in a situation where he knows or ought reasonably to know that he may be the subject of compulsion by them or their associates, he cannot rely on the defence of duress to excuse any act which he is thereafter compelled to do by them.

Note that the defendant no longer has to foresee himself being forced to commit crimes by his criminal associates in order to be denied the defence. It will suffice that he foresaw that he might be subject to compulsion. Note further that there is an ambiguity in the House of Lords' decision. Is the test objective or subjective? Will it suffice that the defendant *ought* to have foreseen that he might be subjected to compulsion? Although not arising directly on the facts in *R v Hasan*, the question arises as to whether the restrictive approach would extend to those cases of duress of circumstance where a drug addict becomes indebted to a drug dealer and is told that he will be killed if the debt is not paid. The drug dealer does not nominate a crime to be committed by the defendant, but the defendant is subject to compulsion and has voluntarily associated with criminals. Perhaps the driving force here is the public policy interest in deterring individuals from becoming involved with drug dealers—if they do so, duress will not be permitted if a situation such as that just described arises.

7. Duress and murder

Traditionally, duress has never been recognized as a defence to murder, *Blackstone's Commentaries on the Law of England* (1857) stating that a man under duress 'ought rather to die himself than escape by the murder of an innocent'. However, in *DPP for Northern Ireland v Lynch* [1975] AC 653, the House of Lords made an inroad into this blanket rule by holding that duress was available as a defence to an accused charged as an accomplice to murder, and shortly afterwards Lords Wilberforce and Edmund-Davies, in a much acclaimed minority judgment in the Privy Council decision in *Abbott v R* [1976] 3 All ER 140, concluded that the decision in *Lynch* should be extended to cover a principal offender. The Law Commission (Law Com. No. 83) also recommended this approach, but this trend was abruptly halted by the House of Lords in *R v Howe* where their Lordships not only confirmed the traditional approach, but also, using the Lord Chancellor's Practice Note [1966] 3 All ER 77, overruled their earlier decision in *Lynch*.

A number of reasons were given for this decision, although there are equally strong reasons for recognizing the defence. First, Lord Hailsham pointed out that following superior orders is not a defence to murder (Article 8 of the chapter of the International Military Treaty series no. 26 of 1946), and *R v Dudley and Stephens* [1881–5] All ER Rep 61 also ruled out the similar defence of necessity. It is submitted that both necessity and duress should be a defence to murder and that the analogy with superior orders is inappropriate.

Secondly, the principle underlying the denial of both defences (duress and necessity) is the special sanctity that the law attaches to human life and which denies a person the right to take an innocent life even at the price of his own or another's life. However, developments such as the Suicide Act 1961 and the House of Lords' decision in *Airedale NHS Trust v Bland* [1993] 1 All ER 821 have recognized that life does not have to be preserved at all costs, and it is not beneficial simply to adopt a blanket rule without good reason. Thus an accused should have the defence of duress considered if he or she was forced to take one life but in doing so save more. *Re A (Children) (Conjoined Twins: Surgical Separation)* [2000] 4 All ER 961, does envisage necessity being available as a defence to murder, precisely because the case concerned a situation where the doctors causing the death of one of the conjoined twins would not have been acting to save their own lives at the expense of another conjoined twin.

Thirdly, Lord Hailsham stated in *R v Howe* (at p. 579): 'I do not at all accept in relation to the defence of murder it is either good morals, good policy or good law... that the ordinary man of reasonable fortitude is not to be supposed to be capable of heroism if he is asked to take an innocent life rather than sacrifice his own'. However, as the Law Commission have recognized (Law Com. No. 122), it is not fair to expect the standard of the reasonable person to be one of heroism and it should be for the jury to decide if the threat was one which an accused could reasonably be expected to resist.

Two other weak arguments were also advanced for maintaining the *status quo*: first, Parliament has made no attempt to change the law despite the recommendations of the Law Commission, and therefore Parliament must be taken to agree with the present principle; and, secondly, any injustice that might result from application of the present law would be alleviated by the exercise of executive discretion not to prosecute or to release on licence a person serving a life sentence. It is submitted that reliance on executive discretion is not an adequate response in principle or practice; and as no Bill has been introduced proposing that duress be available as a defence to murder, Parliament has never had the opportunity of expressing an opinion on the matter. The Law Commission, in its Report 'Murder, Manslaughter and Infanticide' (Law Com. No. 304) in 2006 has reaffirmed its commitment to the view that duress should be a full defence to murder and attempted murder.

Although in *R v Kingston* [1994] 3 All ER 353, Lord Mustill in the House of Lords stated that 'the Court should when faced with a new problem acknowledge the justice of the case and boldly create a new common law defence', their Lordships again refused so to do in *R v Gotts* where duress was held to be not available as a defence to attempted murder. This approach continues to fly in the face of the Law Commission's recommendation (No. 122), the Commission believing that all uncertainties surrounding the defence could be removed by a clear statutory definition.

Shifting the burden of proof to the accused is another safeguard against unmeritorious defences succeeding; but leaving the law as it is, it is submitted, is the least satisfactory solution. This has been recognized by the Law Commission, who state: 'If however it were decided that duress should not be available as a complete defence, we would regard its statutory recognition as a partial defence reducing murder to manslaughter as the second best option.' Unsurprisingly, this view had already been rejected by the House of Lords in *Howe*.

Duress

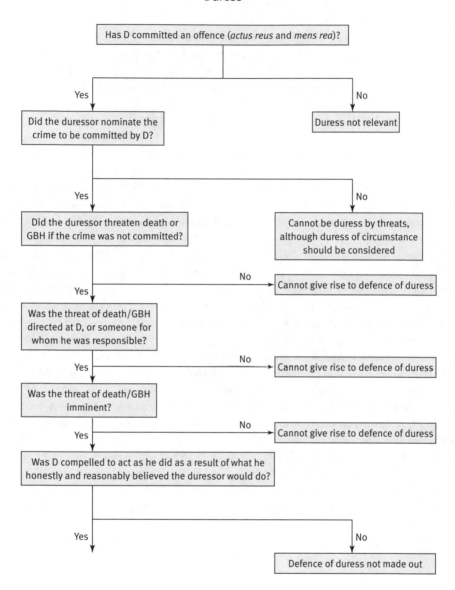

Continued

Continued from page 156.

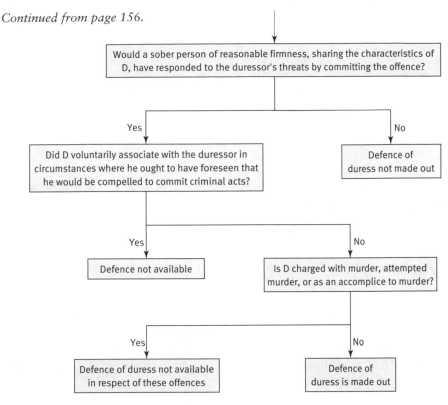

Further reading

Clarkson, C.M.V., 'Necessary Action: A New Defence' [2004] Crim LR 81.

Douglas, G.R., *'Dudley and Stephens*—Revisited and Updated', Justice of the Peace (Vol. 166) 40.

Douglas, G.R., 'Self-defence in the Light of *R v Martin*', Justice of the Peace (Vol. 166) 368.

Elliott, D.W., 'Necessity, Duress and Self-defence' [1989] Crim LR 611.

Rogers, J., 'Necessity, Private Defence and the Killing of Mary' [2001] Crim LR 515.

Smith, K.J.M., 'Duress and Steadfastness' [1999] Crim LR 363.

Wilson, A., 'Self-defence' [2006] 150 Sol Jo 524.

7

Inchoate offences and accessories

Introduction

Inchoate offences and issues of accessorial liability can feature on exam papers in the form of questions dealing with discrete topics, but typically they will feature as part of a problem question dealing with a range of substantive offences. For this reason candidates sometimes fail to prepare properly to deal with these areas. There is also the fact that accessorial liability is amongst the most confusing and conceptually difficult areas of criminal liability.

The inchoate offences are encouraging and assisting crime (under Part 2 of the Serious Crime Act 2007, which abolished the common law offence of incitement), conspiracy and attempt. It remains to be seen to what extent criminal law syllabuses cover the 2007 Act, but as it replaces incitement and overlaps significantly with the rules on accessorial liability, it is included here. The 2007 Act is a very complex piece of legislation, hence the solutions in this chapter do not necessarily go into every possible aspect of liability under that Act. The key is to provide examiners with a sensible overview of what the potential liability of a defendant might be under that 2007 Act. Conspiracy is now by and large a statutory offence based upon the Criminal Law Act 1977 as amended. It would be a surprise if an examiner set a problem question involving common law conspiracy to defraud, but candidates may want to have at least a working knowledge of it if only as a residual offence that might apply in theft and fraud questions where no other statutory offence seems to apply. Attempt is now a fairly straightforward offence following the enactment of the Criminal Attempts Act 1981. There may be queries regarding whether or not a defendant has got close enough to the commission of an offence to have committed the *actus reus* of attempt, but it should be borne in mind that this is, in any event, a question for the jury to determine. The task of candidates answering criminal law exam questions is to advise on the law that will be applied.

The abolition of incitement at common law means that impossibility has become a more straightforward issue than was previously the case, with a statutory solution in place for both attempt and statutory conspiracy.

As indicated above, accessorial liability can be a very complicated issue for candidates to deal with—largely because the law is not entirely logical in its approach, and because the case law is somewhat inconsistent in its treatment of the issues. Methodology is the key to finding a way through these complexities. Always start by identifying the liability of the principal offender. If candidates fail to do this the whole answer will be a muddle—it needs to be made clear what offence the accomplice is a party to.

Assuming the liability of the principal offender is dealt with, the next task is to identify the mode of participation. For the most part, the only really important distinctions are: (i) between procurers on the one hand and aiders, abettors and counsellors on the other; and (ii) between those accomplices involved in helping the principal offender prior to the commission of the offence, and those engaged in a joint enterprise at the scene of the crime. For procuring, the prosecution will have to prove a causative link between the accomplice's acts and the commission of the offence, along with an intention that the offence be committed. With the other forms of accessorial liability, a causal link will suffice along with contemplation of the type of offence committed by the principal offender. The joint enterprise distinction is one that has emerged largely in respect of murder and manslaughter cases. On the basis of *R v Powell and Daniels* [1997] 4 All ER 545, a defendant can be convicted as an accomplice to murder provided he foresaw the possibility that the principal offender might kill or cause grievous bodily harm with intent to kill or cause grievous bodily harm. If the accomplice intended the death of the victim, it matters not if the principal offender actually caused death by a means not contemplated by the accomplice. Where, however, the accomplice contemplated only that the principal offender might kill or intentionally cause grievous bodily harm, complications can arise if the evidence reveals that the principal offender caused death by taking steps that went beyond the actions foreseen by the accomplice.

Suppose, for example, that an accomplice contemplates the principal offender attacking the victim with a piece of wood, intending thereby to cause the victim grievous bodily harm. The principal offender then decides of his own volition to use a gun to shoot the victim through the head, fatally injuring him. The accomplice obviously contemplated grievous bodily harm, he may even have foreseen the risk that death might result from the grievous bodily harm, but he will not incur any liability in respect of the murder as the death results from deliberate actions by the principal offender that are fundamentally different and more dangerous than those contemplated by the accomplice as part of the joint enterprise. In terms of 'just deserts' candidates find this confusing as the accomplice was clearly willing to be involved in some wrongdoing. The key to understanding the logic of the outcome is to remember that in using the gun the principal offender is effectively 'off on a frolic of his own' to borrow a phrase from the law of torts. Issues of accessorial liability in respect of murder cease to arise because the principal is now acting independently of the accomplice. The example given is a simple clear-cut one. In real life, and sometimes in exam questions, the facts are far more challenging. What if the accomplice is at the scene and sees the principal produce the gun? Does the accomplice's failure to stop the use of the gun suggest he is adopting the actions of the principal offender? Can the nature of the joint enterprise evolve as the crime develops? Suppose the joint enterprise is to scare the victim with a loaded gun, causing him grievous bodily harm by hitting him with it. The principal offender fires the gun killing the victim.

The principal offender claims it was an accident. If this is true he will be guilty of manslaughter and so will his accomplice. The accomplice, on the other hand, might argue that the firing of the gun was deliberate—this would mean the principal was guilty of murder, and possibly that the accomplice escapes liability altogether if he can show that firing the gun was a deliberate departure from the common design. These examples only scratch the surface of the possible complexities, but they give a flavour as to why this is a fascinating topic for legal academics, and a frightening one for exam candidates! Bear in mind that in many cases, a defendant who is an accomplice can also be charged under Part 2 of the Serious Crime Act 2007 with assisting in the commission of an offence—these possibilities are flagged in general terms in the solutions that follow.

Question 1

Amy, Betty, Claire, and Debbie plan to break into X's warehouse in order to steal. Amy, Betty, and Claire know that there will be a night-watchman on the premises, but Debbie does not know this fact. Amy gives Betty a loaded revolver, telling her not to hesitate to use it if the occasion should so require. When they set off to X's warehouse, Debbie knows that Betty has a revolver in her possession but Claire does not. Once inside the warehouse the four are interrupted by the night-watchman, Victor. As Betty is about to fire the revolver at Victor, Amy, recognizing Victor as her cousin, knocks Betty's hand to one side crying out 'Don't shoot'. Amy's act causes the bullet to miss Victor, but it strikes and kills Peter, a police officer who is entering the room.
    Discuss the criminal liability of the parties.

 Commentary

This is a complex and challenging question. There are various ways in which an answer could be structured, but the preferable approach is to take the liability of Betty first and deal with her as the principal offender. Bear in mind that the facts leave open whether her liability could be for murder or manslaughter in respect of the death of Peter, complicating the answer considerably. Betty does not kill Victor, but attempted murder must be covered. Consideration of the other three defendants involves looking at variations upon the *R v Powell and Daniels* **[1997] 4 All ER 545** problem. If Amy, Claire, or Betty intend the death of the night-watchman in the course of the joint enterprise it matters not how this comes about. If, however, they contemplate that, in the course of their joint enterprise, the night-watchman might be killed by a co-principal acting with the *mens rea* for murder, thought needs to be given to whether or not Betty deliberately exceeded the scope of the joint enterprise. This is where the accomplices' knowledge of the gun, or of Victor's presence becomes crucial. Although homicide is the main substantive offence it is necessary to point out that there are burglary offences committed here, possibly aggravated by possession of the gun. Although the conspiracy is mentioned first in the question it is perhaps best to leave inchoate offences until the end and present them as alternatives to other forms of accessorial liability. A comprehensive model answer to this question would be very lengthy indeed but would not provide any realistic indication of what could be achieved in a typical exam scenario—hence consideration of some of the more abstruse aspects of liability is deliberately curtailed in the answer that follows, the focus being on the main aspects of liability.

 ## Answer plan

- Betty's liability as a principal offender

  - burglary

  - attempted murder

  - murder and manslaughter

- Amy's liability—burglary

  - as an accomplice to attempted murder—does she withdraw?

  - as an accomplice to murder or manslaughter

- Liability of Claire and Debbie—accomplices to murder or manslaughter

- Residual inchoate offences

Suggested answer

Betty's liability

Betty kills Peter by causing his death in fact and in law. The fact that Amy grabs her arm to stop her firing at Victor does not amount to a *novus actus interveniens*. Even though her gun points at Peter not Victor, her pulling the trigger is still a voluntary act. The *mens rea* of murder is satisfied by the prosecution proving that Betty intended to kill or intended to cause grievous bodily harm (*R v Moloney* [1985] 1 All ER 1025). Following *R v Woollin* [1998] 4 All ER 103, the jury should be directed that they will be entitled to infer that Betty intended to kill if there is evidence that she foresaw death or grievous bodily harm as virtually certain to result from her actions. Given that Betty was intending to fire the revolver at Victor, foresight of some grievous bodily harm on her part seems evident.

Betty may argue that, as she intended to fire the gun at Victor, she did not intend to harm Peter. The court will apply the doctrine of transferred malice. Thus if the accused has the necessary *mens rea* of the offence, but the actual victim is different from the intended victim, the *mens rea* will be transferred and the accused will be guilty (*R v Mitchell* [1983] 2 All ER 427).

Betty might argue that she was simply firing a warning shot in Victor's direction, and that it was Amy's act of hitting her arm, which caused her aim to alter, resulting in Peter's death. In the unlikely event of this argument being accepted, Betty would still be guilty of involuntary (unlawful act) manslaughter on the constructive basis. The prosecution would need to prove that Betty intended to do an act that was unlawful and dangerous (*R v Newbury and Jones* [1976] 2 All ER 365). Simply drawing and pointing a gun at someone would be unlawful, i.e., assault; and as the test for dangerous is objective ('the unlawful act must be such as all sober and reasonable people would inevitably recognize must subject the other person to at least the risk of some physical harm resulting therefrom, albeit not serious harm' *per* Edmund Davies J in *R v Church* [1965] 2 All ER 72), this element of the offence would be made out. The intention to assault is evident.

In light of the above it should be noted that Betty might also have incurred liability for attempting to murder Victor, contrary to s. 1(1) of the Criminal Attempts Act 1981. There is evidence to support the assertion that she takes steps more than merely preparatory to killing Victor (indeed she seems to have committed the 'last act' within her power). The *mens rea*, however, requires proof that she intended to kill Victor—intention to cause grievous bodily harm will not suffice for a charge of attempted murder; see *R v Walker and Hayles* (1989) 90 Cr App R 226. For reasons outlined above, proof of this might be doubtful unless she confesses that killing him was her intention.

Although Betty's main liability would be for homicide of some sort, it should be noted that she commits a s. 9(1)(a) **Theft Act 1968** burglary when she enters the warehouse as a trespasser intending to steal and, because she is armed, could be charged with the more serious offence of aggravated burglary under s. 10 of the Theft Act 1968.

Amy's liability

Amy will, in all likelihood, be guilty of a s. 9(1)(a) Theft Act 1968 burglary, as outlined above. She could also be charged with counselling Betty's offence of aggravated burglary under s. 10 of the Theft Act 1968. Amy encourages Betty to go armed with the gun and it is her intention that Betty should do so.

Turning to Amy's liability in relation to the death of Peter, it could be argued that she incurs liability as a principal offender, as she does contribute to causing his death; but for her pushing Amy's hand to one side Peter would not have been killed. Her actions in causing the gun to be fired at Peter can also be seen as the operating and substantial cause of his death. *Mens rea* would be problematic, however, as her intention when she pushes Betty's hand is to prevent harm. There is no evidence that she intends any harm to occur to Peter as opposed to Victor. Indeed it might be impossible to identify any fault that would suffice for her to be convicted of a form of manslaughter as principal offender. There is no obvious dangerous criminal act as is required for unlawful act manslaughter, and it is far from obvious that the duty of care and grossly negligent breach of duty of care needed for killing by gross negligence can be identified.

The prosecution will almost certainly seek to charge Amy with either the murder or manslaughter of Peter as an accomplice to Betty's actions. Amy supplies Betty with a loaded gun, knowing that there is a night-watchman on the premises. There is compelling evidence on these facts that she contemplates a scenario in which the gun will be discharged by Betty—especially given the evidence that she told Betty to use the gun if necessary. At the very least Amy contemplated that Betty might kill or do grievous bodily harm either with intent to kill or with intent to do grievous bodily harm. In *R v Powell and Daniels*; *R v English* [1997] 4 All ER 545 the House of Lords held that, to found a conviction for murder, it was sufficient for a secondary party to have realized, in the course of a joint enterprise, that the primary party might kill with intent to do so or with intent to cause grievous bodily harm. On this basis, therefore, Amy could be convicted as an accomplice to the murder of Peter if she foresaw the possibility of Betty intentionally killing someone, or intentionally causing grievous bodily harm.

Could Amy argue that she contemplated harm being caused to a guard at the warehouse (such as Victor) but not a police officer called to the scene? Normally in criminal law, the identity of the victim is irrelevant, the doctrine of transferred malice applying. In respect of accessorial liability, however, there is authority to support the view that the identity of the victim can be material, if the joint enterprise is aimed at a specific victim; see *R v Saunders and Archer* (1573) 2 Plowd 473. In the present case, there is no evidence to suggest that the death of Peter is caused by Betty deliberately choosing a different victim—hence this argument will not avail Amy.

If Betty was found guilty of manslaughter, Amy might contend that she could not be found guilty as an accomplice to murder. This point arose in the Privy Council case of *Hui Chi Ming v R* [1991] 3 All ER 897, where the court upheld the conviction of the accused for murder even though the principal offenders had in an earlier trial been found guilty of manslaughter only. The principle is that if the *actus reus* has been committed, the court will look at the *mens rea* of the individual participants in order to ascertain their criminal responsibility.

In the event that there is any difficulty in establishing the *mens rea* of Amy as an accomplice to murder, the prosecution is most likely to contend that Amy incurs liability as an accomplice to the manslaughter of Peter by Betty on the basis that his death was an unforeseen and accidental consequence of the common design (committing a burglary armed with a loaded weapon) being carried out. Both *R v Betts and Ridley* (1930) 22 Cr App R 148, and *R v Baldessare* (1930) 22 Cr App R 70, support the conclusion that an accomplice will be a party to the accidental consequences of the principal offender's acts, provided the principal offender's actions were within the scope of what the accomplice contemplated or agreed. In *R v Baldessare*, the court held that an accused who agreed to take and drive away a car was guilty of abetting manslaughter when the principal offender drove so negligently as to cause a pedestrian's death, as although this consequence was unforeseen it arose when the principal offender was acting within the scope of the agreement.

As noted above, Betty could be charged with the attempted murder of Victor. Similarly Amy could be charged as an accomplice to the attempted murder—for an example of accessorial liability for attempt see *R v Dunnington* [1984] QB 472.

The facts indicate that Amy does try to stop Betty firing at Victor. Hence Amy may argue that, notwithstanding her supply of the gun, she had, at the last minute withdrawn from the joint enterprise, and should not incur any liability as an accomplice to the attempted murder. The key case on withdrawal is *R v Becerra and Cooper* (1975) 62 Cr App R 212, where before the principal offender in the course of a burglary killed the victim, the accomplice had said 'Come on let's go' and had left the building. The Court of Appeal, in upholding his conviction for murder, held that something vastly more substantial and effective was required to constitute a valid withdrawal, such as shouting a warning or physical intervention. Amy would argue that in shouting 'Don't shoot' and knocking Betty's hand, she had done all that she reasonably could to prevent the crime. It will be a question of fact for the jury to determine whether or not this is the case. As was confirmed in *R v O'Flaherty* [2004] Crim LR 751, whether or not withdrawal is effective is a matter of fact and degree. The later it is left the more is required by way of positive action.

Claire's liability

As with Amy, Claire could be charged under s. 9(1)(a) Theft Act 1968 as a principal offender. As she does not know Betty had the gun the prosecution would not charge her as an accomplice to Betty's offence of aggravated burglary under s. 10 of the Theft Act 1968.

Claire knew that there was a night-watchman on the premises, providing evidence that she did contemplate some harm being caused to him if the burglary was to succeed. For her to be convicted of murder there would have to be evidence that she at least contemplated death or grievous bodily harm being caused with the necessary *mens rea* for murder; see *R v Powell and Daniels*; *R v English* [1997] 4 All ER 545. The key point for Claire would be the use of the weapon. Provided she did not intend the death of any person, she could avail herself of the 'fundamentally different' rule, under which even an accomplice who contemplates that death or serious injury might occur, can escape liability if the principal offender causes death by the use of a fundamentally different (more dangerous) *modus operandi*—such as the use of a gun instead of a cosh.

If Claire contemplated some harm being caused to a person, not amounting to actual bodily harm, she could be convicted as an accomplice to manslaughter on the given facts, but again she would escape liability if she was able to avail herself of the 'fundamentally different' rule; see *Attorney-General's Ref (No 3 of 2004)* [2005] EWCA Crim 1882.

Debbie's liability

Debbie could be charged with offences contrary to s. 9(1)(a) Theft Act 1968 burglary, as outlined above, and as an accomplice to Betty's offence of aggravated burglary under s. 10 of the Theft Act 1968.

Regarding accessorial liability for homicide, Debbie's position is slightly different from Claire's. Debbie knows about the gun, but not that there will be a night-watchman. It is submitted that her knowledge regarding the gun will put her in a much worse position than Claire however. The prosecution will argue that as she knew about the gun she contemplated its use—why else did she think Betty was taking it? Regarding her liability both as an accomplice to the attempted murder of Victor, and the murder of Peter, in order to escape liability Debbie would be forced to use the weak argument that although she knew that Betty had a gun, she did not contemplate that Betty would actually use it. Applying *R v Powell and Daniels*; *R v English* [1997] 4 All ER 545, considered above, Debbie could be held to have had sufficient *mens rea* to be an accomplice to the murder of Peter, and the attempted murder of Victor. If the prosecution cannot establish that Debbie had the requisite *mens rea*, she might still be convicted as an accomplice to the manslaughter of Peter, as explained above in relation to Amy.

Other inchoate offences

Even before the four parties enter the warehouse, they would be guilty of the crime of conspiracy to burgle under s. 1 of the Criminal Law Act 1977, as they have agreed to pursue a course of conduct which would necessarily involve a criminal offence. Amy would also be guilty of encouraging and assisting Betty to commit burglary, assault, and possibly murder when supplying her with the gun and encouraging her to use it; see s. 46 of the Serious Crime Act 2007.

Question 2

Alf planned to beat up Steve. Barry, Chris, and Desmond told Alf that they would help him. On the appointed day, Barry failed to turn up, but Chris and Desmond held Steve while Alf hit him causing some minor bruising. Chris then said 'I can't do this anymore' and walked away to the other side of the room. Shortly after, Desmond said 'Come on let's go' and he left with Chris. Alf then hit Steve again, breaking his jaw.

　Discuss the criminal responsibility of the parties.

 Commentary

A fairly straightforward question combining accessorial liability with conspiracy. Candidates should deal with Alf's liability for the actual bodily harm before turning to consider the potential accessorial liability of the other parties. Withdrawal from the criminal enterprise features largely in this question and should be considered in some depth. It makes sense to deal with the broken jaw as a discrete incident as the accessorial liability issues may not be the same in respect of this incident. Leave the residual conspiracy charge to the end of the answer, as this is an alternative for the prosecution should any elements of substantive liability prove problematic.

Answer plan

- Alf's liability for the **s. 47** offence
- Accessorial liability of Chris and Desmond at the scene of the crime
- Whether Barry has withdrawn by not attending
- Alf's liability for **s. 18, Offences Against the Person Act 1861**
- Accessorial liability of Barry, Chris, and Desmond for the **s. 18** offence
- Issues of withdrawal reconsidered
- *Rook* [1993], *Baker* [1994]
- Conspiracy and offences under **Part 2 of the Serious Crime Act 2007**

Suggested answer

Actual bodily harm by Alf

Alf, when he deliberately hits Steve causing him some bruising, could be guilty of assault occasioning actual bodily harm under s. 47 of the Offences Against the Person Act 1861. *R v Miller* [1954] 2 QB 282 confirms (*per* Lynskey J) that actual bodily harm encompasses any hurt or injury calculated to interfere with the health or comfort of the victim. The actual bodily harm can be caused by an assault in the narrow sense but the facts indicate that Alf has committed a battery, which will suffice. The *mens rea* required was confirmed in *R v Savage; R v Parmenter* [1992] 1 AC 699, as intention or recklessness as to whether the victim suffered a battery or apprehended immediate physical violence. The recklessness here is subjective, meaning the defendant must at least have contemplated the risk that the victim would suffer an assault or battery. It will not avail Alf to argue that he did not foresee actual bodily harm. Liability under s. 47 is constructive, meaning that the accused only needs *mens rea* for the assault that causes the actual bodily harm, as opposed to foreseeing the actual bodily harm itself.

Accessorial liability of Chris and Desmond

Chris and Desmond could be charged as accomplices to Alf's s. 47 offence. Under s. 8 of the Accessories and Abettors Act 1861: 'Whosoever shall aid, abet, counsel, or procure the commission of any misdemeanour whether the same be a misdemeanour at common law or by virtue of any Act passed or to be passed, shall be liable to be tried, indicted, and punished as a principal offender'.

By holding Steve down, Chris and Desmond are clearly aiding and abetting Alf's offence at the scene of the crime. On the basis of *R v Bainbridge* [1959] 3 All ER 200, and *R v Bryce* [2004] EWCA Crim 1231, the prosecution must prove that the accomplices did the acts (constituting the participation) deliberately, realizing that their acts were capable of assisting the offence by Alf. It will suffice that they each contemplate Alf's offence as a real possibility. Given that there has been an agreement to beat up Steve, it would seem to be evident that the elements of accessorial liability are established here.

Withdrawal by Barry and Chris

Barry fails to attend at the appointed time and therefore does not take part in the attack on Steve. Chris pulls out after Steve has suffered minor bruising. On these facts, Chris has left it too late to disassociate himself from the actual bodily harm suffered by Steve, but Barry has a stronger case. Even though not present at the scene Barry could still be an accomplice on the basis that he counselled the commission of the s. 47 offence. Following *R v Calhaem* [1985] 2 All ER 266, as confirmed in *R v Luffman* [2008] EWCA Crim 1379, it will suffice that Barry contemplated the s. 47 offence, and that when Alf committed it he was acting within the scope of Barry's authority or encouragement. The problem for Barry is that although he fails to turn up as agreed, he does not take active steps to prevent the commission of the offence by the other defendants. In *R v Rook* [1993] 2 All ER 955, the Court of Appeal, on similar facts, stated that the defendant's absence on the day could not possibly amount to an unequivocal communication of his withdrawal. As Rook knew that there was a real risk that the murder would take place, his conviction was upheld. In order to constitute a valid withdrawal there must be evidence that the accomplice has taken all reasonable steps unequivocally to abandon the enterprise. This will depend on the accomplice's involvement. Thus in *R v Whitefield* (1984) 79 Cr App R 36, where the accomplice had given the principal offender information that would enable him to commit burglary, the Court of Appeal recognized that a valid withdrawal could be effected by the accomplice simply telling the principal offender that he was no longer prepared to assist. It is submitted that the court would take an unsympathetic view of Barry's withdrawal argument—given that he could have gone to the police to warn them of the planned attack (albeit at the risk of exposing himself to conspiracy or incitement charges—see below).

Alf's liability for grievous bodily harm

When Alf hits Steve causing Steve's jaw to break he almost certainly commits grievous bodily harm. The most serious form of the offence would be a charge under s. 18 of the 1861 Act, wounding or causing grievous bodily harm with intent. Whether a broken jaw would amount to grievous bodily harm is a question of fact for the jury, but in *R v Wood* (1830) 1 Mood CC 278, a broken collar bone was held to constitute grievous bodily harm; see further *R v Doyle* [2004] EWCA Crim 2714. Under s. 18 the prosecution also must establish that Alf intended to cause grievous bodily harm, but it appears from the facts of the question that either this was Alf's purpose, or he knew that grievous bodily harm was a virtual certainty, and this would be sufficient. The House of Lords stated in *R v Moloney* [1985] 1 All ER 1025 that as 'intention' is a word in common use, the trial judge should simply leave it to the jury without giving them an involved direction unless the issue on the facts of the case is complicated. It is submitted that the jury would not require guidance on these facts and would be most likely to convict Alf under s. 18. See further *R v Woollin* [1998] 4 All ER 103, which presumably applies here to the extent that Alf's foreseeing grievous bodily harm as virtually certain would be evidence of his intention to cause the harm.

In the unlikely event of the prosecution not being able to establish the intention required for s. 18, Alf would be convicted under s. 20 of the 1861 Act (wounding or inflicting grievous bodily harm maliciously). The *mens rea* 'maliciously' would be established by proof that Alf foresaw the risk of some physical harm occurring to Steve (see *R v Savage*; *R v Parmenter*). Again, the *mens rea* seems evident on the facts.

Withdrawal by Barry, Chris, and Desmond

Whether or not Barry would be an accomplice to the s. 18 or s. 20 offences depends on the outcome of the discussion above in respect of his failure to attend as agreed and whether or not this is evidence of his having effectively withdrawn. If his withdrawal argument fails, he will contend that he did not contemplate grievous bodily harm, and thus lacked the *mens rea* to be an accomplice to the more serious assaults committed by Alf. Whether or not he had this contemplation is a question of fact to be determined by the jury. If Alf deliberately exceeded the scope of what was agreed in terms of beating up Steve, Barry will not be an accomplice. Unfortunately the facts given do not provide enough evidence to resolve this. Alf does not use a weapon to break Steve's jaw. The crucial issue will be whether or not there was an express or implied agreement that the harm caused would not exceed the legal definition of actual bodily harm.

Chris and Desmond leave the scene before Alf breaks Steve's jaw. They would rely on this as evidence of their having withdrawn from any subsequent harm that Alf caused to Steve. In *R v Becerra* (1975) 62 Cr App R 212, the leading case on withdrawal, the Court of Appeal stated that something vastly more substantial and effective was required than simply saying 'Come on let's go' and leaving, where the accomplice had given the principal offender a weapon, which he later used to kill a night-watchman who interrupted their burglary. The court stated that to be an effective withdrawal, the accomplice should have tried to recover the weapon, shouted a warning to the victim, or physically intervened to prevent the attack. Similarly in *R v Baker* [1994] Crim LR 444, the Court of Appeal, in upholding a murder conviction, stated that an accomplice who had moved a few feet away from the spot where the victim was killed, uttering words 'I'm not doing it', had given far from unequivocal notice that he was wholly disassociating himself from the entire enterprise and had not effected a valid withdrawal.

These authorities would suggest that Chris and Desmond might not have done enough to effectively withdraw from being accomplices to the more serious assaults on Steve. Again, they make no attempt to prevent further harm to Steve. As explained above in respect of Barry, if their withdrawal argument fails, their accessorial liability in respect of the broken jaw will hinge upon the extent to which it involved a deliberate escalation of harm by Alf going beyond what was agreed as part of the joint enterprise.

Conspiracy

All four defendants could be charged with conspiracy to commit some form of assault, contrary to s. 1 of the Criminal Law Act 1977. There is clearly an agreement on a course of conduct which, if carried out in accordance with their intentions, would necessarily result in the commission of a criminal offence. Barry may try to argue that his failure to attend as agreed is evidence that he never really agreed to the assault, but *R v Siracusa* (1989) 90 Cr App R 340, makes clear that agreement can be inferred if it is proved that the defendant knew what was planned and his intention to participate in the furtherance of the criminal purpose can be established by his failure to stop the unlawful activity. In effect, therefore, Barry's initial agreement and his failure to prevent the plan being carried out would be sufficient to uphold his conviction for conspiracy.

Serious Crime Act 2007

Barry, Chris, and Desmond all agree to help Alf to attack Steve, hence all three could incur liability under s. 44 of the Serious Crime Act 2007 for encouraging the commission of an offence. The fact that the attack is actually carried out is no bar to liability under the 2007 Act. The s. 44 offence requires proof that the defendant intended the principal offender to commit a specific offence. Given the vagueness surrounding the plan to 'beat up' Steve, a charge under s. 46 might be more appropriate as this deals with the situation where the defendant encourages one or more offences, believing that any one of them will be committed by the principal offender. The s. 46 offence may be particularly appropriate in the case of Barry, who fails to turn up at all.

Question 3

Alvin contacted Bernard suggesting that they kill Zac because he had refused to pay them a debt. After hearing Alvin's proposals, Bernard secretly decided that he would not do anything to help Alvin, but he told Alvin that he would do anything he could to assist. Their conversation was overheard by Ceri and Desmond, who both agreed to help. Ceri obtained a loaded revolver and gave it to Alvin, and Desmond agreed to drive them in his car to Zac's house.

On the appointed day, Bernard failed to arrive; and after Desmond had taken them to their destination he telephoned the police in time to stop Alvin shooting at Zac.

Discuss the criminal responsibility of the parties.

 Commentary

This is a relatively straightforward question concerning the inchoate offences and accessorial liability. The two areas often overlap, but in practice if the substantive offence is attempted or committed the Crown Prosecution Service should normally charge those not involved as principal as accomplices. The alternative is to charge them with various inchoate offences.

This question requires candidates to consider offences of encouraging and assisting crime under the **Serious Crime Act 2007**, conspiracy and attempt with regard to Alvin, although, as there is little factual information surrounding the attempted shooting, candidates cannot deal with this topic in great detail. The other defendants may be guilty of conspiracy, and for Bernard consideration must be given to the troublesome House of Lords' decision in *R v Anderson* [1985] 2 All ER 961 as interpreted by the Court of Appeal in *R v Siracusa* (1989) 90 Cr App R 340.

Lastly, the position of the parties' liability for abetting must be considered, in particular whether there is an offence of aiding and abetting an attempt.

Answer plan

- Encouraging the commission of crime—**Serious Crime Act 2007**
- Conspiracy to murder

  - *Anderson* [1985], *Siracusa* [1989]
- Attempted murder

  - s. 1(1), **Criminal Attempts Act 1981**
- Accomplice liability

Suggested answer

There are a number of inchoate offences with which Alvin could be charged. His initial action in contacting Bernard suggesting that they kill Zac could amount to the crime of encouraging murder, contrary to s. 44 of the Serious Crime Act 2007. Alvin clearly intends the offence of murder should be committed and that the necessary course of conduct should be followed with the requisite fault element for murder. Liability is inchoate, so the fact that the killing never takes place is irrelevant. The offence focuses on Alvin's state of mind—hence the fact that Bernard does not want to go through with the plan will be no bar to liability.

All four participants could be charged with conspiracy to murder under s. 1 of the Criminal Law Act 1977. Formerly conspiracy was a common law offence, but since 1977 the only remaining common law conspiracies are conspiracy to defraud, conspiracy to corrupt public morals, and conspiracy to outrage public decency (see *Shaw v DPP* [1961] 2 All ER 446). In order to establish a statutory conspiracy, it must be shown that two or more persons agreed that a course of conduct should be pursued which, if the agreement were to be carried out in accordance with their intentions, either:

(a) would necessarily amount to or involve the commission of any offence or offences by one or more of the parties to the agreement; or

(b) would do so but for the existence of facts which render the commission of the offence or any of the offences impossible.

The prosecution must prove that an agreement existed between the parties, and if they are still in the course of negotiations this would not be sufficient. It is submitted that there is an agreement on the facts and, as they intend that death will result, the parties could be guilty of conspiracy to murder. However, Bernard will argue that as he had no intention to assist, and did nothing to assist, he cannot be guilty. The key case on this point is the House of Lords' decision in *R v Anderson* [1985] 2 All ER 961. In this case the accused was convicted of conspiring with a number of people to help one of them escape from jail. He had agreed to supply wire to cut the prison bars, but said he never intended the plan to be put into effect and believed that it could not possibly succeed. However, his conviction was upheld as he had agreed that the criminal course of conduct should be pursued, and it was not necessary to prove that he intended that the offence be committed. In this case Lord Bridge also stated (at p. 965) that the *mens rea* of conspiracy is established 'if and only if it is shown that the accused when he entered into the agreement, intended to play some part in the agreed course of conduct in furtherance of the criminal purpose which the agreed course of conduct was intended to achieve'. On this basis Bernard would have a defence, but unfortunately for him Lord Bridge's *dictum* was clarified by the Court of Appeal decision in *R v Siracusa* (1989) 90 Cr App R 340, where O'Connor J stated that 'participation in a conspiracy is infinitely variable: it can be active or passive. There is no need for the prosecution to prove an intention on each accused's part in the carrying out of the agreement'. It is submitted that Bernard would therefore be found guilty of conspiracy to murder.

Desmond may also be able to argue that he lacked the *mens rea* for conspiracy to murder, as his informing the police demonstrated that he had an intention to frustrate the intention of the conspiracy. In *R v McPhillips* [1990] 6 BNIL, Lord Lowry CJ in the Court of Appeal of Northern Ireland, held that an accused who had joined in a conspiracy to plant a bomb, timed to explode on the roof of a hall of a disco, was not a party to a conspiracy to murder because he intended to give a warning in time for the hall to be cleared. However, in *Yip Chiu Cheung v R* [1994] 2 All ER 924, the Privy Council held that an undercover police officer posing as a drug dealer would have the necessary *mens rea* for conspiracy, when he deliberately carried drugs to entrap other drug dealers. Neither his good motive nor the instructions of his superiors would have been a valid defence.

Bernard may incur liability under s. 45 of the Serious Crime Act 2007 on the basis that he does encourage Alvin by saying he would assist in the murder. The question for the jury will be whether or not there is evidence that Bernard believed that the offence would be committed, and that his actions would encourage or assist its commission. The fact that he did not intend to help does not necessarily mean that his apparent enthusiasm was not capable of encouraging the others. As to *mens rea*, it would suffice that Bernard believed that, were the killing of Zac to take place, it would be done with the fault required for murder.

As withdrawal is recognized as a defence for an accomplice, it is submitted that a conspirator should have a similar defence, if only to provide an incentive for a conspirator to make efforts to stop the conspiracy succeeding. It is submitted that Desmond should not be found guilty of conspiracy. Perhaps the Crown Prosecution Service would decide it is not in the public interest to prosecute Desmond, and instead make him chief prosecution witness!

Alvin may also be guilty of attempted murder. Clearly he has the necessary *mens rea,* an intention to kill (*R v Whybrow* (1951) 35 Cr App R 141), but has he committed the *actus reus* of attempt? The test the prosecution must satisfy under s. 1(1) of the Criminal Attempts Act 1981 is that the accused has done an act that is more than merely preparatory to the offence. This is a question of fact for the jury after the trial judge has decided that there is sufficient evidence to be left to them to support such a finding. Thus in *R v Jones* (1990) 91 Cr App R 356, the Court of Appeal upheld the jury's decision that the accused had done more than a merely preparatory act for attempted murder in pointing a sawn-off shotgun at the victim, even though he had still to remove the safety catch. Whether Alvin would be guilty of attempted murder would therefore purely depend on what precise point the plan had reached before he was stopped.

Bernard, Ceri, and Desmond may also face charges under the Accessories and Abettors Act 1861 of counselling, procuring, aiding and abetting. It is often difficult to identify precisely the specific involvement (see *R v Richards* [1974] 3 All ER 1088), but counselling and procuring are acts done before the principal offence whereas aiding and abetting take place at the time of its occurrence. Clearly, as they intended to assist and contemplated the type of crime (*Chan Wing Siu v R* [1984] 3 All ER 877) they appear to have the necessary *mens rea*. Desmond would argue that he had validly withdrawn by contacting the police in time for them to stop the murder (*R v Becerra* (1975) 62 Cr App R 212), and Bernard would contend that his failure to arrive constituted a withdrawal. It is submitted that whereas Desmond's argument would succeed, Bernard's would fail as in *R v Rook* [1993] 2 All ER 955 the Court of Appeal held merely not turning up to be insufficient, suggesting that a positive act may be required. As was confirmed in *R v O'Flaherty* [2004] Crim LR 751, whether or not withdrawal is effective is a matter of fact and degree. The later it is left the more is required by way of positive action.

Ceri does not appear to have any defence available, and his act of giving Alvin a loaded gun satisfies the ingredients of this offence.

Thus, Ceri and Bernard could be found guilty of abetting an attempted murder. Although the offence of attempt to aid and abet was abolished by s. 5 of the Criminal Law Act 1977, there is an offence of attempting to abet (see *R v Dunnington* [1984] 1 All ER 676).

Ceri and Desmond could also incur liability under s. 45 of the Serious Crime Act 2007 (see Bernard above) on the basis of their offering to help Alvin. Again this would be seen as committing acts capable of encouraging murder, intending that Alvin should commit murder.

Question 4

Kirk hires Miles and Chaka to attack Patti, a business rival. Kirk makes it clear that he wants Patti frightened off so that she will no longer be a threat to Kirk's business. One evening Miles and Chaka follow Patti as she leaves her office to go home at the end of the day. Miles picks up a large stone from the gutter, grabs Patti from behind and beats her on the head with the stone. Patti dies of a brain haemorrhage. Chaka is standing close to Miles as he carries out the attack and does not take steps to intervene and stop him.

Kirk, Miles, and Chaka are subsequently arrested in connection with Patti's death. Under questioning Chaka admits that she knew Miles had a history of violent behaviour and previous convictions for grievous bodily harm, but claims that she had no idea Miles had a stone in his hand when he hit Patti. Kirk admits hiring Miles and Chaka to frighten Patti but denies any intention that Patti should be physically harmed.

Advise the Crown Prosecution Service as to the criminal liability of Kirk, Miles, and Chaka in respect of the death of Patti.

Commentary

The main thrust of this question relates to the complex issues surrounding accessorial liability, and candidates should give due weight to this in their answers. Note that the facts are vague on the nature of the attack by Miles—leaving open issues of causation, *mens rea*, and 'dangerousness' as regards unlawful act manslaughter. As with all exam problem questions involving accessorial liability candidates should first establish the potential liability of the principal offender as the liability of the secondary parties will be derived from this. Because the question is deliberately unclear in terms of Chaka's contemplation of Miles' actions, all possibilities have to be considered—ranging from her contemplating death caused by Miles using a weapon, through to her not comtemplating physical harm being caused at all.

Answer plan

- Liability of Miles for the death of Patti—causation
- Whether Miles has the *mens rea* for murder
- Unlawful act manslaughter if Miles lacks the *mens rea* for murder
- Chaka as an accomplice to Miles—joint enterprise—whether Miles deliberately goes beyond what was contemplated by Chaka
- Liability of Kirk as an accomplice to Miles
- Residual liability of Kirk regarding conspiracy and offences of encouraging and assisting under the **Serious Crime Act 2007**

Suggested answer

Liability of Miles for the death of Patti

The prosecution will need to prove that Miles was the cause in fact and in law of Patti's death. As for causation in law, the application of the 'but for' test would suggest that but for his having attacked Patti with the stone she would not have suffered the injury resulting in her death—see *R v White* [1910] 2 KB 124. The facts provide that Patti dies of a brain haemorrhage. This may be a reasonably foreseeable consequence of the attack by Miles, but the facts do not indicate the ferocity of the attack, the amount of force used or the weight of the stone (although the facts indicate that the stone is 'large'). Miles may try to argue that the harm was not a foreseeable consequence of his actions, and that he did not cause the death as a matter of legal causation. He may, for example, seek to adduce evidence that Patti had a 'thin skull' and was more prone to serious injury as a result of the attack than would have been the case with the average person. It is unlikely that such an argument would succeed. *R v Blaue* [1975] 1 WLR 1411 provides that Miles must take his victim as he finds him or her. The fact that Patti might have been more susceptible to injury will not be relevant in law. The ratio ale for this approach is that Miles should not have launched the attack at all.

Assuming causation can be established the question arises as to whether or not Miles had the *mens rea* for murder. The prosecution would have to prove that he intended to kill Patti or intended to cause her grievous bodily harm. Alternatively it would suffice for the prosecution to prove that Miles foresaw her death, or her suffering grievous bodily harm as being a virtually certain consequence of his actions; *R v Woollin* [1998] 4 All ER 103. Foresight is to be determined in accordance with s. 8 Criminal Justice Act 1967 by looking at what Miles foresaw, not what the reasonable person would have foreseen. On the one hand, to beat a person on the head with a large stone suggests evidence of at least an intention to do some grievous bodily harm. It should also be borne in mind that Miles had a history of violent behaviour and previous convictions for grievous bodily harm—suggesting a propensity towards violence. On the other hand the jury would need to review the evidence indicating the force used, and Miles' own direct testimony. Although not relevant to the issue of causation, evidence that Patti was more susceptible to this type of harm might influence a jury in concluding whether or not Miles did foresee death or grievous bodily harm as virtually certain. If convicted of murder Miles will be sentenced to life imprisonment.

Given the uncertainty regarding the *mens rea* for murder, Miles' potential liability for unlawful act manslaughter must be considered. The attack on Patti is clearly an unlawful (i.e., criminal) act—specifically an assault. Patti also presumably suffers wounding in that the surface of the skin on her skull may well have been broken. It should not be too difficult for the jury to apply the test for dangerousness here in relation to the unlawful act; see *R v Church* [1965] 2 All ER 72, as developed in *R v Dawson* (1985) 81 Cr App R 150. The prosecution would have to prove that a sober and reasonable bystander, at the scene of the attack on Patti, would have foreseen the risk of her suffering some physical harm. This should be self-evident on the facts, as should the *mens rea* for the unlawful act—i.e., Miles being at least reckless as to whether Patti suffers a battery or actual bodily harm.

Liability of Chaka as an accomplice

The prosecution will allege that Chaka was party to a joint enterprise in the attack on Patti—see *R v Petters and Parfitt* [1995] Crim LR 501. Chaka is at the scene of the crime acting in concert with Miles.

A number of issues arise for consideration. First, can Chaka argue that by not physically participating in the attack she played no part in it? Mere presence at the scene of a crime will not normally result in accessorial liability. There normally has to be evidence that the presence actively helped or encouraged the commission of the offence and that the accomplice was aware of this—see *R v Coney* (1882) 8 QBD 534, and *R v Clarkson* [1971] 1 WLR 1402. Chaka's case is hardly one of the innocent bystander happening to witness a crime, however. She set out with Miles to carry out some sort of unlawful attack on Patti that would result in Patti being frightened off. Indeed the prosecution will in all likelihood rely upon her failure to prevent Miles from carrying out the attack as evidence that she passively adopted his actions in hitting Patti with the stone—see further *R v Uddin* [1998] 2 All ER 744.

Secondly, if Chaka is to be convicted of murder as a party to a joint enterprise, what *mens rea* has to be proved on her part? On the basis of *R v Powell and Daniels*; *R v English* [1997] 4 All ER 545 Chaka can be convicted of murder if she intended the death of Patti (unlikely on the facts); intended that Patti should suffer grievous bodily harm (doubtful on the facts); or where she realizes that, in the course of pursuing the joint enterprise, Miles might kill or cause grievous bodily harm with intent to produce either of those consequences (possible, given the facts). A key piece of evidence here is that Chaka confessed that she knew Miles had a history of violent behaviour and previous convictions for grievous bodily harm. This would help to prove that she foresaw death or grievous bodily harm as possible consequences of an attack by Miles.

The third issue is as to whether or not Chaka can argue that Miles' deliberate use of the large stone as a weapon amounted to a conscious departure from the joint enterprise. The law on this point is complex and not altogether clear, but in *R v Powell and Daniels*; *R v English* (above) the House of Lords held that where a party to a joint enterprise 'only' foresaw the principal offender causing grievous bodily harm, and the principal offender in fact killed the victim by using a 'fundamentally different' (i.e., more deadly *modus operandi*—for example firing a gun at the victim instead of punching him) the accomplice could escape liability on the basis that the principal had exceeded the scope of the joint enterprise. By contrast, in cases where the accomplice's intention was that the principal offender would kill the victim with intent to kill or do grievous bodily harm, the 'fundamentally different' rule will not apply because one who intends the death of the victim can hardly argue that he should be absolved from liability because the principal offender opted to kill by a more deadly means.

In *R v Rahman and others* [2008] UKHL 45, however, the House of Lords was willing to extend the scope of the 'fundamentally different' rule to the benefit of an accomplice who foresaw that the principal *might* kill with intent to kill or with intent to some grievous bodily harm—see further *R v Yemoh* [2009] EWCA Crim 930. The rationale for this can be found in *Gamble* [1989] NI 268, where it was held that one who assists in a 'kneecapping' (which involves the victim being shot through the back of the kneecap), could escape liability for murder where the principal offender opted to cut the victim's throat with a knife thereby killing him. The accomplice who contemplates kneecapping obviously contemplates grievous bodily harm, but he must also contemplate that this grievous bodily harm might result in the victim's death. The use of the knife to cut the victim's throat rather than the gun to kneecap the victim is a fundamentally different *modus operandi*—one that carries with it a much more obvious risk of death. Hence Chaka may argue that she foresaw grievous bodily harm (especially in light of her knowledge of Miles) or even that she foresaw Miles causing death as a result of his intentionally inflicting grievous bodily harm, but that she did not foresee the use of a weapon. If this argument is accepted on the basis that an attack with a large stone is something fundamentally different to an attack with bare hands she will not be an accomplice to the murder of Patti.

A fourth point is that Chaka may argue, notwithstanding her knowledge of Miles' past, that she did not even contemplate grievous bodily harm being caused. She would cite in support of this the fact that Kirk asked them simply to frighten Patti. If this is the case Chaka clearly cannot be guilty as an accomplice to murder. The prosecution may, however, argue that she should be convicted as an accomplice to manslaughter. If Chaka only contemplated some harm falling short of grievous bodily harm, it is possible she could be convicted as an accomplice to manslaughter, provided the actions of Miles were not a deliberate departure from the conduct that she contemplated. Hence if she contemplated the use of a weapon, Miles' use of a stone will not amount to a departure from the joint enterprise. If Chaka did not contemplate the use of any weapon she may escape liability altogether; see *R v Stewart and Schofield* [1995] 1 Cr App R 441. There is a further moot point here to the effect that Chaka might argue that she foresaw Miles causing some physical harm with the stone, but did not foresee him hitting Patti with the stone accompanied by an intention to kill her or cause her grievous bodily harm. The essence of this argument being that it was Miles carrying out contemplated acts but with more *mens rea* than that foreseen by Chaka that took the act outside the scope of the common design. This is a very fine distinction and is not one that has yet found any real favour with the courts. As Laws LJ observed in *R v Roberts, Stephens and Day* [2001] EWCA Crim 1594, it does not seem right that if (assuming Chaka foresaw the use of a weapon) Miles had killed whilst harbouring only an intention to do some slight harm that Chaka would have been guilty as an accomplice to manslaughter, but if he had acted with intent to do some grievous bodily harm she would have escaped liability completely. It seems Chaka's liability will derive from what she foresaw Miles doing, not the intent with which she foresaw him acting.

Note that the prosecution will also have the option of charging Chaka with encouraging the commission of the offence by Miles on the basis that she was supporting him at the scene of the crime by her presence—see ss. 44–46 of the Serious Crime Act 2007. There will still be an issue here regarding which crime Chaka was encouraging Miles to commit—but at the very least she can be said to have encouraged him to commit an assault, and to have believed that her encouragement would lead to the commission of the offence; see s. 45.

Kirk's liability

Kirk was not present at the scene of the attack on Patti, hence he would be regarded as a secondary party—an accomplice involved prior to the commission of the offence. Hiring Miles and Chaka to carry out the attack on Patti would amount to counselling— see *R v Calhaem* [1985] 2 All ER 266 and *R v Luffman* [2008] EWCA Crim 1379. The problem lies in whether or not Kirk could be charged with counselling murder or manslaughter. As noted above *R v Powell and Daniels*; *R v English* (above) provides that an accomplice can be guilty of murder provided he at least contemplates that the principal might kill the victim or cause him grievous bodily harm. Although strictly speaking *R v Powell and Daniels*; *R v English* applies to cases of joint enterprise it is hard to see any rationale for not applying it also to cases of participation by counselling. The problem or the prosecution in this case is fairly obvious. Kirk will say that he only intended that Patti should be frightened and that he did not contemplate any serious harm, or possibly that he did not contemplate any harm at all. Even if he did contemplate some physical harm being caused Kirk, like Patti, might escape liability for manslaughter by arguing that the use of the weapon was a deliberate and fundamentally different act from that which he contemplated. If Kirk really did not foresee any physical harm being caused to Patti he can incur no liability; this much is clear from *Attorney-General's Reference (No. 3 of 2004)* [2005] EWCA Crim 1882.

Inchoate offences

Kirk, Miles, and Chaka could be charged with conspiring to cause Patti actual bodily harm, or even grievous bodily harm, contrary to s. 1(1) of the Criminal Law Act 1977. The fact that Kirk intended to play no active part in the attack is no bar to liability—see *R v Siracusa* (1989) 90 Cr App R 340. It would be enough that he agreed with others that the course of conduct should be pursued. The problem for the prosecution is that Kirk will contend that he only agreed to Patti being frightened hence he did not agree on a course of conduct that would necessarily involve actual bodily harm, wounding or grievous bodily harm. Chaka might raise similar arguments if she and Miles are charged with a similar form of conspiracy, although her argument is weaker given her knowledge of Miles' background.

Finally, Kirk could be encouraging Miles and Chaka to assault (in the narrow sense) Patti—the fact that they act on the encouragement would be no bar to his liability for the offence created by s. 44 of the Serious Crime Act 2007. He encourages the commission of the offence of (narrow) assault and intends that it should be committed.

Question 5

Louise, the leader of a criminal gang, believes that Tracey, a member of a rival criminal gang, has information about where a consignment of heroin is being stored. Louise has Tracey brought to her house by Gaye, another member of Louise's gang. Gaye ties Tracey to a chair so that she cannot escape. Under questioning Tracey refuses to divulge the information sought by Louise.

Louise then loads her gun with one bullet and tells Tracey that she will pull the trigger unless Tracey provides the information about the heroin. Tracey still refuses to answer Louise's questions. Louise fires the gun at Tracey's head from point blank range, killing Tracey instantly.

The gun used by Louise is a 'revolver' type having six bullet chambers. Louise understood, therefore, that there was a one in six chance that the gun would fire a live bullet at Tracey when she pulled the trigger. She had no way of knowing whether or not, when she pulled the trigger, the live bullet would be fired.

Gaye remained at the scene throughout these events, also aware that, because there was only one bullet in the six-chamber gun, there was a one in six chance that the gun would fire a live bullet when Louise pulled the trigger.

(a) Advise the Crown Prosecution Service as to the criminal liability of Louise for the murder of Tracey.

How, if at all, would your advice regarding Louise's liability for murder differ if Louise had killed Tracey having loaded her six-chamber revolver gun with three bullets rather than one?

(b) Advise the Crown Prosecution Service as to the criminal liability of Gaye for murder as an accomplice to Louise, on the basis that, as described above, Louise used a six-chamber revolver loaded with a single bullet to kill Tracey.

How, if at all, would your advice regarding Gaye's liability as an accomplice to murder differ in (b) if Gaye had wrongly believed that Louise's gun had been loaded with three bullets when in fact it was only loaded with one bullet?

Note: Candidates are not required to consider the liability of either Louise or Gaye in respect of manslaughter.

 Commentary

The question involves a classic 'is it murder or not?' scenario—in that most lay persons would regard firing a loaded gun and killing the victim as a result the simplest case of murder imaginable. Lawyers, however, know that this is not the case. The question is designed to test whether candidates are capable of thinking like lawyers when giving advice, rather than providing an emotive answer. This is also a very difficult question for those who are not confident with the more subtle aspects of the decision in *R v Powell and Daniels*; *R v English* [1997] 4 All ER 545. Note that much depends upon Gaye's foresight of the *mens rea* with which the principal offender will be acting. Although the rubric confines the question to liability for murder, some reference to related inchoate offences under the **Serious Crime Act 2007** is necessary.

Answer plan

- Louise—causing death
- Louise—*mens rea* for murder—degree of foresight
- Gaye—mode of participation
- Gaye—foresight of death or GBH
- Gaye—foresight of the *mens rea* that Louise would have when firing the gun
- Liability for assisting murder under the **Serious Crime Act 2007**

Suggested answer

The liability of Louise for the murder of Tracey

Murder is a common law offence that requires proof that the defendant caused the death of the victim with the requisite *mens rea*. On the given facts there is no doubt that Louise has caused the death of Tracey in fact—but for Louise's actions Tracey would not have died; see *R v White* [1910] 2 KB 124. Louise's firing of the gun is the operating and substantial cause of Tracey's death—there is no evidence here to suggest a *novus actus interveniens*, or break in the chain of causation—hence Louise will be regarded as having caused the death of Tracey as a matter of law; see *R v Smith* [1959] 2 QB 35.

The *mens rea* for murder requires proof that Louise intended to kill Tracey, or at least that she intended to do Tracey some grievous bodily harm; see *R v Woollin* [1998] 4 All ER 103. The difficulty for the prosecution is that there is no legal definition of intention for these purposes. It might be thought (by the lay person) that any person firing a loaded gun at another, knowing the gun to be loaded, would inevitably be held to have had the intention to kill. On the facts, however, Louise could not be certain that the gun was going to fire a live bullet. The odds on this happening were one in six. Hence the question becomes one of whether or not that is a high enough probability to support a conviction for murder.

In *R v Nedrick* [1986] 1 WLR 1025, Lord Lane CJ observed that, in those murder cases where some direction to the jury as to intent was necessary, the jury should be directed that they are not entitled to infer the necessary intention, unless they feel sure that death or serious bodily harm was a virtually certain (barring some unforeseen intervention) result of the defendant's actions and that the defendant appreciated that such was the case. This approach was reaffirmed by the House of Lords in *R v Woollin* (above), where Lord Steyn emphasized that the *Nedrick* direction was a 'tried and tested formula' which trial judges should continue to use, subject to the substitution of the words 'to find' for the words 'to infer'. More recently in *R v Matthews*; *R v Alleyne* [2003] EWCA Crim 192, Rix LJ observed that, whilst there was no definition of intent in murder cases as a matter of substantive law, the model direction, as approved by the Judicial Studies Board, provided that a jury was not entitled to find the necessary intent unless it felt sure that the defendant appreciated that death was virtually certain to result from his actions. Hence what is required is proof that Louise appreciated that the death of Tracey would be a virtually certain consequence of pulling the trigger of the gun. It is submitted that the facts simply do not support this conclusion. Louise will not be guilty of murder, but should be convicted of unlawful act manslaughter.

The liability of Gaye for murder as an accomplice to Louise

By bringing Tracey to the house where the killing takes place, tying her to the chair, and remaining at the scene whilst the killing is carried out, Gaye could be charged as an accomplice to the murder of Tracey. Her mode of participation could be procuring, in causing the offence to be committed (see *Attorney-General's Reference (No. 1 of 1975)* [1975] 3 WLR 11), although she is more likely to be charged with aiding and abetting the offence as she remains at the scene of the crime. Aiding and abetting does not require proof that Gaye's action caused the commission of the offence as such—the *actus reus* simply requires proof of some causal connection between Gaye's acts of assistance and the commission of the offence by Louise.

As to the fault element, under the basic principles of accessorial liability, Gaye will have sufficient *mens rea* to be convicted as an aider or abettor if it can be proved that she was aware of the type of crime Louise was going to commit; see *R v Bainbridge* [1959] 3 All ER 200. Like Louise, Gaye realised there was a one in six chance of the gun firing a live round, hence murder must have been within her contemplation, even if she could not be sure that death would necessarily occur. Further, *R v Bryce* [2004] EWCA Crim 1231, provides that it is sufficient that Gaye deliberately did the acts constituting the participation, realizing that they were capable of assisting Louise in the commission of the offence.

Given that Gaye and Louise were acting together, the prosecution is likely to argue that there was a joint enterprise, where Louise and Gaye were involved together in the offence committed against Tracey. On this basis reliance will be placed on *R v Powell and Daniels*; *R v English* (above), where one of the certified questions was put in these terms: 'Is it sufficient to found a conviction for murder for a secondary party to a killing to have realized that the primary party might kill with intent to do so or must the secondary party have held such intention himself?'

The House of Lords, in *R v Powell and Daniels*; *R v English*, held that, in cases of joint enterprise, where the victim of an unlawful attack is killed, an accomplice can incur liability for murder where she realizes that, in the course of pursuing the joint enterprise, the principal offender might kill, intending to do so, or might kill whilst acting with at least an intent to cause grievous bodily harm.

On the facts there is clear evidence that Gaye was aware that Louise might kill Tracey if a live bullet was fired. A more difficult issue for the prosecution is whether Gaye foresaw the possibility that Louise would be acting with the *mens rea* for murder at the time of the killing. Gaye can be said to have foreseen:

(a) that Louise might kill without an intent to kill or cause grievous bodily harm or

(b) that Louise might kill being reckless as to whether death or grievous bodily harm resulted.

However, neither of those is enough for Gaye to be liable for murder as an accomplice in a joint enterprise, since neither of those establishes that she foresaw Louise committing the *actus reus* of murder with the requisite intent as a possibility. There is nothing in the facts to suggest that Gaye might have foreseen that Louise might form, or might have believed that Louise did form, an intent to kill. The most that Gaye can be said to have foreseen or appreciated is that Louise was creating a risk that Tracey would suffer death or grievous bodily harm.

As an alternative Gaye could be charged with an offence of assisting or encouraging murder under Part 2 of the Serious Crime Act 2007. The inchoate offences created by ss. 44–46 can be relied upon by the prosecution even where the completed offence is committed. Gaye clearly does assist by bringing Tracey to Louise and tying Tracey to the chair. The problem would be in respect of *mens rea*. A charge of assisting murder under s. 44 requires proof that Gaye assisted Louise with purpose-type intent that Louise's actions should result in Tracey's death. The points made earlier in this answer explain why that would be problematic. Section 45 could be charged where Gaye believed her actions would assist in the murder of Tracey—this is a better option for the prosecution—but believing a consequence will occur is not the same as believing it might occur, which is the case where there is only a one in six chance of death.

Advice to Louise if she had loaded her six-chamber revolver gun with three bullets rather than one

By loading three bullets instead of one Louise would have increased the odds on a live bullet being fired from one in six to one in two—effectively a 50/50 chance of shooting Tracey. Again, this might be seen by the lay person as ample evidence of the culpability required for murder, but as has been noted above, the jury would have to be directed to look for evidence that Louise foresaw death or grievous bodily harm as a virtually certain consequence of her firing the gun. Only then would the jury be entitled to find that she intended to kill or do grievous bodily harm. It is submitted that foreseeing a consequence as a 50/50 chance is not to be equated with foreseeing it as virtually certain. Indeed, it might not be possible to find the evidence of intent on Louise's part unless she loads the gun with six bullets.

Advice to Gaye if Gaye had wrongly believed that Louise's gun had been loaded with three bullets when in fact it was only loaded with one bullet

In this alternative scenario there may be no change to the liability of Gaye. Even with one bullet in the chamber of the gun Gaye foresees that the death of Tracey is a possibility. The problem of proving that Gaye foresaw Louise acting with sufficient *mens rea* for murder remains. Gaye's belief that Louise has loaded the gun with three bullets simply provides stronger evidence that she foresaw Louise acting with intent to kill or cause grievous bodily harm. Arguably, Gaye could only be an accomplice to murder if she (mistakenly) believed the gun was fully loaded with six bullets and that Louise knew this to be the case when she pulled the trigger. As to potential liability under the Serious Crime Act 2007, see above.

Further reading

Clarkson, C., 'Complicity, Powell and Manslaughter' [1998] Crim LR 556.

Dennis, I.H., 'The Rationale of Criminal Conspiracy' [1997] 93 LQR 39.

Ormerod, D., 'Making Sense of *Mens Rea* in Statutory Conspiracies' (2006) 59 CLP 185.

Ormerod, D. and Fortson, R., 'Serious Crime Act 2007: The Part 2 Offences' [2009] Crim LR 389

Rogers, J., 'The Codification of Attempts and the Case for "Preparation"' [2008] Crim LR 937

Simester, A.P., 'The Mental Element in Complicity' (2006) 122 LQR 578.

Smith, K.J.M., 'Withdrawal in Complicity' [2001] Crim LR 769.

Sullivan, G.R., 'Participating in Crime: Law Com No. 305—Joint Criminal Ventures' [2008] Crim LR 19

Taylor, R., 'Procuring, Causation, Innocent Agency and the Law Commission' [2008] Crim LR 32

Wilson, W., 'A Rational Scheme of Liability for Participating in Crime' [2008] Crim LR 3

Joint enterprise (1): Assume A is involved in a joint enterprise with P in the course of which P kills V intending to kill or with intent to do some GBH

Did A intend the death of V?

No → See Joint enterprise (2) flowchart

Yes →

In killing V did P depart from the course of conduct contemplated by A? (For example using a weapon, using a more dangerous weapon, or using a weapon in a more dangerous way than was contemplated by A)?

No → A guilty as an accomplice to murder

Yes → A guilty of murder as an accomplice – makes no difference that P chose for example to use a weapon where A did not contemplate this, or that P used a more dangerous weapon, or used a weapon in a more dangerous way than was contemplated by A – see *obiter* Lord Rodger in *R v Rahman* [2008] para 33; effect of *Rahman* confirmed by the Court of Appeal in *R v Yemoh* and others [2009] EWCA Crim 930

Joint enterprise (2): Assume A is involved in a joint enterprise with P in the course of which P kills V intending to kill or with intent to do some GBH

Did A intend the death of V?

Yes → See Joint enterprise flowchart (1)

No ↓

Did A foresee either that P might kill V (with suficient mens rea for murder); or that P might intentionally cause V some GBH?

No → See Joint enterprise flowchart (3)

Yes ↓

Did the act of P that caused the death of V involve the use of a weapon that A was unaware of, the use of a weapon more lethal than that contemplated by A, or the use of a weapon in a manner that was more dangerous than that contemplated by A so that P's acts could be regarded as fundamentally different from the acts contemplated by A?

Yes → As P deliberately departed from the common design, A will not be an accomplice to murder or manslaughter – see *R v Rahman* [2008] HL. But see criticism of *R v Gamble* in *R v Rahman*. Query – does P depart from what A contemplated if he uses a contemplated weapon in a way that is much more dangerous than was contemplated by A? Note that in any event A could be guilty of encouraging or assisting the commission of an offence by P under Part 2 of the Serious Crime Act 2007

No ↓

Did P nevertheless act with more *mens rea* than contemplated by A (i.e.. P intended to kill whereas A contemplated P acting with intent to do GBH)

Makes no difference – A contemplated the act committed by P – P acting with more *mens rea* does not bring those acts within the 'fundamentally different' exception – see *R v Rahman* [2008] HL (Query – what if P uses a contemplated weapon but in a much more dangerous way?)

Joint enterprise (3): Assume A is involved in a joint enterprise with P in the course of which P kills V intending to kill or with intent to do some GBH

Did A intend the death of V?

- **Yes** → See Joint enterprise flowchart 1
- **No** → **Did A foresee either that P might kill V (with sufficient *mens rea* for murder); or that P might intentionally cause V some GBH?**
  - **Yes** → See joint enterprise flowchart (2)
  - **No** → **Did A foresee that P might cause some harm – but not anything amounting to GBH?**
    - **Yes** → **Was the act of P that caused death fundamentally different from the acts contemplated by A?**
      - No – A will be an accomplice to manslaughter e.g. *R v Stewart and Schofield* and *R v Gilmour*. Can P exceed the scope of what was contemplated by acting with more *mens rea* than an A foresaw? Doubtful following *R v Rahman* [2008] HL. See further *R v Roberts, Stevens and Day* [2001] (which also suggests not) and A-G's Ref (**No** 3 of 2004)
      - Yes – A not guilty as an accomplice to murder or manslaughter – see *R v Perman* and *A-G's Ref (No 3 of 2004)*. Not that A might have a residual liability for encouraging or assisting an offence contrary to ss. to 46 of the Serious Crime Act 2007
    - **No** → A not guilty as an accomplice to murder or manslaughter. Note that A might have a residual liability for encouraging or assisting an offence contrary to ss.44 to 46 of the Serious Crime Act 2007 although proof of *mens rea* is likely to be problematic

8

Theft, fraud, and criminal damage

Introduction

Unlike other areas of the criminal law syllabus, both theft and criminal damage are governed by comparatively modern legislative measures: the Theft Act 1968 and the Criminal Damage Act 1971. The Theft Act 1968 was enacted to replace complex larceny laws. As Lord Diplock observed in *R v Treacey* [1971] AC 537: 'the Theft Act 1968 makes a welcome departure from the former style of drafting in criminal statutes. It is expressed in a simple language as used and understood by ordinary literate men and women. It avoids as far as possible those terms of art which have acquired a special meaning understood only by lawyers in which many of the final enactments which it supersedes were couched.'

Whatever Parliament's good intentions, however, the operation of the Theft Act 1968 in practice has thrown up many difficulties. Principal amongst these is the problem of consensual appropriation. Can a defendant steal property even though the 'victim' is giving it to her willingly? If the victim is tricked into parting with the property by the use of false pretences a fraud offence should be used (see ss. 2–4 of the Fraud Act 2006). The problem cases have proved to be those where the defendant is seen to have behaved dishonestly in persuading the owner to transfer property, but no false pretences can be proved.

As a result of decisions such as *R v Hinks* [2000] 4 All ER 833, it is now possible for a defendant to be guilty of theft even though the victim validly transferred property to the defendant. The effect of this decision is that a civil court may declare that there was a valid gift of property from V to A, and therefore A has become the owner of that property, but this will not prevent a criminal court from holding that A had still dishonestly appropriated that property and is therefore guilty of stealing it. When one considers that theft is a property offence and ownership of property is a civil law issue, it is remarkable that the House of Lords has confirmed this approach.

This situation is partly the draftsmen's fault, but also stems from the fact that the law of theft is dependent on civil concepts of ownership, possession and passing of property—complicated topics which are constantly being analysed and altered by the civil courts (e.g., does a bribe received by an employee belong to the employer: *Attorney-General for Hong Kong v Reid* [1994] 1 All ER 1). As Lord Lane recognized in *Attorney-General's Reference (No. 1 of 1985)* [1986] 2 All ER 219: 'There are topics of conversation more popular in public houses than the finer points of the equitable doctrine of the constructive trust.' Yet knowledge of this topic is essential in determining if the accused is under a legal obligation to retain and deal with property in a particular way.

In approaching theft problems it pays to be methodical. Go through the five elements in turn. Some parts can be dealt with in a sentence without any reference to authority, others will require considerable coverage. Candidates often ask how they are to know which parts of the question require depth, and which can be dealt with quickly. The answer is really self-evident. If the point is an obvious one it will not provide many marks—state the obvious and move on. If the point is tricky and can be argued a number of ways—it requires depth (and will attract more marks). Deal with the *actus reus* first. If there is no property belonging to another there may be little need to consider *mens rea*. Bear in mind that the combined effects of the House of Lords' rulings on appropriation is that virtually anything can now be appropriation—hence this element will rarely be in doubt. Sections 5(3) and 5(4) of the Theft Act 1968 can raise tricky issues about when property passes, so be prepared to deal with these.

Because of the way the law of theft has developed, however, it is increasingly dishonesty that becomes the crucial issue. Candidates should remember that if they are considering liability for theft, s. 2(1)(a)–(c) of the 1968 Act should be considered first. If a defendant can show that he was not dishonest because he comes within one of the three exceptions there will be no need to consider *R v Ghosh* [1982] QB 1053. As regards intention to permanently deprive (ITPD), remember that in most cases it will be self-evident. Resort should only be had to s. 6(1) and 6(2) in cases of difficulty where the defendant needs to be deemed to have an intention to permanently deprive. Avoid a common mistake that candidates make. There is no need to prove that the owner was permanently deprived. The prosecution needs to prove the defendant's state of mind.

Criminal damage

Whilst theft questions nearly always appear on criminal law exam papers, criminal damage is more likely to arise as part of a question. Note in particular that it may be used as the unlawful act in cases of constructive manslaughter. Examiners also used to mix criminal damage in with assault questions in order to bring out the divergent approaches to recklessness depending on whether the defendant was charged with assault or criminal damage. However, now that *Metropolitan Police Commissioner v Caldwell* [1981] 1 All ER 961 no longer holds sway, the House of Lords' decision in *R v G* [2003] 4 All ER 765 marking a return to subjective recklessness under the Criminal Damage Act 1971—that type of question may be less likely. Indeed questions dealing solely with criminal damage may become something of a rarity. That said, some examples are included at the end of this chapter for the purposes of exposition.

There are five offences under the Criminal Damage Act 1971, but by far the two most important for exam purposes are s. 1(1) ('simple' criminal damage) and s. 1(2) ('aggravated' criminal damage). An important point to remember regarding the offence of criminal damage under s. 1(1) is the fact that in addition to the general defences there are two specific defences contained in s. 5(2) and there are many interesting cases interpreting these provisions. Aggravated criminal damage is an odd offence as it is a combination of an offence against property and an offence against the person. It is very useful for the prosecution, as its ingredients are very easily satisfied.

Question 1

A hurricane has left much of the Isle of Wight devastated and severe weather continues to prevent any form of travel to the mainland. Katrina has been without food or fresh water for four days and she has small children to feed. In desperation she goes to her local supermarket, which has been partly destroyed, and takes items of food off the shelf. On her way back home she sees the body of Madge, an elderly woman, in the road. Realizing that Madge is dead, Katrina takes the loaf of bread she finds in Madge's carrier bag.

Katrina's neighbour Phil has a stock of bottled water he is selling off at £10 a bottle. Katrina thinks Phil has a nerve making money from the disaster, but she reluctantly purchases a bottle, handing Phil a £10 note. In haste, Phil hands the bottle to Katrina and a £10 note, saying 'Here's your change from £20'. Katrina takes the note and says nothing.

Later that day Katrina decides it would be wrong to keep the £10 note from Phil and, meeting him in the street, she tells him of his mistake with the money. Phil, incensed, grabs Katrina's handbag from her shoulder, causing her to lurch forward, and he helps himself to two £5 notes from the purse in her bag.

Advise the Crown Prosecution Service as to the criminal liability of Katrina and Phil.

 ## Commentary

There are several incidents of theft in this question and a lot of issues to cover. Hence it is not a good strategy to dwell at any length on those elements of theft that are evident from the given facts. Simply mention them and move on to the more knotty aspects of the problem because that is where the marks will be awarded. In the theft of food and bread by Katrina note the interplay of dishonesty and necessity—to some extent if she succeeds with necessity she must too succeed in arguing she is not dishonest—the law would be slightly contradictory otherwise. The issue of dishonesty comes up several times—there is no need to repeat all the legal principles in detail each time—adopt an economical style by 'referring above' as necessary. Take care also not to try too hard to resolve issues of fact that are really in the province of the jury. If it is not possible to tell how a jury might decide, indicate this in the answer.

Answer plan

- Theft of food from the supermarket—clearly appropriated property—still belongs to another against Katrina—not abandoned—is she dishonest—s. 2(1)(b) Theft Act 1968 and *R v Ghosh*—ITPD is evident

- Burglary—does the supermarket still constitute a building—she would be trespassing unless the supermarket agreed to her being there to take the bread—requires an intention to steal or a theft—as to the elements of which see above

- Taking bread from Madge—bread is property, it is appropriated—does the bread have an owner—lost/abandoned issue—is Katrina dishonest—claim of right—belief owner would consent—*R v Ghosh*—ITPD evident

- Any defence of necessity regarding the taking of the food from the supermarket and from Madge, or just an aspect of dishonesty?

- Money got by mistake—remains property belonging to another by virtue of **s. 5(4) Theft Act 1968**—appropriated by Katrina

- Is Katrina dishonest—claim of right—*R v Ghosh*—appears to have ITPD but query given later events

- Katrina's change of mind does not 'undo' the theft if the five elements coincided when she first took the money

- Phil—robbery—uses force in order to steal at the time of stealing or before doing so—use of force on bag is the same as use of force on person

- Does Phil steal—not the same notes so the money could be property belonging to another—but query whether the £5 notes are the proceeds of the £10 note—no evidence of this

- Phil appropriates with ITPD—live issue is dishonesty—claim of right—*R v Ghosh*

- Phil has residual liability for assault

Suggested answer

Taking food from the supermarket

In taking the food from the supermarket Katrina may have committed theft contrary to s. 1(1) of the Theft Act 1968. The food is clearly property belonging to another as against her, and she appropriates it by taking it; see ss. 4(1), 5(1) and 3(1) of the 1968 Act respectively. As to *mens rea*, there seems to be little doubt that she intends to permanently deprive the store owners of the food—hence no recourse to s. 6(1) of the 1968 Act is required. The only remaining issue as regards the elements of theft is, therefore, dishonesty.

Consideration needs to be given in the first instance to whether or not Katrina can rely on any of the 'escape routes' provided by s. 2(1) of the 1968 Act which provides for a number of situations where a defendant is not to be regarded as dishonest. Katrina may seek to rely on s. 2(1)(a) under which she will not be dishonest if she took the food honestly believing she had the right in law to do so. Note that she does not have to prove that any such right in law actually exists. She bears an evidential burden of providing evidence as to why she honestly believed she had such a right. Hence it may be the case that she really did believe it was legal to help herself to the food because of the emergency—in which case she would have to be acquitted. Under s. 2(1)(b) Katrina might argue that she honestly believed that the owner of the food would have consented to her taking the food if he or she had known of the circumstances. Given the facts this must be a very strong point for Katrina. Again she does not have to prove that the owner actually did consent, or would have done—simply that she honestly believed the owner would have. Section 2(1)(c)—honest belief that the owner cannot be found—does not have any application here.

If Katrina was not able to succeed under s. 2(1)(a) or (b) the issue of whether or not she was dishonest will fall to be determined by the jury following a direction in accordance with *R v Ghosh* [1982] QB 1053. The jury will be asked to consider whether, according to the ordinary standards of reasonable and honest people, it was dishonest of Katrina to take the food. It is always dangerous to try and guess how a jury might apply this test, but the facts are compelling and Katrina might well be regarded as having acted in a way that was not dishonest. Even if she is regarded as having acted dishonestly, the jury would then have to consider the second limb of the *Ghosh* direction by asking themselves whether or not Katrina must have realized that what she was doing was by those standards dishonest. Again, Katrina may have genuinely believed she was doing the right thing—thus justifying an acquittal.

If there is liability for theft in relation to the food it should be pointed out that there could also be liability for burglary contrary to s. 9(1)(b) of the Theft Act 1968. Assuming that the supermarket, albeit partly destroyed, still constituted a building, she would have entered it as a trespasser provided she did not have permission to do so (for example because it was off-limits to the public after the storm damage) or because she entered intending to steal (as to which see above). If the trespass and the theft can be established there could be liability for burglary.

As a general defence to either theft or burglary Katrina may want to rely on necessity. Traditionally the courts have been reluctant to recognize a common law defence of this nature, not least because it could open the floodgates in terms of 'excuses' raised by defendants, but there are now precedents in the sphere of motoring offences—see for example *R v Martin* [1989] 1 All ER 652—where the courts have been willing to recognize a form of duress of circumstances where the accused is regarded as having acted reasonably and proportionately in order to avoid a threat of death or serious injury. On the given facts stealing food to keep children alive would probably meet these requirements.

Against this, in *R v Quale and other appeals; Attorney-General's Reference (No. 2 of 2004)* [2005] EWCA Crim 1415, the court held that necessity could not be relied upon as a defence to the cultivation of cannabis in breach of the Misuse of Drugs Act 1971— on the basis that Parliament had created a statutory scheme to regulate an activity and it was not for the courts to legitimize conduct which was contrary to the clear legislative policy. It could be argued that similar arguments apply to the scheme established by the Theft Act 1968.

The issue of necessity can be circumvented if the facts are sufficiently compelling as it seems unlikely Katrina would be regarded as dishonest (see above).

Taking bread from Madge

In taking the bread from Madge Katrina may have committed another theft. Again there is clearly an appropriation of property, but there is some debate as to ownership and whether the property can be regarded as property belonging to another as against Katrina. Technically, as Madge is dead, the bread passes as part of her estate to her successors in title. It does not become ownerless or abandoned property. The fact that Madge is dead, however, may be relevant to whether or not Katrina was dishonest in taking the bread. The structure of dishonesty under s. 2 of the Theft Act 1968 has already been outlined in respect of the food taken from the supermarket. Applying these subsections in turn. Katrina may again believe that she had the right in law to take the bread, because of the emergency and the fact that Madge no longer had any use for it. Katrina might also have believed that, under s. 2(1)(b), the owners of the bread (for the purposes assumed to be Madge's estate) would have consented to Katrina having it given the circumstances. Note here that the bread would have perished if not eaten by someone, so presumably Katrina could plausibly argue that the owners of the bread would not have wanted it to go to waste during the emergency. Subsection 2(1)(c) is of more relevance on this occasion as Katrina could argue that she honestly believed that the legal owners of the bread (Madge's successors in title) could not have been found by taking any steps that were reasonable in the circumstances. The emphasis here is on what Katrina thought would be reasonable steps—not the view of the reasonable person.

Katrina's intention to permanently deprive Madge's estate of the food is self-evident and does not require any recourse to s. 6(1)(a) of the Theft Act 1968. As to a possible defence of necessity—see above in relation to the theft of the food.

Theft of Phil's £10 note

Katrina can be guilty of theft in respect of her retaining the £10 that Phil gives her by mistake. When she takes possession of the money she appropriates property that, by virtue of s. 5(4) of the Theft Act 1968, will be regarded as property belonging to another as against her. It may appear as a matter of fact that Phil makes Katrina the owner of the money, but s. 5(4) operates to stop property in the money passing to Katrina because she obtains it as a result of a mistake on Phil's part, and at the time she is under a legal obligation to return the money to Phil. The legal obligation is not created by s. 5(4) but exists in quasi-contract—Katrina has been unjustly enriched by Phil's error and Phil could (in theory) bring an action for money had and received to recover it; see further *Attorney-General's Reference (No. 1 of 1983)* [1984] 3 All ER 369, and *R v Shadrokh-Cigari* [1988] Crim LR 465.

The facts indicate that Katrina took the £10 and said nothing. If she was not aware that she was receiving the money she cannot be guilty of theft, but this seems unlikely. Assuming she was aware of the overpayment it appears that when she first took the £10 note she intended to keep it—otherwise why the evidence of her subsequently changing her mind? Thus the only issue to be determined is whether or not she was dishonest when she took the money. As explained above recourse would be had first to s. 2(1)(a) of the 1968 Act. Katrina might claim she believed she had the right in law to keep the money because it somehow made up for Phil profiteering—although this may be asking too much of the jury to believe. Subsections 2(1)(b) and (c) do not seem to offer anything to Katrina in this situation; hence the jury would be invited to consider her actions in light of a *Ghosh* direction—as outlined above. This would offer an alternative to s. 2(1)(a) in as much as that asks whether Katrina thought she was legally justified in keeping the £10 note, whilst the *Ghosh* test invited the jury to look at the morality of Katrina's actions. It is impossible to offer a categorical view of how a jury would determine this matter.

The fact that Katrina subsequently has a change of heart and decides to return the money to Phil is irrelevant to the question of whether or not she committed theft when she first took the money. If the five elements of theft came together at that time, her subsequent decision to return the money cannot undo the theft, although it might be evidence in mitigation of sentence.

Phil's liability

In grabbing Katrina's bag and taking two £5 notes from her purse Phil may have committed theft, and possibly robbery. The £5 notes are property belonging to another as against Phil. The fact that the notes equal the value of the property he parted with by mistake does not make them his as a matter of law, although as will be seen this may be relevant to the issue of dishonesty. Phil appropriates the money by taking it and clearly has intention to permanently deprive Katrina of the money. As to whether or not he is dishonest in doing so, s. 2(1)(a) provides him with the opportunity to argue that he honestly believed he had the right to the £10 because it represented the property he had transferred to Katrina by mistake. If this is his honest belief he must be acquitted. Subsections 2(1)(b) and (c) do not seem to offer anything to Phil in this situation; hence the jury would be invited to consider his actions in light of a *Ghosh* direction—as outlined above. Again this will involve the jury in a moral assessment of Phil's behaviour—would the jury sympathize with someone seeking to make money in an emergency, who resorts to force to recover what he believes to be his by right? Perhaps not.

If the elements of theft are present Phil could be guilty of robbery under s. 8 of the Theft Act 1968, which requires proof that he stole and immediately before or at the time of doing so, and in order to do so, he used force on Katrina. The facts clearly state that Phil grabbed Katrina's handbag from her shoulder, causing her to lurch forward—hence there is evidence of his using force on her before stealing and in order to do so. Therefore it is submitted that, provided Phil is found by the jury to have acted dishonestly, he could be convicted of either theft or robbery. In addition it should be noted that Phil commits a common assault (technically a battery) in causing unlawful force to be used on Katrina, being at least reckless as to whether or not this would result from his actions.

Question 2

Susan owns and runs a convenience store. Martina opens up a rival business in the same shopping precinct. Susan enters Martina's shop and, for fun, swaps price labels on two boxes of chocolates so that a £10 box is now priced at £2, and a £2 box is now priced at £10.

Stephen enters Martina's shop and, unaware of Susan's actions, selects the box of chocolates now (wrongly) priced at £2, knowing full well that it should be priced at £10. Stephen takes the box of chocolates to the counter and buys it for £2. The cashier, Gavin, does not realize that the item is wrongly priced.

Natasha goes to the delicatessen counter in Martina's shop and asks Joanne, the assistant, for six spicy sausages. The sausages cost 50p each. Joanne selects eight spicy sausages by mistake and wraps them up for Natasha. Joanne writes on the bag that it contains six sausages. Aware of Joanne's mistake, Natasha takes the bag to the counter where Gavin, unaware that the bag contains eight, not six, sausages, charges her £3.00.

Advise the CPS as to the criminal liability, if any, of:

(i) Susan;

(ii) Stephen;

(iii) Natasha; and

(iv) Martina.

Commentary

This question comprises four incidents, each of which can effectively be dealt with individually. As with all theft offence questions a methodical examination of each element is required. Candidates find that this sometimes throws up issues that were not immediately apparent. The facts of a problem like this can sometimes present candidates with a choice of advising as to liability for theft or fraud. Prior to the enactment of the Fraud Act 2006 candidates were normally advised to consider liability for deception before theft, but the provisions of the 2006 Act perhaps make that unnecessary. Note the way in which civil law concepts come into play in determining criminal liability, for example the contract law of offer and acceptance as regards mispriced goods. Be prepared to advise that the prosecution may not be able to establish criminal liability for some of these incidents, especially where dishonesty is an issue.

Answer plan

- Susan's liability

  - s. 1, Theft Act 1968

  - fraud by false representation

  - burglary

- Stephen's liability

  - fraud by false representation or by failing to disclose information

  - theft contrary to **s. 1 Theft Act 1968**

  - making off without payment

- Natasha's liability

  - theft contrary to **s. 1 Theft Act 1968**

  - fraud by false representation

  - making off without payment

- Martina's liability

  - liability for theft

  - problem of intention to permanently deprive

  - *R v Lloyd*

  - **s. 2, Theft Act 1968**—dishonesty

  - *Ghosh* [1982]

Suggested answer

Susan's liability

When Susan enters Martina's shop and, for fun, swaps price labels on two boxes of chocolates so that a £10 box is now priced at £2, and a £2 box is now priced at £10 she may have committed the offence of theft contrary to s. 1(1) of the Theft Act 1968. The two boxes of chocolates are clearly property (see s. 4(1)), and can be regarded as belonging to another as against Susan—see s. 5(1) of the 1968 Act. Swapping the price labels over would be regarded as an appropriation of property belonging to another. On the basis of s. 3(1) an appropriation is any assumption of the rights of the owner. In *R v Morris* [1983] 3 All ER 288, this was interpreted as any assumption of any right of the owner. There is no need to show an outright taking of the property. Swapping labels is effectively an assumption of the owner's right to determine the level of what contract lawyers would describe as the 'invitation to treat'. Hence the *actus reus* is made out. The live issue is dishonesty. As this was a practical joke it is unlikely that Susan can 'escape' under s. 2(1)(a)–(c) of the 1968 Act. There is no evidence that she honestly believed she had the right in law to play practical jokes, and no evidence that she honestly believed Martina would have consented had she known. Assuming s. 2(1)(a)–(c) does not avail her, the issue of dishonesty will be a question of fact for the jury, directed in accordance with *R v Ghosh* [1982] QB 1053:

(i) ...whether according to the ordinary standards of reasonable and honest people what was done was dishonest. If it was not dishonest by those standards, that is the end of the matter and the prosecution fails. If it was dishonest by those standards, then the jury must consider

(ii) …whether the defendant himself must have realized that what he was doing was by those standards dishonest.

It is hard to tell how a jury might regard Susan's actions. As the value involved is small, and given that there is no direct personal gain for her, a jury might be reluctant to conclude that she was dishonest.

Susan has no actual intention to permanently deprive. The issue is whether she can be deemed to have had this intent by virtue of s. 6(1) of the Theft Act 1968. Is it a situation where it was her intention to treat the property as her own to dispose of regardless of the other's rights? Compare and contrast *R v Cahill* [1993] Crim LR 141 and *DPP v Lavender* [1993] Crim LR 297 on this point. It could be argued that switching labels is evidence of her treating it as her own to dispose of, as she is creating the risk that someone might buy the goods at an undervalue. On the other hand, there is no disposal as such. This is very much a moot point. Any ambiguity under the statute should be resolved in the defendant's favour, but criminal courts often disregard this maxim.

There are two other possible offences to consider. The first is fraud by false representation contrary to s. 2 of the Fraud Act 2006. The offence requires proof that Susan dishonestly made a false representation, and intended by that representation to make a gain for herself or another, or to cause loss to another or to expose another to a risk of loss.

Switching price labels would constitute the false representation (see further s. 2(3) of the 2006 Act). Susan is representing the selling price to be something other than the correct amount—this satisfies s. 2(2), which provides that a representation is false if it is untrue or misleading. Obviously the wrong price label is likely to mislead. As to *mens rea*, the prosecution will have to prove three elements. First that Susan intended, by making the representation, to make a gain for herself or another, or intended to cause loss to another or to expose another to a risk of loss. The facts indicate that Susan swaps the price labels 'for fun'. She may argue that she just wanted to cause confusion, as opposed to loss of property. Note that recklessness as to whether loss will be caused is not enough. If the jury thinks that Susan was just playing a practical joke she may escape liability on this point. Against this is the fact that she has a financial interest in Martina's business not doing well, and this may lead the jury to infer an intent to cause Martina loss. The second element of *mens rea* is that Susan must be shown to have known that the representation as to price was or might have been untrue or misleading. Her knowledge that the label indicated the wrong price is evident from the facts. Thirdly it must be proved that Susan was dishonest.

There is no definition of dishonesty in the Fraud Act 2006, hence the jury would again be asked to consider her actions in the light of a *R v Ghosh* [1982] QB 1053 direction (considered above).

The second offence is burglary—although this would be a rather artificial charge. If she had the intention to swap labels before entering the store, and if this could be equated with an intention to steal (doubtful, see above), it might be possible to charge her with burglary contrary to s. 9(1)(a) of the Theft Act 1968—entering a building as a trespasser with intent to steal. By entering intending to switch labels, even as a joke, she would be trespassing as she would be entering for a purpose in excess of the express or implied permission granted to the public at large as customers: see *R v Jones and Smith* [1976] 3 All ER 54. Similarly if she does commit theft in swapping labels she could be guilty of burglary under s. 9(1)(b) of the 1968 Act. Having entered a building as a trespasser she committed theft therein.

Stephen's liability

At the time Stephen selects the box of chocolates it is property belonging to another—see s. 4(1) and s. 5(1) of the Theft Act 1968. Does he commit an offence of fraud by false representation contrary to s. 2 of the Fraud Act 2006 when he offers to buy the chocolates for £2? Whilst the offence under s. 2 is effectively an inchoate offence (there is no need to prove that he obtains anything as a result of the false representation, unlike the previous offence under s. 15 of the Theft Act 1968) there is still a need to show that Stephen makes a representation. The prosecution will argue that he is presenting himself as an honest shopper who believes £2 to be the correct price, and perhaps rely on s. 2(3) of the 2006 Act, which provides that a representation can include a representation as to the state of mind of the person making the representation. Against this Stephen will argue that he did not make any representation as to price. He did not switch labels. At present there is no case law to indicate how the courts will apply s. 2(3), but it is submitted that any ambiguity should be construed in favour of the defendant. To hold that his offering to buy the chocolates knowing they were wrongly priced amounted to a false representation by the defendant would be to extend the scope for liability—is this what Parliament intended in passing the 2006 Act? Even if this was the case *mens rea* (as outlined above in relation to Susan's liability under s. 2) would have to be established and a jury might not regard his attempt to buy the chocolates at less than the normal selling price to be dishonest (see also a discussion of this in relation to theft below).

Section 3 of the Fraud Act 2006 creates the offence of fraud by failing to disclose information. Liability would arise if it could be shown that Stephen dishonestly failed to disclose information that he was under a legal duty to disclose, and that he intended to make a gain for himself thereby. Stephen knew that the chocolates were mispriced, but there is serious doubt as to whether he was under any legal duty to disclose this fact. Any such duty would have to arise either from statute (not relevant here) or from a contract. As no contract exists at the time he tries to buy the chocolates there is no obvious basis for any legal duty.

Turning to his possible liability for theft, did he appropriate the chocolates when he selected the box? As explained above, any assumption of the rights of the owner will suffice. Further, appropriation can be conduct to which the owner consents. In *Lawrence v Metropolitan Police Commissioner* [1970] 3 All ER 933, the House of Lords confirmed that, by omitting the phrase '…without the consent of the owner…'

from s. 3(1), Parliament had intended to relieve the prosecution of the burden of establishing that a taking of property belonging to another was without the owner's consent. This has subsequently been reaffirmed in decisions such as *Dobson v General Accident (etc) plc* [1989] 3 WLR 1066, and *R v Gomez* [1993] 1 All ER 1. The *actus reus* of theft is therefore made out when Stephen selects the chocolates. Was he dishonest? Stephen will rely on s. 2(1)(a) of the 1968 Act, contending that he appropriated the property in the belief that he had, in law, the right to deprive the store of it. If he had studied any contract law he would argue that he believed he had the legal right to select the goods, even though wrongly priced, because the price tag was, in any event, only an invitation to treat. He will contend that anyone could pick up any item in a store and, regardless of the marked price, make an offer to buy it. It is up to the store to decide whether or not to accept the purchaser's offer. It is submitted that this provides a compelling basis from which he can refute dishonesty. The other provisions under s. 2(1)(b) and s. 2(1)(c) are less relevant. Again, if the s. 2(1)(a) argument does not succeed he could still rely on the jury. Directed as per *R v Ghosh* (above), the jury might not consider his actions as dishonest. Most people love a bargain and would try to buy an item at a lower price if given the chance. Given that these facts seem to indicate a possible loophole in the law, the prosecution might seek to rely on the House of Lords' decision in *R v Hinks* [2000] 4 All ER 833. In a very questionable ruling, a majority of their Lordships held that a defendant could commit theft even where he acquired a valid title to property under a valid *inter vivos* transfer. In other words a defendant can steal property whilst becoming the owner of it. On this basis it could be argued that, notwithstanding that Stephen becomes the owner of the chocolates when he buys them, he nevertheless appropriates property belonging to another. The prosecution would still have the difficulties outlined above in relation to dishonesty, however.

If fraud and theft charges fail, the prosecution might fall back on a charge of making off without payment, contrary to s. 3 of the Theft Act 1978. The offence requires proof that Stephen dishonestly made off without having paid as required or expected, that he knew payment was expected from him, and that he had intent to avoid payment of the amount due. The obvious problem is that he will argue that he did pay as required and expected— he paid the amount requested by the cashier. Even if this issue is surmounted there might still be difficulties in establishing dishonesty: see the *R v Ghosh* direction outlined above.

Natasha's liability

Does Natasha steal the sausages when she first takes possession of them? The sausages are property—see s. 4(1). Does property pass to her at the deli counter? Possibly not as she has not yet paid—hence she appropriates by taking them. Does she have *mens rea* at this point? As to dishonesty see s. 2(1)(a)–(c) and *R v Ghosh* (above). She may believe that it is her good luck that she has been given the extra sausages and that she has the legal right to keep them (see s. 2(1)(a)). She has intention to permanently deprive. If property in the sausages does pass to Natasha at the deli counter, notwithstanding that she has not paid, s. 5(4) of the Theft Act 1968 (property got by mistake), cannot operate to prevent property passing here as she is not under any legal obligation to make restoration of the sausages. Section 5(4) does not create the legal obligation to make restoration, it applies if there is, in civil law, a legal obligation to make restoration.

Natasha may have committed a fraud offence at the checkout. She knows the bag is wrongly labelled but says nothing. The prosecution may argue that her conduct amounted to an implied representation that she believed the bag to be correctly marked-up—see *DPP v Ray* [1974] AC 370 (an authority on the pre-Fraud Act 2006 law, but still persuasive on this point). If her conduct can amount to a representation it is clearly untrue or misleading. As the s. 2 offence does not require anything more by way of *actus reus*, liability would therefore hinge upon proof of *mens rea*. Natasha knows the price on the bag is too low—hence the jury would have to determine whether or not her actions were dishonest following a direction in accordance with *R v Ghosh* (considered above). Some jurors might be minded to think that the mistake by the assistant is Natasha's good luck and that she ought to be allowed to benefit by it, especially as she did not induce it.

As with Stephen's liability considered above, it is hard to see how there could be liability under s. 3 Fraud Act 2006 (fraud by failing to disclose information), the issue again being the absence of any legal (as opposed to moral) duty on the part of Natasha to point out the shop assistant's error.

On a similar basis to Stephen, Natasha could be charged with making off without payment contrary to s. 3 of the 1978 Act, and could also be charged with theft if *R v Hinks* (above) was relied upon by the prosecution. In each of these offences dishonesty might still prove the stumbling block for reasons outlined above.

Martina's liability

Martina cannot incur liability for theft of the DVD if she had no intention to permanently deprive Susan of the property. Assuming the other elements of theft are made out, under s. 6(1) Martina can be *regarded* as having the intention of permanently depriving Susan of the DVD if it was her intention to treat the thing as her own to dispose of regardless of Susan's rights—it is a question of fact whether taking the DVD for one night amounts to a disposal. The court may be persuaded by the argument that it was a borrowing for a period and in circumstances making it equivalent to an outright taking, given that Susan was deprived of the chance of hiring out the DVD whilst Martina had it: see by contrast *R v Lloyd* [1985] QB 829. If intention to permanently deprive cannot be established the obvious charge is one of making off without payment contrary to s. 3 of the Theft Act 1978—all elements are present, subject to proof of dishonesty. There is no evidence to suggest the use of any false representation in relation to Martina's taking of the DVD, hence no Fraud Act 2006 liability under ss. 2–4 arises. It is also hard to see how any liability could arise under s. 11 of the 2006 Act—obtaining services dishonestly. What Martina obtains is property, in the form of the DVD. It would be straining the words of s. 11 to extend the concept of 'service' to include the watching of the DVD in her own home—compare with watching a film in a cinema which clearly would fall within the scope of services.

Question 3

Alison visits her local library to borrow a book. The loan period is three weeks. On her way out of the library she stops at a vending machine to buy a bar of chocolate. She puts a £1 coin (the correct amount) into a vending machine to obtain a bar of chocolate. Because of a malfunctioning of the vending machine ten bars of chocolate are dispensed. Alison takes all ten bars.

Alison then visits Grace, her mother. Whilst Grace is busy making a cup of tea Alison takes a silver ornament from the mantelpiece and places it in her pocket intending to sell it later. Whilst they are having tea Grace tells Alison that she has bought her a silver ornament as a present.

Grace searches for the ornament but is unable to find it. Alison says nothing about the fact that she has already taken it.

Alison telephones for a taxi to take her home from her mother's house. On arriving at her destination Alison tells the taxi driver that she has no money to pay for the ride. This is untrue. The taxi driver is furious and tells her to get out of his cab. He drives off without having been paid. Three months later Alison comes across the library book and realizes that it is overdue. She has not received any reminders from the library so decides to keep the book.

Advise the Crown Prosecution Service as to the possible criminal liability of Alison.

Commentary

A number of discrete incidents here, the library book, the chocolate, the ornament and the taxi ride. Note the need to consider burglary in relation to the ornament. Candidates might think that the incident with the chocolate bars involves issues of obtaining property by mistake, but care must be taken not to automatically bring in **s. 5(4) of the Theft Act 1968**. Remember that the subsection only applies where D is under a legal obligation to return the property, circumstances that normally only arise where money is received by mistake. Theft is the obvious charge in relation to the silver ornament, leading possibly to burglary, but the **Fraud Act 2006** offences should also be considered as there are issues about false representations being made by silence—the question here is whether liability can be imposed even though Alison has already taken possession of the ornament. Take care over Alison's liability in relation to the taxi ride. Is it obvious from the facts as to when she decided not to pay for the journey? Examiners often leave the issue open—liability for certain offences may depend very much on when Alison decided not to pay. If this information is not provided candidates may have to argue in the alternative, as demonstrated in the suggested answer that follows.

Answer plan

- Theft of library book—problems with intention to permanently deprive
- Subsequent appropriation of library book by keeping—dishonesty in issue
- Theft of chocolate bars—dishonesty problems and consideration of **s. 5(4)**
- Making off without payment

- Burglary and theft in relation to the ornament
- Possible fraud offences in relation to the ornament
- Fraud and making off offences in relation to the taxi ride

Suggested answer

Library book

When Alison borrowed the book she appropriated property belonging to another, as defined by ss. 4(1) and 5(1) of the Theft Act 1968. There is no liability for theft at this stage, however, as she does not appear to be dishonest—neither does she have any intention to permanently deprive at this point. Her decision several months later to keep the book could amount to theft. Under s. 3(1) she can appropriate property where she has come by it innocently, without stealing it, if she later assumes the rights of the owner by keeping it. Her intention to permanently deprive is self-evident when she decides to keep the book hence the only live issue is dishonesty. Consider first s. 2(1)(a)–(c) of the Theft Act 1968. Alison has not been asked to return the book. Might this cause her to believe that she has, in law, the right to deprive the library of it? The test is subjective. On the facts this seems like a weak argument. More promising is s. 2(1)(b) whereby Alison can argue that she honestly believed that the library would have consented had it known of the appropriation and the circumstances of it. Again the test is subjective. Alison might believe that the failure of the library to chase up the non-return of the book is evidence of the library not caring about her keeping it. Section 2(1)(c) is not relevant on the facts. If Alison cannot bring herself within s. 2(1)(a)–(c) she may have to rely on the jury, following a *R v Ghosh* [1982] QB 1053 direction. Under *Ghosh* the jury will be asked to consider two questions: whether according to the ordinary standards of reasonable and honest people Alison acted dishonestly in keeping the library book? If 'No', Alison must be acquitted. If 'Yes', the question will be whether or not Alison must have realized that what she was doing was by those standards dishonest. It seems unlikely that a jury would regard her behaviour as dishonest.

Vending machine

Alison could be liable for theft of the additional bars of chocolate. The extra bars of chocolate are property—see s. 4(1) of the Theft Act 1968. There was no intention on the part of the owner that property should pass to Alison without her inserting the required amount of money. Hence the additional bars remain property belonging to another. There is no need to resort to s. 5(4) of the Theft Act 1968 here (property got by mistake), as s. 5(1) can be relied upon to establish that the property belongs to another. In any event it is doubtful that s. 5(4) could apply—was Alison under any legal obligation to make restoration of the additional bars of chocolate? Alison appropriates the bars of chocolate by taking them. Her intention to permanently deprive the owner is evident. Again dishonesty is the element that will provoke most argument. Referring again to s. 2(1)(a) of the Theft Act 1968, she might argue that she had the right in law to keep the chocolate. She does not have to establish any such legal right—merely provide evidence that she honestly thought she had such a right. She might well believe this. Section 2(1)(b) seems less compelling here, but s. 2(1)(c) might be worth considering. Did she believe the owner of the chocolate bars could not be found by taking reasonable steps? She could have alerted the library and returned them there and then, but she may have believed that the machine was nothing to do with the library. The subjective nature of the s. 2(1)(c) provision should be stressed here. If Alison cannot avoid a finding of dishonesty under s. 2(1) of the Theft Act 1968, she may still escape liability on the basis that she was not dishonest according to the common law approach to that concept, see *R v Ghosh* (above). Was Alison dishonest in keeping the chocolate according to the ordinary standards of reasonable and honest people? If 'No', Alison must be acquitted. If 'Yes', the question will be whether or not Alison must have realized that what she was doing was by those standards dishonest. It is very hard to predict what view a jury might take on applying this test.

As a last resort the prosecution might consider liability for making off without payment contrary to s. 3 of the Theft Act 1978. Having obtained the chocolate bars, however, how is Alison meant to make the additional payment? Dishonesty would also be a problem as outlined above.

Silver ornament

In taking the silver ornament Alison appears to appropriate property belonging to another with intention to permanently deprive. It subsequently transpires that her mother intended to give her the ornament as a gift but at the time it was taken it was still property belonging to another as against Alison. The only issue that Alison can argue to avoid liability is dishonesty. Under s. 2(1)(b) of the Theft Act 1968, she can argue that she honestly believed her mother would have consented to the taking had she known of it. Alison will rely on the fact that her mother intended to give her the ornament as a present. The problem for Alison is that she did not know this when she took the ornament. Alternatively Alison might argue that if her mother had known how desperate she was for money she would have agreed to her taking the ornament to sell. This is a weak argument—if that was the case why did she not ask her mother outright?

Again, if an argument under s. 2(1) of the Theft Act 1968 fails, Alison will have to rely on the jury determining that she was not dishonest following a direction under *R v Ghosh* (above). It is submitted that this is unlikely to avail her.

If it can be shown that Alison intended to steal the ornament (or indeed anything) before she entered the house, she could be charged with burglary contrary to s. 9(1)(a) of the Theft Act 1968—entry as a trespasser with intent to steal; or s. 9(1)(b)—having entered as a trespasser she therein stole.

Alison might try to argue that she could not be a trespasser in her mother's house, but see *R v Jones and Smith* [1976] 3 All ER 54—if she enters intending to steal she enters for a purpose in excess of her express or implied permission—her mother does not give her permission to enter in order to steal.

Although theft and burglary are the obvious offences here, consideration ought also to be given to the possibility of fraud offences, as these may prove less complicated. Under s. 2

of the Fraud Act 2006 it could be argued that by her silence when Grace talks about giving the ornament to Alison and not being able to find it, Alison makes a false representation. She is giving the impression that she does not know where it is when in fact she does. Section 2(3) provides that a representation for these purposes can include a representation as to a person's state of mind. The fact that Alison has already taken the ornament should not be a bar to liability as, unlike under the previous deception offences, there is no need under s. 2 to prove that the false representation actually causes anything. The offence is really inchoate in nature. Hence there is no need to show that the false representation occurs before Alison obtains the ornament. If the false representation is established the *mens rea* issues will be: (i) whether or not Alison was dishonest within the terms of *R v Ghosh* (above), as to which see above in relation to the library book; and (ii) whether or not she made the false representation with a view to gain. On this latter point s. 5(3) provides that 'gain' can extend to keeping what one has—hence the gain here could be Alison keeping possession of the ornament. It is submitted that s. 3 of the Fraud Act 2006—fraud by failing to disclose information—ought not to be pursued as the prosecution might have difficulty in proving that Alison was under a legal duty to tell her mother that she had already taken the ornament. A moral duty will not suffice for these purposes.

Taxi ride

Alison's liability depends on when she decided not to pay—if she never intended to pay she may have dishonestly obtained services contrary to s. 11(1) of the Fraud Act 2006. Calling the taxi not intending to pay would constitute the required dishonest act. The taxi ride was a service provided on the understanding that it had been or would be paid for. The dishonest act must be shown to have caused the provision of the service—in other words to have been operative. It can be reasonably safely assumed that the taxi driver would not have provided the service had he known he was not going to be paid. The *mens rea* is evident—dishonesty (as per *R v Ghosh* (above)) and the knowledge that the service will only be provided on the basis that it has been or will be paid for, and an intention not to pay for it. If Alison decided not to pay on arriving at her destination she could be charged with making off without payment contrary to s. 3(1) Theft Act 1978. She clearly fails to pay as required and as expected for services provided, and she knows that payment is required on the spot. The only argument might be as to whether she makes off—it is the taxi driver who throws her out of the taxi. It is submitted that Alison's behaviour is the type of 'mischief' the s. 3 offence was intended to cover—hence she should be liable. An alternative charge might be s. 2(1) of the Fraud Act 2006—Alison dishonestly makes a false representation with view to gain, or more likely in this case causing loss to the taxi driver. The false representation is evident in the lie that she tells about not having any money. There seems to be little argument here as to her dishonesty and her intention to gain by keeping the fare money or causing loss to the taxi driver by not paying. There is no need to prove that the driver is in any way taken in by Alison's lies. The offence under s. 2 is effectively inchoate—liability arises once the false representation is made with the requisite intent.

Question 4

Answer both parts.

(a) Christina sends Britney a £50 note as a gift because Christina believes that Britney has passed her CPE Criminal Law exam. Britney has not in fact passed her CPE Criminal Law exam and knows that Christina is acting under that misapprehension.

(b) Does Britney commit theft when she keeps the £50 note and uses it to purchase some bottles of wine for herself?

(c) Kashif takes a £50 note from the cash register of his employer Ahmed on a Friday evening because he has no money to go out with his friends that night. Kashif, who earns £400 a week working for Ahmed, is normally paid in cash on Saturdays. Kashif leaves a note in the cash register explaining that he has taken the money and that Ahmed should deduct it from the wages due to Kashif the following day.

Does Kashif commit theft when he takes the money from the cash register?

Commentary

On one level a very standard theft question—and note that the rubric limits answers specifically to liability for theft. Candidates are not being asked to consider liability under the **Fraud Act 2006**. This should serve as a clue, however, to the fact that the examiner is looking for a little more depth on the difficult points. Without question, in part (a) this is the vexed question of whether or not property in the money has passed. Candidates should be well acquainted with the decision in *R v Hinks* as examiners are likely to weave it into their theft questions. The decision may not be supported by a logically reasoned majority argument, but it is compelling evidence of the willingness of the House of Lords to allow public policy (the conviction of dishonest persons) to drive the interpretation of the **Theft Acts**. Part (b) centres on a detailed run through of the possible arguments on dishonesty that all properly prepared exam candidates should be in a position to undertake.

Answer plan

(a) Britney's liability

- Does property in the money pass?
- Application of ss. 5(1) and 5(4) of the Theft Act 1968
- Possible reliance on *R v Hinks* by the prosecution
- Arguments on dishonesty

(b) Kashif's liability

- Elements of *actus reus* established
- Detailed consideration of dishonesty
- s. 2(1)(a)–(c)
- *Ghosh*
- Intention to permanently deprive
- Deeming provisions of s. 6(1)

Suggested answer

Part (a)

The £50 note is clearly property for the purposes of the offence of theft; see s. 4(1) Theft Act 1968. When Britney receives the £50 note it appears that it is her own property. Christina has made her a gift of the money, and there is no evidence presented here to suggest that the gift is anything other than a valid *inter vivos* transfer of property. If that argument were to be accepted by the courts there could be no liability on the part of Britney as a key element of the *actus reus* of theft (property belonging to another) would be absent.

Are there any grounds upon which it could be argued that property in the money does not pass to Britney? First, s. 5(1) of the Theft Act 1968 provides that property shall be regarded as belonging to any person having in it any proprietary right or interest. It might be argued that, as Christina has parted with the money under a misapprehension, she should in equity be regarded as retaining an equitable interest in the money; see *R v Shadrokh-Cigari* [1988] Crim LR 465 (although this argument was raised in relation to a mistake as to the amount of the money being transferred, not the basis on which it was being transferred).

Secondly, the prosecution might argue that s. 5(4) of the 1968 Act operates to prevent property passing because Britney got the money as a result of Christina's mistake, and was thus under a legal obligation (arising from quasi-contract) to restore the money (or proceeds thereof). Again, it might be argued that this subsection was enacted to deal with mistakes as to the amount of money transferred, not a mistake as to the basis for the transfer itself (see *Moynes v Cooper* [1956] 1 QB 439), but it is submitted that the wording of the sub-section is wide enough to cover the situation described in the facts. In *Attorney-General's Reference (No. 1 of 1983)* [1984] 3 All ER 369, Lord Lane CJ observed that s. 5(4) came into play once a defendant received money transferred under a mistake on the part of the giver as to a material fact (i.e. mistake as to a fundamental or essential fact), provided the payment was due to that fundamental or essential fact.

Note that if Britney got the money by mistake she would have been, as a result, under an obligation to make restoration of the money or its proceeds to Christina. If the money was spent on bottles of wine the obligation would be to return the bottles of wine to Christina (as the proceeds). If Britney consumes the wine it is not clear what 'proceeds' of the £50 note Britney would be under an obligation to restore other than the empty bottles!

If s. 5(1) or s. 5(4) cannot be relied upon to establish that property has not passed to Britney, the prosecution could argue its case on the basis of the House of Lords' ruling in *R v Hinks* [2000] 4 All ER 833, where it was held that the recipient of a valid gift could be guilty of theft, even where the donor retained no residual interest in the property simply because the recipient was dishonest in accepting the gift.

Lord Steyn, giving the majority view in *R v Hinks*, observed that in *R v Gomez* [1993] 1 All ER 1, the House of Lords was expressly invited to hold that there could be no appropriation (and therefore no theft) where the entire proprietary interest in the property in question passed to the defendant, but the majority in *R v Gomez* rejected the proposition. He accepted that the certified question in *R v Gomez* concerned a situation where consent to the taking of the goods had been obtained by deception (see now ss. 2–4 of the Fraud Act 2006), but concluded that the majority judgments did not differentiate between cases where there had been fraud and those where there had not.

What is clearly unsatisfactory about the majority speeches in *R v Hinks* is their failure to engage with the argument that if the transfer of property was valid, the property could no longer be regarded as property belonging to another as against the defendant. As Lord Hobhouse (dissenting in *R v Hinks*), observed, once the donor has done his part in transferring the property to the defendant, the property (subject to s. 5 of the Theft Act 1968) ceases to be 'property belonging to another'. Lord Hobhouse felt that, however wide a meaning one were to give to 'appropriates', there could not, in those circumstances, be a theft. In his view Britney would not be assuming the rights of Christina, she would be acquiring them by way of gift.

Assuming the prosecution relies successfully on one of the three routes outlined above to establishing that the £50 note remains property belonging to another as against Britney, and taking the appropriation as read (keeping and spending the money) attention will turn to the issue of *mens rea*. As the charge under consideration is theft, attention first has to be given to s. 2(1)(a)–(c) of the 1968 Act. Under s. 2(1)(a) Britney could argue that she appropriated the property in the belief that she had in law the right to deprive Christina of it. The test is subjective. Britney merely has to provide evidence that she honestly believed that she had the right—there is no need for her to prove that any legal right to the money in fact existed. Britney is less likely to rely on s. 2(1)(b)—that she appropriated the money in the belief that Christina would have consented if she had known of the appropriation and the circumstances of it. The 'circumstances' here must encompass the fact that Britney has not passed her exams, hence it is hard to see how Britney could argue that she honestly believed that Christina was nevertheless still happy for her to keep the money. Sub-sections 2(1)(c) and 2(2) have no application here.

If the argument under s. 2(1)(a) does not sway the jury Britney will have to rely on the argument that, notwithstanding that she does not fall within the negative definition of dishonesty in s. 2(1)(a)–(c), she is not dishonest in light of the standard direction to the jury on dishonesty at common law; see *R v Ghosh* [1982] QB 1053. The jury will be directed to consider whether according to the ordinary standards of reasonable and honest people Britney was dishonest in keeping and spending the money. If the jury conclude that what she did was not dishonest by those standards, she will not be guilty of theft. If the jury conclude that she was dishonest by those standards they will have to go on to consider a second question: whether Britney realized that what she was doing was, by those standards, dishonest. It is not possible to predict how a jury might view Britney's actions, hence the advice would have to be that this issue could go either way.

Britney clearly had intention to permanently deprive Christina of the money, as evidenced by her spending it, hence this element can be made out without reference to s. 6(1) of the 1968 Act.

Part (b)

When Kashif takes the £50 note from Ahmed's cash register he appropriates property belonging to another. The £50 note is property—s. 4(1) of the Theft Act 1968 refers; the money clearly belongs to another as against Kashif—s. 5(1) of the 1968 Act refers; and by taking the money Kashif is assuming some of the rights of the owner—s. 3(1) of the 1968 Act refers. The *actus reus* of theft is clearly made out.

Regarding dishonesty, attention first has to be given to s. 2(1)(a)–(c) of the 1968 Act. It is unlikely that Kashif would be able to rely on s. 2(1)(a)—honest belief that he appropriated the property in the belief that he had in law the right to deprive Ahmed of it. Even though Kashif does not have to prove the existence of any such legal right, there is no evidence to suggest that he believes any such legal right exists. The only rational basis for such a belief could be the evidence that Kashif is owed more in wages for the work he has already done that week than the amount of money he takes from the cash register without permission.

Kashif is more likely to rely on s. 2(1)(b)—that he appropriated the money in the belief that Ahmed would have consented if he had known of the appropriation and the circumstances of it. The 'circumstances' here must encompass the fact that Kashif has left a note making it clear that he has taken the money, and the fact that he has accrued an entitlement to wages that would more than cover the amount of money he is taking. It would be prudent to ascertain whether there was any previous custom and practice of employees acting as Kashif has done that had been expressly or impliedly accepted by Ahmed. The key point to bear in mind here is that the test is subjective—if Kashif honestly believes Ahmed would have consented then he must be acquitted, regardless of whether or not Ahmed actually did consent, or would have done had he known.

If the arguments under s. 2(1)(a) and 2(1)(b) do not prevail Kashif will have to rely on the argument that, notwithstanding that he does not fall within the negative definition of dishonesty in s. 2(1)(a) and (b), he is not dishonest in light of the standard direction to the jury on dishonesty at common law; see *R v Ghosh* (above). The jury will be directed to consider whether according to the ordinary standards of reasonable and honest people Kashif was dishonest in taking the money. The fact that he leaves a note, and the fact that he is due far more in wages the next day suggest strongly that a jury might take a benign view of his actions. Even if they do not, he might still escape liability if there is evidence that he did not realize that what he was doing was, by the standards of ordinary decent people, dishonest.

As to intention to permanently deprive, Kashif may argue that he was not intending to cause any real loss to Ahmed, as the £50 would have been deducted from his wages.

The fact remains, however, that Kashif was intending to permanently deprive Ahmed of the particular £50 note in question; see *R v Velumyl* [1989] Crim LR 299. By taking the money and spending it he is unquestionably treating it as his own to dispose of regardless of Ahmed's rights—s. 6(1) of the Theft Act 1968 refers.

Question 5(a)

Jerry is the managing director of, and majority shareholder in, Barnham Ltd, a company that owns an old people's home. Mike is an employee of Barnham who works at the home. The business is going badly and the home is deteriorating rapidly. This fact has been noted by Ben, an eccentric resident, who has complained on many occasions that the fire-fighting equipment is totally inadequate and that the residents and the adjoining local church are in danger from the risk of fire. Jerry instructs Mike to start a fire, so that Barnham Ltd will be able to make a claim for damage to the home on their insurance policy. Mike starts a small fire.

At the same time, and independently of Mike, Ben decides to test his theory and also starts a fire. Both fires spread, the home is badly damaged and, although nobody is injured, the residents have to be evacuated.

Before Jerry submits an insurance claims form, the police arrest Jerry, Mike, and Ben.

Advise Mike, Jerry, and Ben as to their criminal liability.

 Commentary

This question involves a detailed analysis of a number of issues under the **Criminal Damage Act 1971**. In particular, the offences under **s. 1** and the two specific defences to **s. 1(1)** contained in **s. 5(2)** must be analysed in detail. These principles have been applied in a number of decisions that have emphasized the peculiarities of the law on this topic.

The advice on the *mens rea* required will need to reflect the fact that *Metropolitan Police Commissioner v Caldwell* [1981] 1 All ER 961, no longer determines the definition of recklessness in relation to the offence of criminal damage, *R v G* [2003] 4 All ER 765, reasserting the subjective approach to this type of fault. In addition inchoate offences should be considered: encouraging the commission of an offence contrary to **ss. 44 and 45 of the Serious Crime Act 2007** and attempt contrary to **s. 1(1) of the Criminal Attempts Act 1981**, and conspiracy contrary to **s. 1(1) of the Criminal Law Act 1977**.

 Answer plan

- Mike's liability as principal offender—simple and aggravated criminal damage
- Jerry's liability as an accomplice to Mike

- Availability of lawful excuse to s. 1(1) charge

  - *Denton* [1982]

  - *Appleyard* [1985]

- Liability for related inchoate offences

- **Serious Crime Act 2007**

- Statutory conspiracy

- Attempted fraud—s. 2, **Fraud Act 2006**

- *Ben*

  - Criminal damage

  - **s. 1(1), Criminal Damage Act 1971**

  - **s. 5(2), Criminal Damage Act 1971**—*Hunt* [1977]

Suggested answer

The facts indicate that Mike starts a small fire. Given that he does so on Jerry's instructions, and given that Jerry wants the elderly persons' home destroyed, it is assumed that Mike damages and destroys some property in starting the fire. For an offence of criminal damage contrary to s. 1(1) of the Criminal Damage Act 1971 to be made out, the prosecution must prove that, as against Mike, the property belongs to another. Given that Mike is an employee of Barnham Ltd, the company that owns the premises, this should be easy to establish. Mike clearly intends to damage and destroy property by his actions, hence *mens rea* would be established. As Mike has used fire, the charge may actually be one of arson under s. 1(3) of the 1971 Act as the maximum sentence is greater (life as opposed to ten years).

Jerry could be charged as an accomplice to Mike on the basis that he counselled the commission of the offence and Mike did nothing outside the scope of the authority given to him by Jerry. Jerry clearly intended that the property should be damaged or destroyed.

Both defendants, however, might to seek to rely on a defence under s. 5(2) of the 1971 Act, which provides that a person charged with a s. 1(1) offence can be regarded as having had a lawful excuse for his actions if, at the time of the act, he believed that the person or persons whom he believed to be entitled to consent to the destruction of or damage to the property in question had so consented.

Although their positions may seem identical, on analysis of the two leading cases on this section (*R v Denton* [1982] 1 All ER 65; *R v Appleyard* (1985) 81 Cr App R 319) there may be a difference in Jerry's and Mike's criminal responsibility. In *R v Denton*, an employee (D) had been instructed by his employer (X) to damage X's property by fire, so that X could make a fraudulent insurance claim. At D's trial, the judge ruled that s. 5(2) of the 1971 Act could not provide D with a lawful excuse, as he knew that his employer had consented to his starting the fire and damaging the property purely for fraudulent purposes. The consent, ruled the trial judge, was therefore invalid. However, D's conviction was quashed on appeal, the court holding that no offence was committed under s. 1(1) or s. 1(3) of the Act by a person who burnt down his own premises; neither could that act become unlawful because of the intent to defraud the insurers.

On application of *Denton*, Mike would have a defence; and it would appear that Jerry could use the same argument. However, Jerry's liability appears to be governed by the decision in *R v Appleyard*. In this case, A, the managing director and majority shareholder of a company, X Ltd, set fire to X Ltd's property, with a view to making a fraudulent insurance claim. A argued on the authority of *Denton* that he could not be guilty of damaging his own property, but this argument was rejected on the basis that the company is a separate legal entity and, as the building was owned by the company, A was damaging property belonging to another. A also contended that, as he was in control of the company and could make decisions on the company's behalf, he had the defence under s. 5(2) as he had the consent of the company. Again, the court rejected the argument on the basis that company decisions must be made for a proper purpose and in the company's best interests. As this was clearly not the case, there was no consent or belief in the owner's consent. A's conviction was upheld by the Court of Appeal.

It is therefore submitted on authority of these cases that whereas Mike may be acquitted of these charges on the basis of having honestly believed he had the owner's consent, Jerry would be convicted.

It should be further noted that when Jerry instructs Mike to start a fire, he will have committed the offence of intentionally encouraging or assisting another person to commit an offence, contrary to s. 44 of the Serious Crime Act 2007. Jerry clearly intends that Mike should commit the *actus reus* of criminal damage, and although Mike might have a lawful excuse, Jerry can be convicted by virtue of s. 47(5)(a)(iii) of the Serious Crime Act 2007 on the basis that, regardless of Mike's state of mind, had Jerry committed the *actus reus*, he would have done so with the requisite intent.

Jerry and Mike could also be charged under s. 1(2) of the 1971 Act, which provides that it is an offence, without lawful excuse, to destroy or damage any property, regardless of who owns it, where the defendant intentionally or recklessly destroys or damages any property intending by the destruction or damage to endanger the life of another or being reckless as to whether the life of another would be thereby endangered.

The facts demonstrate that as the home was evacuated, life may have been endangered; it is only necessary that the prosecution show that life could have been (not actually was) endangered (*R v Dudley* [1989] Crim LR 57).

Jerry and Mike may argue that they lacked the *mens rea* for this offence because they did not foresee this consequence. As indicated above, the House of Lords in *R v G* [2003] 4 All ER 765, confirmed that a defendant could not be guilty unless he had foreseen the risk of criminal damage (or the endangerment of life thereby), had gone on to take that risk, and that in the circumstances known to the defendant, it had been unreasonable for him to take the risk.

Again Jerry may be charged with an offence of encouraging the commission of the s. 1 (2) criminal damage offence, contrary to the Serious Crime Act 2007. Section 45 of the 2007 Act may be the appropriate charge on the basis that Jerry encouraged Mike in a course of conduct that he believed would assist in the commission of the offence.

Further inchoate offences may be made out. The prosecution may contend that Jerry and Mike agreed that the fire should be started, and thus conspired to commit either the s. 1(1) criminal damage offence, or the aggravated form of the offence under s. 1(2), contrary to s. 1(1) of the Criminal Law Act 1977. Such a charge might be appropriate where the prosecution feels that the substantive offence cannot be made out, as indicated above. Jerry may be charged under s. 1(1) of the Criminal Attempts Act 1981 with an attempt to commit fraud by false representation contrary to s. 2(1) of the Fraud Act 2006. Had Jerry made the insurance claim, the claim itself would have constituted a false representation, given the fact that he had ordered the fire to be started. By making the claim he would have been implying that he was in no way responsible for the fire being started deliberately. This implied representation would have been untrue. The dishonesty accompanying such a claim would have been self-evident, given the facts, as would the intention to gain from making the false representation. The issue for the prosecution would, therefore, be as to whether or not Jerry had gone far enough towards committing the s. 2 Fraud Act offence to be regarded as having attempted to commit it. To establish liability for attempt the prosecution would have to show that Jerry went beyond a merely preparatory act with the appropriate *mens rea*. Whether an act is more than merely preparatory is a question of fact for the jury (Criminal Attempts Act 1981, s. 4(3)). Each case depends on its own particular facts, but in the similar case of *R v Robinson* [1915] 2 KB 342, D's conviction for attempting to obtain money by false pretences (as the offence was then known) was quashed on the basis that as D had not actually submitted the fraudulent claim form, his conduct had not amounted to the *actus reus* of attempt. Although this case was before 1981 and therefore did not apply the present test, *R v Widdowson* (1985) 82 Cr App R 314 was decided in the same way, and it is therefore submitted that Jerry may not have gone beyond a merely preparatory act and could not be found guilty of attempting to commit the offence under s. 2 of the Fraud Act 2006. Mike, in starting the fire, could be charged with assisting Jerry in attempting to commit the s. 2 fraud offence, contrary to s. 44 of the Serious Crime Act 2007, provided the prosecution can prove that it was Mike's intention that the fraud should be committed. As purpose type intent is required this may be problematic—Mike may have been indifferent as to whether or not the fraud was carried out.

Provided the prosecution can prove that he was aware of the risk of harm, Ben would appear to be guilty of criminal damage under s. 1(1) of the 1971 Act. He may, however, be able to argue that the defence of lawful excuse is available under s. 5(2)(b), to the effect that he destroyed or damaged the property in order to protect property belonging to himself or another, and at the time of the act he believed that the property was in immediate need of protection, and that the means of protection adopted or proposed to be adopted were or would be reasonable having regard to all the circumstances.

At first sight, this subsection appears to offer a defence in many circumstances, as it is written in subjective terms. However, an objective element has been imported by the cases, and in *R v Hill and Hall* (1988) 89 Cr App R 74, the Court of Appeal ruled that the trial judge has to decide whether the evidence submitted by D is sufficient to enable this defence to be left to the jury; see also *R v Kelleher* [2003] EWCA Crim 2846, where D was convicted of 'decapitating a statue of Margaret Thatcher claiming that he was doing so to save the world from the consequences of materialism'. In *R v Hunt* (1977) 66 Cr App R 105, the court, on similar facts to the problem, held that D's act in setting fire to property was not done in order to protect the property—which was not in any case in immediate need of protection, until D started the fire! Further, in *Blake v DPP* [1993] Crim LR 586, it was held that s. 5(2) is not satisfied by D's belief that God is the owner of all property and that God consents to the damage.

Consequently, Ben may also be guilty under s. 1(2) of the 1971 Act on the same basis as Jerry and Mike.

Question 5(b)

Tracey, aged 14, often played in a small wood above concealed waste ground. She and her friends were in the habit of throwing stones down on to the waste ground, in the knowledge that as nobody ever went on that ground there was no risk of injury.

One day a sign was erected by the woods: 'New greenhouses, do not throw stones'. Although she saw the sign, Tracey was of low intelligence and could not read. Unaware of the warning, she threw a stone to the waste ground. The stone smashed a pane of glass in a greenhouse and narrowly missed Bill the gardener. Bill was so shocked by the incident that he became depressed and suffered headaches for a month.

Discuss the criminal responsibility (if any) of Tracey.

 ## Commentary

There are many interesting areas within the Criminal Damage Act 1971, a statute that has also attracted a number of odd cases (*Jaggard v Dickinson* [1980] 3 All ER 716, for example).

It is difficult to set a question exclusively related to criminal damage, and examiners will often involve an offence against the person to test the students' awareness of the different offences. Again the answer to this question should reflect the shift from objective recklessness, as determined by *Metropolitan Police Commissioner v Caldwell* [1981] 1 All ER 961, towards subjective recklessness as laid down in *R v G* [2003] 4 All ER 765. Section 47 of the Offences Against the Person Act 1861 must also be considered; in particular, can psychiatric injury constitute actual bodily harm?

Answer plan

- Criminal damage—s. 1(1), Criminal Damage Act 1971
- Recklessness
  - *R v G* [2003]
- Aggravated criminal damage—s. 1(2), Criminal Damage Act 1971
  - *Steer* [1987]
  - *Webster and Warwick* [1995]
- s. 47, Offences Against the Person Act 1861
  - *Chan Fook* [1994]
  - *Savage and Parmenter* [1992]

Suggested answer

Tracey could face charges under the Criminal Damage Act 1971 and the Offences Against the Person Act 1861, although she will be able to contend that she did not possess the necessary *mens rea* for these offences.

Under s. 1(1) of the Criminal Damage Act 1971, a person who without lawful excuse destroys or damages any property belonging to another, intending to destroy or damage any such property or being reckless as to whether any such property would be destroyed or damaged, shall be guilty of an offence. There are specific defences to s. 1(1) in s. 5 of the Act, but as they relate either to a belief in the owner's consent, or to a necessary and reasonable act to prevent further damage to property, Tracey will be unable to use them. However, although she has clearly committed the *actus reus* of the offence, she can argue that she lacked the *mens rea*, on the basis that as she did not foresee the consequence, she neither intended it nor was reckless as to its occurrence.

Following the House of Lords' decision in *R v G* [2003] 4 All ER 765, where the objective approach to recklessness laid down in *Metropolitan Police Commissioner v Caldwell* [1981] 1 All ER 961, was abandoned, the prosecution will have to prove that Tracey was at least aware of the risk of harm, consciously took that risk, and that it was, in the circumstances known to her, unreasonable for her to take the risk.

Section 1(2) of the Criminal Damage Act 1971 is the most serious offence facing Tracey; and although there is the possibility of a life sentence if the accused is found guilty, the ingredients of the offence can be easily satisfied by the prosecution. It is not necessary to show that someone's life was actually endangered, simply that it could have been endangered (*R v Dudley* [1989] Crim LR 57); and *mens rea* can be satisfied by proof of (subjective) recklessness. Hence Tracey could incur liability if she foresaw the risk of criminal damage endangering life. It should be noted, however, that the endangerment to life must arise as a result of the criminal damage. This was confirmed by the House of Lords in *R v Steer* [1988] AC 111, where the accused fired bullets, which narrowly missed V, through the window of a house. The prosecution contended that as the accused had caused criminal damage and V's life had been endangered, the offence under s. 1(2) had been established. However, the House of Lords stated that this offence was committed only if the life had been or could have been endangered by the criminal damage.

It will sometimes be difficult on the facts to make this key distinction. Thus in *R v Webster and Warwick* [1995] 2 All ER 168, where the accused threw bricks at a moving police car, smashing a window and causing glass to fall over the officers, the court held that this ingredient for s. 1(2) could be satisfied, as the driver might lose control as a result of being showered with glass. Thus, if the gardener was endangered by the stone thrown by Tracey, she would not be guilty; but if endangerment was caused by the splintering glass, she would be!

Tracey might also be charged under s. 47 of the Offences Against the Person Act 1861: 'Whosoever shall be convicted upon an indictment of any assault occasioning actual bodily harm shall be liable...to [imprisonment for five years]'. Although Bill has not suffered direct physical injury, psychiatric injury can amount to actual bodily harm (*R v Mike Chan-Fook* [1994] 2 All ER 552); and in *R v Ireland* [1997] 4 All ER 225, the Court of Appeal and the House of Lords held that psychiatric injury can amount to grievous bodily harm for the purpose of s. 20 of the 1861 Act. However, minor emotional harm (e.g., fear or mild hysteria) will not be sufficient, and the prosecution must call expert psychiatric evidence to establish that Bill's depression and headaches constitute actual bodily harm.

Assault can be defined as intentionally or recklessly putting a person in fear of being then and there subjected to unlawful force (*Fagan v Metropolitan Police Commissioner* [1968] 3 All ER 442). It is quite clear that objective recklessness does not apply to common assault or s. 47 of the 1861 Act (*R v Savage; R v Parmenter* [1992] 1 AC 699); and although the *mens rea* for s. 47 is satisfied by proving the *mens rea* of common assault (i.e., the prosecution does not have to prove that the accused foresaw the risk of actual bodily harm: *R v Roberts* (1971) 56 Cr App R 95)—it is submitted that as Tracey was unaware of any danger to the person, she could not be found guilty of this offence.

Further reading

Elliott, D.W., 'Directors' Thefts and Dishonesty' [1991] Crim LR 732.

Griew, E., 'Dishonesty—The Objections to *Feely* and *Ghosh*' [1985] Crim LR 341.

Heaton, R., 'Deceiving without Thieving' [2001] Crim LR 712.

Hickey, R., 'Stealing Abandoned Goods: Possessory Title in Proceedings for Theft' (2006) 26 Leg Stud 584.

Shute, S., 'Appropriation and the Law of Theft' [2002] Crim LR 445.

Smith, J.C., 'Stealing Tickets' [1998] Crim LR 723.

Theft—*actus reus*

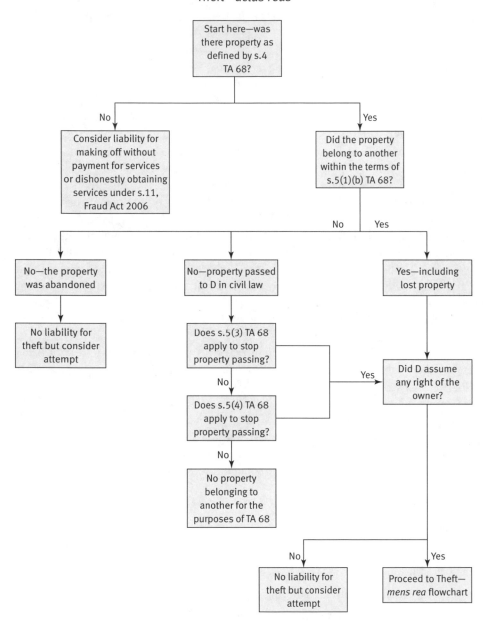

Theft—*mens rea*

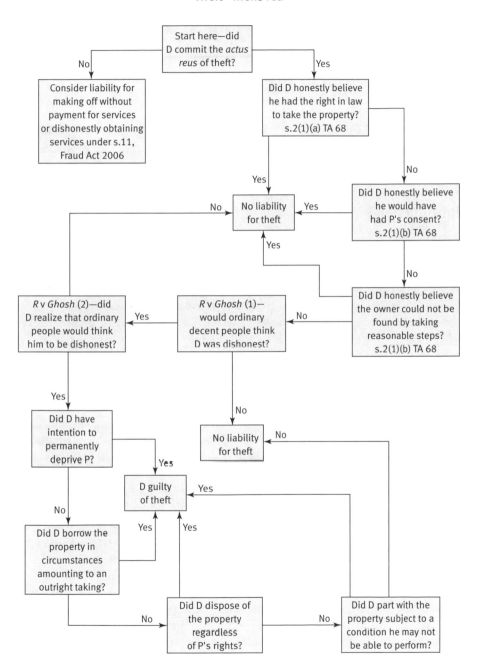

9

Fraud and other theft-related offences

Introduction

Many criminal law syllabuses will cover only theft and a few other theft-related offences, such as robbery and burglary. In the past deception offences were covered in most criminal law courses, but these have now been abolished by the Fraud Act 2006. It is assumed that most criminal law courses will seek to cover the main offences in the Fraud Act 2006, i.e., ss. 2–4 and s. 11, and those offences are dealt with in some of the questions comprising this chapter. There is less uniformity of practice in respect of coverage of offences such as blackmail, handling, taking a conveyance and going equipped. Again these are given some coverage in the answers set out in these chapters, and indeed in answers elsewhere in this book. There are many other offences under the Theft Act 1968, such as forgery and false accounting, but normally only specialist bodies would set questions on these crimes.

The questions included in this chapter are typical examination problems. It is rare that essay questions are set on these offences, as the rationale of the criminal law is best explored in other areas of the syllabus, such as *actus reus* and *mens rea*. Because there is not such a vast amount of material to cover on these offences as, for example, on causation or recklessness, the questions will often involve consideration of three or four offences. Some questions are set simply to test a student's ability to differentiate between closely related offences (for example, Question 2 concerning fraud). Others may require detailed analysis of cases and concepts on one crime only—burglary and handling stolen goods lend themselves to this type of question.

Because of the diverse material, and the fact that studying theft and theft-related offences almost seems like studying a separate subject from criminal law, many students are very apprehensive about tackling questions on these topics. Candidates should not be intimidated, however, as questions tend to be set on the well-known areas of difficulty which have been discussed in leading cases. A well-prepared student should be confident of scoring high marks on these questions, which may often be easier to answer than those from other parts of the syllabus.

Question 1

Ken is employed by Infinity plc and has his petrol paid for by his employer. The arrangement is that when he fills his tank at his local petrol station, owned and operated by Randy, the account held there by Infinity plc is debited to the extent of the amount due. Following a downsizing of Infinity plc Ken is made redundant on 1 March, but he continues to obtain his petrol from Randy's petrol station, telling him to charge the amount due to the Infinity plc account.

On one of these visits to the petrol station Ken sees a car stereo for sale priced at £9.99. A number of identical models are displayed for sale priced £99.99, and Ken realizes that this one item has been mispriced. Ken, who notices that Randy's 12-year-old son Fred is minding the counter whilst Randy is dealing with another customer, takes the stereo to the counter where Fred sells it to him for £9.99.

A week later, Ken visits Randy's petrol station and fills his petrol tank as usual, but, on attempting to charge the amount due to the Infinity plc account, he is challenged by Randy who tells him that he will have to pay, and that he owes Randy for all the petrol he has obtained since 1 March. As Ken moves to run away, Randy grabs his car keys to stop him making off. Ken punches Randy in the face causing him to become concussed. Ken takes his car keys, and grabs a bag of sweets from the counter. Ken's actions are captured on Randy's security video and he is later apprehended.

Advise the Crown Prosecution Service as to the criminal liability of Ken.

 Commentary

This is a good example of a **Theft Act 1968** and **Fraud Act 2006** question that covers a wide range of offences. Note how one incident, such as the non-payment for the petrol, raises the possibility of a number of different charges. The task for candidates is to determine which might be the most appropriate. As a general rule concentrate on the offence that most accurately reflects the defendant's criminality. For example, technically Ken may have stolen the petrol, but to prove this involves a rather difficult argument on appropriation. It may be much better to proceed with a fraud charge if possible. Dishonesty arises many times in a question such as this and it is often impossible to do more than hazard a guess as to how a jury might view the defendant's actions. Where candidates are given relevant facts, such as the circumstances of the victim, or the value of the property, they should bring these in to inform the advice given—see for example the advice regarding the mispriced stereo.

 Answer plan

- Fraud in relation to the purchasing of the petrol on account
- Theft of petrol
- Making off without paying for the petrol
- Selection of mispriced goods—theft and fraud

- Fraud in attempting to purchase more petrol on account
- Assault and robbery

Suggested answer

Fraud

The facts indicate that Ken continues to charge the cost of petrol to the Infinity plc account despite the fact that he is no longer employed by the company. Each time he did this he may have committed the offence of fraud by false pretences contrary to s. 2(1) of the Fraud Act 2006. The prosecution will argue that Ken exercised a false representation by purporting to be a person who was going to use a valid means for payment. This representation was untrue and misleading as Ken intended to charge the petrol to his previous employer's account when he no longer had authority to do so—see *DPP v Ray* [1974] AC 370. Under s. 2 of the 2006 Act there is no need to prove that this false representation actually causes any result, such as the obtaining of the petrol. In effect liability is inchoate. It is enough that the false representation is made with the relevant *mens rea*. Provided Ken realized that his line of credit had been terminated with his job it is submitted that the *mens rea* should be self-evident. He intends, by his false representation to gain (by keeping his money rather than using it to pay for the petrol) and he intends to cause loss to another (in this case Randy). Either intent will suffice for liability. Assuming these elements of s. 2 are made out the only live issue would then be dishonesty. As this is a fraud offence there is no statutory definition of dishonesty. The jury would be directed according to *R v Ghosh* [1982] QB 1053. According to the ordinary standards of reasonable and honest people was what Ken did dishonest? If it was dishonest by those standards, did Ken himself realize that what he was doing was by those standards dishonest? It is submitted that a jury would regard Ken's actions as dishonest.

Theft

Theft of the petrol is problematic as property in it passes to Ken as it fills his tank. The prosecution could argue that he appropriates it by pouring it into his tank, but this would be a little artificial. The prosecution might seek to rely on *R v Hinks* [2000] 4 All ER 833, to contend that Ken steals the petrol even though property in it has passed to him, but this involves a strained use of the Theft Act 1968 that seems unnecessary given the more obvious deception charge.

Making off without payment

In failing to pay for the petrol Ken may have committed the offence of making off without payment contrary to s. 3 of the Theft Act 1978. Ken knew that payment on the spot for goods supplied was required or expected from him. He made off without having paid as required or expected. He clearly had intent to permanently avoid payment: see *Allen* [1985] 2 All ER 641. Dishonesty, following a *Ghosh* direction as outlined above, would appear to be evident.

Liability for the mispriced item

The prosecution may allege that Ken committed theft in relation to the mispriced stereo. The stereo was property belonging to another: see s. 4(1) and s. 5(1) of the Theft Act 1968. Ken appropriates it simply by selecting it, even if the owner consents: see *Lawrence v Metropolitan Police Commissioner* [1970] 3 All ER 933, and *R v Gomez* [1993] 1 All ER 1. Ken evidently had intention to permanently deprive, hence the live issue is dishonesty, especially s. 2(1)(a). Ken will argue that he honestly believed he had the right in law to select the item and try to buy it at the lower price. The price tag is, in law, nothing more than an invitation to treat. A shopper who selects an item offers to buy it at the marked price. It is up to the retailer to decide whether or not to accept the offer. If the nuances of contract law prove to be beyond the average juror, Ken will seek to rely on the common law approach to dishonesty based on the *Ghosh* direction. According to the ordinary standards of reasonable and honest people was the selection of the mispriced item dishonest? If it was dishonest by those standards, did Ken himself realize that what he was doing was by those standards dishonest? Much depends on the extent to which the average juror would be prepared to take advantage of a mistake by a retailer. Some will see large companies as 'fair game' but may take a different view where family-run businesses are concerned. Also, the difference between the correct price and the erroneous price will be a factor. Here the difference is considerable, and the jurors might view Ken's actions as exploitative. The fact that he decides to buy the item when Randy's son is serving at the counter is suggestive of this. The prosecution might prefer to charge theft on the basis that Ken appropriates the stereo when he leaves the petrol station. One obvious problem with this approach is the argument that property has passed to Ken, hence he cannot steal the stereo. Even though there is a mistake as to price it is almost certainly the case that Ken acquires voidable title to the goods. The prosecution might seek to rely on *R v Hinks* (above), where the House of Lords, by a majority, held that a defendant could be guilty of theft even where he acquired title to property under a valid *inter vivos* transfer. Their Lordships were at a loss to explain how the property could still be regarded as property belonging to another if property in the goods had passed, but it provides an answer for the prosecution as regards Ken. Again, dishonesty would be an issue, as to which see above.

An alternative basis for liability might be that Ken committed a Fraud Act offence in attempting to purchase the mispriced item. The first argument could be that he committed an offence contrary to s. 2 of the Fraud Act 2006 when he offered to buy the car stereo for £9.99. Whilst the offence under s. 2 is effectively an inchoate offence (see above) there is still a need to show that Ken makes a representation. The prosecution will argue that he is presenting himself as an honest shopper who believes £9.99 to be the correct price. The prosecution might further rely on s. 2(3) of the 2006 Act, which provides that a representation can include a representation as to the state of mind of the person making the representation. Against this Ken will argue that he did not make any representation as to price. He did not switch labels. The representation as to price was being made by whoever put the £9.99 sticker on the car stereo. It is submitted that Ken should succeed on this point as to hold that his offering to buy the car stereo, knowing it to be wrongly priced, amounted to a false representation would arguably be to extend the scope of liability further than Parliament intended in passing the 2006 Act. The Act seeks to remove the need to prove that the false representation caused the obtaining of property. The definition of false representation under s. 2(3) of the Fraud Act 2006 is remarkably similar to the definition of deception that was contained in s. 15(4) of the Theft Act 1968—this creates a strong presumption that in passing the 2006 Act Parliament did not intend to extend the concept of false representation.

On this basis it is further submitted that Ken would not incur liability under s. 3 of the Fraud Act 2006 (the offence of fraud by failing to disclose information). It is true that he did not point out the error in the pricing of the car stereo—but then again why should he? It is not the customer's responsibility to ensure that items are correctly priced. Liability could only arise if it could be shown that Ken dishonestly failed to disclose information that he was under a legal duty to disclose, and that he intended to make a gain for himself thereby. It is not clear how this legal duty to point out the error in pricing could be established.

Finally, the prosecution may give consideration to charging Ken with making off without payment contrary to s. 3 of the Theft Act 1978 on the basis that he did not pay the full price for the car stereo. Notwithstanding that Ken knew that payment on the spot for goods supplied was required or expected from him. He may have been dishonest—this would have to be established by the jury following the *Ghosh* direction as outlined above—and he clearly intended to permanently avoid paying the full amount. The problem for the prosecution may lie in proving that Ken failed to pay as required and expected. In contract law terms he made an offer to buy the car stereo for £9.99 and this offer was accepted. Hence he will argue that he paid what was required within the terms of the contract of sale. The contract of sale might have been vitiated by the mistake as to price, but the error would have only rendered the contract voidable. It is submitted that Ken should succeed with the argument in defending any charge under s. 3 of the 1978 Act.

Assault/robbery

Ken punches Randy in the face causing him to become concussed. Concussion is likely to amount to actual bodily harm—see *T v DPP* [2003] All ER (D) 20—the harm caused involved an injurious impairment of the victim's sensory functions. The punch is clearly an assault and it causes the actual bodily harm. *Mens rea* is evident. A more serious charge would be robbery, contrary to s. 8 of the Theft Act 1968. Ken steals the sweets. His taking of the bag of sweets involves the dishonest appropriation of property belonging to another with intention to permanently deprive. Immediately before or at the time of stealing he uses force on Randy. The problem lies in whether or not he can be shown to have used the force in order to steal. The facts suggest that he used the force in order to recover his car keys. This in turn throws up the possibility that a charge of theft could be based on Ken using force to recover his keys. The problem then becomes one of whether or not he stole his keys when he grabbed them from Randy. The keys are property under s. 4(1). They could be regarded as property belonging to another as against Ken because they were in Randy's possession at the time—see s. 5(1). The problem for the prosecution is that Randy's possession may not have been lawful, however *R v Kelly* [1998] 3 All ER 741, confirms that it is possible to steal from one whose possession is unlawful. The taking of the keys would be the appropriation, and there is clearly intention to permanently deprive. The only remaining issue is dishonesty. Ken will rely on s. 2(1)(a)—he honestly believed he had the right in law to recover his keys—but given the context in which this occurs he is unlikely to engage the sympathy of the jury. Hence a conviction for robbery is technically possible.

Finally, in relation to the sweets, a charge of making off without payment contrary to s. 3 of the Theft Act 1978 would be sustainable.

Robbery—s. 8 Theft Act 1968

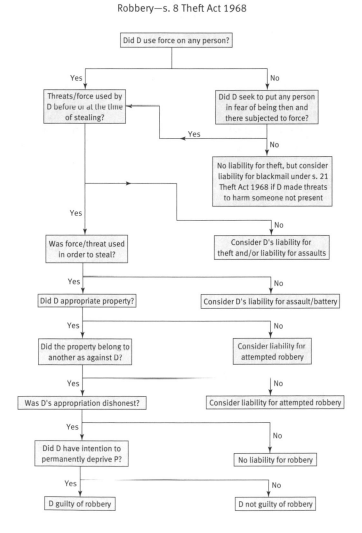

Question 2

Eric goes to *The Bottom Line*, a local restaurant, where he orders a meal. Eric is offended by what he feels to be the patronizing manner of the waiter Frederick and, when he has almost finished eating the meal, he decides to take a matchbox out of his pocket that contains two cockroaches. Eric opens the matchbox and releases the cockroaches onto his plate. Eric then calls Frederick and complains loudly about the restaurant's poor hygiene standard, threatening to inform the local environmental health officer. Frederick apologizes and tells Eric that no charge will be made for the meal.

The following evening Eric visits *Bone Appetite*, another local restaurant, where he orders a meal. Later, when Grégoire the waiter presents the bill, Eric discovers that he has no money with him. He offers to come back the next day in order to settle up, and gives Grégoire his name and address. Grégoire allows Eric to leave without paying. Once outside the restaurant Eric decides that he will never return to pay for the meal.

Advise the Crown Prosecution Service as to the criminal liability, if any, of Eric.

Commentary

This is a deceptive question as at first glance it might seem as though the main bases for liability are fairly obvious. A careful reading shows, however, that imposing liability on Eric may be highly problematic. In relation to blackmail there is the issue of whether he actually makes any demand—he does not say what he wants when he threatens the waiter. This in turn causes problems with determining whether he intends to gain from his actions, and in determining whether or not his demands are warranted. Note that he cannot be charged with making off as there was no requirement to pay. It is doubtful whether the incident at *Bone Appetite* involves any criminal liability at all—it is probably just a debtor–creditor relationship. Examiners sometime set such problems to test the confidence of candidates who typically think there must be some criminal liability. The marks here lie in explaining why there might not be any.

Answer plan

- Eric's liability for blackmail
- Eric's liability for fraud under **s. 2 Fraud Act 2006**
- No liability for making off without payment
- No liability for theft or fraud
- No liability for making off
- Very doubtful liability under **s. 3 Fraud Act 2006**
- Civil law—debtor–creditor relationship

Suggested answer

In making his threats Eric may have committed the offence of blackmail contrary to s. 21 of the Theft Act 1968. The offence requires proof that Eric made an unwarranted demand with menaces with a view to gain or with a view to causing another loss. A problem for the prosecution will be as to whether or not Eric makes a demand as such. His comments could be perceived as a demand, i.e., it could be implicit that he will continue with the demand unless he is given something, but the facts do not make this clear; see further *R v Collister and Warhurst* (1955) 39 Cr App R 100. If no demand is identified there can be no liability under s. 21. Given that he has deliberately released the cockroaches in order to cause trouble a jury might be willing to infer that he is demanding to be allowed to leave without paying for the meal, as it is most unlikely that any restaurateur faced with such a situation would press his claim to be paid for the meal.

Assuming there is a demand, the menaces are fairly self-evident—the threat to inform the local environmental health officer—see further *R v Clear* [1968] 1 QB 670. There may be an issue in relation to s. 34(2) of the Theft Act 1968. Is the demand made with a view to gain in the sense that by making the demand Eric seeks to keep what he has? He does not expressly ask for anything. Again the prosecution would have to rely on the inference that Eric seeks to gain by not paying for the meal. Note that liability now depends on two inferences—the making of a demand and the desire to gain from it in keeping property or causing another to not get what he might. Assuming all other elements of blackmail are made out the prosecution would still have to establish that the demand was unwarranted. Eric's demand will be unwarranted unless he made it believing that he had reasonable grounds for making the demand; and that the use of the menaces was a proper means of reinforcing the demand. The tests are essentially subjective—hence if Eric did really believe that the attitude of the waiter warranted his taking some sort of revenge he may satisfy the first test. Satisfying the second limb may be more difficult. There were other courses of action he could have pursued, such as complaining to the manager. It may be difficult for him to convince a jury that he really thought releasing cockroaches was a proper means of enforcing his demands. Note again that the issue of whether or not a demand is warranted relates to the nature of the demand. As noted above this point is difficult to resolve on the facts as it is not clear what demand he is making at the time.

It is possible that the releasing of the cockroaches amounted to a false representation for the purposes of s. 2 of the Fraud Act 2006. It is clear from the facts that Eric was implying to the waiter that the cockroaches had been found in the restaurant, not imported and released by Eric. This implication is clearly untrue given the facts. The offence under s. 2 creates an inchoate form of liability inasmuch as the false representation does not have to be shown to have caused any benefit to be conferred on the defendant. It is sufficient that Eric commits acts constituting the false representation with the requisite *mens rea*. For these purposes the prosecution would need to establish that: (i) Eric knew the implied representation to be false (clear on the given facts); (ii) Eric intended to make a gain for himself, or cause loss to another; and (iii) that he acted dishonestly. As to acting with a view to making a gain or causing another loss, Eric may contend (as with blackmail—see above) that he simply wanted to embarrass a waiter who had upset him. The jury, on the other hand, may be willing to infer that he was acting with a view to being let off paying for the meal. If the jury takes this view they can conclude that he acted with intent to cause loss to the restaurant. The only remaining issue under s. 2 would then be whether or not Eric was dishonest in releasing the cockroaches. As there is no definition of dishonesty in the Fraud Act 2006, the jury would be directed in terms of *R v Ghosh* [1982] QB 1053. According to the ordinary standards of reasonable and honest people was what Eric did dishonest? If it was dishonest by those standards, did Eric himself realize that what he was doing was by those standards dishonest? It is submitted that whether or not a jury would regard Eric's actions as dishonest would depend very much on the issue of whether he acted for personal gain. If he did, then the conclusion is likely to be that he was dishonest. If he simply wanted to make trouble, some members of the jury might disapprove of his actions but might not actually regard them as dishonest. Perhaps the most significant point here is that Eric leaves without offering to pay anything—that might be a clue as to his real intentions.

Finally, it should be made clear that there can be no liability on the part of Eric for making off without payment contrary to s. 3 Theft Act 1978. Clearly Eric leaves without paying, but the problem is the absence of any understanding on Eric's part that payment for the goods or services is required or expected from him at the time he leaves. The waiter makes it clear that no payment is requested. Of course if the waiter had known the truth payment would not have been waived, but that is why a fraud charge may be far more suitable than a making-off offence.

Regarding his not paying for the meal at the *Bone Appetite*, Eric does not incur any criminal liability in ordering and eating the meal as he was honest at all times. When he leaves without paying he cannot incur liability for making off without payment contrary to s. 3 of the Theft Act 1978 as there is no expectation of payment—hence again his making off cannot be seen as dishonest (indeed he leaves his name and address). When Eric decides not to return to settle his bill it is clearly too late for any theft liability to be imposed—property will have passed. Neither can there be liability under s. 2 of the Fraud Act 2006 as there is no evidence of Eric making any false representations. The prosecution may consider pursuing a charge under s. 3 of the 2006 Act. This offence involves proof that Eric dishonestly failed to disclose to the restaurant information that he was under a legal duty to disclose. The information in question would be his decision not to return and pay his bill. The question for the prosecution to consider is whether or not Eric was under any legal obligation to disclose this change of mind. The argument would hinge on establishing a legally binding agreement between the restaurant and Eric to the effect that he would be allowed to leave provided he intended to return and settle the bill, and that it was implicit in this agreement that he would let them know if he was not going to do this. The prosecution may be unwilling to bring a charge that relies so heavily on a jury having to deal with some rather abstruse aspects of contract law. There may not have been an agreement, and even if there was it may not have been legally enforceable. If these obstacles can be overcome the prosecution would have to prove that Eric acted with a view to gain by not paying for the meal (evident on the facts), and that he was dishonest.

Question 3

Paul is very short of money and decides to remedy the situation. He sees an open window of a house and enters with a view to stealing anything inside which he might find of value. However, after examining the contents he decides that there is nothing worth anything to him and he leaves without taking anything.

He then meets Steve, who is having an affair with a secretary. Paul tells Steve that unless Steve gives him £500 he will tell Steve's wife about the affair. Steve replies that, as his wife already knows, he will give Paul nothing.

While driving home, Paul is stopped by the police who find a crowbar and other items that could be used for burglary, and Paul admits that he intended to use them to gain access if he found an unoccupied property.

Discuss the criminal liability of Paul.

Commentary

At first glance this appears to be a question on attempt, as Paul has not succeeded in his criminal ventures. Although this topic should be mentioned briefly, the answer must concentrate on three substantive offences under the Theft Act 1968, namely: burglary (s. 9), blackmail (s. 21), and going equipped (s. 25). They do to some extent resemble the inchoate offences, as they do not require the accused to obtain anything in order to be guilty; but the answer must state that Paul will be guilty of the full offence, not merely attempt.

If these pitfalls can be avoided, candidates should be able to obtain a high mark, as all that is required a knowledge of the basic ingredients of the three offences.

Answer plan

- s. 9, Theft Act 1968

  - *Attorney-General's References (Nos 1 and 2 of 1979)* [1979]

- s. 21, Theft Act 1968—blackmail

  - *Clear* [1968]

  - *Lambert* [1972]

- **s. 25, Theft Act 1968**—going equipped

  – *Rashid* [1977]

  – *Hargreaves* [1985]

Suggested answer

As a result of entering another's property with intent to steal, Paul will be charged with burglary. This is defined under s. 9 of the Theft Act 1968, and the relevant part in this case is s. 9(1)(a), whereby a person is guilty of burglary if he enters any building or part of a building as a trespasser with intent to commit any such offence as is mentioned in s. 9(2), which includes stealing or attempting to steal anything therein. Thus it is not necessary for the prosecution to prove that Paul actually stole something, only that when he entered he intended to steal something. This will be sufficient for the full offence of burglary, not simply an attempt.

Paul has clearly entered a building as a trespasser with the requisite *mens rea* for these ingredients of the offence (*R v Collins* [1972] 2 All ER 1105), and therefore the only doubtful issue is whether his conditional intent to steal is sufficient. This particular question has caused difficulties. In *R v Easom* [1971] 2 All ER 945, where the accused had taken and then (after rifling through its contents) abandoned a ladies handbag, because there was nothing of value to him which he wanted to steal, his conviction for theft was quashed on the basis that his conditional intent was not regarded as an intention permanently to deprive for the purposes of theft. However, the position is different with burglary, as the law recognizes the fact that most burglars do not intend to steal a specific thing, but will take anything they may find of value. The indictment should therefore state that Paul intended to steal 'some or all of the contents of the house'. On this basis, the Court of Appeal confirmed in *Attorney-General's References (Nos 1 and 2 of 1979)* [1979] 3 All ER 143, that the accused would be guilty of burglary. The fact that there is nothing in the building worth stealing is no bar to Paul's conviction.

Paul could also be charged with the offence of blackmail under s. 21 of the Theft Act 1968. Section 21(1) provides that a person is guilty of blackmail if:

> with a view to gain for himself or another or with intent to cause loss to another, he makes any unwarranted demand with menaces; and for this purpose a demand with menaces is unwarranted unless the person making it does so in the belief—
>
> (a) that he has reasonable grounds for making the demand; and
>
> (b) that the use of the menaces is a proper means of reinforcing the demand.

Paul has clearly made a demand, but this was not accompanied by the threat of physical violence, so can it be said that it was a demand with menaces? 'Menaces' was chosen by the Law Commission in preference to 'threats', as being the most appropriate term for blackmail, and was defined in *Thorne v Motor Trade Association* [1937] AC 397 as 'not limited to threats of violence but…including threats of any action detrimental to or unpleasant to the person addressed'. Further, it is not necessary for the prosecution to prove that the victim was affected by the demand, merely that it was of such a nature and extent that the mind of an ordinary person of normal stability and courage might be so influenced or made apprehensive as to accede unwillingly to the demand. Thus in *R v Clear* [1968] 1 All ER 74, an accused who demanded money from a litigant (for giving evidence) in a civil case was convicted of blackmail, although the victim was unaffected by the demand as his insurance company had agreed to settle any damages award.

A threat to tell Steve's wife could therefore be deemed a menace by the jury. Whether or not it is unwarranted depends on the accused's ability to convince the jury that he believed that he had reasonable grounds for making the demand and that the use of menaces was a proper means of reinforcing it. This is a subjective test, and in *R v Lambert* [1972] Crim LR 422 the trial judge directed the jury that they would find the menaces 'proper' if the accused honestly believed that they were proper. This again was a case where the accused demanded money as compensation for keeping quiet about a sexual liaison. If, on the other hand, the accused threatens to kill or harm the victim, he cannot claim that he thought this was 'proper' (*R v Harvey, Uylett and Plummer* (1981) 72 Cr App R 139). On the facts, it appears that Paul could not succeed with this argument; and as he has clearly made an unwarranted demand with menaces, it is submitted he will be found guilty of blackmail.

As Paul has equipment that could be used for burglary in his car, he could be charged under s. 25 of the Theft Act 1968 with 'going equipped'. Section 25 (as amended by the Fraud Act 2006) provides that a person shall be guilty of an offence if, when not at his place of abode, he has with him any article for use in the course of or in connection with any burglary or theft. From the prosecution's viewpoint, s. 25 has a great advantage over a charge of attempted burglary as for that offence the prosecution must prove that the accused has done more than a merely preparatory act (under s. 1(1) of the Criminal Attempts Act 1981). In practical terms this would require Paul to be on the very point of entering a particular property. Even this may not be sufficient, as in *R v Campbell* (1991) 93 Cr App R 350, the Court of Appeal quashed a conviction of attempted robbery where the accused was arrested on the entrance steps of a post office armed with an imitation gun and ransom demand, on the basis that as he was still outside the building his act was still only merely preparatory. No such difficulty arises under s. 25, and there have been convictions of British Rail stewards arrested on the way to their trains armed with sandwiches and coffee which they intended to pass off as British Rail products to passengers on the train (*R v Rashid* [1977] 2 All ER 237; *R v Corboz* [1984] Crim LR 302).

Paul would be able to argue that he lacked the necessary *mens rea* as he had not specifically formed the intention to use the equipment on a particular property. However, s. 25(3) provides that proof that the accused had with him any article made or adapted for use in committing burglary shall be evidence that he had it with him for such use; and in *R v Hargreaves* [1985] Crim LR 243, the Court of Appeal held that the prosecution had to prove only that the accused had formed the intention to use the article if a suitable opportunity arose.

Although it was recognized in *R v Bundy* [1977] 2 All ER 382 that a motor vehicle could in certain circumstances be a place of abode, it is submitted that it could not be in Paul's case as he was driving around in it at the time he was stopped. It is submitted that Paul has therefore committed all three offences: burglary, blackmail, and 'going equipped'.

Blackmail—s. 21 Theft Act 1968

```
                    ┌──────────────────────────────────┐
                    │ Does D make a demand addressed to P? │
                    └──────────────────────────────────┘
              Yes │                              │ No
       ┌──────────────────────┐         ┌──────────────────────┐
       │ Was the demand made  │         │   D has no           │
       │ with menaces?        │         │ liability under s. 21 │
       └──────────────────────┘         └──────────────────────┘
              Yes │                              │ No
       ┌──────────────────────┐         ┌──────────────────────┐
       │ Was the demand made with │     │  Consider possible   │
       │ a view to a loss or gain? │    │  liability for       │
       └──────────────────────┘         │  attempted blackmail │
                                        └──────────────────────┘
              Yes │                              │ No
       ┌──────────────────────────┐     ┌──────────────────────┐
       │ Did D believe that he had │     │ No liability under s. 21 │
       │ reasonable grounds for making the demand? │ └──────────────────┘
       └──────────────────────────┘
              Yes │                              │ No
       ┌──────────────────────┐         ┌──────────────────────────────┐
       │ No liability under s. 21 │      │ Did D believe that the threat was │
       └──────────────────────┘         │ a 'proper' means of reinforcing │
                                        │ the demand?                     │
                                        └──────────────────────────────┘
              Yes │                              │ No
       ┌──────────────────────┐         ┌──────────────────────┐
       │ No liability under s. 21 │      │ D is guilty of blackmail │
       └──────────────────────┘         └──────────────────────┘
```

Question 4

Ron knew that X had recently committed a serious criminal offence. He threatened to tell the police unless X gave him some property. As a result X gave Ron a watch, a ring and a lighter. Ron then gave the ring to Steve as a birthday present. He sold the watch at an undervalue to Trevor and asked William to look after the lighter for him until he wanted it returned. Steve, Trevor, and William took these articles in good faith, not knowing how they had been obtained by Ron. However, three days later Ron told them the full story. Nevertheless, all three kept possession of the articles.

Advise the Crown Prosecution Service regarding the liability of Ron, Steve, Trevor, and William for completed offences under the Theft Act 1968.

Commentary

This is a difficult question requiring detailed knowledge of, and an ability to apply, the principles relating to handling stolen goods under **s. 22 of the Theft Act 1968**. In addition candidates need to be able to demonstrate an understanding of the relationship between **s. 22** and theft (**s. 1**), with particular reference to the important protection for a bona fide purchaser for value contained in **s. 3(2)** of the 1968 Act. There are many important cases on these points that must be used to illustrate the application of the principles. Consideration must also be given to blackmail (**Theft Act 1968, s. 21**). Note the rubric constrains the advice required to the Theft Act 1968. An examiner may use this device to ensure candidates are not distracted by the somewhat convoluted possibilities of liability under **Part 2 of the Serious Crime Act 2007** for assisting and encouraging crimes.

Answer plan

- Blackmail—s. 21, Theft Act 1968
- Handling stolen goods—s. 22, Theft Act 1968
    - *Bloxham* [1982]
    - *Pitchley* [1972]
- Theft
    - s. 1, Theft Act 1968
    - s. 3(2), Theft Act 1968

Suggested answer

As a result of his dealings with X, Ron may have committed blackmail (Theft Act 1968, s. 21) and compounding (Criminal Law Act 1967, s. 5). Ron is guilty of blackmail if, with a view to gain for himself or another or with intent to cause loss to another, he makes any unwarranted demand with menaces; and for this purpose a demand with menaces is unwarranted unless the person making it does so in the belief:

(a) that he has reasonable grounds for making the demand; and

(b) that the use of menaces is a proper means of reinforcing the demand.

It is clear on the facts that Ron will have no defence to this charge and it appears he will also be guilty of compounding. Under s. 5(1) of the Criminal Law Act 1967:

Where a person has committed an arrestable offence, any other person who, knowing or believing that the offence or some other arrestable offence has been committed, and that he has information which might be of material assistance in securing the prosecution or conviction of an offender for it, accepts or agrees to accept for not disclosing that information any consideration other than the making good of loss or injury caused by the offence, or the making of reasonable compensation for that loss or injury, shall be liable on conviction on indictment to imprisonment for not more than two years...

However, it is the possibility of charges under s. 22 of the Theft Act 1968 for handling stolen goods that will provoke the most argument. All four parties could be charged with this offence since, under s. 22(1), a person handles stolen goods 'if (otherwise than in the course of the stealing) knowing or believing them to be stolen goods he dishonestly receives the goods, or dishonestly undertakes or assists in their retention, removal, disposal or realization by or for the benefit of another person, or if he arranges to do so'. Further, although the goods have been obtained by blackmail they are still regarded as stolen goods as a result of s. 24(4) of the 1968 Act.

Ron could be charged on the basis that he has assisted in the goods' disposal or realization, by or for the benefit of another. As he has given the lighter to William only temporarily, to look after for Ron's benefit, this cannot constitute the offence; but his dealings with Steve and Trevor may satisfy this condition. The key case on this point is the House of Lords' decision in *R v Bloxham* [1982] 1 All ER 582. D had bought a car in good faith and later discovered that it had been stolen. He then sold it at an undervalue to V. As he had purchased in good faith he could not be guilty of theft, as a result of s. 3(2) of the Theft Act 1968 (the protection given to a bona fide purchaser), or of handling on the basis of dishonest receipt. But he was found guilty of handling on the basis that when he sold the car at an undervalue, he was assisting in its disposal for the benefit of another, namely the purchaser. However, their Lordships, in quashing his conviction and reversing the decision of the Court of Appeal, held that a purchaser of stolen goods is not 'another person' within the meaning of s. 22. So, although the sale was at an undervalue it was not deemed to be for the benefit of another. Thus Ron would not be guilty of handling as a result of the sale of the watch to Trevor.

Ron could use this argument if he was charged with handling as a result of giving the ring to Steve. However, in *Bloxham* their Lordships were clearly influenced by the fact that as D had bought in good faith and could not therefore be guilty of theft, it would be going against the spirit of the Theft Act 1968 to convict him of handling, where the maximum sentence is greater. Ron's position differs in this respect, and also in the fact that it is hard to argue that an outright gift benefits the donor and is not for another's benefit (i.e., the donee). It is therefore submitted that *Bloxham* can be distinguished and that Ron could be found guilty of handling in this instance.

Neither Steve, nor Trevor or William could be guilty of handling on the basis that they had dishonestly received the goods, but they may be found guilty on the alternative ground involving acting by or for the benefit of another. However, as Steve is given the ring as a present and keeps it for his own use, he is not doing an act for the benefit of another and cannot be found guilty of handling.

William, on the other hand, in keeping the lighter in custody for Ron, is clearly assisting in its retention for the benefit of another. Thus as soon as he knows the true position he has the necessary *mens rea* and would therefore be guilty. This was the case in *R v Pitchley*

(1972) 57 Cr App R 30, one of the few cases where an omission to act was sufficient for the *actus reus* of the offence. There the accused had been given a sum of money to look after for his son. He received it in good faith and placed it in his bank account, where he allowed it to remain after discovering that his son had acquired it dishonestly. The court held that this was sufficient to constitute handling, on the basis that he assisted in its retention by or for the benefit of another.

As far as the crime of handling is concerned, Trevor would appear to be in the same position as Steve as he has not done an act by or for the benefit of another. However, there is a marked difference in their criminal responsibility for theft. This is because Trevor has the protection of s. 3(2) of the 1968 Act, which provides:

> Where property or a right or interest in property is or purports to be transferred for value to a person acting in good faith, no later assumption by him of rights which he believed himself to be acquiring shall, by reason of any defect in the transferor's title, amount to theft of the property.

The only way in which Trevor could be guilty is if the jury decided that as he bought the watch at an undervalue he was not acting in good faith and that s. 3(2) of the 1968 Act therefore does not apply.

Because Steve is not a purchaser he does not have the protection of s. 3(2). Further, under s. 3(1), 'appropriation' includes, where D has come by the property (innocently or not) 'without stealing it, any later assumption of a right to it by keeping or dealing with it as owner'. As the other ingredients of theft appear to be satisfied, it is therefore submitted that Steve will be guilty of theft.

Question 5

Answer all parts.

(a) On Monday mornings Nigel's hair salon offers haircuts to customers over the age of 65 for £5, rather than the £9 charged at other times. Buster, who is 59, goes to Nigel's on a Monday morning and asks for an 'over 65's haircut'. Nigel cuts Buster's hair and charges him £5.

What offences, if any, has Buster committed?

(b) Zak, who is 17, asks Xerox, his father, to lend him £100 to purchase some books he needs for his studies. Xerox gives Zak the money. Zak, who is in fact an addict, spends the money on heroin for his personal use. Xerox knows that Zak is a heroin addict.

What offences, if any, has Zak committed?

(c) Hanif goes to Lorenzo's café where he orders a meal and drinks. The bill should total £45, but Paulo, the waiter, has forgotten to add several items and presents Hanif with a bill for £25. Hanif, who thinks the meal and the service to be rather poor, puts £25 in cash on the table and leaves the restaurant.

What offences, if any, has Hanif committed?

Commentary

A collection of fraud and possibly theft related scenarios each of which is deceptively simple! The methodology to apply when answering these questions is very predictable—go through each element in turn looking out for any difficulties the prosecution might have. For those students familiar with the deception offences that were in force prior to the enactment of the **Fraud Act 2006** it may be interesting to reflect on how the liability of the parties varies according to whether one considers it from the perspective of deception or fraud, but do bear in mind that examiners will now want to see the **Fraud Act** applied. There is little scope in answering problem questions for digressions into what the law used to be. Note that this question provides an opportunity in particular to demonstrate the change from obtaining services by deception under the **Theft Act 1978** to obtaining services dishonestly under the Fraud Act 2006. Ultimately the issues thrown up by these scenarios are not difficult, but they need to be explored fully to extract maximum marks.

Answer plan

Part (a)

- Buster's liability for

  - fraud by false pretences
  - obtaining services dishonestly
  - making off without payment

Part (b)

- Zak's liability for

  - fraud by false pretences
  - theft
  - whether £100 is property belonging to another
  - whether Zak is dishonest

Part (c)

- Hanif's liability for

  - no fraud offences
  - making off without payment as an alternative
  - whether any dishonesty

Suggested answer

Part (a)

The haircut provided by Nigel is a service within the definition provided by s. 11(2) of the Fraud Act 2006—i.e., a something made available on the understanding that payment has been or will be paid for it. The haircut is not provided as a gratuitous service, even to those over the age of 65, hence it falls within s. 11(2). As May LJ observed in *R v Sofroniou* [2003] EWCA Crim 3681, when referring to the offence of obtaining services by deception under s. 1 of the Theft Act 1978 (the forerunner of the revised s. 11 offence):

> [The definition of services]...is...intended to cover situations where nothing explicitly is said about payment, but where there is a common understanding that the services will not be provided gratuitously. I can induce someone to mow my lawn on the understanding that he will do so for nothing: or the understanding may be that he will be paid. If, in the latter instance, I induce him to mow my lawn dishonestly...as for instance by representing that I am able to pay him when I am not, I commit an offence....

The prosecution will have to establish a dishonest act on Buster's part that occurs prior to his obtaining the haircut. There is evidence of an express statement by Buster in that he asks for an 'over 65s haircut' that would presumably be the dishonest act that the prosecution will allege caused the provision of the service. Had Nigel known the truth he would presumably have refused to provide the haircut at a discount. Given that Buster does not pay the normal price for his haircut the requirement under s. 11(2) that he obtains the service '....without payment having been made in full...' seems to be satisfied.

The first element of *mens rea* is dishonesty. As this is a fraud offence the jury will be given a '*Ghosh*' direction following *R v Ghosh* [1982] QB 1053. The jury will be directed to consider whether, according to the ordinary standards of reasonable and honest people, what Buster did was dishonest. If it was dishonest by those standards, the second question will be as to whether Buster himself realized that what he was doing was by those standards dishonest. It is submitted that a jury would regard Buster's actions as dishonest. There is no evidence here to suggest that Buster believed he was in any way entitled to the cheaper haircut.

The second element of *mens rea* is proof that Buster knew that the haircut was being provided on the basis that payment was to be made for it—on the facts this is evident. The third element of *mens rea* is that Buster intended not to pay in full. Again this may seem obvious on the facts, but Buster might argue that he intended to pay what he was asked to pay (the £5) in full. Such an argument would be specious as the only reason he is asked to pay £5 is because of his dishonest act in purporting to be over the age of 65. Hence liability should be approached on the basis that he did not intend to pay what for him would have been the correct charge. One further argument Buster might try to raise is that he did not lie about his intention to pay, but lied about his age. Although the point is not dealt with explicitly in s. 11 of the 2006 Act it is notable that the s. 11 offence is constructed so as to require proof of a dishonest act, and then proof that the service was obtained in breach of s. 11(2). It is s. 11(2) that requires proof that the service was not provided on a gratuitous basis, that D knew this, and that D intended not to pay, or not to pay in full. There is nothing to suggest that the dishonest act referred to in s. 11(1) must relate to D's intention not to pay referred to in s. 11(2).

There are two alternative charges open to the prosecution on these facts. The first involves charging Buster with fraud by false representation contrary to s. 2 of the Fraud Act 2006. Purporting to be over the age of 65 would constitute the false representation—the falsehood is implicit in his requesting an 'over 65s' haircut. The prosecution will argue that he is implying that, as a matter of fact, he is over the age of 65 when this is untrue. The s. 2 offence is useful to the prosecution as it is an inchoate type of liability—there is no need to prove that the false representation has any consequences. What is required is proof that Buster knew the representation to be untrue (not a problem on the facts), that Buster was dishonest (presumably established as discussed above in relation to s. 11) and that Buster made the representation with a view to gain (keeping money he would otherwise have had to pay Nigel). A s. 2 charge therefore looks very promising for the prosecution.

The second alternative charge is less certain. Buster could be charged with making off without payment contrary to s. 3 of the 1978 Act, but the difficulty would be in establishing that Buster had not paid as required and expected—he did pay what he was asked. For this reason alone the prosecution would be advised not to pursue this possibility.

Part (b)

Zak may be guilty of fraud by false representation contrary to s. 2 of the Fraud Act 2006 in asking his father for the £100 in order to buy books. The prosecution will allege that the false representation is Zak's statement of fact that he wants the money to buy books when in fact he later spends the money on drugs; see s. 2(3). This statement can only be a false representation if it was untrue at the time it was made. Care is needed here because the facts do not clearly provide that, at the time he asked for the money, Zak had any intention other than to use the money to buy books. If he did indeed intend to buy the books when he asked for the money there can be no fraud offence, although a charge of theft when he spends the money on drugs might be sustainable (as to which see below).

Assuming Zak's statement about intending to buy books was untrue when he made it, the prosecution will not have to show any causal link between the statement and the obtaining of the money. Section 2 of the Fraud Act 2006 creates an inchoate form of liability that is complete once the false representation is made. The prosecution must, however, establish three aspects of *mens rea*. At the time of the statement did Zak know it to be untrue or realize that it might be? If he did, did he make the statement with a view to gaining property? In this case the intention to obtain the £100 would suffice. Finally it would have to be shown that he was dishonest. If Zak was lying to his father, the jury will have to judge his actions in the light of the standard *R v Ghosh* (above) direction on dishonesty. The jury will be directed to consider whether according to the ordinary standards of reasonable and honest people Zak was dishonest in asking for the money. If the answer is 'Yes', the second question will be as to whether or not Zak realized that what he was doing was, by those standards, dishonest. Much will depend on whether the jury has any sympathy with the fact that Zak is a drug addict.

A fraud offence seems the most likely charge on the facts provided the prosecution can show Zak was dishonest from the outset. If it transpires that a fraud offence cannot be used because he only decided to buy the drugs after obtaining the money matters become much more difficult for the prosecution. A charge of theft could be brought, but it would be problematic. The money would clearly be property within s. 4(1) of the Theft Act 1968, but if his father has made him the owner of the money Zak will argue that, in spending the money on drugs he is not appropriating property belonging to another. There are two arguments the prosecution can use. The first is that, by virtue of s. 5(3) of the Theft Act 1968, the £100 remained property belonging to another as against Zak because he was under a legal obligation to retain it and deal with it in a particular way. The difficulty with this is that the facts do not reveal any basis for the existence of that legal duty. Section 5(3) does not create the legal duty—it operates if there is a legal duty. This is a domestic arrangement. Typically the courts have treated domestic agreements as non-enforceable in law. The second argument the prosecution might use is *R v Hinks* [2000] 4 All ER 833, where the House of Lords, by a majority, ruled that a defendant could commit theft even where he acquired a valid title to property under a valid *inter vivos* transfer. In other words Zak could steal the £100 whilst becoming the owner of it. The decision is unsatisfactory as it does not explain how the £100 remains property belonging to Zak for the purposes of civil law, but remains property belonging to another for the purposes of the criminal law. Section 5(3) and 5(4) of the Theft Act 1968 achieve such an outcome by means of express statutory intervention when certain preconditions are met. *R v Hinks* attempts to achieve this as a matter of common law. Even if *R v Hinks* were successfully relied on in Zak's case the prosecution would still face difficulties with dishonesty. Under s. 2(1)(a) of the Theft Act 1968 Zak will not be dishonest if he believes he has the right in law to spend the money as he pleases. Given that his father has made him the owner of the money he may well believe he can do as he pleases with it. Under s. 2(1)(b) of the 1968 Act he will not be dishonest if he believed his father would have consented to his purchasing the drugs if he had known of the circumstances. It may seem a strange argument but Zak may contend that as his father knows he is an addict his father would not want to see him suffer the effects of not being able to secure a supply of drugs. He might even contend that his father would rather have him spend the £100 on drugs rather than steal money to feed his addiction. Zak would be advised to rely on these two arguments to establish that he was not dishonest, as predicting how a jury might view his actions following a direction in terms laid down in *R v Ghosh* (above) is a very uncertain enterprise. Zak's intention to permanently deprive in relation to the £100 is evident, assuming it is property belonging to another.

Part (c)

On the evidence provided Hanif is honest throughout the period when he enters the café, orders the food and eats the meal. There can be no liability, therefore, in relation to obtaining the food, or the services of the waiter, by any dishonest act. Neither can there be any liability for theft of the food or drink as he is honest at the time of consumption.

Does Hanif commit a fraud offence in not advising the waiter as to the error in respect of the bill? Under s. 2 of the Fraud Act 2006 the prosecution would need to establish a false representation by Hanif. On the facts it is hard to see what this could be. At best the prosecution could cite his silence and the fact that he left the restaurant like an honest diner who had paid his bill in full. Hanif would, of course, argue that that was exactly what he had done—hence there was no false representation. More promising might be a charge under s. 3 of the 2006 Act, that Hanif dishonestly failed to disclose information to another person whilst he was under a legal duty to do so, and that he acted with a view to make a gain for himself or to cause loss to another. Clearly Hanif fails to draw the waiter's attention to the incorrectly totalled bill, but was he under anything more than a moral duty to do so? It is submitted that he was not, unless the prosecution can conjure up an implied term in the contract under which the meal is supplied that the diner has to tell the waiter if the bill is incorrectly totalled. It is hard to see the basis for any such argument. If this submission is correct consideration of *mens rea* issues is otiose—but it perhaps ought to be noted that in any event dishonesty would be problematic given Hanif's view of the service and food. Perhaps it would have been wiser for Hanif to raise these issues rather than sneaking out having paid the incorrect sum required by the bill.

Approaching the problem in a different way the prosecution could charge Hanif with making off without payment contrary to s. 3 of the Theft Act 1978. Clearly Hanif knows that payment on the spot for the food supplied and service done is required or expected from him. There may, however, be an issue as to whether or not he makes off without having paid as required or expected. He pays the amount asked of him. Is this the same as the amount required and expected? If it is, there can be no liability under s. 3. It should also be noted that, by virtue of s. 3(3) of the Theft Act 1978, no liability can arise where the service done is such that payment is not legally enforceable. Could it be argued that if the quality of the food and the service in the café was really poor, there was no enforceable contractual obligation on Hanif to pay the £45? See further, *Troughton v The Metropolitan Police* [1987] Crim LR 138. Even if the prosecution surmounts this problem, there are issues of dishonesty, as discussed above in relation to the deception offences that will have to be addressed.

In summary it is submitted that Hanif may not have committed any offence on these facts.

Question 6

Maysa, a vastly wealthy widow, is a neurotic anorexic with a pathological fear of being without a male partner. She meets Bluey through a dating agency. Bluey, aware of Maysa's wealth, declares his undying love for her, although in reality he is involved in a longstandingrelationship with Sara, and is only interested in how much money he can get out of Maysa. Over the course of the next three months Maysa gives a total of £50,000 in cash to Bluey to reward him for his devotion.

Maysa then discovers that Bluey has been living with Sara for many years and asks him to return the money. Bluey, who has taken a number of nude photographs of Maysa with her consent, tells her that if she takes steps to recover the money he will send copies of the photographs to *The Stunna*, a lurid national tabloid newspaper.

Maysa hires Ray, a private detective, to retrieve the pictures and negatives from the darkroom in Bluey's house. That night the part of Bluey's house that includes the darkroom is demolished in an explosion caused by a gas leak. No one is hurt in the blast, but the pictures and negatives are among the items destroyed. Ray discovers what has happened when he pulls up outside Bluey's house the following morning.

Advise the Crown Prosecution Service as to the criminal liability of: (i) Ray; (ii) Bluey; and (iii) Maysa.

Commentary

This question combines theft, blackmail, burglary plus some general principles of criminal liability. It is essential that a clear structure is adopted taking each of the incidents in turn. The issues relating to the £50,000 clearly require a good understanding of *R v Hinks*. Be prepared, however, to acknowledge situations where there may not be any criminal liability. Hence Bluey may not have exercised any false representations in respect of Maysa, or he may not have been dishonest. In the context of blackmail his demands may not be unwarranted. Where there are issues about accessorial liability, establish the liability of the principal offender before dealing with the liability of the accomplice. Maysa's liabilities regarding the hiring of Ray will require candidates to address the complex issues surrounding liability for encouraging crime under **Part 2 of the Serious Crime Act 2007**.

Answer plan

- Fraud by false pretences
- Theft of the money
- Problems with appropriation—*R v Hinks* [2000]
- *Mens rea* for theft
- Blackmail—whether demands warranted
- Attempted burglary—whether steps more than merely preparatory
- Whether any ulterior intent
- Maysa's liability as an accomplice
- Maysa's liability for conspiracy and under **Part 2 of the Serious Crime Act 2007**

Suggested answer

Fraud by false representation

As a general rule, where the facts indicate that there may be liability for fraud or theft the prosecution would be advised to consider fraud first. Does Bluey commit a s. 2 Fraud Act 2006 offence in respect of Maysa? The first issue is as to whether or not he acts in a way that could be regarded as involving a false representation. Bluey's declaration of love could be a false representation (by words), and s. 2(3) makes clear that a false representation can include representations as to the present intentions of the defendant. There are likely to be evidential problems here, however. The facts indicate that Bluey was involved in a long-standing relationship with Sara, and was only interested in how much money he could get out of Maysa. However, unless he confesses that he never loved Maysa, how would the prosecution ever prove this? It might be possible to establish the falsity of Bluey's statements by virtue of the evidence given by Maysa—inferences would have to be drawn by the jury. If this obstacle can be overcome, liability under s. 2 becomes a possibility. There is no need for the prosecution to prove that Bluey's statements actually induced Maysa to part with her money. The offence under s. 2 is, in that sense, inchoate. Once the false representation is established it is for the prosecution to prove that Bluey knew it to be untrue (depends on the evidence), that he made the false representation with a view to gaining the money (seems evident on the facts) and that Bluey was dishonest. A jury might well regard him as dishonest following a direction based on *R v Ghosh* [1982] 2 All ER 689. The jury would have to consider two questions:

(a) Were Bluey's actions dishonest according to the ordinary standards of reasonable and honest people? If not, Bluey is not guilty.

(b) If they were, did Bluey realize that reasonable and honest people would regard what he did as dishonest? If so, he is guilty; if not, he is not guilty.

If the false representation cannot be established, the prosecution will have to consider theft as an alternative.

Theft of the money

In respect of a charge of theft under s. 1(1) of the Theft Act 1968, the money is clearly property, but whose money is it? If the property in the cash passes to Bluey, it would be difficult to show that he has appropriated property belonging to another. Earlier cases such as *R v Mazo* [1996] Crim LR 435, proceeded on the basis that the receiver of a valid *inter vivos* gift could not be guilty of stealing it. This appeared to amount to a 'gloss' upon *R v Gomez* [1993] AC 442, suggesting that the *Gomez* approach to appropriation may only be relevant where there is evidence of fraud on the part of D. In *R v Hinks* [2000] 4 All ER 833, the House of Lords held, by a majority of 3–2, that the recipient of a valid gift could still be a thief, provided dishonesty was established.

Lord Steyn expressed the view that *R v Gomez* 'unambiguously ruled out' any submission to the effect that appropriation as defined in s. 3(1) of the 1968 Act could not occur where a gift of property was effected on the grounds that the entire proprietary interest would have passed to the recipient (i.e., the defendant). He went on to approve the approach taken in *Gomez* to the effect that 'appropriation' was a neutral word which should be taken to cover 'any assumption by a person of the rights of an owner'. This he felt was wide enough to encompass 'gift' situations.

The problem with the majority viewpoint in *Hinks* is that if one accepts, for the sake of argument, that there can be an appropriation even though the donor validly consents to D having the property, it must still be an appropriation of property *belonging to another*. It is not made clear how the property gifted to D by P remains property belonging to P. As Lord Hobhouse (dissenting) observed, D is not 'assuming the rights of an owner', when he appropriates the property, D has them already.

If the court applies *R v Hinks* as it is bound to do, a difficult problem arises whereby Bluey could be convicted of theft (subject to proof of *mens rea*) of the property received as a matter of criminal law, but would be able to resist moves to recover it as a matter of civil law, because in civil law the transfer would be valid and he would have an absolute title to it.

Assuming (for the purposes of criminal law) that the property remains property belonging to Maysa notwithstanding her gift, Bluey appropriates the money when he assumes the rights of the owner in respect of it—he can appropriate even though Maysa consents to his having it—*Gomez*.

Bluey may still escape liability on the basis that he was not dishonest at the time of the alleged appropriation. With reference to s. 2(1)(a) Theft Act 1968, did he appropriate the property belonging to another in the belief that he had in law the right to deprive the other of it? This is at least arguable—it was a valid gift to him. Did he act in the belief that he would have had Maysa's consent if she had known of the appropriation and the circumstances of it—s. 2(1)(b)? This is less promising—especially if the circumstances include his true feelings. Alternatively Bluey could still escape liability following a *Ghosh* direction—as to which see above in relation to the s. 2 Fraud Act 2006 offence. Again Bluey's intention to permanently deprive is self-evident.

Blackmail

Maysa's request for the return of the money does not, *prima facie,* indicate any liability. She does not make any threats about what she might do if the money is not returned.

Bluey may have incurred liability for blackmail contrary to s. 21 of the Theft Act 1968. Arguably he does make a demand—he is indirectly asking her to stop pursuing him for the money. A reasonable person would realize that a demand was being made—see *R v Collister and Warhurst* (1955) 39 Cr App R 100. The 'menaces' are evident. On the basis of *R v Clear* [1968] 1 QB 670, the threat is such as would influence the mind of an ordinary person of normal stability and courage so as to make them accede unwillingly to the demand.

Bluey's threat could indirectly be made with a view to gain—either keeping the pictures or the money. Under s. 34(2)(a)(i) Theft Act 1968 'gain' and 'loss' are to be construed as extending only to gain or loss in money or other property. The prosecution would have to prove that the demand was unwarranted. For these purposes a demand with menaces is unwarranted unless the person making it does so in the belief—(a) that he has reasonable grounds for making the demand; and (b) that the use of the menaces is a proper means of reinforcing the demand. The test is subjective. Does Bluey believe he has reasonable grounds for the demand? Does he believe that the menaces are a proper way of reinforcing the demand? It is significant that he is not threatening to commit a serious criminal offence if his demand is not met—see by contrast *R v Harvey* (1981) 72 Cr App R 139.

Ray's liability

Ray could be charged with attempted burglary contrary to s. 1(1) of the Criminal Attempts Act 1981. The *actus reus* would require proof that he took steps more than merely preparatory to committing an offence contrary to s. 9(1)(a) of the Theft Act 1968—entry into a building as a trespasser with intent to steal. Whether or not he took steps more than merely preparatory is a question of fact: see *R v Gullefer* (1990) 91 Cr App R 356, and *R v Geddes* [1996] Crim LR 894. Assuming this is made out, the prosecution would have to prove *mens rea* for the attempt—in this case that Ray intended to enter as a trespasser with intent to steal. There was clearly intention to enter, and it seems safe to assume that Ray would have known that he would have been trespassing had he done so. The uncertainty arises because he may not have had an intention to steal because he was not dishonest. Ray might argue that he was doing the 'right thing' by seeking to retrieve the pictures and negatives. Much would depend on the view of the jury following an *R v Ghosh* (above) direction. The impossibility of the enterprise will not afford Ray any defence to a charge of attempt— *R v Shivpuri* [1987] AC 1, makes it clear that the Criminal Attempts Act 1981 succeeds in imposing liability on a defendant who took steps that he believed would be more than merely preparatory to the commission of the offence, regardless of whether the commission of the offence was possible. In effect the defendant is judged on the facts as he believed them to be. As a residual offence Ray could be charged with having committed conspiracy to burgle with Maysa, unless it can be argued that the taking of the pictures and negatives would not have constituted theft (see above). Neither party can raise impossibility as a bar to liability for statutory conspiracy—see the Criminal Law Act 1977 as amended by the Criminal Attempts Act 1981.

Maysa's liability

Maysa could be charged with statutory conspiracy to steal or commit burglary contrary to s. 1(1) of the Criminal Law Act 1977 (as amended), even though she does not intend to play any active part in the enterprise. This latter point is made clear by the Court of Appeal decision in *R v Siracusa* (1989) 90 Cr App R 340. Maysa could also be charged with counselling what transpires to be an attempted burglary. This is an unusual charge, but it is possible to be an accomplice to an attempt: see *R v Dunnington* [1984] QB 472.

Given the facts, perhaps the most likely charge brought against Maysa would be one of assisting and encouraging the commission of offences contrary to Part 2 of the Serious Crime Act 2007. Maysa clearly encourages Ray to commit theft of the negatives, and given that the property in question is in a dwelling, she also encourages him to commit burglary. She intends that the course of conduct that would constitute the offence should be committed by Ray; she believes that Ray, in carrying out her instructions would be acting with the requisite *mens rea*, or is at least reckless as to whether he would; and she is aware of the circumstances that would make Ray's actions an offence (e.g. that the negatives are property belonging to another). Hence, the elements of the offence under s. 44 of the 2007 Act appear to be made out. The fact that the offence cannot subsequently be committed is irrelevant to a charge under s. 44—the offence looks at Maysa's actions and her *mens rea*, not whether the offence could ever be committed by Ray. The only moot point here might be as to *mens rea*—could Maysa argue that she was not dishonest in seeking possession of the negatives? Section 50 of the 2007 Act provides for a defence of acting reasonably that Maysa might seek to rely on. She would have to show that she knew of the relevant circumstances—i.e. the threat of blackmail—and that it was reasonable for her to act as she did in those circumstances.

Further reading

Ormerod, D., 'The Fraud Act 2006—Criminalising Lying?' [2007] Crim LR 193.

Withey, C., 'Comment—The Fraud Act 2006—Some Early Observations & Comparisons with the Former Law' (2007) 70 Journal of Criminal Law 220

Yeo, N., 'Bulls-Eye' (2007) 157 NLJ 212.

Burglary—s. 9(1)(a) and (b) Theft Act 1968

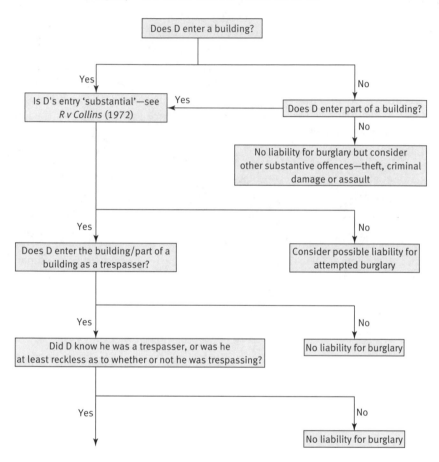

Continued

Continued from page 242.

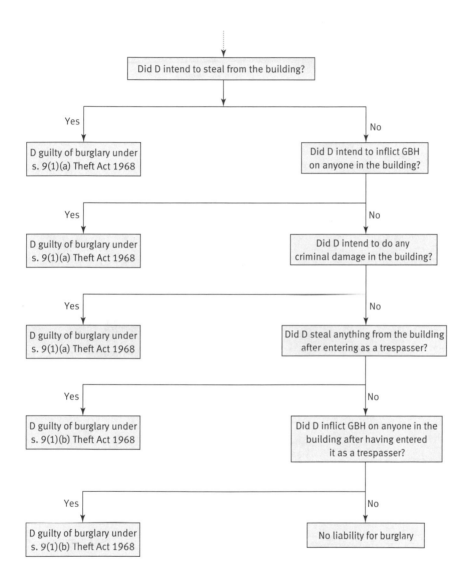

Section 2 Fraud Act 2006 liability flowchart

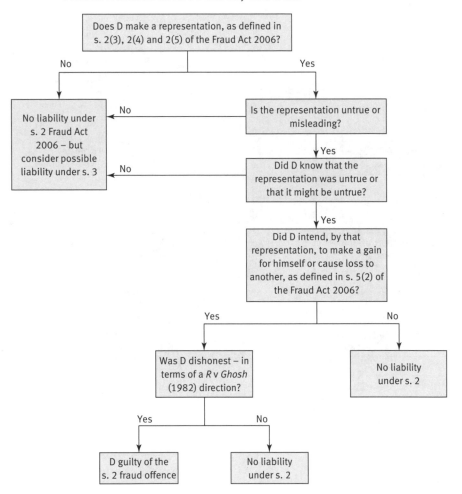

Section 3 Fraud Act 2006 liability flowchart

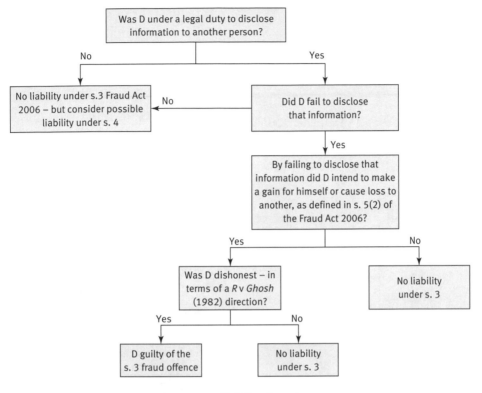

Section 4 Fraud Act 2006 liability flowchart

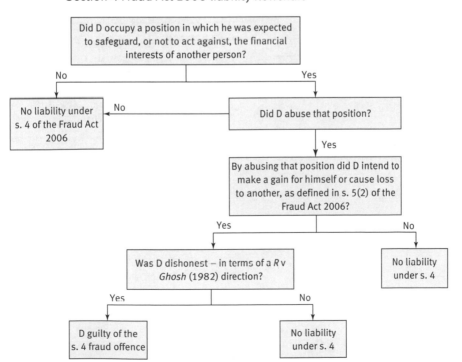

Section 11 Fraud Act 2006 liability flowchart

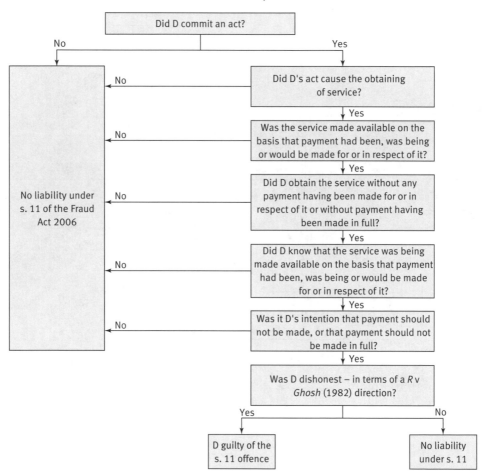

10

Mixed questions

Introduction

The styles adopted for criminal law examination questions can vary enormously. Some examiners will set problem questions that focus largely on one area. Others will set mixed questions that cut right across the syllabus, perhaps in the hope that this will wrong-foot students who 'question spot'. A mixed question will, therefore, require knowledge of a wide variety of topics from different parts of the syllabus. Quite often these topics are unrelated, so candidates could have to deal with criminal damage, manslaughter, theft, conspiracy and duress in the same answer. Mixed questions will generally be of two types: (1) where candidates have to cover a vast number of issues briefly; (2) where candidates need to cover some issues briefly, but others in some depth. Type two questions are obviously the more difficult, as candidates have to decide which are the points requiring detailed discussion. However, this should be fairly obvious for the well-prepared student.

Because a mixed question may cover so many diverse points, it will often yield comparatively high marks. This is sometimes because a student who does not cover one particular point will not lose so many marks, as the student may do when tackling a question with only three or four major points to cover. So don't be intimidated!

Question 1

Aaron works with Belinda and over a period of time they become close friends. One day Belinda invites Aaron over to her house to show him her paintings. Aaron and Belinda are in Belinda's bedroom looking at one of her paintings when Aaron grabs Belinda and begins to kiss her. Belinda enjoys being kissed by Aaron, but does not want to have sex with him. Aaron, wrongly believing that Belinda wants to have sex with him, takes his trousers off and pushes Belinda onto the bed lying on top of her.

Belinda is just about to repel Aaron's advances when Cameron, Belinda's husband, unexpectedly returns home from work. Aaron flees the scene by climbing out of the bedroom window and climbing down a drainpipe.

Aaron, whose house is nearby, runs home in his underpants. When he arrives at his house Aaron realizes that his keys and his wallet are still in the pocket of the trousers he left in Belinda's bedroom. Aaron persuades his friend Duncan to drive back to Belinda's house with him and climb in through an open ground floor window in order to retrieve the trousers without anybody noticing, whilst Aaron waits outside in his car. Duncan agrees.

Duncan enters Belinda's bedroom, where Belinda and Cameron are in bed together. Duncan retrieves Aaron's trousers but is seen by Cameron as he is crawling along the floor on his way out of the bedroom. Cameron chases after Duncan, but Duncan manages to get back in the car before Cameron can catch him. Aaron drives off at high speed with Cameron clinging to the car. The car swerves violently as Aaron takes a corner at high speed and Cameron falls off, suffering severe bruising when he hits the ground.

Advise the Crown Prosecution Service as to the criminal liability of Aaron and Duncan. (Ignore issues arising in relation to road traffic offences.)

Commentary

There is quite a lot going on in this question, hence fact management skills are needed to isolate the key issues and to ensure a careful organization of the answer. Examiners may choose to link together issues of burglary and sexual offences, hence candidates should be clear as to whether **s. 63 of the Sexual Offences Act 2003** is covered by the syllabus on which they are being examined. In theft the live issue is frequently dishonesty, as this question shows, but note the link to the 'ownership' point here. Beyond that, the question covers a wide gamut of material from assault, self-defence to accessorial liability and inchoate offences. Where so much has to be dealt with the style should be direct and succinct without being superficial.

Answer plan

- Aaron

  - s. 63, Sexual Offences Act 2003
  - sexual assault/rape
  - attempted rape

- Duncan

  - theft—whether dishonest
  - burglary

- Aaron's accessorial liability
- Aaron's liability under s. 18/s. 20, Offences Against the Person Act 1861
- Aaron's reliance on self-defence
- Duncan as an accomplice to Aaron

Suggested answer

It is possible, given the evidence, that Aaron entered Belinda's house (or her bedroom) intending to engage in some sexual activity with her if he had the opportunity. This alone would be enough to establish that he entered her house (or part of her house) as a trespasser—i.e., he entered for a purpose in excess of the implied or express permission that she gave him—see *R v Jones and Smith* [1976] 3 All ER 54. The problem for the prosecution would be in establishing that, at the time he enters either the house or the bedroom, he has any of the ulterior intents identified under s. 9(1)(a) of the Theft Act 1968. There is no evidence that he intends to steal, do criminal damage or cause grievous bodily harm.

Kissing Belinda is unlikely to amount to a sexual assault contrary to s. 3 of the 2003 Act, as this requires proof that: (i) Aaron touched her in a manner that was sexual; (ii) Belinda did not consent to the sexual touching; and (iii) that Aaron did not reasonably believe that Belinda was consenting. The kissing would obviously constitute touching as defined by s. 79(8) of the Sexual Offences Act 2003, but it is questionable that it would be considered as 'sexual', as defined by s. 78 of the 2003 Act. Under that section the kissing would be held to be sexual if the jury concluded that it was an act that, by its very nature, was sexual, or if because of its nature it could be sexual, and because of the circumstances or Aaron's purpose it was sexual. In the absence of direct evidence from Aaron in the form of a confession it is not clear how this could be established.

Even if the sexual nature of the kissing is established, Belinda's consent would place a complete block in the path of any prosecution. Kissing Belinda could also be a common assault in that it involves physical contact—but again the fact that she consents would provide Aaron with a complete defence.

An alternative charge might be that Aaron committed an offence contrary to s. 63 of the Sexual Offences Act 2003 when he decided to have sexual intercourse with Belinda. The basis of liability would be that, when he formed the intent to have sexual intercourse he became a trespasser, as she would not have given him permission to be there for that purpose. It would have to be shown that he either knew he had become a trespasser at that point, or was at least reckless as to whether or not he had become a trespasser. Evidence that he intended to engage in non-consensual sexual activity with Belinda would be persuasive in leading the jury to the conclusion that he knew he did not have permission to be in her house for that purpose. The problem for the prosecution is that if Aaron honestly believes Belinda will consent to sexual intercourse, he may not realize that he has no permission to be in her room for that purpose.

Aaron lying on top of Belinda in a state of undress would constitute a sexual assault contrary to s. 3 of the 2003 Act. Clearly there is touching. Given that he is in a state of undress there is evidence on which the jury can conclude that the touching is sexual (see explanation above). It is evident that Belinda is not consenting, but the difficulty will lie in establishing that Aaron had no reasonable belief that she was consenting. The irrebuttable presumption that he had no reasonable belief that she was consenting provided by s. 76

of the 2003 Act cannot apply, as there is no deception by Aaron. Similarly the conditions that, under s. 75, would justify a rebuttable assumption that Aaron had no reasonable belief in Belinda's consent are not present. Hence the issue becomes one of the jury looking at the evidence, including any steps taken by Aaron to ascertain Belinda's consent, to determine whether or not he had any reasonable belief that she was consenting. Clearly, Belinda's previous consent to the kissing would be used by Aaron to substantiate an argument that the reasonable man would have believed she was consenting to more intimate contact.

The prosecution may also consider a charge of attempted rape contrary to s. 1(1) of the Criminal Attempts Act 1981 and s. 1 of the Sexual Offences Act 2003. The first issue with any such charge will be whether or not Aaron can be regarded as having taken steps more than merely preparatory to raping Belinda. On the basis of *R v Gullefer* (1990) 91 Cr App R 356, and *R v Geddes* [1996] Crim LR 894, it is clear that there does not have to be evidence that Aaron went as far as almost committing penile penetration, of Belinda, but the prosecution must prove that he had gone as far as actually trying to commit the act in question, rather than merely putting himself in a position, or equipping himself, in order to do so.

It is unclear how a jury would conclude on this point. Assuming the *actus reus* is made out, the *mens rea* for attempt requires proof that Aaron intended to have sexual intercourse with Belinda, being at least reckless as to whether or not she would have been consenting; see *R v Khan* (1990) Cr App R 351, where it was held that recklessness as to circumstances would suffice for rape, although this point has not been tested yet in relation to the definition of rape provided for in the 2003 Act.

When Duncan entered Belinda's house, he may have committed burglary contrary to s. 9(1)(a) of the Theft Act 1968. He clearly entered a building as a trespasser and had no permission to be there. If he thought he would be welcome in the house why did he not knock on the door? As explained above, *mens rea* requires proof that he knew he was trespassing, or was at least reckless as to whether he was trespassing. Proof of the ulterior intent could be difficult. The only one that is relevant on the facts is the intention to steal. The trousers are property belonging to another in the sense that they are in the possession and control of another (Belinda and Cameron). The fact that Aaron is the owner is no bar to the trousers being deemed to be property belonging to another person for the purposes of theft; see s. 5(1) Theft Act 1968 as interpreted in *R v Turner (No. 2)* [1971] 1 WLR 901. Duncan obviously intends to appropriate the trousers and similarly intends to permanently deprive (Belinda and Cameron). The problem is dishonesty. Duncan could argue, under s. 2(1)(a) of the Theft Act 1968, that he honestly believed he had the right in law to retrieve Aaron's trousers. Alternatively this might be a case where a direction in terms approved in *R v Ghosh* [1982] QB 1053 might be needed—would the ordinary decent person have regarded his actions as dishonest? If so, did Aaron realize that his actions would be so regarded?

It is clearly difficult to guess at how a jury would view his actions here. He is actually seeking to return the trousers to the rightful owner—on that basis alone a jury might be willing to acquit.

Duncan's actions in grabbing the trousers arguably creates the possibility of a s. 9(1)(b) charge—on the basis that, having entered as a trespasser, he therein stole—but again this depends on proof of dishonesty as discussed above.

Aaron could be charged as an accomplice to any burglary committed by Duncan. He suggests the course of action, drove Duncan to Belinda's house, and is at the scene of the crime. Given the discussion above relating to the absence of dishonesty on Duncan's part, however, Aaron might argue that he did not contemplate any crime being committed. The facts would not appear to support the *mens rea* requirement for aiding and abetting identified in *R v Bryce* [2004] EWCA Crim 1231, to the effect that the accomplice must be shown to have realized his actions were capable of assisting the offence, and that he must have contemplated the principal's offence as a 'real possibility'.

Similarly, there would be difficulties with any inchoate offences—Aaron encouraging Duncan to commit burglary contrary to s. 44 of the Serious Crime Act 2007, or Aaron and Duncan conspiring to commit burglary. For reasons outlined above regarding lack of dishonesty, there may not be evidence that Aaron thought he was suggesting the commission of a crime or that Aaron and Duncan thought they were agreeing to commit burglary.

When Aaron drives off at high speed causing Cameron to fall from the car he might have caused grievous bodily harm—severe bruising would suffice to establish the degree of harm required; see *R v Doyle* [2004] EWCA Crim 2714. To succeed with a charge under s. 18 of the Offences Against the Person Act 1861, the prosecution would need to prove intent to do some grievous bodily harm. On the facts this may be questionable if Aaron was frightened and panicking. As an alternative Aaron could be charged, under s. 20 of the 1861 Act, with maliciously inflicting grievous bodily harm. Assuming the harm is made out, proof of *mens rea* would require evidence that Aaron at least foresaw the possibility of some physical harm albeit slight; see *R v Mowatt* [1967] 3 All ER 47, approved in *R v Savage; R v Parmenter* [1992] 1 AC 699.

A crucial issue here is whether or not Aaron realizes Cameron is clinging to the car— he was aware that Cameron was giving chase, but the facts leave open the question of whether Aaron knew where Cameron was when he drove off at high speed. If Aaron was not aware of the risk that Cameron might be hurt, not only is a s. 20 charge likely to fail, but also any lesser charge such as s. 47 assault occasioning actual bodily harm. Even a s. 47 charge requires proof that the defendant was aware of the risk of assault or battery. Again, ignorance that Cameron was hanging on to the car could be evidence that Aaron had no such awareness.

Even if an assault charge is made out, Aaron might seek to rely on self-defence in that he was using reasonable force to protect himself in driving so as to shake Cameron off the car; see *R v Julien* [1969] 1 WLR 839. He is clearly retreating from the threat, and this will be a factor that will register with the jury; see *R v McInnes* [1971] 3 All ER 295. Whether what he did was reasonable or not should be looked at in the context of the perceived threat. As Lord Morris observed in *Palmer v R* [1971] AC 814, the person defending himself cannot 'weigh to a nicety the exact measure of his necessary defensive action'. Hence if the jury conclude that, in a moment of unexpected anguish, Aaron had only done what he honestly and instinctively thought was necessary, that would be potent evidence that only reasonable defensive action had been taken.

Section 76 of the Criminal Justice and Immigration Act 2008 simply confirms this position at common law. Sub-section 76(3) in particular provides that the question of whether the degree of force used by a defendant was reasonable in the circumstances is to be decided by reference to the circumstances as the defendant believed them to be. Hence much turns on what sort of attack Aaron feared.

If Aaron succeeds with this argument he must be acquitted of the possible assault charges.

Duncan might be charged as an accomplice to Aaron's actions that cause the injuries suffered by Cameron, but there would be problems in establishing the *actus reus* of participation. In what sense did Duncan encourage Aaron to drive as he did or help him do so? Can it be said that Duncan 'adopted' Aaron's actions by remaining in the car with him? Duncan will argue that Aaron was acting on his own in driving the car as he did and as such no issues of accessorial liability arise. Again, there is no clear evidence that Duncan had any idea the car was being driven with Cameron clinging on to it. If such evidence could be established there might be a case for arguing that the injuries to Cameron were an accidental consequence of the common design to drive off at high speed. In which case Duncan might incur liability as an accomplice to the possible assault charges; see *R v Betts and Ridley* (1930) 22 Cr App R 148. There is even the possibility that Duncan was aware of Cameron clinging to the car and Aaron was not—thus opening up the prospect of Aaron being acquitted in respect of the injuries suffered by Cameron, but Duncan being an accomplice to the *actus reus* committed by Aaron. The facts given lack the degree of certainty to pursue this particular point any further.

Question 2

Justin and Tintin, having been partners for several years, split up when Tintin discovered that Justin was having a relationship with Roger. Tintin, incensed by what Justin had done, decided to seek revenge.

Tintin enters Justin's flat, using the front door key that he still has, armed with a pair of scissors that he intends to use to stab Justin. Tintin goes into Justin's bedroom and finds him asleep in bed. Instead of stabbing Justin, Tintin decides to use the scissors to cut off Justin's ponytail whilst he is asleep, and does so without waking Justin. Tintin rummages through the drawer of Justin's bedside table and removes some nude photographs that he took of Justin in the shower.

As he is about to leave the flat Tintin is confronted by Roger, who is just arriving. Tintin, who is still holding the scissors, fears that Roger is about to attack him. He pushes the scissors into Roger's arm, causing a deep cut, and runs off. Tintin subsequently writes to Justin telling him that if he does not return the ring he gave to Justin to celebrate the fifth anniversary of their being partners, he intends to put the nude photographs of Justin on the internet. Justin, who is a secondary school headmaster, is worried that if Tintin carries out his threat he might have to resign from his job.

Advise the Crown Prosecution Service as to the criminal liability of Tintin.

Commentary

This question may (superficially) look easy, but it bristles with little traps and uncertainties. The basic burglary issues should be obvious but note the possibility of aggravated burglary. The distinction between wounding and grievous bodily harm needs to be dealt with carefully, as this in turn affects whether or not there might be liability for burglary. There may be no liability for theft of the photographs at all. Whose pictures are they? Is Tintin dishonest when he takes them? Did he ever have intention to permanently deprive when he removed them? These uncertainties explain why a blackmail charge may be more appropriate, but even with that offence there are uncertainties regarding whether or not the demand is unwarranted. The attack on Roger is complicated by the issue of whether or not a trespasser can claim to act in self-defence, and whether or not the defence can be relied upon in order to launch a pre-emptive strike.

Answer plan

- Entering the flat with a key—is this trespass with intent contrary to **s. 9(1)(a) Theft Act 1968?**
- Aggravated burglary?
- Does Tintin progress far enough to have attempted GBH/wounding?
- ABH in cutting the ponytail
- Theft of the photographs—is he dishonest—does he have ITPD?
- If theft—consequent **s. 9(1)(b)** burglary under **Theft Act 1968**
- Injuries caused to Roger—is self-defence available?
- Blackmail—the demand unwarranted?

Suggested answer

Burglary

When Tintin enters Justin's flat armed with the scissors he may have committed burglary contrary to s. 9(1)(a) of the Theft Act 1968, or aggravated burglary contrary to s. 10 of the 1968 Act. Was he a trespasser when he entered? He may have had express or implied permission to enter the flat when he was in a relationship with Justin, but as the relationship has now ended it could be argued that the permission has been expressly or impliedly revoked. In any event, if he enters intending to stab Justin, or even simply armed in order to do some physical harm, the prosecution will argue that this is entry in excess of any implied permission Tintin may have had: see *R v Jones and Smith* [1976] 3 All ER 54. Under s. 9(1)(a) Tintin can be convicted of burglary if he entered as a trespasser with intent to do some grievous bodily harm on a person in the building. Grievous bodily harm for these purposes means 'serious' harm; see *R v Doyle* [2004] EWCA Crim 2714. The intent to stab is established on the facts, but a stabbing (whilst almost certainly involving a wounding) does not necessarily involve grievous bodily harm. Liability under this limb of s. 9(1)(a) would require more evidence as to Tintin's precise intentions. The alternative formulations under s. 9(1)(a) are that Tintin entered as a trespasser intending to steal, or that he intended to cause criminal damage. Again the evidence as to his state of mind at the time of entry is inconclusive. If it can be shown that he intended to steal photographs, human hair, or indeed commit criminal damage to Justin's hair, a s. 9(1)(a) charge might be sustainable—but it is submitted there is no direct evidence of this.

Burglary contrary to s. 9(1)(a) could be based on Tintin's entry into the flat with a key, or indeed his entry into Justin's bedroom as a trespasser, given that burglary can be committed by a defendant entering part of a building as a trespasser. The prosecution would be advised to base liability on the act of trespass that carried with it the strongest evidence of the necessary ulterior intent to steal, cause grievous bodily harm, or criminal damage.

Under s. 10 of the 1968 Act a person is guilty of aggravated burglary if he commits any burglary and at the time has with him any weapon of offence. Clearly the scissors could constitute a weapon of offence for these purposes, but it should be noted that liability for the aggravated offence requires proof of the basic offence under s. 9. As indicated above this may be the matter of some dispute.

Attempt and assault

Once inside Justin's bedroom Tintin decides not to stab Justin. Has Tintin nevertheless gone far enough to be charged with attempting to commit wounding contrary to s. 1 of the Criminal Attempts Act 1981 and s. 20 of the Offences Against the Person Act 1861? Under the 1981 Act the prosecution will have to prove that Tintin has taken steps more than merely preparatory to wounding Justin. Whether or not entering Justin's bedroom armed with scissors is sufficient to satisfy this requirement will be a question of fact to be determined by the jury; see for example *R v Gullefer* (1990) 91 Cr App R 356 and *R v Geddes* [1996] Crim LR 894. Again, much will hinge upon the evidence of Tintin's state of mind, as liability for attempt cannot be established without proof that Tintin intended to wound Justin. Even if Tintin confesses that this was his initial intent when he set out to seek revenge, he is unlikely to be foolish enough to admit that he still intended to do this when he approached Justin's sleeping figure in the bedroom. If he does confess, then the prosecution might have the evidence for an attempt charge.

In cutting off Justin's ponytail Tintin will have committed the offence of causing actual bodily harm contrary to s. 47 of the Offences Against the Person Act 1861. *DPP v Smith* [2006] All ER (D) 69 (Jan) establishes that cutting off another's hair without consent amounts to actual bodily harm. There is no doubt that Tintin intended to cause this result and there would appear to be no defence available (revenge not being a defence at common law—perhaps not even a mitigating factor in sentencing). As will have been noted above, a burglary charge could be sustained if Tintin entered the bedroom intending to do grievous bodily harm. Entering intending to cut hair would not suffice for these purposes. In any event the facts indicate that he only decided to cut Justin's hair once he had entered the bedroom. For the same reason a charge of burglary contrary to s. 9(1)(b), alleging that Tintin, having entered Justin's bedroom as a trespasser, therein committed grievous bodily harm would not be sustainable as the cutting of the hair would only be actual bodily harm.

Theft of the photographs

The prosecution may consider charging Tintin with theft of the photographs of Justin. The photographs are clearly property; see s. 4(1) of the Theft Act 1968. The facts indicate that the photographs were taken by Tintin—hence he may argue that they still belong to him. The prosecution may need to clearly establish that Tintin made Justin the owner of the photographs, but in any event s. 5(1) of the 1968 Act extends the concept of 'belonging to another' to encompass situations where, even though the defendant is the legal owner of the property in question, it can still be deemed to be property belonging to another as against the defendant if the property is in the possession or control of another. On the facts the photographs would clearly be regarded as having been in Justin's possession or control; see further *R v Turner (No. 2)* [1971] 1 WLR 901.

Tintin's removal of the photographs would constitute an appropriation—see s. 3(1) of the Theft Act 1968. Hence the live issues will be those relating to *mens rea*. The prosecution must prove that Tintin's appropriation of the pictures was dishonest. Under s. 2(1)(a) of the 1968 Act Tintin will not be dishonest if he can show that he honestly believed he had the right in law to take the photographs. He does not have to show that any such right does exist in law, simply that he believed he had the right. The fact that he was the photographer may be supportive evidence here. It is also significant that he does not appear to have had the intention to use the pictures for blackmailing purposes (considered below) until after he removed them. Tintin could cite this as evidence that he had an 'honest' motive in his initial removal of the pictures. It is submitted that s. 2(1)(b) (honest belief in the owner's consent) and s. 2(1)(c) (honest belief that the owner cannot be found) have no application on these facts. If, therefore, Tintin cannot rely on s. 2(1)(a), he will have to rely on the jury and their view following a direction in terms laid down in *R v Ghosh* [1982] QB 1053. The jury must first decide whether, according to the ordinary standards of reasonable and honest people, what Tintin did was dishonest. If it was not dishonest by those standards he is not guilty of theft. If he was the jury must go on to consider whether Tintin himself must have realized that what he was doing was by those standards dishonest. Given the facts it is almost impossible to tell how a jury would determine this, although they may well take a dim view of a defendant who, having entered a flat without permission, armed with a weapon, subsequently threatens to embarrass the victim by publishing the pictures.

If dishonesty is established the prosecution will have to prove the second element of *mens rea*, namely an intention on the part of Tintin to permanently deprive Justin of the photographs. It should be noted that the intention to permanently deprive must exist at the time of appropriation. Tintin's intentions in this regard are not clear at the time he removes the pictures from Justin's bedroom. It subsequently becomes clear that he intends to use the pictures for what may be blackmailing purposes. The prosecution could argue that even if Tintin lacked the necessary intention to permanently deprive in relation to the pictures when he was in the bedroom, it is later evidenced by his threats to publish them. Tintin will argue that he did not intend to keep the photographs but was simply using them as a bargaining factor in respect of the ring. Under s. 6(1) of the 1968 Act, in cases where the defendant does not actually have an intention to permanently deprive, he can nevertheless be deemed to have such an intent if he intends to '...to treat the thing as his own to dispose of...'. In *R v Raphael and another* [2008] EWCA Crim 1014, the appellant took P's car and then told P that it would be returned to him provided he paid £500. The Court of Appeal had little hesitation in concluding that the taking of property in such circumstances could amount to theft—the requirement that money be paid by the owner for the return of his property falling very much within the scope of s. 6(1).

In the present case Tintin is seeking the return of a ring as exchange for the photographs—essentially the same issue as in *R v Raphael*. Assuming, therefore, that the photographs are property belonging to another, and assuming Tintin is dishonest, theft should be made out.

If Tintin did commit theft when he removed the pictures from Justin's bedroom, he may also be guilty of burglary contrary to s. 9(1)(b) of the Theft Act 1968—having entered the bedroom as a trespasser he therein stole.

Wounding and self-defence

In cutting Roger's arm Tintin caused a wound—see *JCC v Eisenhower* [1983] 3 WLR 537. Thus Tintin may have committed an offence under either s. 18 ('wounding with intent...') or s. 20 ('maliciously wound') of the Offences Against the Person Act 1861. The key factor will be *mens rea*. More evidence is needed on the type of harm Tintin intended to cause. If he intended to cause serious harm, an intention to do some grievous bodily harm could be established, thus making out a case under s. 18. It is submitted that there should be ample evidence to sustain a charge under s. 20. Malicious wounding requires evidence that Tintin was at least aware that his actions created the risk of causing some physical harm albeit slight; see *R v Savage; R v Parmenter* [1992] 1 AC 699.

Tintin will presumably argue that, in attacking Roger, he acted in self-defence using reasonable force to protect himself; see *R v Julien* [1969] 1 WLR 839. The fact that Tintin may have been 'in the wrong' inasmuch as he was trespassing in Justin's flat (possibly committing burglary—see above) does not remove his right to act in self-defence if threatened with unlawful violence from Roger; see *R v Rashford* [2005] All ER (D) 192.

The facts indicate that Roger had not actually attacked Tintin, hence Tintin will have to provide evidence that he honestly believed Roger was about to use unlawful violence on him. *R v Williams* [1987] 3 All ER 411, and subsequent cases, make clear that Roger is entitled to be judged on the facts as he honestly believed them to be, a position now confirmed by s. 76 of the Criminal Justice and Immigration Act 2008. Assuming Tintin did honestly believe he was about to be attacked by Roger, was the force he used reasonable in the circumstances as he believed them to be? On the basis of s. 76(7) the jury should be directed to take into account the fact that Tintin may not have been able to weigh to a nicety the exact measure of any necessary action. Evidence that he only did what he honestly and instinctively thought was necessary for a legitimate purpose will constitute strong evidence that only reasonable action was taken by him. If self-defence is made out Tintin will have a complete defence. If the jury conclude that there was a basis for Tintin acting in self-defence but he used more force than was reasonable he will have no defence at all; see *R v Clegg* [1995] 2 WLR 80.

Blackmail

When Tintin subsequently wrote to Justin telling him that if he did not return the ring he would put the nude photographs of Justin on the internet, Tintin may have committed blackmail contrary to s. 21 of the Theft Act 1968. There is clearly a demand. The accompanying threat would amount to the required menaces. The test is essentially objective— what would the effect be on the reasonable person? See *R v Clear* [1968] 1 QB 670. In cases where the reasonable person would not be threatened, the menaces can still be made out where the defendant has knowledge of the victim that indicates a particular sensitivity to the threats—see *R v Garwood* [1987] 1 WLR 319. The fact that Justin would be particularly embarrassed because of his job may be a factor here. The demand must be made with a view to gaining property or causing loss to another. In this respect the obtaining of the ring would constitute the gaining of property (even if Tintin is getting back something he thinks belongs to him anyway—see s. 34(2) Theft Act 1968). The most difficult aspect of establishing blackmail may lie in showing that the demand was unwarranted. Under s. 21 the prosecution must prove that Tintin had no belief that he had reasonable grounds for making the demand; and that he had no honest belief that the use of the menaces was a proper means of reinforcing the demand. Tintin will argue that he honestly believed he had a reasonable basis for making the demand as the relationship with Justin was over, and that he had no, or perhaps only doubtful, recourse to law in order to get the ring back. Whether this argument succeeds will be a matter for the jury to determine.

Question 3

Joy is hosting a fireworks party in her garden. She drinks a large quantity of alcohol and becomes very drunk. Fiona, a guest at the party who has not been drinking, encourages Joy to throw a large firework over the hedge into the next door neighbour's (Leonora's) garden.

The firework hits Leonora who is badly burnt. Leonora's partner Sanjeet decides to exact revenge on Joy. The next morning, when Joy's milk is delivered, Sanjeet hides the bottles in the bushes in her garden. When she eventually finds the bottles the milk has gone sour. Sanjeet also lets the air out of the tyres on Joy's car causing them to go flat.

A few days later Sanjeet persuades Allan to make a series of threatening and abusive telephone calls to Joy. Allan agrees to do this but, unknown to him, he repeatedly dials the wrong number leaving his threatening messages on the answer-phone of Pauline, a frail elderly woman who lives alone. Pauline is terrified by these calls, becomes depressed, and has to receive psychiatric help for the resultant neuroses.

Advise the Crown Prosecution Service as to the possible criminal liability of Joy, Fiona, Sanjeet and Allan.

Note: Candidates should ignore, for the purposes of this question, offences under the Protection from Harassment Act 1997, and offences relating to explosives and the misuse of public telephone systems.

Commentary

A question that brings in so many issues, any candidate would be hard pressed to provide much more than a cursory examination of each point in the time allowed in most examinations. If this were set as a coursework question with a reasonable word limit rather more could be achieved. The more issues there are, the more important it becomes for candidates to isolate them clearly and deal with them in a logical order—the use of sub-headings is generally to be welcomed. Most of the criminal damage issues are very straightforward, as is the theft—but do not make the mistake of dwelling at length on non-contentious points. The difficult issue in relation to theft, for example, is whether or not there is intention to permanently deprive. The accessorial liability issues raise some tricky points. Many exam questions deal with a deliberate departure from the common design, but candidates should also be aware of the rules on accidental departure from the common design. As this question demonstrates, general issues such as intoxication and transferred malice can be inserted just about anywhere by an examiner.

Answer plan

- Joy—s. 18/s. 20, Offences Against the Person Act 1861—*mens rea* and intoxication
- Section 47 as a residual offence
- Fiona—accomplice—accidental consequences of the common design—liability under Part 2 of the Serious Crime Act 2007
- Sanjeet—theft of milk—intention to permanently deprive
- Sanjeet—criminal damage to milk and tyres—note *R v G*
- Allan—psychological injury—transferred malice
- Sanjeet—accomplice—different victim—deliberate or accidental?

Suggested answer

Joy's liability for the injuries to Leonora

An examination of Joy's liability in respect of the harm caused to Leonora must start by considering the harm done. The expression 'badly burnt' is suggestive of grievous bodily harm, thus opening up the possibility of offences contrary to both s. 18 and s. 20 of the Offences Against the Person Act 1861. Under s. 18 there would have to be proof that Joy had caused grievous bodily harm—which for these purposes would be satisfied by evidence that the burns constituted serious harm: see *R v Saunders* [1985] Crim LR 230. There are no causation issues. The throwing of the firework causes the harm in fact and there is no evidence of any *novus actus interveniens*.

The problem for the prosecution would be as regards the *mens rea*. Did Joy intend to cause grievous bodily harm to any person? Unless there is evidence that Joy foresaw such harm as virtually certain (see *R v Woollin* [1998] 4 All ER 103) there will be no basis for a s. 18 charge. Proof of such foresight seems unlikely, especially if the throwing of the firework was meant as a prank. Further problems would arise under s. 18 in respect of Joy's alcohol consumption. The offence is one of specific intent—hence if Joy was intoxicated i.e., she could not and did not form the specific intent because of her self-induced intoxication—she cannot be guilty of the s. 18 offence: see *DPP v Majewski* [1976] 2 All ER 142. Whether or not Joy was so intoxicated will be a question of fact for the jury.

Bearing these points in mind a charge under s. 20 of the Offences Against the Person Act 1861 would seem more promising. The prosecution will have to prove that Joy maliciously inflicted grievous bodily harm on Leonora. The harm will be made out as discussed above in the context of s. 18. For all practical purposes the term 'inflicting' can be regarded as synonymous with 'causing' see *R v Burstow; R v Ireland* [1998] AC 147. The mental element here requires proof that Joy foresaw the possibility of some physical harm, albeit slight, occurring to someone as a result of her actions: see *per* Diplock LJ in *R v Mowatt* [1967] 3 All ER 47. On the facts it is possible that Joy did not foresee any physical harm—especially if she gave no thought to the possibility of there being anyone on the other side of the hedge. If Joy was intoxicated, she could still incur liability under s. 20 (a basic intent crime) if there is evidence that she was reckless in becoming intoxicated and, as a result, was unaware of a risk of physical harm being caused that she would have been aware of had she been sober: see *DPP v Majewski* (above), and subsequent decisions such as *R v Richardson and Irwin* [1999] Crim LR 494 and *R v Hardie* [1984] 3 All ER 848.

If the harm done does not amount to grievous bodily harm, or the *mens rea* for s. 20 cannot be established, Joy may be charged under s. 47 of the Offences Against the Person Act 1861—that she assaulted Leonora (i.e., assaulted and/or battered) and thereby occasioned actual bodily harm. The burns would undoubtedly satisfy the definition of actual bodily harm: see *R v Miller* [1954] 2 QB 282. The only *mens rea* required would be the intention to assault or recklessness, but it is subjective recklessness: see

R v Cunningham [1957] 2 QB 396. Joy must, therefore, be proved to have been aware of the risk that another person might be assaulted or battered by her actions. There would be no need to show that she foresaw any actual bodily harm: *R v Savage*; *R v Parmenter* [1992] 1 AC 699. Again s. 47 is a basic intent crime—hence the comments above regarding the significance of intoxication in relation to s. 20 apply here.

Fiona's liability as an accomplice to Joy

Fiona encourages Joy to throw the firework and can thus be described as someone who abetted the offence by Joy—i.e., Fiona was at the scene of the crime and spurred Joy on. Fiona will argue that she did not think that anyone would be hurt, but this will not avail her. An accomplice will be a party to all the unforeseen or accidental consequences of the agreed course of conduct carried out by the principal offender. In the present case Joy does precisely what Fiona suggests she should do, hence Fiona will be a party to the resulting offences: see *R v Betts and Ridley* (1930) 22 Cr App R 148 and *R v Baldessare* (1930) 22 Cr App R 70. It is possible that Fiona, as an accomplice, may be charged with and found guilty of a more serious offence than that which Joy is charged with. Note that Fiona is sober—hence she may be capable of greater foresight of harm occurring to another. There is nothing in principle to prevent Fiona being charged with a more serious offence than that charged against Joy.

Fiona could also be charged with encouraging or assisting offences believing one or more will be committed, contrary to s. 46 of the Serious Crime Act 2007. The prosecution case would be that Fiona encouraged Joy to commit one or more of a number of offences; and that Fiona believed that one or more of those offences would be committed (the prosecution does not have to prove which) as a result of her encouragement. On the facts the offences would range from narrow assault to criminal damage. Provided the prosecution can prove Fiona believed that one of these offences would be committed as a result of Joy throwing the firework, liability can be made out. The prosecution will rely on evidence that Fiona was either reckless as to whether or not Joy would have acted in response to the encouragement with the necessary fault, or on the evidence that Fiona's state of mind was such that, had she thrown the firework, she would have acted with the required fault.

Sanjeet's liability regarding the milk

Sanjeet may be guilty of theft of the milk. It is clearly property belonging to another: see s. 4(1) and s. 5(1) of the Theft Act 1968. He appropriates the milk by hiding it: see s. 3(1) of the 1968 Act. Any assumption of any right of the owner can amount to an appropriation of property. It is hard to see any argument by which he could claim not to be dishonest. The only issue here is intention to permanently deprive. Sanjeet will argue that he had no such intention, but s. 6(1) of the Theft Act 1968 provides that even if he did not actually intend Joy to permanently lose the milk, his dealing with it can be *regarded* as evidence of his having the intention of permanently depriving her of it, because he chose to treat the milk as his own to dispose of regardless of Joy's rights. *R v Cahill* [1993] Crim LR 141, suggests that removing another's property to another place as a prank falls outside s. 6(1) but the courts are likely to follow *DPP v Lavender* [1993] Crim LR 297, which suggests that such action can be theft. The perishable nature of the commodity will strengthen the prosecution case on this point. In the event that intention to permanently deprive poses a problem, note that the damage to the milk could also provide the basis for a criminal damage charge contrary to s. 1(1) of the Criminal Damage Act 1971.

Sanjeet's liability regarding the deflated tyres

Deliberately deflating the tyres could be criminal damage contrary to s. 1(1) of the Criminal Damage Act 1971—the point to note here is that the tyres can be 'damaged' simply by being altered. The *mens rea* is evident. A charge of aggravated criminal damage contrary to s. 1(2) might also be considered, but if the car cannot be driven because the tyres are flat it would be difficult for the prosecution to prove that Sanjeet intended to endanger life or was reckless as to whether his action would have that effect. Tampering with the brakes, by contrast, would support a s. 1(2) offence. It should be noted that, following *R v G* [2003] 4 All ER 765, the recklessness involved in the offence of criminal damage is subjective—hence (assuming his intention to damage property can be taken as evident from the facts) the prosecution would have to prove that Sanjeet was aware of the risk that life would be endangered as a result of the damage to the property, and that in the circumstances known to him, it had been unreasonable for him to take the risk.

Allan's liability regarding the telephone calls

Lord Steyn in *R v Burstow*; *R v Ireland* [1998] AC 147, held that both grievous bodily harm and actual bodily harm could take the form of neurotic disorders induced by a defendant's conduct. It was also accepted in that case that such harm could be caused without any direct assault on the victim by the defendant. Whether a case involved grievous bodily harm or actual bodily harm would simply be a matter of degree. The House of Lords also held in that case that although in s. 47 actual bodily harm cases an assault had to be proven, it could be committed by the use of words alone, by a telephone call, even by a silent telephone call. The prosecution would have to prove, however, that the victim apprehended *immediate* physical violence as a result of the telephone calls. On this basis Allan could be charged under s. 20 or s. 47 in respect of the harm he causes to Pauline. There is no problem in relation to causation. As to *mens rea,* the fact that he telephones the wrong victim by accident is irrelevant—the principles of transferred malice would apply, the identity of the victim being irrelevant: see *R v Latimer* (1886) 17 QBD 359. Problems might arise under s. 20 in establishing that Allan acted maliciously: see *R v Mowatt* (above). He might not have foreseen the risk of any physical harm occurring to anyone. On this basis a s. 47 charge seems more likely. The only *mens rea* requirement would be evidence that Allan foresaw the risk of another person apprehending immediate physical violence as a result of his telephone calls. Whether or not this could be established would depend to a large extent on the evidence of what he said when making the calls. The statement 'I am coming to fire bomb your house in two minutes' would be an example of a threat where the required intent would probably be made out.

Sanjeet's liability as an accomplice to Allan

Sanjeet counsels Allan in the commission of the offences against Pauline in the sense that he persuades him to make the calls—there is a connection between Sanjeet's requests and the actions of Allan. Allan acted within the scope of the authority given by Sanjeet: see *R v Calhaem* [1985] 2 All ER 266, as confirmed in *R v Luffman* [2008] EWCA Crim 1379. That Allan hurts Pauline, not Joy, is irrelevant. Only if Allan had deliberately chosen a different victim would Sanjeet have escaped liability as an accomplice; see *R v Saunders and Archer* (1573) 2 Plowd 473, as applied in *R v Leahy* [1985] Crim LR 99. Sanjeet contemplates the actions of Allan that cause the harm to Pauline, hence Sanjeet has the *mens rea* to be an accomplice. There is no deliberate departure from the common design by Allan.

Question 4

Marvin owes £5,000 to Paul, a drug dealer with a formidable reputation for resorting to violence against those who cross him. Paul tells Marvin that he must get the money he owes or he will have Marvin tortured and killed.

Marvin decides to burgle Harriet's house. Hoping to avoid any trouble Marvin watches the house to see when it might be unoccupied. Having called at the house to check that there is no one in, Marvin enters via an unlocked ground floor window. Unknown to Marvin, Harriet is at home. She had been fast asleep upstairs when he had earlier knocked on the door. On confronting Marvin, Harriet attacks him with a hammer. Seeking to protect himself Marvin pushes Harriet downstairs. She suffers a fractured skull when her head hits the stone floor.

Advise the Crown Prosecution Service as to the possible criminal liability of Marvin and Paul. Candidates are not required to consider Harriet's liability.

How, if at all, would your answer differ if:

(a)   Marvin had taken a large quantity of cocaine prior to the burglary in order to give himself the courage to carry it out?

(b)   Paul had told Marvin to burgle Harriet's house?

 Commentary

This question explores issues such as burglary, assault, self-defence, duress, and accessorial liability. Given the debate regarding the right of householders to defend themselves against burglars, examiners will quite commonly use a question like this—and as will be seen it is not free from difficulty.

It is important to read the instructions carefully. Two very common errors with questions such as this are: first to advise on Harriet's liability despite the clear statement in the question instructing candidates not to do this; secondly, to assume that Harriet has died, thus necessitating advice on liability for homicide. Saving (one hopes) rare cases where an examiner has been sloppy in drafting a question, candidates should assume that a victim has not been killed unless the facts of the question make this explicit.

This question also provides a warning about the way in which duress issues might arise— note the distinction between duress *per minas* and duress of circumstances.

Finally, there are some tricky issues here regarding the extent to which an accomplice can be held responsible for the actions of a principal offender. Candidates should distinguish clearly between issues of law, upon which they can be expected to advise, and issues of fact that should be left to the jury to determine. The **Serious Crime Act 2007** adds further complications as it creates a layer of liability that overlaps considerably with accessorial liability.

 ## Answer plan

- Marvin—burglary—s. 9(1)(a), s. 9(1)(b) Theft Act 1968—conditional intent
- **Section 18 and s. 20, Offences Against the Person Act 1861**, against Harriet—availability of self-defence where D is 'in the wrong'—s. **76 of the Criminal Justice and Immigration Act 2008**
- Duress *per minas*— no crime nominated
- Duress of circumstances—policy limitations where self-induced and where threat not nullified
- Paul's liability—not accessorial—blackmail—assault by words
- Marvin's liability if intoxicated—specific/basic intent dichotomy—*DPP v Majewski*
- Paul specifies burglary—Marvin has duress *per minas*—Paul as a counsellor—liability under the **Serious Crime Act 2007**
- Query extent of Paul's accessorial liability—burglary and assaults

Suggested answer

Marvin burgles Harriet's house

Marvin clearly enters a dwelling as a trespasser and with intent to steal: see s. 9(1)(a) of the Theft Act 1968. The fact that he does not have a specific item in mind that he wants to steal does not prevent him from having a present intention to steal: see *Attorney-General's References (Nos 1 and 2 of 1979)* [1980] QB 180. This rather liberal reading of the 1968 Act reflects the reality that most burglars enter a property hoping that there will be something worth stealing—whether there is or not has no bearing on the burglar's state of mind at the point of entry. If it can be shown that Marvin entered prepared to use force if necessary he may also be said to have entered with intent to do some grievous bodily harm. His careful planning to avoid confrontation would militate against this, however. The *mens rea* for theft seems evident. As discussed below, Marvin may have committed grievous bodily harm to Harriet, hence a further burglary charge could be one under s. 9(1)(b) of the Theft Act 1968, to the effect that he entered the house as a trespasser and therein inflicted grievous bodily harm.

The injuries to Harriet

Harriet's fractured skull would be grievous bodily harm—i.e., serious harm: *R v Saunders* [1985] Crim LR 230. Marvin has caused this harm—there is no suggestion of a *novus actus interveniens*. Whether Marvin had the intent necessary for the offence under s. 18 of the Offences Against the Person Act 1861 will depend on whether there is evidence that he foresaw grievous bodily harm as virtually certain to result from his actions: applying *R v Woollin* [1998] 4 All ER 103. It is submitted that unless such foresight can be shown the jury would not be entitled to infer the intent required by s. 18. The facts suggest this may be doubtful. An alternative charge under s. 20 of the Offences Against the Person Act 1861 would be maliciously inflicting grievous bodily harm.

Marvin must be shown to have foreseen at least the possibility of physical harm occurring to Harriet: see *R v Mowatt* [1967] 3 All ER 47. An intention merely to frighten her would not suffice: see *R v Sullivan* [1981] Crim LR 46. These decisions were confirmed by the House of Lords in *R v Savage; R v Parmenter* [1992] 1 AC 699. On the facts the *mens rea* for s. 20 would seem to be beyond doubt, hence a s. 20 charge would be appropriate.

Marvin could raise the defence of self-defence, although the jury is likely to look askance at any burglar who seeks to rely on this. Marvin will argue that Harriet's actions were excessive and thus unlawful. He was therefore attempting to prevent harm to himself arising from an unlawful attack. On the basis of *R v Julien* [1969] 1 WLR 839, he will have to provide evidence that he did not want to fight and that he was prepared to 'temporize and disengage'—even run away—although *R v McInnes* [1971] 3 All ER 295 suggests that a failure to retreat is only one element of the various considerations upon which the reasonableness of an accused's conduct is to be judged. On the basis of *R v Rashford* [2005] All ER (D) 192, it is not accurate to contend that a person who injures another having started a quarrel should thereby be denied self-defence if his victim retaliates. The jury should be asked to consider whether or not Harriet's retaliation was such that Marvin was entitled then to defend himself. That will depend on whether the violence offered by Harriet was so out of proportion to Marvin's own act as to give rise to the reasonable apprehension that he was in immediate danger from which he had no other means of escape, and whether the violence which he then used was no more than was necessary to preserve his own life or protect himself from serious injury.

Section 76 of the Criminal Justice and Immigration Act 2008 was enacted to clarify some aspects of self-defence, but in reality it largely restates the common law position outlined above. It makes it clear that a defendant is entitled to be judged on the facts as he honestly believed them to be. Where the evidence is that Marvin was mistaken as to the degree of force required to defend himself, the jury can have regard to the reasonableness of his belief in determining whether he genuinely held that belief. Once a jury determines that Marvin did genuinely believe that he was about to be the victim of unlawful violence they have to judge him on the facts as he believed them to be regardless of the fact that his belief was mistaken, and regardless of the fact that the mistake may not have been one made by a reasonable person.

Bearing these factors in mind it will be for the jury to consider whether the force used by Marvin was excessive. It is the force that should be considered, not the fact that Harriet suffered a fractured skull in the fall downstairs: see further *Shaw (Norman) v R* [2002] Crim LR 140.

Duress

Marvin may try to argue that he was forced to commit the crimes by Paul and thus acted under duress. The courts will reject this, however. Paul threatened to kill Marvin if he failed to pay his debt. He did not threaten to kill him if he refused to commit a crime: see *R v Cole* [1994] Crim LR 582. Whilst this would rule out the defence of duress *per minas*—i.e., duress based on threats, Marvin may nevertheless try to argue that he is entitled to raise the defence of duress of circumstances: see *R v Martin* [1989] 1 All ER 652. The defence is available only if, from an objective standpoint, the accused can be said to be acting reasonably and proportionately in order to avoid a threat of death or serious injury. The jury should be directed to determine two questions: (i) was the accused, or may he have been, impelled to act as he did because as a result of what he reasonably believed to be the situation he had good cause to fear that otherwise death or serious physical injury would result? (ii) if so, might a sober person of reasonable firmness, sharing the characteristics of the accused, have responded to that situation by acting as the accused acted? Both questions would have to be answered in the affirmative for the defence to be made out.

There are two policy limitations that apply to duress *per minas* (and presumably therefore to duress of circumstances) that might prevent the defence even being left to the jury in this case. The first limitation arises as a result of Marvin voluntarily associating with Paul in the criminal activity of drug dealing, and thereby exposing himself to the risk of being subjected to threats if he failed to pay for his drugs. In *R v Hasan* [2005] UKHL 22, in the context of duress *per minas,* Lord Bingham observed that the law on this point could be summarized as follows:

> If a person voluntarily becomes or remains associated with others engaged in criminal activity in a situation where he knows or ought reasonably to know that he may be the subject of compulsion by them or their associates, he cannot rely on the defence of duress to excuse any act which he is thereafter compelled to do by them.

It is submitted that this is wide enough to encompass Marvin's situation, subject only to an argument that Marvin had not agreed to commit crimes with Paul, but had simply become involved with him through being a client. Against this, however, is the public policy argument that denying the defence of duress to drug dealer's clients might inhibit the unlawful activity of drug dealing to some extent. The second policy limitation arises from the fact that Marvin may have had the opportunity to obtain protection against Paul's threat (for example by going to the police). Again, in *R v Hasan* [2005] UKHL 22, Lord Bingham signalled a much more restrictive approach to the defence of duress where he stated that juries should be directed that the defence would not be available where the evidence was that the retribution threatened against the defendant was not such as he reasonably expected to follow immediately or almost immediately on his failure to comply with the threat.

On the given facts it is impossible to advise further with any degree of certainty as to whether or not the defence would succeed.

Paul's liability

Paul may be guilty of blackmailing Marvin. With reference to s. 21 of the Theft Act 1968, Paul makes a demand that is clearly supported by menaces. It is with a view to gain, as this encompasses the situation where a defendant makes threats in order to recover debts—see s. 34(2) Theft Act 1968—and gain is to be construed as extending to keeping what one has.

To secure a conviction the prosecution will have to show that Paul's demand was unwarranted—i.e., that he did not believe he had reasonable grounds for making the demand; and he did not believe that the use of the menaces was a proper means of reinforcing the demand. As a violent criminal Paul may think death threats are a reasonable way of forcing indebted addicts to pay up, but *R v Harvey* (1981) 72 Cr App R 139, makes it clear that such demands can never be warranted. As Bingham J explained, no act, which was not believed to be lawful, could be believed to be proper within the meaning of the subsection: 'Where…the threats were to do acts which any sane man knows to be against the laws of every civilized country no jury would hesitate long before dismissing the contention that the defendant genuinely believed the threats to be a proper means of reinforcing even a legitimate demand.'

Paul will, therefore, be guilty of blackmail.

A further possible charge against Paul would be common assault. His words may have had the effect of causing Marvin to apprehend immediate physical violence. That an assault can be committed by words alone has been established by the House of Lords' decision in *R v Burstow; R v Ireland* [1998] AC 147. The *mens rea* required is intention or at least recklessness as to whether or not Marvin would apprehend immediate physical violence. Given that the threat is made in circumstances where Marvin is given the opportunity to go away and obtain the money it is hard to see how the element of immediacy can be satisfied on these facts.

On these facts the prosecution would have difficulty in establishing that Paul was an accomplice to Marvin's offences, as Paul does not order Marvin to commit a crime; neither did he encourage him to do so. In *DPP for Northern Ireland v Maxwell* [1978] 3 All ER 1140, Lord Scarman observed that an accomplice who leaves it to the principal offender to choose the offence to be committed will incur accessorial liability, but only where the choice is made from the range of offences from which the accomplice contemplates the choice will be made. Paul, if he has any sense, will presumably contend that he contemplated Marvin arranging a loan in order to repay the debt. The prosecution will be left to fall back on the rather weak argument that, as Paul knew Marvin was unable to pay the debt, and hence had no funds, it was foreseeable that Marvin would resort to crime to get the money needed. This would still not be sufficient to satisfy the test in *R v Bainbridge* [1959] 3 All ER 200, which requires proof that Paul contemplated the type of crimes Marvin chose to commit. On this basis it seems doubtful that Paul would be an accomplice to the s. 9(1)(a) or (b) burglaries, or the s. 18 and s. 20 offences that may have been committed by Marvin. The prosecution may seek to rely on a charge under s. 46 of the Serious Crime Act 2007, to the effect that Paul, in threatening Marvin regarding the debt, was effectively encouraging him to commit a range of possible offences. Section 65(1) of the 2007 Act provides that encouraging the commission of an offence includes doing so by threatening another person or otherwise putting pressure on another person to commit the offence. The problem for the prosecution here is that Paul does not specifically encourage the commission of an offence. There would have to be evidence that Paul believed that the only way Marvin could get the money was by resorting to crime, and that by implication he therefore believed he was encouraging Marvin to commit one of a range of offences, contrary to s. 46 of the 2007 Act. In the absence of a confession from Paul this seems to be an unlikely outcome.

(i) How, if at all, would your answer differ if Marvin had taken a large quantity of cocaine prior to the burglary in order to give himself the courage to carry it out?

If Marvin was in a state of self-induced intoxication at the time he committed these offences he may be able to plead intoxication as a defence to specific intent crimes. For these purposes that would encompass the burglary offences and s. 18 of the Offences Against the Person Act 1861: see *DPP v Majewski* [1976] 2 All ER 142. There are no lesser-included offences in s. 9(1)(a) of the Theft Act 1968, hence Marvin would have a complete defence. His liability under s. 18 would be reduced to s. 20. It should be noted, however, that the courts have recognized exceptions in those cases where there is evidence that the defendant deliberately got himself intoxicated in order to have the courage to commit the crime: see *Attorney-General for Northern Ireland v Gallagher* [1963] AC 349. In such cases intoxication is not allowed even as a defence to crimes of specific intent.

If the evidence was that Marvin had been mistaken as to the amount of force needed to protect himself against the attack by Harriet, he would not be permitted to rely on the defence of self-defence. As s. 76(5) of the Criminal Justice and Immigration Act 2008 makes clear, a defendant who is in a state of voluntarily induced intoxication will not be permitted to rely on his mistaken belief as a basis for self-defence at common law. Note that the sub-section sweeps over any distinction between crimes of basic intent and crimes of specific intent in this respect.

Again Paul would probably avoid any liability as an accomplice as he had not ordered Marvin to commit a crime; neither had he encouraged him to do so; see above.

(ii) Alternatively how, if at all, would your answer differ if Paul had told Marvin to burgle Harriet's house?

As regards Marvin, the defence of duress *per minas* (as opposed to duress of circumstances) could be available if the evidence is that Paul nominates the crime that Marvin must commit, but see comments above regarding policy limitations on the availability of duress defences where a defendant knowingly puts himself at risk of being threatened with death or grievous bodily harm.

Paul could incur liability as an accomplice to the burglary on the basis that he counselled the commission of the offence. In *R v Calhaem* [1985] 2 All ER 266, the Court of Appeal explained that counselling did not require a causal connection between the counselling and the offence, there simply had to be a connection between the counselling and the offence committed by the principal offender. This was more recently confirmed in *R v Luffman* [2008] EWCA Crim 1379. There seems little doubt that the *actus reus* of counselling is established on these facts. As to *mens rea*, *R v Bainbridge* (above), provides that it is sufficient that the accomplice contemplated the 'type' of crime committed by the principal offender. If the evidence is that Paul specified burglary there would seem to be little doubt about this. As detailed above, whether Paul's liability would extend to his being an accomplice to the attack on Harriet would depend on the application of the tests in *R v Bainbridge* [1959] 3 All ER 200, and *R v Bryce* [2004] EWCA Crim 1231, the Court of Appeal in the latter case holding that liability would require proof that the accomplice intentionally committed the acts of participation and contemplated the offence committed by the principal offender, in the sense that the accomplice knew what the principal intended to do, or at least realized that there was a real possibility that the principal would commit the offence. The court went on to hold that, in cases where the defendant accomplice provided assistance in the preliminary stages of a crime later committed by the principal offender in the absence of the accomplice, the prosecution would have to prove intentional assistance by the accomplice, in the sense of an intention to assist (and not to hinder or obstruct) the principal offender in acts which the accomplice knew were steps taken by the principal offender towards the commission of the offence.

Applying this to the facts, Paul intentionally encouraged Marvin to burgle Harriet's house, not appearing to care whether she would be in occupation at the time or not. The question of whether or not he contemplated physical violence as a 'real possibility' has to be left as a question of fact for the jury. The prosecution might argue, however, on the basis of *R v Betts and Ridley* (1930) 22 Cr App R 148 and *R v Baldessare* (1930) 22 Cr App R 70, that the attack on Harriet (arising from Marvin's instinctive actions in defending himself from his attack upon him) was an unforeseen and unintended consequence of the common design (the burglary) being carried out, and on that basis Paul should be a party to the consequences.

The prosecution would have a much stronger case in respect of a charge under s. 44 of the Serious Crime Act 2007 to the effect that Paul encouraged the commission of the burglary, intending that the offence should be committed by Marvin. As noted above, threats can be treated as encouragement for these purposes. A charge under s. 44 can be sustained even where the substantive offence is committed by the principal offender. Liability for encouraging the offences in respect of Harriet would be more difficult to establish—the prosecution would need to establish that he intended Harriet to be attacked (s. 44); believed she would be (s. 45); or believed that an attack on Harriet was one of a number of offences that would be committed if Marvin acted as he suggested (s. 46).

Index